BECOMING ELEKTRA

THE TRUE STORY OF JAC HOLZMAN'S VISIONARY RECORD LABEL

MICK HOUGHTON

Becoming Elektra
The True Story Of Jac Holzman's
Visionary Record Label
Mick Houghton

A Jawbone book
Second edition 2016
Published in the UK and the USA by Jawbone Press
3.1D Union Court
20–22 Union Road
London SW4 6JP
England
www.jawbonepress.com

ISBN 978-1-911036-03-6

EDITOR Tony Bacon
JACKET DESIGN Mark Case
BOOK DESIGN Tom Seabrook

Printed in China by Everbest Printing Investment Ltd.

1 2 3 4 5 21 20 19 18 17

Contents

4 Foreword *by John Densmore*
7 Introduction *by Mick Houghton*

13 CHAPTER 1 **Da Capo**
19 CHAPTER 2 **New Songs**
28 CHAPTER 3 **O Love Is Teasin'**
44 CHAPTER 4 **Folk Song & Ballad**
52 CHAPTER 5 **Dueling Banjos**
65 CHAPTER 6 **When Maidens Lost Their Heads**
73 CHAPTER 7 **Spirituals & Blues**
84 CHAPTER 8 **Those Were The Days**
93 CHAPTER 9 **Folk Songs From Just About Everywhere**
112 CHAPTER 10 **Where I'm Bound**
126 CHAPTER 11 **High Flying Bird**
138 CHAPTER 12 **All The News That's Fit To Sing**
158 CHAPTER 13 **Blues, Rags & Hollers**
174 CHAPTER 14 **Quality Recordings At The Price Of A Quality Paperback**
196 CHAPTER 15 **East-West**
215 CHAPTER 16 **Maybe The People Should Be The Times**
233 CHAPTER 17 **Extracts From A Continuous Performance**
247 CHAPTER 18 **Take A Journey To The Bright Midnight**
262 CHAPTER 19 **Happy Sad**
279 CHAPTER 20 **Accept No Substitute**
298 CHAPTER 21 **Down On The Street**
322 CHAPTER 22 **Anticipation**
335 CHAPTER 23 **Goodbye & Hello**

345 Afterword *by Jac Holzman*
346 Appendix 1 *A 70s Miscellany*
357 Appendix 2 *Elektra 1973–2016*
362 Appendix 3 *Discography by Andy Finney*
372 Bibliography and Sources
376 Index

Foreword
by John Densmore

Without Jac Holzman, there would be no Jim Morrison. Without Jac Holzman, The *Doors* would never have opened. Without Jac Holzman there would be no Judy Collins, Arthur Lee and Love, Paul Butterfield, The Stooges, MC5, Queen, Tim Buckley, Harry Chapin, or Carly Simon, to name but a few.

As a teenager, if Jac hadn't tied his Nagra tape recorder to the back of his moped and ridden all over Manhattan looking for music acts, we wouldn't have all those great folk singers from Greenwich Village. He fed the scene that launched a thousand songwriters.

Long before Jac ventured out to the Whisky A Go Go on the West Coast to hear our band, we were well aware of the Greek demigoddess who presided over the muses: Elektra. She had a wonderful classical- and ethnic-music wing, Nonesuch, which really was the first world-music label. We adored Judy Collins, who was covering (doing other songwriters' material) then-unknown folks like Joni Mitchell and Leonard Cohen. We idolised The Paul Butterfield Blues Band from Chicago, which was so earthy you could smell the dirt.

The Doors became the house band at the Whisky. Arthur Lee, lead singer of Love, graciously tipped his hat in our direction by telling the president of his record company (Jac) to check us out. Love was a racially mixed folk-rock band that broke the mold. Black musicians were playing funk at the time, and here comes Arthur Lee with his guitar player, Johnny Echols, making music like The Byrds. The last album by Love's original line-up, *Forever Changes*, is a friggin' masterpiece! It's up there with *Sgt Pepper's Lonely Hearts Club Band.*

At the time, we were signed to Columbia, a behemoth who ignored us, and eventually dropped our little quartet (a year doesn't go by when the recording giant doesn't call and ask if we actually recorded anything, hoping there is something, anything, in their vaults). But we never met the head of the Columbia, and I don't even know who dumped us. That was the difference between a boutique and a giant corporation. Suddenly we had a relationship with the president of the label to which we were signed. Trying to talk to anyone at Columbia was like trying to call the IRS, but at Elektra we could call up Jac and he would listen.

What did Jac see in us? He was attracted to the same thing I was with The Doors. He heard a band that was not only playing rock, but rock infused with jazz and flamenco and the blues. The late, great Ray had the blues from Chicago. I had the jazz, Robby had the flamenco, and then on top of that, you had the word man with Jim Morrison. His lyrics were so poetic, and Jac recognised we were intellectuals playing rock'n'roll.

And there was something even more important for us than accessibility to the record company. *Jac had ears.* Good ears. Ears that built his very respected boutique label into one of those giants (which eventually brought on its own problems). Don't want to get ahead of myself … we'll talk about the poisoned chalice a little later. Jac's ears liked what they heard; he signed us and assigned Paul Rothchild to produce. Paul Butterfield's producer!

Our relationship with the prez never changed much over the years. He hovered and helped orchestrate our career, choosing singles, sequencing album cuts, and hiring the most sophisticated sound people in the biz, i.e. Bruce Botnick. Jac also endured excessive personalities such as Iggy Pop, Tim Buckley, the MC5, etc … let alone our lead singer.

When we were working on the first album, Jim got inebriated after recording 'Light My Fire', broke into the studio at two in the morning that same night, and hosed the place down with fire extinguishers, 'cos he thought the song was going to burn up the building. Jac graciously paid for the damages and kept the whole thing under wraps, even though we hadn't hit it big yet. That's true commitment for you.

But nothing could douse the rocket-like ascension of LMF, which quickly landed at Number One on the *Billboard* charts. A Robby Krieger-penned 60s anthem that would change Jac's life, the band's life, and even the culture. I remember driving in my car when the song came on the radio, and I rolled down the window and shouted out to whoever could hear, "That's me!"

Recently, Jac said that the hardest thing he had to deal with in terms of the label was coping with success on a level that largely came about through The Doors. Success meant that almost overnight, Elektra was no longer a 'boutique' label and had to compete with more corporate labels. For the band, the pressure to play the 'hits' took away our incubation period for nurturing a song. Jim wanted to go away to an island to re-inspire our band, but by then the spirit in the bottle had seduced him. There were already too many rummies on islands, so that idea didn't, and wouldn't, come to fruition.

So the pressures and repercussions of 'suckcess' had their Achilles' heel, but we all drank the poisoned chalice and don't regret it! Maybe, besides paying the rent, we helped compose a part of the soundtrack for people's lives, and music is one of the great elixirs that make life much more than bearable. As Jim's hero Nietzsche said, "Without music, life would be a mistake." Jac brokered that sound for millions and millions of eager listeners, and for that we are extremely grateful.

JOHN DENSMORE SPRING 2016

Introduction
by Mick Houghton

"*You can never learn less.*" **BUCKMINSTER FULLER**

I bought my first Elektra LP in 1966. I was 16 years old and still at school in London. That record was the self-titled debut by The Incredible String Band, and its sound of scratchy fiddles, whistle tunes, and ragtime banjo was just a little too strange for me. My taste was more for The Kinks, The Pretty Things, The Searchers, and The Rolling Stones. I was drawn to that Incredible String Band album by the weird photo on the front – three beatnik-looking folkies holding strange instruments – and the intriguing liner notes that I'd read in the shop. It was a typically seductive marketing triumph for Elektra's eye-catching jackets.

I stuck with *The Incredible String Band*, not least because I'd invested five times the price of a single, but it only made sense to me several years later. Singles were the main currency at the time, and I made no connection between artist and label. My collection divided equally between Decca, EMI (Parlophone and Columbia), Pye, and Fontana, although I had no idea that they were the four major labels who dominated the UK music industry. That meant nothing to me.

Albums were gradually replacing singles in my life, guided by John Peel's essential Radio London programme *The Perfumed Garden* and his subsequent BBC Radio 1 shows *Night Ride* and *Top Gear*. Within a couple of years I had a dozen or so albums, virtually all American. I was snotty enough to dismiss acknowledged must-haves like *Sgt Pepper*. At least half my meagre collection were Elektra albums: Love's *Da Capo*, *Strange Days* by The Doors, another Incredible String Band, *The 5000 Spirits Or The Layers Of The Onion*, The Paul Butterfield Band's *East-West*, and Tim Buckley's debut and his *Goodbye And Hello*. By now, I'd discovered essential shops in central London like One Stop Records and Musicland, which sold these as imports. My local shops no longer catered for my needs, aside from the odd Doors or Love single – even though, mysteriously, classics such as 'Light My Fire', '7 And 7 Is', and 'Alone Again Or' never troubled the British charts.

Peel's influence aside, the fact that I owned so many Elektra albums was more by luck than judgement. I was hooked on Elektra without realising, and only gradually over the next few years did I join the dots. I would notice the distinctive, perfectly-positioned Elektra logo and the imaginative and colourful jackets, and I would recognise almost subliminally the names on the back of those jackets – Jac Holzman, Paul Rothchild, Bruce Botnick – and that the jacket design or art direction was by William S. Harvey. No other pop label told you who designed the jackets.

As the years went by, I met more Elektra fanatics. The trainspotting aspect never attracted me. I was only drawn to the music, and I soon picked up albums by Clear Light, David Ackles, Tom Rush, and Zodiac Cosmic Sounds, with its mad astrological narrative and pulsating electronic score. It was an extraordinary time for music, and my taste, expanded by Elektra's daring possibilities, now widened to take in more British folk and underground releases by Pink Floyd, Family, Traffic, Fairport Convention, and Pentangle as well as American albums on Warner Bros, CBS, and Verve.

But Elektra's records marked the first time I discovered the concept of label identity. I realised that great music was not happenstance, that it was the result of a nurturing, guiding hand – the hand of that very astute label boss Jac Holzman. Plenty of people before me had made the same kind of connection with Sun or Chess or Atlantic. But in a new age when pop music suddenly acquired critical and intellectual standing, it was Elektra that led the charge for like-minded entrepreneurs in the UK to mould independents – Island, Charisma, Transatlantic – and for major labels to preach similar music-first ideals with spin-offs like Harvest, Deram, Vertigo, and Dawn.

For an independent American label, Elektra holds a special place among British music fans, particularly during those years when Holzman was running the label, between 1950 and 1973. For me, it was a particularly proud moment when Stuart Batsford and I were commissioned by Rhino UK to put together an Elektra boxed set. Along with designer Phil Smee, we compiled and produced the five-disc *Forever Changing* in 2006. As a result I met Jac Holzman – 40 years after that leap of faith when I'd bought *The Incredible String Band.* Jac was gracious, friendly, supportive, and encouraging, just as he must have been toward the hundreds of artists he signed down the years.

When Jac suggested that I write this book, it was a more daunting prospect, because the indispensable oral history *Follow The Music* by Jac Holzman and Gavan Daws had been published in 1998. However, my intention with *Becoming Elektra* is not so much to follow the music as to explore the motivation behind the music.

I can't thank Jac enough for subjecting himself to hours and hours of my questions during the summer and autumn of 2009. I also had access to the invaluable *Follow The Music* interview transcripts, an indispensable source for comments from key figures such as Paul Rothchild, Mark Abramson, Bill Harvey, and Cynthia Gooding, all of whom have died since the book's publication. *Becoming Elektra* is, I hope, a worthy companion to *Follow The Music*, telling the story more subjectively from the perspective of someone living the other side of the world.

I felt it was important to focus on the story of Elektra as much during the 50s as later decades, during the time when the label brought folk music to a wider audience through Jean Ritchie, Josh White, Theodore Bikel, Bob Gibson, and others. Their lives are no less compelling than the more celebrated artists from the 60s. Elektra's achievements as a folk label are too often eclipsed by its success with The Doors and the enduring fascination with Arthur Lee and Love or with the troubled singer-songwriters Fred Neil, Tim Buckley, and Phil Ochs. We called the boxed set *Forever Changing* simply because Elektra was always changing. It's a long journey from the obscure art song and the pure Appalachian folk of Jean Ritchie, on Elektra's earliest LPs, to Jobriath and Queen, among the last signings during Holzman's reign.

Becoming Elektra is not only the story of Elektra but also the story of Jac Holzman. It tells how a nerdy underachieving 19-year-old launched and cultivated one of the hippest record labels of all time and became one of the most significant figures in the American music industry. Jac's honesty, insight, and reminiscences are at the heart of this book.

I want to thank others, too. The following helped me along the way: Stuart Batsford, Max Bell, Joe Black, Rick Conrad, Julian Cope, Gavan Daws, Peter Doggett, Jason Draper, Kevin Howlett, Cory Lashever, John

Mulvey, Neil Scaplehorn, Phil Smee, and Terry Staunton. Thanks to Mark Brend, Nigel Osborne, and Tony Bacon at Jawbone Press, and to Andy Finney for the discography. And not forgetting Sara.

My grateful thanks to those who agreed to be interviewed and those who helped put us in touch (in most cases specifically for *Becoming Elektra* or *Forever Changing*): Janice Ackles, David Anderle, Ron Asheton, Scott Asheton, Joan Baez, Elvin Bishop, Bruce Botnick, Joe Boyd, Herb Cohen, Judy Collins, John Densmore, Cyrus Faryar, Danny Fields, David Gates, Bill Harvey Jr, Richie Havens, Mike Heron, Jorma Kaukonen, Lenny Kaye, Robby Krieger, Ray Manzarek, Roger McGuinn, Frazier Mohawk, Mickey Newbury, Van Dyke Parks, Tom Paxton, Jean Ritchie, John Renbourn, Joshua Rifkin, Tom Rush, Buffy Sainte-Marie, John Sebastian, Clive Selwood, John Sinclair, Michael Stuart, David Stoughton, and Lee Underwood. (All quotes in the text without credits are from my own interviews; quotes from other sources are credited by numbers keyed to the Endnotes pages at the back of the book.)

October 2010 marks Elektra's 60th anniversary. A few months earlier, I reach the same landmark. Jac Holzman will turn 80 next year, and I can only hope that if I reach that venerable age I will be even half as mentally and physically agile as Jac is today. He still tirelessly provides the Warner Music Group with the benefits of his experience and expertise. *Becoming Elektra* is a testament to Jac's extraordinary accomplishments and achievements. I thoroughly enjoyed our conversations and learned so much in process, far beyond our discussions and dissections of Elektra Records. He is a man of remarkable taste, perception, grace, and style. A cut above.

About this revised edition

When I was writing the first edition of *Becoming Elektra* I was very conscious that Jac Holzman had already collaborated with Gavan Daws to create *Follow The Music*, their wonderful, collective testament to Elektra Records and the culture it grew from. It was an invaluable template and, needless to say, it presented a daunting challenge. My aim with *Becoming Elektra* was always to dig a little deeper in certain areas, and to fill in some of the gaps that I saw from my perspective. This time around I'm equally conscious of my own collaboration with Jac but I was still able to discover ground that hadn't been excavated, stories that hadn't been told, and artists and albums that I felt were worth another look.

As a result, there are two new full chapters here. One is *A 70s Miscellany*, which re-examines and re-evaluates 23 albums released during the last three years that Jac was running the label he had founded 20 years before. The other new chapter is a more thorough look at Elektra's operation in Britain throughout the 60s. That was when I first discovered Elektra in my teens, and as a Brit I felt it was a largely unexplored story. There's absolutely no doubt that Elektra provided a model and a source of inspiration to contemporary independent labels such as Transatlantic, Island, and Charisma in the UK, as well as major-label-funded underground labels, particularly Harvest and Vertigo, all of which sought to forge a uniqueness through distinctive repertoire and visual identity.

Elsewhere, this edition includes eight new, standalone interviews and draws from many others, some of which came about through other commissions: the Sonny Ochs interview about her brother Phil was done for a feature in *Uncut* magazine; Larry Beckett's recollections about Tim Buckley drew from '20 Questions' in *Shindig!* and Spencer Leigh's interview for *Record Collector*; and new interviews with John Renbourn, Joe Boyd, Georg Kajanus, and Gerry Conway were part of the research for my biography of Sandy Denny, *I've Always Kept A Unicorn.* I'm delighted to find a home for an interview with Jean Ritchie that came through too late for the first edition of *Becoming Elektra*. I was surprised to find that the great Tom Paley lives nearby me in North London, having moved to Britain in 1965 where he's still wowing audiences in folk clubs wherever he can find them. My thanks to Bonnie Dobson for hooking me up with Bernie Krause, who has a fascinating story to tell, while Stefan Grossman – another enthralling new voice in this edition – put me in touch with Peter K. Siegel, one of Jac Holzman's brilliant team of engineer/producers during the 60s. Peter speaks eloquently about the many great albums he engineered and/or produced for both Elektra and Nonesuch Explorer. It was Siegel who brought Peter Rowan to Elektra, and he explains the difficulties in translating bluegrass music to a rock audience via the music of Eric Dolphy and John Coltrane. Only on Elektra.

You really can never learn less; the story of Elektra Record and all those who sailed in her continues to fascinate me, although I think I'll leave it to somebody else to find any further gaps in the story and to discover and reappraise their own overlooked gems and curios in Jac Holzman's all-encompassing catalogue.

My thanks to the following people either expressly interviewed for this edition or whose utterances under other circumstances were relevant: John Barham, Joe Boyd, Gerry Conway, Michael Fennelly, Stefan Grossman, Georg Kajanus, Lenny Kaye, Bernie Krause, Sonny Ochs, Tom Paley, Glenn Phillips, John Renbourn, Jean Ritchie, Peter Rowan, Ed Sanders, Peter K. Siegel, and Billy Swan.

Second time around, the following people were most helpful, each in their own way: Stuart Batsford, Max Bell, Daniel Coston, Nigel Cross, Adam Dineen, Bonnie Dobson, Al Evers, Colin Harper, Ken Hunt, Spencer Leigh, Henry Lopez Real, Richard McIlroy, Henry McGroggan, Jon Mills, Andy Morten, Gray Newell, Les Ong, Tom Pinnock, Mark Rye, Emily Sulman, and Jim Wirth.

Particular thanks to Nigel Osborne and Tom Seabrook at Jawbone for responding to a post-lunch idea of a revised, re-formatted edition and running with it; and to John Densmore for his warm and incisive foreword.

I'm indebted as ever to Jac Holzman, not least for undergoing further inquisition with typical grace and patience.

MICK HOUGHTON SUMMER 2016

CHAPTER

Da Capo

> *"I never forgot something Freddie Hellerman once said to me – and it really stuck – that if you exercise reasonable intelligence and taste, and hang in there, you are bound to be standing in the right place at the right time at least once. That made a lot of sense to me. I just didn't expect once to take so long."* **JAC HOLZMAN**

Fred Hellerman is the epitome of 50s folk music in America. He was a founding member of The Weavers with Pete Seeger and he played guitar on the debut recordings of Joan Baez and Judy Collins. When he gave Jac Holzman that piece of advice, Hellerman would never have envisaged that the "right place" would be a rock'n'roll nightclub like the Whisky A Go Go on the Sunset Strip in Los Angeles. It was there, in May 1966, that Jac Holzman saw The Doors for the very first time.

"I had just flown to LA," says Holzman. "Arthur Lee was playing the Whisky and expected me to drop by. It was 11pm LA time, 2am New York metabolism time. I was beat, but I went. Arthur urged me to stick around for the next band. I could easily have not gone that night. Sometimes it's those little decisions in life that make a difference, not the major ones." That night, The Doors did nothing for him.

It was The Doors who took Elektra to a whole new level some 16 years after Holzman founded Elektra Records while a student at St John's College in Annapolis, Maryland. There were plenty of other pivotal if perhaps less transparently vital moments for him: when he was introduced to Jean Ritchie, resulting in Elektra's first folk release, in 1952; when he first saw and heard Theodore Bikel at a party; when he was approached about recording the blacklisted Josh White. When he recorded Bikel and White in 1955, it was a revelation to Holzman that their names above the title would be as significant as the music they proffered.

Come the 60s, this was the norm and music was increasingly artist-driven. When Holzman saw Judy Collins at the Village Gate in 1960, he knew she was now ready to make a record, and she went on to become Elektra's most enduring artist, remaining with the label until 1984. With Elektra's offices in the West Village, Holzman was ideally placed to sign Phil Ochs and Tom Paxton, two contrasting singer-songwriters playing in Greenwich Village. A no less significant moment occurred when the *Blues, Rags & Hollers* record by Koerner Ray & Glover arrived in the mail one day in 1963 and helped get Holzman back on track at a time when he felt the label was beginning to lose direction.

When producer Paul Rothchild joined Elektra that year, it was Rothchild who helped guide Elektra into the electric age. Significantly, it was Rothchild who discovered The Paul Butterfield Blues Band at Big John's in Chicago and signed them to Elektra. They were the bridge between acoustic folk and the rock era that Holzman knew was coming. He found what he was looking for when he saw Love at Bido Lito's in 1965, which led to The Doors. Without this confluence of events, Elektra Records would never have signed The Doors or known how to handle them.

Elektra Records was hardly the 'small independent folk label' that so many accounts of Doors history would have us believe. Elektra's survival of tough times in the 50s and its ability to break a group like The Doors by the mid 60s was largely due to the vision, intelligence, drive, and passion of Jac Holzman. Only Jac Holzman would have initiated a series of *Authentic Sound Effects* records that made a million, or would have launched a novel baroque–classical label, Nonesuch Records, in 1964. Nonesuch offered 'Quality Recordings At The Price Of A Quality Paperback' and revolutionised the classical-record world. Within 12 months the label was netting half a million dollars a year.

Jac Holzman is a thinker. He likes to let ideas marinate, and something in his inner ear whispered that there was more to The Doors than he saw and heard that first night. It took another three nights before he got it. "I have to find something," he says, "a song or something that's like a Rosetta stone, a portal through which I go to better understand the music. It took me four nights before I found that, and it was 'Alabama Song' – which I knew thoroughly, but what they did with it was pure Doors. And then I got it; I needed that point of reference, that one navigational fix. With Love, it was 'My Little Red Book'. That told me they were more than just another band on the strip."

When Holzman heard the piano bassline that Doors keyboard man Ray Manzarek played under 'Light My Fire', he was ready to sign them. Manzarek was impressed by Holzman. "He was the only person who was interested. He was an intellectual, the cowboy from New York. He was like Gary Cooper riding into town, but with brains. Jac even knew that 'Alabama Song' was written by Kurt Weill and Bertolt Brecht. He was the only person who ever understood, which was one of the things that encouraged him to sign us. 'My God, these guys play rock'n'roll and they're smart: they're doing Brecht and Weill!'"

Holzman laughs. "As Ray once said to me, I spoke in whole sentences, which wasn't always the norm with music people. He was a bit full of himself when he said it, but he meant it well."

The Doors weren't consistent, says Holzman. They needed some fine-tuning before they would be ready to record – but he knew this was no ordinary rock'n'roll band. "The Doors are unique to this day and nobody has ever sounded like them. They were special. That was the number one question: am I hearing something I've never heard before? And the answer was certainly yes."

Three of the four Doors already knew about Elektra Records when Holzman first approached them, but perhaps their singer did not. Van Dyke Parks was a friend of Holzman from the time before Elektra became successful on both Coasts, and he recalls the Doors signing coming out of nowhere. "Elektra put a bid in for something that was decidedly not pandering to pop-music tastes, totally outside the box in terms of what they'd been known for previously. It was surprising to everybody, probably even The Doors themselves. I was living in Laurel Canyon at that time and was fairly close to Jim Morrison, and I knew it was an offer he wasn't expecting."

According to Manzarek, The Doors "were excited that Elektra was interested. The Paul Butterfield Blues Band was on Elektra. We knew they were a well established folk label, but they had done very well with Love, in our eyes, and we wanted nothing more than to be as big as Love."

Doors guitarist Robby Krieger was ecstatic. "I was almost an exclusive Elektra listener when I was in high school. I went to a private school in Menlo Park, in the Bay Area, which had a lot of guys from back East, and they turned me on to folk. It was pretty eye-opening. Before I thought about being a rock'n'roll player, I was very much into folk music. We had a jug band which was called The Back Bay Chamber Pot Terriers.

"Elektra had a lot of great flamenco stuff – I had the Sabicas records – and they did a lot of great blues and folk music. I loved The Paul Butterfield Blues Band, Koerner Ray & Glover – this was stuff that I listened to every day in high school. I had listened to Josh White and Judy Collins. A lot of the stuff I got from Elektra was produced by Paul Rothchild, which was very foreboding. I thought man, that's perfect. It was amazing when we heard that Paul Rothchild might produce us."

Elektra was already moving away from being that 'small folk label'. Holzman says, "We were considered a label that was definitely on the come, and I was always considered a guy who was on the make. I have a hard time seeing myself that way, but I would go after opportunities if I was committed to something, and I just wouldn't let up." He chased The Doors for months and didn't understand why Columbia rejected them, even though he was thrilled that they had. He made his approach after seeing the band play four or five nights. "They liked me," he says. "Our success with Love mitigated any concern as to whether we could deliver on The Doors. They were reticent because they had been burned by Columbia, and I finally realised what the closure might be: not to guarantee that I would release a record, but to guarantee I would release three albums. I knew they had enough for two full albums, and I would give them what no other label would give them. If the first release did less well, The Doors wouldn't be out on the street, another disheartened and discarded LA band."

This was a magnet for the group, says Krieger. "The three-album deal was unusual in those days, because it was always discretional on the part of the record company. There were no offers on the table when we signed to Elektra, although I'm sure there would have been, because we were getting pretty hot around LA – and there were guys who wanted to produce us and do production deals."

Krieger mentions Terry Melcher, even Frank Zappa, as producers keen to work with the band. But the band wanted a record deal rather than a production deal. "Those kinds of deals were pretty loaded against the artist. You had no control."

Manzarek agreed. "Columbia had signed us for a single or two and then never recorded us, and dropped us – and Jac said three albums! That meant we could record all our songs. There was no stopping us. 'Light My Fire', 'Break On Through', 'Soul Kitchen', 'The End', 'When The Music's Over', 'Moonlight Drive' – all those songs were written and going to be out there. That was amazing. I was shocked that he gave us three guaranteed albums – not just recorded, but put out on the street."

Ultimately, it was the combination of Elektra's flexibility and its unswerving reputation plus Holzman's acumen and commitment that won over The Doors. Those factors brought so many to the label. After Herb Cohen sent Holzman a demo by an extraordinary young singer and songwriter, Tim Buckley, Holzman signed Buckley to Elektra in 1966, captivated by his voice. Buckley heralded yet another swathe of singer-songwriters who didn't fit the existing folk template: David Ackles, Paul Siebel, Pat Kilroy, even Nico, who recorded the dauntingly experimental album *The Marble Index* for Elektra in 1968.

These elements would even draw the MC5 and The Stooges to Elektra – two bands signed in the course of one weekend purely because Holzman trusted the judgement of the label's publicity man, Danny Fields. Their debut albums, released in 1969, were *Kick Out The Jams* and *The Stooges*, and both are seen as milestones today. But Holzman caused considerable consternation among his fellow executives within Elektra by bringing these enfants terribles to the label. Ironically, there was no less puzzlement when, later the same year, Holzman signed a bunch of soft-rock sessionmen who would soon became Bread. Bread's phenomenal success in turn paved the way for Elektra to sign Carly Simon and Harry Chapin in the 70s, two exceptional singer-songwriters who, stylistically, went against the grain of early 70s trends and represented the sort of intelligent, articulate artists Holzman attracted and so admired.

Holzman reflects on an interesting parallel with Ahmet Ertegun, who founded Atlantic Records in 1947. "He and I have a similar educational background – we both went to St John's College – but he used that background differently. Ahmet always wanted to 'get down'; I wanted to 'get up'. And the artists he was with wanted to get down. I preferred the artists where I could talk about something, or they could talk about things other than music. Jim Morrison and I would hang for a couple of hours and we would mostly talk about film and film technology – which he appreciated. You talk music but you talk life: you talk about everything. It's not just about intellectual understanding but about emotional understanding, and to be able to convey that. And you also have to get their music on the most fundamental level, to be passionate about it."

Barely a year after The Doors signed to Elektra, the band hit Number One in the *Billboard* charts with 'Light My Fire' in July 1967. This was the supreme validation for Holzman. "It was a kind of euphoria I feel impossible to describe, to have your personal taste and judgement confirmed by others. It was not just the music but the label that was held in such respect. It was wonderful. There was excitement. People were running up and down the halls. We were heroes. We had a smash hit label in Nonesuch, and Elektra was happening. People were paying attention to what we were doing and people were saying: it must be worthwhile, it's on Elektra."

It was an astonishing year. With 'Light My Fire' barely out of the charts, the *Strange Days* album proved The Doors were no mere one-shot band. That year, Elektra also released Love's *Forever Changes*, Tim Buckley's *Goodbye And Hello*, and Judy Collins's *Wildflowers*. All were recorded in Los Angeles, where Elektra had established a parallel studio and office to its New York base. Over in Britain, where Elektra already defined the notion of a cult label, Holzman had established a small office. There, Joe Boyd signed the quintessential eclectic folk duo, The Incredible String Band, whose record *The Hangman's Beautiful Daughter* was an unlikely Top Five album, while Love were bigger in the UK than they were in America, certainly outside of California.

"1967 was the moment when it all came together," says Holzman, with justifiable pride. "I knew the label was solid. We had brought ourselves up from nothing and could prove to people who needed us to prove it to them what our capabilities were, but we were still a small company. I was just knocked out by that year – it was a great year. Suddenly I had this massive vindication, after having struggled all these years, and knew, for the first time, that maybe I really did know what I was doing. It was a wonderful feeling."

CHAPTER

New Songs

> *"I decided instinctively, without much thought, just to pretend I knew what I was doing and charge ahead."* **JAC HOLZMAN**

No question: 1967 was an extraordinarily momentous year for Elektra. "We were now contenders," Jac Holzman justly claims. It was also the year when the folk boom could be said to be well and truly over. No longer was Elektra the small New York-based independent folk label that had begun life in 1950, and few of the label's releases during 1967 could be traced back definitively to its folk beginnings.

Perhaps simplistically, it's been said that the folk musicians of the 50s revival were either Seeger's children or Woody's children. On October 3 1967, one of those founders of modern folk music, Woody Guthrie, finally gave in to the illness that had plagued him for years. Huntington's chorea had left him confined to a hospital bed in New Jersey during his later life. At a tribute concert the following January at Carnegie Hall, a celebration of Guthrie's life and work was overshadowed as the spotlight fell on the most famous of his children, Bob Dylan, whose presence hovers over the 60s.

Dylan's performance at Carnegie Hall was the first since his self-imposed exile following his August 1966 motorcycle accident. The bill included Odetta, Ramblin' Jack Elliott, Judy Collins, Tom Paxton, and Arlo Guthrie, with Pete Seeger appropriately closing the show. Seated in the audience that night was Phil Ochs, once Dylan's most driven rival in the Greenwich

Village scene of the early 60s, and the most committed of Elektra's topical songwriters. Ochs left before the end of the concert, seething that he hadn't been asked to perform.

Ochs had been released from his Elektra contract by Jac Holzman after three perfectly time-capsuled albums, and he left New York City for Los Angeles in an attempt to cast off his folk troubadour image. LA was rapidly replacing New York as the focal point of the music industry, in which Elektra Records was a player on both coasts.

Holzman could never have imagined this when, in 1950, as a 19-year-old student, he took his first tentative steps at forming a record label that would merge his two great passions: folk music and audio engineering.

Jac Holzman was born in September 1931 and grew up on the Upper East Side of New York City, on 84th Street, between Park and Madison. He was the son of a successful doctor, but to say he enjoyed the advantages of his parents' support would be far from the truth. He felt disengaged from them, particularly his silent, domineering father. From the age of five, he ran away every year, only to be dragged back home. By the time he was twelve, he had discovered that he could escape by going to the movies.

"I must have seen eight out of every ten Hollywood movies made every year of my young life," he recalls. "For me, film was a connection with an emotional life on the screen that I didn't have at home. I speak of my father as being a silent, dominant force – he didn't rant and rave, which I would have preferred. I was always adrift and never knowing how my parents felt about me. If it hadn't been for my absolutely incredible grandmother, I would never have accomplished anything. Children need stability in their life: you need a couple of givens amid all the unknowns, and film was one of those givens. Most of my life's lessons came out of the movies, and I would try and imitate what I saw on the screen until it became part of me."

At 16, Holzman graduated from high school, and this provided an opportunity to permanently run away from his unhappy home life. His first choice was his father's alma mater: Reed College in Portland, Oregon, a liberal institution with the special benefit of its location on the other side of the continent. But his father, surprised that Jac had even been accepted, vetoed it. Holzman says his father rejected the idea for fear his son's "mischief" might "tarnish the family name".

Holzman was adamant that he would find somewhere far enough away from home. And he did: St John's, an unorthodox liberal arts college in Annapolis, Maryland. To his father, says Holzman, getting to St John's College was simply "Jac taking the easiest way out". St John's did not even require an interview. "They accepted me because my father could pay the full fee and they were short of students," he explains. "The government subsidy of the GI Bill, which helped returning servicemen attend college, wasn't sufficient to keep the school in business."

Among St John's collective of post-war students, Holzman fell into the latter section of what he calls a "ragtag collection of dilettantes, pragmatic war veterans, parental escapees, and dedicated bookworms – with a sprinkling of well off, mentally undernourished prep school graduates with grades so poor or indifferent that only St John's could find any virtue in us".

Aside from providing an emotional awakening, St John's played a huge part in Holzman's intellectual development. "What I discovered in St John's College, which was so important to me, was that the college experience was more formative than anything I had been surrounded by before. First of all it required a great deal of discipline, which I had assuredly lacked. There were no easy textbooks, no CliffsNotes. I was thrown into an environment of intellectual rigour and philosophical jousting that was, for me, fearful in the extreme but quietly exciting. I didn't really communicate who I was because I wasn't much at the time. I was very much a work in progress, but what held me in good stead later in life was to question everything and to have acquired a facility with language. I didn't think I was very smart – that was the message I was always getting from my father."

Holzman says that St John's College is wrapped up in what he later achieved at Elektra. It underlined his approach and his decision-making process. "The function of college is to find a vocation around which you can build a happy and productive life. I found it at St John's, but it was the context of the experience more than the content of the curriculum that informed so much of what I did and what I became."

Holzman was captivated by folk music, largely due to his dormitory friend Bob Sacks, who had a rich collection. Sacks had cerebral palsy, and Holzman would occasionally help him load the breakable 78rpm shellac discs onto the thin turntable spindle. He was sucked into the world of Woody Guthrie, Josh White, Leadbelly, John Jacob Niles, Richard Dyer-Bennet, Burl Ives, and Susan Reed.

"I connected with people's simple lives, not my Park Avenue silver-plated-spoon early life," says Holzman. "The kind of life I had been living at home didn't feel real to me. It wasn't until I got to folk music that I understood some of the more basic drives. The manner in which I was listening to folk music with a friend who had cerebral palsy and whose movements were a bit limited was a powerful contact element which added to the music. It connected me in ways that I couldn't show to others. Once I started making records, I was very aware that I was making records for me, I was making records that I would want to enjoy listening to years later. I hoped there were enough people out there with similar tastes to keep Elektra afloat."

One of the special attractions of folk music to Holzman was that it was like a movie that took place in just a few minutes. It seemed to give him the same emotional uplift as film. Where films were on a grand scale, and you would sit through a whole film and share the experience with an audience, the beauty of a song was that it went instantly to the heart. "The verse was the narrative and the chorus was the lesson. Music for me was like taking a stronger emotional pill. When I'm listening to music though headphones, I feel the song is being mainlined to me."

Bob Sacks's folk collection offered a glimpse into Holzman's future and the foundations of Elektra Records. Art singer Susan Reed and stylish folk-blues original Josh White would both eventually record for Elektra, and Holzman was honoured to produce and edit boxed sets of both Guthrie's and Leadbelly's Library of Congress recordings in the mid 60s. The other artists he discovered were popular folk singers of the day who helped set the tone for folk music but whose styles soon became outmoded.

Richard Dyer-Bennet's elegant, spindly folk style had long been a steady seller; he played beautiful guitar and had a trained high tenor voice, though his schooling was in the English ballad tradition. Collector and publisher John Jacob Niles, strumming a weird oversized dulcimer, sang in a strangulated falsetto described by Bob Dylan as "bone chilling, eerie, and illogical". The warm-voiced Burl Ives had major folk hits with 'Blue Tail Fly' and 'Foggy Foggy Dew' during the 40s and continued to have pop and country & western hits for the next 20 years.

Something stirred within Holzman when he discovered such simple, direct melodies and affecting words. "I loved music. I found my heart opening to music. It was there I discovered my emotional identity. My heart had always wanted to be open, but I hadn't known how to manage that, coming from a family of suppressed feelings. Now I had found a way to connect to the rest of the world through music."

If at first Holzman saw St John's as an escape from the orbit of his parents, he realised that the college offered many opportunities beyond the scholastic. To him that was the real benefit of attending – even if he was ready to leave at the end of the third year. He barely passed the enabling exam for that final year, and so the dean suggested he take a year off. Holzman wondered if they were kicking him out of school, and they said no … not really. Holzman asked the dean to explain this to his grandmother so that she in turn could break it to his father.

"The way the dean put it was: 'Jac has some genius, and I don't know where it is, but I think he'll do well when he finds it. I don't think St John's is appropriate for him any more.' He was proven right. Fourteen years later, in 1965, I was appointed to the St John's board of governors, which my grandmother thought validated his opinion."

Holzman was a disconnected kid because his parents, and especially his father, did not pay him enough attention. His grandmother Estelle, on the other hand, believed he was something special. She supported him and loved him. It was not untypical of a male-dominated family in the 30s and 40s. Holzman was overweight until he was 13, and then he simply lost the weight, slimming down to become a tough kid, ready to face the world. "So by the 50s, I was out the door as quickly, and on my own by the time I was 19. There was no hesitation about my starting Elektra. I just couldn't imagine failure, and I was totally committed to Elektra."

Although Holzman was inspired by folk music, it was the post-war technological advances in audio engineering that fired his enthusiasm and opened up the possibility that he could record the music himself and on his own equipment. Stretched by the learning programme at St John's, Holzman found solace as the late-40s equivalent of a present-day nerd, hanging out for hours in the school's electronics lab, excited by oscillators and amplifiers. At weekends, he'd rummage in seedy stores in lower Manhattan, in the blocks surrounding Cortlandt Street, for Army and Navy surplus gizmos.

He says his love of electronics allowed him to keep a grasp on reality. "That was something I could wrap myself around: I could comprehend it, I could afford to pick up bits and pieces and form them into something new.

This was after the war, when all the surplus came back and hit these shores, and you could buy odd parts. I spent my time building quite sophisticated equipment with the aid of the Lafayette and Allied radio catalogues and manuals. And after building an FM tuner, you could receive these wonderful radio stations that played classical music."

There was one must-have piece of equipment Holzman couldn't build himself, so he lobbied his parents with unusual devotion and guile. They bought him a Meissner semi-professional disc recorder for his next birthday. He knew it was portable enough to allow him to record piano recitals in the St John's Great Hall. His notion of starting an as-yet-unnamed label was nebulous, but it took a step forward after he attended a recital at St. John's by soprano Georgiana Bannister featuring musical settings of poems by Rilke, Hölderlin, Kafka, and e.e. cummings, accompanied by the music's composer, pianist and art critic John Gruen. Holzman approached them, and Bannister and Gruen agreed to record for his non-existent record company.

In October 1950, Holzman persuaded Paul Rickolt, a friend from St. John's, to help launch a record label. Between them, they provided the initial capital of $600: Rickolt, a few years older, had served in the Navy and put up his $300 veteran's bonus; Holzman's half came from money he'd saved from his bar mitzvah.

The two friends would listen to music and talk about what they heard while they played canasta into the small hours. "The wonderful thing about recorded music, which I also first got from St John's, is that it can be a shared experience as much as a personal experience," says Holzman. "We had very different taste. Paul loved show tunes. I had heard folk music through Bob Sacks, and I'd also discovered Ralph Kirkpatrick, the great interpreter of Scarlatti's works for the harpsichord. That firmed up my interest in baroque."

The name of the label came by changing the usual anglicised spelling of the Greek mythological heroine Electra. As Jac joked in later years, "I gave her the 'k' that I lacked." In truth, Elektra had the right sort of classical connotations for a label originating in such a school of the mind as St John's.

The name of a Greek demigoddess who presided over the artistic muses was admirably suited to Elektra's first musical offering. In December 1950, *New Songs* by John Gruen, sung by Georgiana Bannister and with Gruen on piano, was recorded in one three-hour session in a New York City studio. Holzman took the tapes to RCA for mastering and pressing, at a cost of

$40. When he received the test pressings in February, he was disappointed to find the music was barely audible above the surface noise. RCA agreed to another transfer, which he insisted on supervising. From day one, Elektra Records took pride in audio quality. After all, *New Songs* was the first LP to carry the credit 'Produced by Jac Holzman.' By the close of the 50s, Elektra would notch up close on a hundred releases, mostly produced by Holzman or scrupulously supervised by him.

This was rule one of running a shoestring record label: you have to do everything yourself. "I found out that no matter how much you wanted to concentrate on just the artistic and creative concerns, you were always responsible for everything," says Holzman.

He names Peter Bartók as a very important figure in the early Elektra story. "He had the same reference point for sound quality that I had. Having decided to make the *New Songs* album, I had nowhere to go. I didn't know about anything. John Gruen suggested Peter Bartók. I knew who Béla Bartók was, of course, and here was the composer's son."

Peter Bartók spent a lifetime making exquisite recordings of his father's work, which he paid for by being an engineer. Peter had a small studio, so Holzman booked it on Gruen's recommendation. He found Peter a first-rate engineer and a wonderful man, obsessed with the history of his father and perfecting his approach to sound recording. Holzman learned a lot, gaining a respect for breaking the technological rules and underlining a firm commitment to excellence.

"Peter was a role model in terms of his approach, which was that nothing was ever good enough until you got it absolutely right – and knew it was right. I aspired to his standards. As a result of what I learnt from him, Elektra didn't need a staff engineer for almost ten years. I was able to do all the original recordings on my own."

Peter bent the rules to try to achieve better results unconventionally. Holzman cites one of Elektra's earliest releases, *Voices Of Haiti*, as an example. "It was recorded on wire, pre-tape, and for the transfer Peter constructed a clever filter circuit to eliminate the buzz. People thought *Voices Of Haiti* was high fidelity. He was a real mentor to me, and when he left to live in Florida in 1957, I had been thoroughly schooled through observation of his methodology and attitude. He was a genius of electronic engineering, in my opinion."

In March 1951, Jac Holzman and Paul Rickolt duly received 500 copies of *New Songs*, Elektra EKLP-1, with a jacket designed by John Gruen's wife, Jane. The records were packed and stored in an adjacent dormitory room in St John's.

Rickolt remembers that Holzman made all the arrangements. "This was done during our junior year, but we got the record out. We found it a very difficult market, because we couldn't have picked a more esoteric genre to start with or anything that would have sold more poorly than this kind of art song."[1]

Holzman concurs. "*New Songs* was a combination of an unknown composer's material – literate songs – being sung by an unknown soprano. And I had another early cautionary lesson in the business of music. You could get more records back than you sold."

By the fall of 1951, Holzman had made the decision to stick with his infant dream of running a record company. His partner, Rickolt, remained at St John's, but Holzman took advantage of his option to leave and moved back to New York City, initially under his parents' roof before deciding to take a $5-a-week walk-up at 40 Grove Street in the residential part of the West Village.

By the end of the year, he had started a record store at 189 West 10th Street, taking over the lease from an ailing sheet-music store. He renamed it the Record Loft, with a stock of about 1,000 albums for sale. Half were folk-music titles, the rest baroque and world titles: African, Indian, flamenco. It was just such a combination of styles that would provide the core of Elektra's output throughout the 50s. Now ensconced at the Record Loft, open seven days a week, Holzman stretched makeshift chicken-wire across the front window to display record jackets, highlighted by the Elektra *E* – which was actually a letter *M* turned on its side.

"I was not a businessman," says Holzman. "My business plan was that a record we made would never cost me more than the cost of the tape, and that every artist was paid from the first record sold. Everyone received the same deal: five percent of the list price on all records sold. I couldn't pay an advance and there were never any negotiations. The contract was, perhaps, three pages, and no one hired a lawyer. It was that simple."

Elektra records existed. Holzman was unhappy with *New Songs*, but it had served its purpose: his wish to produce and release a record had come true. "*New Songs* was a little beyond my taste. I liked it, but what I considered as avant-garde song at that time was Brecht & Weill. John Gruen was too eclectic for me. There was no audience for it, so I chose to concentrate on folk music, where I knew there was an audience – not large, but there was one. I could gain a reputation within that."

Holzman looked at the classical models and the baroque models and realised they were not for him. Folk music, however, was perfect. "I could get an idiosyncratic performance that could not be duplicated, and the costs would be low and affordable."

He had been introduced to the Greek passion for immortality at St John's College, in the Iliad and the Odyssey. "The Greeks would talk about how they would be remembered, and that stuck with me. What can you leave behind? Life is so fleeting. It shifts in a second, and we never notice the moment. All those thoughts were with me. In the beginning, I thought the process of making records was everything, and as much as you savour the process, is the result truly worth the effort? Is it good enough to be remembered?"

New Songs acquired a certain immortality as the first release on Elektra Records, at a time when no one could have anticipated that the label would go on to celebrate its 60th year. It is unlikely that *New Songs* would otherwise be remembered, whereas Elektra's second release was the label's first folk recording, and it came from an artist, Jean Ritchie, who proved enduring in her own right.

CHAPTER

O Love Is Teasin'

> *It was necessary to have an abundance of creative ideas, a vibrant personality, a facility to spot talent, a hard work ethic, an awareness of latest trends, a need to move quickly (in thought and deed), and an ability to sell. A slick record company name, distinctive label design, and a stash of capital did no harm, either.* **JOHN BROVEN, *RECORD MAKERS AND BREAKERS*[1]**

After World War II in America, an independent record industry emerged to challenge the supremacy of the major record labels. John Broven's notion of the record man is almost exclusively applied to those whose labels set their sights on the charts as their ultimate goal and focussed on singles, especially after the resilient new 45s had replaced the old, heavy, and breakable shellac 78s. The birth of rock'n'roll only stepped up the game, as men like Art Rupe at Specialty, Leonard and Phil Chess, and Ahmet Ertegun and Jerry Wexler at Atlantic unleashed some of the finest R&B singles of the period. They breached the monopoly of a record industry dominated by the big three in New York City – RCA Victor, Decca, and Columbia – and the insurgent Capitol Records in Los Angeles.

The major labels controlled every aspect of the business, from a record's inception to pressing, manufacturing, and distribution. But for another more unsung group of pioneers, it was the invention of the 33 1/3 vinyl LP that provided an opening in the market.

For the 17-year-old Jac Holzman, a 1948 article in *Life* magazine was something of an epiphany. "They published a full page photograph of Doctor Peter Goldmark, the resident genius of the experimental CBS Laboratories," he says. "The good doctor was shown standing next to an eight-foot-high stack of bulky, fragile, and very heavy shellac record albums. Yet, comfortably tucked underneath one arm was the very same music, on the newly developed, unbreakable, long-playing records." Some 20 years later, Holzman was asked to become a member with Goldmark of the Warner Communications think-tank, which aimed to make technological headway beyond the music and film industries. Holzman and Goldmark became close friends, and Goldmark gave him one of the three existing copies of the original LP – another is in the Smithsonian.

The 50s is often described as the decade when teenagers took over popular music, but as the decade wore on, in economic terms the new trend was that of albums overtaking singles. It was not simply that music could be targeted to adults but that albums presented a format that was more geared to adult tastes: Broadway cast albums, mood music, popular classical titles, and jazz. Until well into the 60s, the bestselling albums were invariably original cast recordings from theatrical productions, such as *Oklahoma!*, *South Pacific*, and *My Fair Lady*, and later even more successful film soundtracks to *South Pacific*, *The Sound Of Music*, and *West Side Story*. Comedy albums were big sellers too and, like folk music, simple and cheap to record. Accountant Bob Newhart's monologues, recorded at a remote club in Texas, helped alleviate cash flow at Warner Bros, with *The Button-Down Mind Of Bob Newhart* its first Number One album, in 1960.

The new format also suited popular singers like Nat King Cole, Frank Sinatra, and Johnny Mathis. Sinatra was one of the first to realise that albums could be more than just collections of songs, and he recorded tastefully structured albums such as *Songs For Swingin' Lovers!* and *Sings For Only The Lonely*, all with now-classic illustrated jackets. If this trend began in the 50s, the arrival of two-channel stereo, after its successful launch by the New York independent label Audio Fidelity in 1957, only widened the potential of the album.

"When I told my father I wanted to start a record label in 1950," recalls Holzman, "he insisted I meet a patient of his, an executive at Decca Records, who immediately told me you could never break through the four major labels. The more he told me why I couldn't do it, the more determined I became. I knew they were wrong because they would never focus on the kind of repertoire I was planning. It was a move on my father's part to save me from myself. I'd had transitory passions before, and he thought this was just one more that I would fail to follow up on."

The advent of the LP meant that pressing plants now opened their doors to a new breed of independent entrepreneur. They could take orders outside of the majors' stranglehold and ship the unbreakable LPs anywhere in the country – to individual distributors or to specialist shops. It was possible now with far greater ease to start a record label without the benefits of major distribution.

Significantly, the new LP accommodated far more music and was blessed with a far less scratchy surface sound. Until the late 50s, record companies used both the ten-inch and twelve-inch format for LPs, and then the larger size prevailed. Five tracks each side was better suited to certain styles of music whose appeal wasn't a simple three-minute thrill.

For Holzman, the invention of the LP changed all the rules. Record companies had survived largely on the money they made from singles, not conceptualised albums. "They might release a Bing Crosby Christmas album, or three or four ten-inch 78s put into an album with no fresh thought behind it. The major record companies did very well with soundtracks which, like classical music, really utilised the format of the album. Broadway-cast albums were tailor-made for the LP and rapidly advanced the format."

He doesn't think the majors saw that the LP might change the music itself, through the format, and certainly saw no evidence that they had an affinity for folk music – or any genre where they had no experience. "When something new comes along, the entrenched order filters it through paradigms of their past experience without being able to invest it with the kind of awe that says: what can I do with this? It was a great adventure. Not only had I been bitten by the bug, but also 400 other people started their own labels about this same time."

For every success story, many more of these independents went out of business as rapidly as they began. But a small number survived through the 50s. One such label was Caedmon Records, formed in 1952 by college graduates Barbara Holdridge and Marianne Roney and specialising in spoken word and other literary content. Caedmon's first release was a collection of poems by Dylan Thomas read by the author. The label's marketing hook-line was 'The Third Dimension Of The Printed Page'. In the CD age, it became Caedmon Audio, but it remained independent until bought by Harper Collins in 1987. Jazz was another specialist genre that flourished. Labels founded between 1948 and 1953 in New York City as well as Los Angeles included Contemporary, Pacific Jazz, Fantasy, Jazzology, Bethlehem, Riverside, and Prestige. The labels that survived were well placed by mid-decade when, only seven years after LPs had been introduced, LPs accounted for around half of all record revenues.

It was a very select group who chose folk music as their speciality genre. Folk music in the 50s had to survive both the onslaught of McCarthyism and the rise of rock'n'roll. Yet by the time folk boomed commercially in the late 50s, rock'n'roll was already in decline. By then, says Elijah Wald, "Polls of college students regularly found them dismissing rock'n'roll as kids' music, and album acts like Dave Brubeck and, a few years later, The Kingston Trio were specifically associated with college listeners – a group which had grown to unprecedented size thanks to the boom in higher education following World War II. The idea of 'good music' no longer meant classical but now included jazz, folk, and adult pop."[2]

It proved to be a resounding vindication for those like Jac Holzman who had hung on. "This was not my vision alone," he says. "It was truly a revolution of the musically undernourished and disenfranchised. They could not find what they wanted on the major labels so they created it themselves."

Just as Holzman was launching Elektra Records from his college dorm, the Solomon brothers, Maynard and Seymour, established Vanguard Records in 1950, borrowing $1,000 from their father to set up a specialist classical label. In the summer of 1950, Seymour Solomon had taken a tape recorder and travelled to Vienna, where he captured the Vienna Philharmonic and the Vienna State Opera performing Bach cantatas. These became the first issues of Vanguard's Bach Guild label, dedicated to recording the complete choral works of J.S. Bach. Aside from an album of Russian folk songs and two by bluesman Brother John Sellers, Vanguard's critical entry into folk didn't come until *The Weavers At Carnegie Hall* in 1957.

Maynard Solomon echoes Holzman's view. "Elektra and Vanguard were unique, and not mainstream at all. We had to find different niches, one of which was folk. Any small company had to have its wits about it in order to survive against the majors. We had to see the cracks where you could make a contribution that the majors didn't see."[3]

Just as Vanguard was adding folk to its roster, two other labels were founded. Irish group The Clancy Brothers set up Tradition Records with Guggenheim heiress Diane Hamilton in 1956, while Bill Grauer and Orrin Keepnews's jazz-based Riverside label began issuing folk records in 1955, persuaded to develop a Folklore Series by producer and writer Ken Goldstein (who by then had co-produced several of Elektra's early albums with Holzman). By the 60s, another jazz label, Prestige, followed suit; their coup was to hire Paul Rothchild, who was effectively the label's folk department. He produced thirteen albums in six months, recording Geoff Muldaur, Eric Von Schmidt, Tom Rush, and many others before Holzman lured Rothchild to Elektra in the watershed year of 1963.

These labels co-existed in open friendly rivalry even as interest in folk music began to snowball. Holzman remembers that there was nothing cutthroat about their competitive camaraderie, that each was struggling to keep its head above the water, not to push the other guy under.

This was the specialist league in which Holzman and Elektra Records played during the 50s. But the premier label, against which all were initially measured, was Folkways Records, which had been steadily recording folk music since before the war. It was run by Moe Asch, who grudgingly tolerated Holzman and his upstart label in the back room of the Record Loft – which, after all, stocked a considerable range of Asch's product.

Recording engineer Moses 'Moe' Asch was the son of novelist and playwright Sholem Asch. Moe made his first recordings of Jewish folk songs by The Bagelman Sisters in 1939. Within a few years he branched out into recording other ethnic music – Ukrainian, Italian, Greek – for the local immigrant community in New York City, and in 1941 Asch recorded Leadbelly for the first time, performing children's songs. He teamed with Herbert Harris of the Stinson Trading Company in 1943, and the two released records for their Asch/Stinson label, with one or other of the names appearing above the title. They parted company at the end of World War II when Asch launched Disc Records, and this in turn became Folkways Records after Disc slid into bankruptcy. By the end of the decade, across these three labels, Asch had recorded all of folk's leading lights: Leadbelly, Woody Guthrie, Sonny Terry, Josh White, and Burl Ives. He would soon forge a lasting relationship with Pete Seeger, who went on to record for Folkways.

Surveying the opposition today, Holzman acknowledges that Folkways was the benchmark. "Moe resembled a rumpled Joseph Stalin in build and facial structure, and his politics also leaned to the left. He considered me a usurper, but the Record Loft was a good customer, and eventually we became friends. Folkways was really just Moe and his associate, Marian Distler. They were devoted to the company and to each other and worked the kind of crazy hours we all did. Theirs was one of the world's great folk and ethnic music libraries. Moe would cagily press 100 copies of one title and sell primarily to educational institutions, scholars, or devoted collectors, from whom he received the cheque before shipping the records. Sales to retailers in large cities and college towns were a bonus."

Folkways and other progressive labels like Keynote had little real competition at first. Essentially a jazz label, Keynote had released the first LP by The Almanac Singers, *Songs For John Doe*, on Almanac Records, and then *Talking Union* on Keynote itself. The commune-like Almanac Singers centred on Pete Seeger, Lee Hays, Fred Hellerman, and often Woody Guthrie. Josh White first recorded for Keynote as a guitarist with the Almanacs, but in 1941 he released one of his most significant albums, *Southern Exposure: An Album Of Jim Crow Blues*, and one of the most significant records of the period. Uniquely, the songs were all originals, written by White with the Harlem poet Waring Cuney. It was the first civil rights album ever recorded and a precursor of the singer-songwriter movement.

The major labels had merely dabbled in folk music, with little conviction. RCA Victor released a number of albums of collected 78s by John Jacob Niles, starting with his debut *Early American Ballads* in 1938, as well as recordings by Leadbelly and Woody Guthrie, but the company did nothing to promote them. RCA also released Susan Reed's debut, *I Know My Love*, which was studied, simple, traditional Irish–English–Scottish folk accompanied by harp and zither. Reed would next record for Elektra.

The great jazz producer John Hammond – who would later bring Bob Dylan and Bruce Springsteen to Columbia – signed The Carolinians, a trio featuring Josh White, and released a bold album of anti-racist songs in 1941. *Chain Gang* was an anomaly on Columbia's schedules; the label had little time for folk. The record featured White plus a backup group that included the future civil rights leader Bayard Rustin, and its collection of prison songs and 'Negro laments' was adapted and rewritten by a left-leaning folklorist, Lawrence Gellert. In 1958, Elektra reworked this material with Josh White as *Chain Gang Songs.*

Popular entertainers occasionally recorded folk material – Bing Crosby, for example – but none more so than Jo Stafford, who recorded a series of singles and an album, *American Folk Songs*, for Capitol in 1948, featuring 'I Wonder As I Wander' and 'Black Is The Color', collected by John Jacob Niles, and 'Poor Wayfaring Stranger'. Stafford had grown up in Tennessee and learned folk songs from her mother, but she believed that "the orchestra lures some listeners who flee in terror at a guitar or zither".[4] The uptempo songs she recorded, though, were more conventionally folk-based, with accompaniment from banjo, guitar, and bass.

Among those who were turned toward folk by Jo Stafford was Judy Collins, at the time a classical pianist. "I heard 'The Gypsy Rover' on the radio," says Collins, "and before I knew it I was hearing other folk material, like Jo Stafford singing 'Barbara Allen', and I was hanging out in record stores listening to Richard Dyer-Bennet records. Then I found there was a Folklore Center in Denver which was run by Lingo the Drifter – he had a radio show that played singers like Woody Guthrie and Pete Seeger. I convinced my father to rent me a guitar and I started learning folk songs, but Jo Stafford was the person who really turned me on to folk music."

Decca was by far the biggest player in the field, enjoying considerable success with Burl Ives, whose 1949 album *A Collection Of Ballads, Folk And Country Songs* included pop hits like 'Big Rock Candy Mountain', 'The Foggy Foggy Dew', and 'Blue Tail Fly'. Richard Dyer-Bennet would eventually release his own records, but this self-styled 20th-century minstrel also recorded for Decca, where his high tenor appealed to those accustomed to art song.

Dyer-Bennet and John Jacob Niles, a Julliard-trained folk-song collector, were important figures in bringing folk song into the concert hall and to the attention of "polite society". Decca also recorded prolific international balladeers Josef and Miranda Marais and would use folklorist and musicologist Alan Lomax as a consultant for a series of albums, including collector and poet Carl Sandburg's *Cowboy Songs And Negro Spirituals*. But the label's most auspicious signing was The Weavers, in 1950.

The Weavers had already recorded two songs in September 1949 for the independent Hootenanny label, co-founded by future *Sing Out* magazine editor Irwin Silber. One of those, Pete Seeger's 'The Hammer Song', later inspired *Sing Out*'s name with the phrase "sing out danger". During the ensuing years Decca sold over four million Weavers records, and in the process they became the first pop folk group to offer a diluted version of folk, with toned-down lyrics and a sweetened sound. It was something of an irony since the group – old campaigners Pete Seeger and Lee Hays with young singer Ronnie Gilbert and singer-guitarist-arranger Fred Hellerman – had appeared from a radical background, although their left-wing past would eventually derail them.

Theodore Bikel, soon to become Elektra's bestselling artist of the 50s, understood the fine line between commercialism and political ideology. The Weavers, he wrote later, made "a fusion of human concerns, of political, people-orientated awareness, and of fine musicianship. The last thing they had in mind was to make show business history: but without intending it, that is exactly what they did."[5]

Few in the music industry saw folk song as anything other than a passing fad, and they were right. The major labels didn't buy a season ticket for the folk bandwagon, and for a good few years folk music would remain in the hands of independent music makers, radicals, academics, bohemians, liberals, lefties, and oddballs. This was folk's small and insular world. Everyone knew everybody else and, rather than in dedicated venues or the coffee house scene that was almost a decade away, folk-singing parties took place in the cramped apartments and drafty lofts of the homes of the musicians themselves or of other artists, writers, and painters.

In the summer, musicians and singers were just starting to gather around the fountain at Washington Square Park in New York City's Greenwich Village. Other establishments provided unlikely social centres: Peter Carbone's Village String Shop, or Allan Block's Sandal Shop, which opened in 1950 on West 4th Street. Block was a self-taught leather worker who learned to play country fiddle as he grew up in Wisconsin. His shop became a centre for anyone interested in folk music, with musicians far outnumbering customers. "God help you," observed Dave Van Ronk, "if you wanted to buy a pair of sandals."[6]

Close by Washington Square was The Record Loft, where Jac Holzman sat nursing unsold copies of *New Songs*. People would come in as much to talk as to buy anything. "I had encouragement – from fans, people who came into The Record Loft," says Holzman. "People would talk about the records and they would be surprised to find that the Elektra Records office was in the store. The whole space was about ten feet wide and twenty feet deep – and the Elektra Records area was next to the sink."

Holzman says that much of what he learned about the immediate reaction people had to albums came from observing them in the Loft: which records they picked up, how long before they flipped to the other side, and so on. "All that made me recognise that I had to have arresting artwork, an attraction which set Elektra apart from other labels." Of the first eight albums, three are by illustrator Maurice Sendak (two by Shep Ginandes and one by Cynthia Gooding). Sendak was just getting his start, but today he is best known for his book *Where The Wild Things Are*, first published in 1963. "Everything came about by one person telling another," says Holzman. "I had landed in the Village with no network whatsoever, but, sooner or later, everyone in the very narrow world of city folk came into the store: singers, guitar players, collectors, and aficionados like George Pickow. He was a photographer, and his wife, Jean Ritchie, was from a family of Kentucky Mountain singers."

Holzman was introduced to Jean Ritchie by his friend Edward Tatnall Canby, a fellow hi-fi enthusiast and son of the founder of the *Saturday Review Of Literature*. Ritchie had grown up in Viper, south-eastern Kentucky, in the heart of the Cumberland Mountains, but was now living in New York. She sang unspoilt traditional songs in the purest of tones. In folk singer Ed McCurdy's phrase, "she had left the mountains but the mountains had never left her".

For a budding folk label like Elektra in 1952, *Jean Ritchie Singing The Traditional Songs Of Her Kentucky Mountain Family* laid down an impressive marker. To everyone who knew anything about authentic folk music, Ritchie was the undisputed queen of New York City. "I can look back now and marvel in the fact that Elektra's first record proper, the first folk record, was by Jean Ritchie," says Holzman proudly. "She has endured and grown in appreciation and importance. I wasn't aware that this was special. Here was an artist, and I had a friend who had a tape recorder, and he had already recorded a bunch of stuff with her. We did additional recording, put it all together, and mastered it. It was that straightforward. I had no idea how long I could carry on doing it. I was focussed on the day when I would have enough records in a catalogue to support myself and to give Elektra sufficient financial runway to explore its future."

In Ritchie's autobiographical book *Singing Family Of The Cumberlands*, published in 1955 by Oxford University Press, she refused to anglicise local dialect to tell her tales. She recounts the history of her family, who even had a visit from Cecil Sharp in 1917 during one of his song-collecting expeditions to the Appalachian Mountains. Raised in the Cumberland Mountains, Ritchie relates how, in the 40s, many mountain people lost interest in the older ballads, preferring the new hillbilly songs they heard on the radio, especially by The Carter Family and Jimmie Rodgers. The Ritchie clan fought against the tide. Jean loved the old songs and carried on the proud tradition, astonished that the New York folk elite couldn't get enough of her homespun material. They were more interested in the old songs than some of her neighbours in Viper.

"She had no idea that what she was doing had value," explains Holzman. "People who were intellectually alert loved the idea of reconnecting to roots. If you look at the Anglo-American ballad tradition, you see a phraseology in the ballads that had survived in the Appalachian area in versions that were purer than those currently existing in the UK and Ireland. Then there was the political aspect – although Jean wasn't political. Going back to The Almanac Singers, Pete Seeger and Woody Guthrie were generally liberal, or left-leaning. People who bought folk music were middle-class – school teachers, bohemians, professionals – who, in what were still quite austere times, could afford to have interests outside of themselves."

Jean Ritchie was born in 1922, the youngest of the 14 children of Balis and Abigail Ritchie. Their Anglo-Scots-Irish heritage was rich in songs sung by generations hidden away in the Appalachians. Jean was the beneficiary of this deep well of material. The whole family sang and played together. "I learned the songs mostly from my folks, my older sisters, neighbours in the community," she explains. "I lived in the coal mining section of the state, and mom and dad taught me songs they had learnt from their ancestors going back to England, Scotland, and Ireland mostly – intermarried with a few other people. They sang along with whatever they were doing. My mother had a sweeping song she liked to sing when she was sweeping because it had a good brushing rhythm. When she was churning it was something else more quick and bouncy to go with the dasher coming down on the butter. For rocking babies there were lullabies, sometimes an old ballad where everybody gets killed in the end, but it had a nice soothing tune and the baby didn't understand the words."[7]

Balis taught her to play the mountain or plucked dulcimer when she was five or six years old. Two of the strings were tuned in unison and played the melody; the third was a drone, like a five-string banjo. Unusually, she strummed it toward herself, and she learned to sing one melody while she strummed another on the dulcimer, creating a fascinating duet with herself. Aside from the old ballads Jean sang with her family at home, she also learned traditional hymns nearby in Viper's small church.

Theodore Bikel, who first encountered Ritchie in London, says, "The fascinating thing about Jean's material was that much of it was culled from her church background – songs originally unaccompanied for fear of secular contamination by instruments that might also be used for such frowned-upon activities as dancing. But her main instrument was her voice, which produced a haunting and pure sound."[8]

Ritchie also learned the instrumentals: the dances and reels and jigs that were played at weddings and social gatherings. And she did not forget or put aside any of this heritage when she went to college – in itself a rare achievement for a girl in the 30s. She graduated in 1946 with a BA degree in social work from the University of Kentucky. After college, she was a teacher and supervisor of elementary education in her native Perry County. She then went to New York City to work in the Henry Street Settlement on the Lower East Side. Part of her work there with seven to nine-year-olds was to play singing games and to teach ballads and songs to New York children. It earned her the nickname 'Kentucky'.

The bohemian New York folkies took no time in discovering her, especially after she played her first formal concert at the Little Greenwich Mews Theatre in 1948. After that, she performed wherever and whenever she could, mostly at country dances in places like the Village Barn, ladies clubs, and later at regular folk shows at the Cherry Lane Theatre. "The Village was a very exciting place," she recalls. "A few of us used to go down into the subways and sing, because the acoustics were so good; we'd sing rounds and madrigals and things down there. Nobody had seen a dulcimer before. I used to carry it on the subway wrapped in a scarf, and once people found out it wasn't a gun, they wanted to see what it was, so I'd take it out and they'd say: play it for us. I'd say you won't hear it because the train is making so much noise, but I'd pluck it – bing! – and they'd all go wow!"[9]

Full of grace and good humour, Jean Ritchie was the complete authentic package. As she sang in the purest of tones and strummed the dulcimer, her songs carried an ancient DNA that reached back to Europe. As Ed McCurdy observed: "She's a very unique character because, with all her knowledge and scholarship, she still sings as a primitive. That's a very difficult thing to do. With all the sophistication around her to soak up the notes, she kept that voice as pure and simple as it started out. A lovely thin straight voice."[10]

She was as much at home with the New York intelligentsia as attending potluck parties and hoots with radicals like Leadbelly, Josh White, and Pete Seeger. Soon she was a regular on Oscar Brand's weekly radio show and often performed with Brand, the two eventually appearing on an album together, *Courting Songs*, released by Elektra in 1954.

Until then, like most people in cities, Jac Holzman had only heard folk songs as performed by interpreters or on recordings preserved in the Folk Culture archive at the Library of Congress, and then usually as poor-quality field recordings. To be able to record someone as unusual as Jean Ritchie and create an intimacy in the speakers was a challenge and opportunity. Although Ritchie recorded for Mitch Miller – an obscure album of children's songs called *Round And Roundelays* – it was her Elektra debut that began to bring international attention to the folk-music heritage of the talented Ritchie clan. (Miller became a major player in the music industry as head of A&R at Columbia in the 50s.)

Since then, following in the footsteps of Cecil Sharp and Alan Lomax, countless song collectors have sought and now acknowledge the Ritchie family as a major source of traditional tunes and songs. Recently, the Library of Congress acquired her memorabilia for its archive.

Ritchie's Elektra debut was largely recorded in the living room of Holzman's friend Ed Canby, at his apartment on West 4th Street. She says: "Ed was propping the mikes on books and sometimes moving it back and forth to get the instrument and the voice. The funny thing was that the tape recorder was running slow. Jac corrected it somewhat but never got it perfectly right, so I sound like I'm about 12 years old, very young and my voice very high, whereas it really was a little bit lower and more serene."[11] Holzman was thrilled with the result. "It was a ten-inch LP, a grand size, I thought, for albums of less than 35 minutes. George [Pickow] did the cover, and he drew an improved logo, yet still preserving my modish E."

In 1950, Ritchie had married Pickow, a magazine photographer. Just as her debut Elektra album was released, she heard that she'd received a Fulbright award and left to study folk music in Britain and Ireland, travelling in 1952 to explore the origins of her family's songs and commit hundreds of them to tape. In 1956, she and Pickow began releasing them on LP, as *Field Trip*.

While in the UK, she appeared at the Royal Albert Hall and Cecil Sharp House, the headquarters of the English Folk Dance And Song Society. On her return to the US in the summer of 1953, she recorded her second LP for Elektra (by now the label's 25th album), *Kentucky Mountain Songs*, released in 1954. Ritchie's reputation has continued to grow, a victory for her insistence that the song and not the artist is the star.

During the sixth decade of her extraordinary career, Ritchie was recognised by the National Endowment for the Arts, which in 2008 finally awarded her a National Heritage fellowship, the country's highest honour in the folk and traditional arts. "Living this long has its advantages," Ritchie told *The New York Times*. "I've seen a lot of revivals in folk music – at least three since I learned that I was a folk singer – in the 50s and the 60s and now. And each time it's slightly different. Today, anything on an acoustic guitar is folk."

Rather more bizarrely, in that same year Ritchie was inducted into the Long Island Music Hall of Fame alongside Public Enemy (based in Roosevelt) and LL Cool J (who owns a Manhasset mansion). Today she resides on Long Island. She had never heard Public Enemy, concluding after their performance, "I think they are very well named, but make sure you add that I was smiling when I said it. They've got a right to invent their music."[12]

After Elektra, Ritchie recorded for Folkways, Tradition, and Riverside, among others, and at the dawn of punk released *None But One* on Sire Records, which won a *Rolling Stone* critics award. She has since re-released many of her albums on her own Greenhays imprint.

Soon after the Jean Ritchie debut LP appeared, Jac Holzman invested in a Magnecord PT-6 tape recorder, the same type that Ed Canby had used to record Jean, and an Electro-Voice EV-650 'hammerhead' microphone. Within a few years this would become Elektra's portable recording set-up. Strapped to the back of a Vespa motor scooter, it enabled Holzman to go off and record in people's homes. Most of Elektra's early recordings were done this way. "Costs for a recording session, generally, were limited to tape – and that was about $7 a reel," says Holzman.

The mobility that this set-up allowed also meant that Holzman could record outside of sterile studios and capture a greater ambience – something that was not lost on Ken Goldstein, who recorded some 500 folk albums himself during the 50s. "Jac took folk music and recorded it well," says Goldstein. "Previously, folk music was determined by people in the field, many of whom didn't have the money to buy decent equipment and had no sense of engineering sound. So the Ritchie recordings, while not made in the field, gave you the feeling that here was something real and authentic – and with superb sound."[13]

Fully equipped and mobile, Holzman had been welcomed into the small world of folk music. This would soon bring other artists to his door.

Remembering Elektra
Jean Ritchie

"I'm very proud that *Singing The Traditional Songs Of Her Kentucky Mountain Family* was Elektra's first folksong album, and it was my first proper album. Jac was a neighbour of ours in Greenwich Village; his tiny storefront office was just round the corner from us. My husband George and I lived in one of the two third-floor apartments at 88 7th Ave. South; the roof just above served as our patio. An older friend of ours, Ed Canby, had introduced us, and Jac really loved the old Appalachian ballads from my family. He recorded most of the songs in Ed's little third-floor apartment, which was so full of books and LPs that the floor would sway when one walked across it, and the landlord made him move out soon after we did our recordings, for fear the floor would collapse. George and I left for England in the fall of 1952, on my Fulbright year, [on] which [I] sought to "trace the sources of Ritchie Family songs". Jac lived in our apartment while we were away. I remember that Jac sent the album to us just before Christmas which we were thrilled about.

Jac always did right by us, and through us he met Frank Warner, Cynthia Gooding, Susan Reid, and other friends of ours, and he went on to record them. I don't think we introduced Jac to Oscar Brand, who was always omnipresent. I'd had certainly met Oscar several years before recording for Jac, and I was a regular on his show, *Folksong Festival*, which was broadcast every week on WNYC radio; we recorded *Courting Songs* together for Jac. George designed the Elektra logo that was used for many years, and he provided photographs for a number of the early recordings.

We can trace the Ritchie family back to the 18th century, which was when the family came over to this country from the old country. And of course they were singing generations and generations before that, too. It's important to understand where a song comes from, the setting for each song, who sang it, and why it was important to them? As a family during the summer, we'd sing on the porch. In the wintertime, it would be sitting around the fire. Everybody knows that lullabies were songs you rocked the cradle to or were sung when you held the baby, but other songs would accompany everyday jobs and activities like sweeping or kneading bread; others were simply dance tunes. Some of the ballads that were sung to the children were terribly sad or actually quite gruesome tales, although some of these would have the loveliest tunes of course.

My father and mother both played the dulcimer, but everyone considered it was Dad's instrument. I used to take it down and I played it without him seeing me; we weren't even supposed to touch it as children. Eventually, when he became aware that I was really interested in playing it he was surprised that I could already play 'Go Tell Aunt Rhody'. That was when I was about seven, but I'd already been playing it for about two years.

After high school I went on to earn a bachelor of arts degree in social work at the University of Kentucky, and to begin with I was teaching close to home. Then I found out about the Henry Street Settlement in New York [on Manhattan's Lower East Side], which appealed to me because social work was not really established back then and opportunities were scarce. So I went to Henry Street in 1947 and began by working for their summer camp program at Echo Hill Farms [Yorkston Heights]. They asked me to work on through the winter. I would do group work with seven, eight, and nine-year-old girls after school. I played the same games I played in Kentucky, and they were fascinated by the dulcimer, as was everybody. It was hard work because it was a twenty-four-hour job; I was living there so I was always on call at all hours to take care of problems or settle disagreements. As much as I enjoyed it, eventually I had to leave because I needed the rest.

People always wanted to hear me play the dulcimer, and word spread, so I would be asked to take it to schools and sing for their kids or when they were having a get-together on a Saturday night. So I was being asked to perform, particularly at ladies' clubs; to bring along the dulcimer and entertain people. And they would pay me, which was something I had never imagined, and that's really how I got started.

I met George Pickow at Henry Street. He came down one night to a square dance. George had a lot of folksong records and knew about folk music. He loved jazz and blues, and some years before he'd seen Woody Guthrie and Cisco Houston perform. He'd been told about me by his then girlfriend, who thought he might like "this Kentucky girl from the settlement who sings". And it turned out that he did like the girl from Kentucky. He was a magazine photographer, and he went away on assignment but we married a year later, on September 29 1950. The following summer we went to North Carolina and we started recording local folk singers, and that was the start of our field recordings.*

After I left the Henry Street Settlement in late 1949, I did similar work in schools and found other work doing music, singing and playing the dulcimer at local dances and ladies' clubs. Another part-time job I had was at a handicraft shop in the Rockefeller Center, which sold a lot of things from back home in Kentucky – woodwork, craftwork, pottery, and dulcimers. Part of my job was to demonstrate dulcimers. I met [conductor and record producer] Mitch Miller there and he liked the dulcimer and the sound of my voice. So he asked me to sing on a record of children's songs called *Rounds And Roundelettes*. So that was my first commercial recording. It was something that I had never envisaged, because singing was part of my heritage and lifestyle at home, and it's been such a joyful experience ever since.”

George Pickow died on March 9 2011; Jean Ritchie died on June 1 2015.

* These recordings are now in the Library of Congress; Jean and George would release their first LP, *Field Trip*, in 1954.

CHAPTER 4

Folk Song & Ballad

> "*Elektra is moving along. We will release ten LPs altogether this year. We have just recorded one with Hally Wood which should be released in the fall. Your album has received magnificent reviews and should do quite well. Our distribution is wider and we have sold about 600 so far. It will sell about 2,000 before it is through.*" **JAC HOLZMAN, LETTER TO JEAN RITCHIE, MARCH 1953**

While Jean Ritchie and George Pickow were travelling in Europe, Jac Holzman sublet their apartment and regularly wrote to them about Elektra's progress. By the end of 1954, Elektra was barely surviving, however much Holzman's willingness to record folk artists and to record them well was becoming a magnet in Greenwich Village. His emotional link to the simplistic power of the music was something that artists understood and respected.

Holzman's appealing watchword was that Elektra wasn't out to sell a lot of records, but to make good ones. "When you had this going for you, people would find you pretty quickly," says Holzman. "And nobody thought they would make much money. Having an album in national distribution was a validation for the artist. I never paid an advance in the first five years, and it rarely cost me more than $50 to make a record. If you sold 500 to 1,000, that was fine, because you never printed more than 250 to begin with. And you hung on. You just hung on."

It would be a few years before Elektra achieved any degree of stability, which came with the release of a series of LPs by Theodore Bikel that began with *Folk Songs Of Israel* in 1955. That year, Holzman bought out Paul Rickolt's interest in the company for $1,000. He'd closed the Record Loft and moved Elektra around the corner to larger premises, at 361 Bleecker Street, to concentrate solely on the label. To help keep afloat, he persuaded the well-off Leonard Ripley, another friend from St John's College, to buy a slice of the company. Over the next five years, Ripley brought a different sensibility and a European accent to some of Elektra's releases, including records by Sabicas and *Songs Of The Abbaye*.

There was a cachet to releasing Jean Ritchie's debut. Ritchie had introduced Holzman to folk cognoscenti such as the Pulitzer Prize-winning poet Carl Sandburg, who had recently published *The New American Songbook*. Folk song books were another indication of a groundswell of interest in the music. The folklorist John Lomax had published his autobiographical *Adventures Of A Ballad Hunter* in 1947, and collections like the *Fireside Book Of Folk Songs* appeared. The most significant and practical work was Pete Seeger's self-published *How To Play The Five-String Banjo* in 1948. Ritchie also brought Holzman together with Frank Warner, who was a banjoist, a song collector, and, since the early 40s, a dedicated singer of Southern Mountain ballads. Warner's 1953 debut LP – Elektra's third release, *Sings American Folk Songs And Ballads* – had been a long time coming for him. His follow-up, *Songs And Ballads Of America's Wars*, came out on Elektra a year later.

Frank Warner brought a necessary gravitas to Elektra. He had none of the hobo mystique of Woody Guthrie or the former convict Leadbelly. He typified the older, more scholastic and collegiate wing, respectable figures who held down steady jobs and weren't to be found hopping freight trains. They were paternal figures who may well have sympathised with Pete Seeger's political dreamscape but were just as likely to have conservative political leanings. They believed that folk song represented an earlier stage of cultural development and should be treated with due respect in the way it was preserved. Recognition in the upper echelons of the folk community almost had to be worn like a hair shirt. Folk music at the start of the 50s had to be anti-commercial, and that was intrinsic to its appeal in most quarters.

The respected musician Dick Weissman, once a member of The Journeymen with Papa John Phillips, says, "There is a sort of implied snobbism among folklorists that assumes that music collected by folklorists is of necessity purer and more authentic than anything recorded by a commercial record company."[1]

The global pop success that Jac Holzman eventually had with Elektra Records has tended to dim its initial achievements as a folk label. Holzman's early co-producer Ken Goldstein recognised Elektra's folk credibility. "It was one of the more important companies to take music out of the exclusive domain of the few cult elites and into a larger domain of popular music," says Goldstein. "So Jac came before, and helped establish, the folk song revival."[2]

Goldstein even draws a connecting line between Holzman and Alan Lomax, America's greatest folk song collector. "Lomax never lost his belief and touch with the music that he thought was America's most important music. He presented it every way he could, through books, records, through producing records, and doing radio programmes. Jac, in a very real sense, is one of his children."[2]

Holzman says he had great respect for collectors like the Lomaxes, Carl Sandburg, and Frank Warner, who had amassed a remarkable heritage of songs by sweating and lugging equipment around. He marvels at these pioneers, who had so little grasp of the technical aspects of recording. The Library of Congress had to maintain about a hundred different playback needles, each with a microscopically different width to match the groove and to compensate for the degree of pressure required by the recording head that cut the various acetate discs of these collectors.

Frank Warner was born and raised in Selma, Alabama, in 1903 and later studied under the folklorists Frank C. Brown and Newman Ivey White at Duke University. With his wife Anne, Warner became a pioneer in the use of portable recording equipment. In 1940, the vice-president of Philco Radio made the couple a battery-powered portable recording machine specifically for their song-catching expeditions. In subsequent years, Warner distinguished himself as president of the New York Folklore Society and vice-president of the Country Dance and Song Society, although he had arrived in New York City in 1931 as program director for the central YMCA.

His greatest contribution to the American folk boom remains his discovery of the outlaw song 'Tom Dooley', which he first heard performed as 'Tom Dula' by folk singer and instrument builder Frank Proffitt in the late 30s. Warner's interpretation of the song, included on his 1952 Elektra album, was a template for the hit version by The Kingston Trio, which sparked the folk boom six years later.

A massive argument broke out over copyright royalties on the song, which The Kingston Trio 'assumed' was public domain. Warner had passed the song on to Alan Lomax, who printed it in his book *Folk Song USA* in 1947. After the courts eventually split the royalty between Alan and John Lomax and Frank Warner – by which time it had already sold millions – Warner split his share with Frank Proffitt.

"Frank Warner's connection to the music was authentic," explains Holzman, "but he would say, 'It's not me singing; I'm channelling the person from whom I collected the song.'"

Warner was among the more scholarly folk singers of the day, and one of the better singers, but he had never recorded professionally until Holzman approached him. Today, Holzman still isn't sure if Warner had harboured such an ambition, but when Holzman asked if he would think about making a record for Elektra, he agreed immediately. "Frank could sing well," says Holzman, "but Carl Sandburg was making records and he couldn't sing at all."

George Pickow describes Warner's novel approach: "He would do a lot of things that today would be frowned upon, comparatively. He would do black songs exactly as he had heard them and be a Negro. And he could mimic the song exactly. Today, of course, people would think he was making fun." According to Jean Ritchie, "He didn't make any bones about it. He said, 'I'm imitating these people and this is the way they sounded. I want you to hear the way they sounded, because I was so excited when I collected this song.' And he could really make you feel like you were there. A very fine man. Good singer."[3]

For Holzman, it was another step forward. Sales of Warner's album were good enough to pay for the next album. "That's all I expected, as I had no overhead, but even in the ten-inch version we probably sold about 3,000 over time. The economics were straightforward. My distributors were paying me $1.67 for each one, and it was costing me half that to manufacture the record. Of course, they were folk songs, so there were no publisher royalties. I would net 80 cents per record. I was doing that on every record. As long as my catalogue was growing, I was making something on every album shipped, and if something didn't work out, I could keep coming back and try again. This was not true of the artist, whose performing life on record was limited."

Holzman would later earn Warner's supreme measure of approval. "His banjo head was graced with the signatures of the great folk singers and folklore preservationists. Years later, when he thought my accomplishments sufficient to add my signature to those of Leadbelly, Woody Guthrie, and Alan Lomax, I signed. I inwardly wept for the joy of being included, accepted, recognised." Warner died in 1978, his unassuming influence on folk music overshadowed by his collecting and recording the song 'Tom Dooley'.

Nothing was more important in the grass-roots tradition of folk music in the 50s than the blues. Sonny Terry and Brownie McGhee were two of the great ambassadors, familiar to folk audiences through their association with The Almanac Singers in the 40s. Holzman was fortunate to grab some time with Sonny Terry, knowing he could do with some blues backbone. "I was afraid of my label being like me – too pasty and white. Even though Jean Ritchie and Frank Warner were very legitimate artists, I felt I needed a little bit more folk-blues foundation. I always thought American roots music was something that had to be preserved as a 'living' document. Sonny Terry breezed into town and I recorded two albums with him over two evenings, *Folk Blues* and *City Blues*. Alec Stewart played guitar on both."

Susan Reed and Cynthia Gooding, two women who sang in highly contrasting styles, brought yet further distinction and variation to Elektra in the 50s. Reed was born into a theatrical family; her father, Daniel Reed, was a noted actor, theatre director, and playwright. She described her upbringing as "on the run", as she spent time in the South, in Los Angeles, and in New York City, where her parents' house guests included Carl Sandburg, Leadbelly, and members of the Abbey Theatre Irish Players, notably Ralph Cullinan, who taught her many traditional Irish songs. She took up the Irish harp and the zither.

By her mid teens, Reed was singing professionally in New York City at the Café Society Uptown nightclub and had recorded an LP for RCA. She was something of an ingénue, playing the circuit of clubs, concerts, and colleges, and was featured in *Life* magazine and on network TV. *Life* described her as "the pet of Manhattan nightclubbers". In 1948, at the age of 21, she made her first and only feature-film appearance, a co-starring role in

Glamour Girl, a low-budget Columbia picture starring Gene Krupa and his orchestra. She played Jennie Higgins, a backwoods girl who sings folk songs and is brought to the big city to perform.

To Ken Goldstein's ears, Reed wasn't a folk singer. "She was an artsy-fartsy singer of songs, some of which were folk, some of which were art in terms of the sources she drew upon. She was called a folk singer because of the lack of definition that existed. Her light, feathery voice appealed to many people and introduced them to folk songs, not to folk music."[4]

By the early 50s, she was running an antiques store on Greenwich Avenue, all but retired, and concerned that she was being grey-listed – a subtle but equally tyrannical variant of blacklisting. Holzman: "She was in her thirties, with the rosy complexion of an Irish lass, crowned with the most vibrant red hair. We talked about recording and she was willing to consider it. But she had previously been on RCA, and it was emotionally difficult for her to move to a fledgling label. No one else was asking her."

Reed recorded the first of her three LPs for Elektra, *Sings Old Airs From Ireland Scotland And England*, in a small Village church one evening in 1954. The reviewer for *The New York Times* described it as the best vocal recording he'd ever heard. Praise indeed, especially as she was a recognised artist before Elektra recorded her. It was three years before she recorded a second Elektra album, simply titled *Susan Reed*, and later there was an expanded version of her debut, called *Sings Old Airs*. By this time, says Holzman, Reed was keeping her head down. "She was always worried that she might have sung for some organisation during the war that would come back to haunt her. If *Red Channels* – an anti-communist publication – looked hard enough, the damning evidence was there. People were really frightened. It was pretty tough, because it could destroy your livelihood, apart from making other people, even friends, very wary." Reed died in 2010.

Cynthia Gooding was also on the move in her younger days. Born in Rochester, Minnesota, in 1924, she was schooled variously between Cleveland and Toronto before taking off to Mexico rather than going to college. She developed her interest in folk song there, studying guitar and learning the language, and performing for the first time in Mexico City. Moving to New York City, she sang regularly at the Soho, a Greenwich Village cabaret club, but Holzman met her at a typical folk fraternity party. He remembers that she blew the lid off the place. "She was an interpreter of folk material which, at first, I was a little leery of – as someone not indigenous to those cultures. The most natural material for Cynthia was Spanish folk song. The Turkish material basically reflected the Moorish impact on Spain and, although the Mexican folk songs she recorded for us were less suited to her, she did them extremely well. She was also knowing and facile on the guitar."

Her first recordings, done over two days at Holzman's apartment, were produced by Holzman with Ken Goldstein. They turned out well enough that Gooding recorded three LPs for Elektra during 1953: *Sings Turkish And Spanish Folk Songs*, *Mexican Folk Songs*, and the less convincing *Queen Of Hearts: Early English Folk Songs*. Even today, her work has a resounding power and presence.

"I always found Pete Seeger's idea that 'let's all clap hands and sing' will bring peace a little simplistic," says Gooding. "I was more into ethnic and music of the world than into American folk songs. It was very hard for me to find American songs to sing, because Jean Ritchie did them so well."[5] Ritchie herself says, "Cynthia sang songs from different cultures, but intricately arranged, with great sort of flamenco licks on the guitar. She didn't sing them like a peasant, but they were ethnic songs to begin with. And she was a very good singer."[6]

A year later, Gooding was at full stretch, and she tackled *Italian Folk Songs* for Elektra before she was teamed with Theodore Bikel on *A Young Man And A Maid*. "Cynthia had a voice with a low register," Bikel joked, "so low that I sometimes took the high harmonies when we sang together."[7]

Gooding only considered herself a collector in that she "spent a great deal of time in the library", yet she carefully documented the sources of the songs on the albums, often with a refreshing disdain, explaining how she learnt songs in bars or from a Mexican street singer, Marcelo Salazar. The most familiar of her Mexican songs was 'La Bamba', long before Ritchie Valens's rock'n'roll hit in the late 50s. Her treatment was, she explains, "somewhat bowdlerized" because in Mexico a woman would not have sung suggestive verses, "even in the interests of pure scholarship".

In 1948, she had married writer Hasan Özbekhan, and while she described her vocation as "singing and mothering", she appeared at the inaugural Newport Folk Festival in 1959. Mark Abramson, later one of Elektra's most gifted producers, was much taken by her towering command. "There was nothing prima donna about her, but very dignified.

At Newport, which was always kind of bedlam and chaos, when Cynthia performed everybody quietened down. It was like, oh, we'd better pay attention."[8]

Gooding's final Elektra release was *A Treasury Of Spanish & Mexican Folk Song,* a double album set. She felt she could no longer compete with the new generation of rising young female folk singers. "I was 38 in 1962. Joan Baez, bless her heart, was 18, and it was a different matter. I made my last record for Jac, the two-record set, which got me the money to go to Spain."[9]

Another aspiring young singer, Judy Collins, was a huge fan. "Cynthia Gooding told me that she quit singing after I signed with Jac and once things started to cook for me. It was like I was the new model – which I found very upsetting. She was someone I listened to and learned songs from. She was wonderful. Some of us respond to competition differently from others."

For Holzman, Gooding was attractive on many levels. "She was regal, very well read, very well spoken. She was about six-two, six-three, same height as me, and she wore low heels or no heels. She was sexy in an intellectual way and I was very drawn to her. I was a kid with a crush but completely uninteresting to her – plus she had a husband. Cynthia was good to have on the label and, in addition, she helped open up Elektra to world music."

Dylan historians remember Cynthia Gooding as the host of *Folksingers Choice* on New York public radio station WBAI. She interviewed the up-and-coming Bob Dylan in March 1962. Her hour-long show featured 11 performances by Dylan, all still without an official release to this day and unheard other than on bootlegs. In the interview, while Gooding happily goes along with his fictitious biographical detail, Dylan is mildly embarrassed when she reminds him that they first met in 1959 in Minneapolis, when he still wanted to be a rock'n'roll singer. "Whatever got you off rock'n'roll and on to folk music?" she asks, politely. Dylan replies in his trademark aw-shucks manner. "I dunno," he says. "I wasn't calling it anything then, you know? I wasn't really singing rock'n'roll."

Dylan had arrived in New York City in January 1961 and, more than anyone, drew attention to a vibrant folk scene in Greenwich Village. But the folk clubs and coffee houses had not sprung up overnight. Folk music had been much more of an underground movement during the 50s. It had no place to go.

CHAPTER

Dueling Banjos

> *"A fabled bohemia since Edgar Allan Poe and Walt Whitman squabbled in its basement drinking halls, the Village had long been infamously tolerant of cultural adventurism, even folk music. The Almanac Singers had rented a loft on East 13th Street as their home base in the 1940s, and Alan Lomax and Harry Smith both worked out of the Village during the 1950s."* **DAVID HADJU, *POSITIVELY 4TH STREET*[1]**

In New York City in the mid 50s there were no dedicated folk clubs, only nightclubs that were ostensibly open for jazz, blues, and comedy or musical revues, but which booked some folk musicians. Primary among these was the Village Vanguard, opened by Max Gordon in 1935 as a variety venue presenting sketch comedy, poetry, and dinner, although later it became known as a focus for progressive jazz, which it presents to this day.

Located at 178 Seventh Avenue South and still with the same seating capacity of 123, the Vanguard has outlived more renowned jazz haunts, Birdland and the Five Spot included. The Vanguard broke new ground back in 1941, booking Leadbelly and Josh White at the recommendation of future film director Nicholas Ray. He told Max Gordon that Leadbelly and White would make the "greatest folk singing act in the country". They opened in November 1941, and Gordon described the scene in his autobiography, *Live At The Village Vanguard*. "I never saw so many guitars in the place. Pete Seeger, Burl Ives, Richard Dyer-Bennet, Millard Lampell, The Almanac Singers, and Woody Guthrie – all present with guitars slung over their shoulders."[2]

It was at the Village Vanguard that The Weavers first played, in December 1949. The show was planned at first as a Pete Seeger solo, but the four-strong Weavers agreed to work for Seeger's $200 fee. It paid dividends. Their Vanguard stint eventually lasted six months, and word spread, reaching Gordon Jenkins at Decca who signed them and produced them, which led to unexpected success.

Café Society was another New York nightclub, opened in the Village by Barney Josephson a few years later, on New Year's Eve 1938, and intended to showcase black artists. It was an L-shaped basement club that began with a three-month engagement of Fletcher Henderson's Orchestra, plus Billie Holiday. This immediately made it one of New York's hottest venues. The name of the racially mixed club was designed to mock upmarket gatherings of middle-class socialites. Josephson even advertised it as 'The Wrong Place for the Right People'. He opened a second and larger club, Café Society Uptown, in 1940, and it was there that folk singers such as Burl Ives, Richard Dyer-Bennet, and Susan Reed often performed. Over a three-year period, Josh White frequently played both clubs, making him a star as well as a leading voice of racial integration in America.

The club also became a haven for New York radicals and, in the McCarthy era, was targeted by red-baiters. Josephson's brother was named as a communist, and by 1949 both the original clubs were forced to shut their doors. Two years later, when Josh White was questioned by the FBI, he was challenged about working for a club "that was run by the Communist Party".

Aside from White, Café Society was a haven for many of the greatest black musicians of the day, famously Billie Holiday, who first sang 'Strange Fruit' there, and it was a breakthrough venue for Lena Horne, Ella Fitzgerald, and Sarah Vaughan, blues artists Big Joe Turner and Big Bill Broonzy, and singer and activist Paul Robeson.

Harry Belafonte was another who popularised folk in the 50s, and he put together a club act of Caribbean songs that he premiered at the Village Vanguard in October 1951. After signing to RCA in 1954, Belafonte helped inspire a small folk-boom all its own, his often-improvised calypso style a further indication of folk's potential audience. After a lengthy engagement at the Vanguard, he moved uptown to the Blue Angel, which Max Gordon opened in 1943 with his partner Herbert Jacoby. For 20 years, the Blue Angel was the number-one showcase for launching acts, with a phenomenal list that included Woody Allen, Carol Burnett, Barbra Streisand, Mort Sahl, Eartha Kitt, and Lenny Bruce. Almost inevitably, Josh White was the first folk artist to play there.

As outlets for folk gradually expanded, the audience was becoming more defined. Rock'n'roll would soon break through and appeal to teenagers, but their parents and elder siblings were more inclined toward folk music. The counter-culture that was evolving in bohemian pockets in most major cities centred on modern jazz, abstract art, and beat writers. However uneasily, beatniks and folk fans co-existed. According to Dave Van Ronk, "To the tourists, folk music was simply part of the beatnik scene. Actually, the beats liked cool jazz, bebop, and hard drugs and hated folk music, which to them was all these fresh-faced kids sitting round on the floor and singing songs of the oppressed masses."[3] Until 1959, the beats held firm, but afterward they were ousted by the sound of folk guitars.

Until that time, outside of major concerts at Carnegie Hall or Town Hall, live folk music in New York City had to find outlets wherever it could: women's clubs, barn dances, Jewish centres, meeting houses, union halls, or on campus. There were also small theatres like the Actor's Playhouse or the Cherry Lane Theatre. At Cherry Lane, The Clancy Brothers asked George Pickow to organise midnight folk shows at the weekend, opening with Jean Ritchie and Oscar Brand, and for a few years everyone in folk would play there – Josh White, Bob Gibson, Richard Dyer-Bennet, Tom Paley, Frank Warner, Theodore Bikel, Ramblin' Jack Elliott, Reverend Gary Davis, Sonny Terry & Brownie McGhee, Ed McCurdy, and the Clancys. The theatre represented "the entire community of folk singers and musicians negotiating the transition from the political folksong movement to the counter-cultural folk revival of the 60s".[4]

The most vibrant and open scene, however, was at private parties – where Jac Holzman was now a regular guest. He would be invited because people knew he had an embryonic record company. "The guitar would get passed around," says Holzman. "Typically, there was cheese and jug wine, and the décor invariably included bullfight posters, candles stuck in Chianti bottles, plus lots of sling chairs. That's how I met Theo Bikel. When I heard Cynthia

Gooding, she blew everybody out of the room – and she was striking to look at, as well. She and Theo stood out in any crowd."

Bikel has fond memories of these gatherings. "I renewed friendships begun in England with Oscar Brand and Jean Ritchie. I met and sang with The Clancy Brothers and Tommy Makem, Ed McCurdy, Jo Mapes, Glenn Yarbrough, and Cynthia Gooding. There were many others as well: some who played ballads, some who played the blues. There were some who played sacred songs, some who sang bawdy songs, and some who sang everything."[5]

A high percentage of these artists recorded for Holzman, who was still just about keeping his financial head above water. "There were records that sustained me, and there were others like Hally Wood's *O' Lovely Appearance Of Death*, which I loved, and if it sold 500 records I'd be surprised. Yet there were people who absolutely adored that record, so I understood the real value of it. I was making just enough money to keep doing it."

Hally Wood, too, was an artist whom Holzman met through Jean Ritchie. She had a degree in musical theory from the University of Texas and was another musicologist who also sang – in a compelling, earthy voice, and not to everybody's taste. Her 1953 album *O' Lovely Appearance Of Death* is highly significant in the annals of Elektra because it bears the first jacket designed by William S. Harvey. Harvey thought it was the "most god-awful music I'd ever heard. I had never been subjected to this kind of music before. Everything is a cappella, no guitar, just this girl, and she sang and she sang. Jac says, 'It's exciting, isn't it? Can you do something with this?' I needed the money, I have kids, and it's 50 bucks. I said, 'Well, let me work on it, you know?"[6]

More than anyone, Bill Harvey came to define Elektra's visual style. *O' Lovely Appearance Of Death* had a stark black-and-white illustration, but within a year an identifiable Elektra approach would evolve. Two-colour and three-colour album jackets were not expensive to do and became a trademark as important to Elektra as its reputation for top-quality recordings.

Holzman was drawn to the flurry of instrumentalists who would play at weekends in Washington Square Park and whose holy grail was the Folkways set generally known as the *Anthology Of American Folk Music*. The set of six LPs consisted of commercial recordings from the 20s and 30s compiled by Harry Smith, an eccentric Bowery-based filmmaker, drawn from his collection of thousands of 78s. It was an essential source of inspiration. The recordings by Mississippi John Hurt, Dock Boggs, Clarence Ashley, The Memphis Jug Band, and plenty more, were barely 25 years old but already sounded ancient in 1952. They provided rich pickings.

Washington Square was the hub in New York City for the new breed of urban folk musicians, sprawling outward from the fountain in the park, across from New York University in Greenwich Village. This was where folk music could flourish freely among musicians and fans who were too young or couldn't afford the late-hours nightspots, many of which still enforced a dress code. More and more players gathered there on Sunday afternoons after 1950, but the Square had begun to draw a crowd five years earlier, purely by chance, when a guitarist named George Margolin played a few impromptu songs for friends. It caught on and the Square became a regular hangout for musicians and a draw for even less desirable characters.

To maintain order, the City passed a bylaw that required a permit-holder to be present before any public performance could be allowed in any of its parks. It was Pete Seeger and his wife Toshi who held the first permit, after which George Sprung took over the responsibility. George's brother Roger is often credited with introducing the bluegrass banjo style to Washington Square. Roger became a member of The Shanty Boys, a trio with Mike Cohen and washtub bassist Lionel Kilberg. The Shanty Boys were omnipresent in Washington Square, and eventually, in 1957, they recorded their sole album for Elektra, *Off-Beat Folk Songs*, a lively crossbreed of bluegrass and jug-band.

By the mid 50s, most of the top musicians and players gravitated to Washington Square at weekends, learning new techniques and freely swapping licks. Among those in the mix were Tom Paley, Mike Seeger, and John Cohen – these three later combined to form the influential New Lost City Ramblers – as well as Erik Darling, Eric Weissberg, Marshall Brickman, Dick Rosmini, and Billy Faier. Those last five pickers all recorded at different times for Elektra, as did Bob Gibson, who would also wind up in the Square on a Sunday when he was in town.

Gibson remembers that when he started out in New York City in 1953 and '54, Washington Square was the place. "That was where you learned everything about folk music. There was an exchange of information: learning banjo licks from Erik Darling, Frank Hamilton, and Billy Faier. You can't underestimate the feeling that everybody in folk music had of being … I don't think *outlaw* is quite the word, but we were definitely doing something out of the mainstream. It was very much ours. We were sort of rebellious. We were aware that what we were doing was not what Tin Pan Alley or what the music industry thought we should do."[6]

Woody Guthrie acolytes Dave Van Ronk, Ramblin' Jack Elliott, Happy Traum, and Paul Clayton regularly sang there, long before the singer-songwriters emerged in the 60s and the numbers turning up to the Square swelled at times into the thousands. Occasionally, Guthrie himself was brought there by friends like Elliott or John Cohen as an escape from his confinement in hospital.

Theodore Bikel soon joined the throng once he'd arrived in New York in 1954. "No one played in the Square for any reason except the satisfaction of playing and honing of musical skills in front of a built-in audience of students," says Bikel.[7] Holzman suggests there were other motives. "The driving force were the folk groupies. If you played a mean banjo with great facility, you got girls. The banjo pickers were folk royalty."

Holzman says the Square was the epitome of urban folk, the result of people in the city getting hold of the music. He recalls how good Tom Paley was, and that he didn't quite realise at the time how good was the ten-inch album that Paley made for Elektra, *Folk Songs From The Southern Appalachian Mountains*. "Pete Seeger," says Holzman, "was never as good a banjo player as Tom Paley – and Pete would always admit it."

Paley's album is one of the forgotten treasures of early Elektra. A maths professor, he was an extraordinary player, steeped in traditional music but not afraid to add variations. Dave Van Ronk recalls seeing Paley in the park and being dumbfounded by the way he picked out the bass notes on the banjo with his thumb while playing the melody with his fingers. Paley's unsung but highly significant 1953 Elektra album, the label's 12th record, was a rare early example of old time folk music played by a Northern urban performer.

Bob Dylan was an ardent fan of The New Lost City Ramblers before he arrived in New York City in 1961. Paley formed the group with Mike Seeger and John Cohen in 1958. "I didn't know that they were replicating everything they did off old 78 records, but what could it have mattered anyway?" Dylan later noted. "For me they had originality in spades, were men of mystery on all counts. I couldn't listen to them enough."[8] In the notes to his 1993 album *World Gone Wrong*, Dylan credits Paley as the conduit for 'Jack-A-Roe' and 'Love Henry', both of which Paley recorded for Elektra.

Paley was renowned for his hot fingerpicking. He was such a perfectionist that he would endlessly retune on stage between numbers. The story goes that he parted from The New Lost City Ramblers with some recrimination because this drove the others to such distraction. And so, in 1962, Paley left America for good and moved to Sweden. Three years later he settled in England (where he still resides today) and with Pete's half-sister recorded a second album for Elektra, called *Tom Paley & Peggy Seeger.*

The Washington Square instrumentalists provided a convenient pool of backup talent for the independent folk labels in New York City, giving accomplished players the opportunity to cut low-budget albums, whether it was for Elektra, Vanguard, Tradition, or Riverside. Holzman knew their value. "Erik Darling, Fred Hellerman, Billy Faier, Alan Arkin … they brought a musical cohesion to the material, allowing us to record more than just a guitar. We had small mixers by that time and were able to record and mix instruments as we went. It also made for a tighter performance by the artist. I always felt I needed something more than an Ed McCurdy or an Oscar Brand just playing guitar."

Billy Faier was a real virtuoso who had his own occasional radio show and edited *Caravan* magazine, essentially a folk fanzine. He recorded very little, but in 1957 he made an album for Riverside, *The Art Of The Five String Banjo*, that provided a focus for many taking up the instrument. For Elektra, Faier compiled *Folk Song Kit*, a how-to-play-guitar set with LP and booklet, and he appeared on Ed McCurdy's *When Dalliance Was In Flower Volume II*, Theodore Bikel and Geula Gill's *Folk Songs From Just About Everywhere*, and Oscar Brand's *Every Inch A Sailor.* The *Sailor* LP also featured Mike Seeger from The New Lost City Ramblers, a committed revivalist but still a jobbing musician.

Erik Darling was typical of the young musicians who got their chops together in Washington Square and went on to have lengthy careers. Darling, who died in 2008, recalled that on his first visit, Roger Sprung played a five-string banjo while his brother, George, held up two loose-leaf books with typed lyrics. "Various people flung their fingers at their guitars with varying degrees of amplitude, aptitude, attitude, and timidity. I didn't dare play that first day, but I became an accepted part of the crowd and did not miss a Sunday for years. My homework was learning what I could remember of the melodies, chord progressions, and words of those songs."[9]

Darling would go on to join The Weavers, replacing Pete Seeger. In 1957, at the age of 24, he cut *Erik Darling* for Elektra. He also recorded for the label as part of The Folksingers. He enjoyed two major commercial successes, both away from Elektra, first with The Tarriers and, later, when he formed The Rooftop Singers. Darling had the idea to record Gus Cannon's jug-band classic 'Walk Right In', driven by the sound of two 12-string guitars. Released by Vanguard, it became one of the biggest hit singles of the folk revival, soaring to Number One in early 1963. "The Rooftop Singers was a total accident," says Holzman, "but it was a good accident, and I didn't begrudge Vanguard or Erik any of the success they had. If anything, it got my competitive juices flowing."

Holzman knew that the bluegrass bands who played in Washington Square were the real deal. "Everyone expected those guys to have the fingers and thumbs of bionic heroes. So when I did *Folk Banjo Styles* in 1963 it brought together Eric Weissberg, Marshall Brickman, Tom Paley, and Art Rosenbaum. They all came to me wanting to do solo albums. Individually, they didn't have enough superior material, so I asked each one to record three or four pieces." Weissberg and Brickman also recorded *New Dimensions In Banjo & Bluegrass* for Elektra the following year.

A decade later, 'Dueling Banjos' appeared in the hit movie *Deliverance*, re-recorded by Weissberg and Steve Mandel. Audiences were captivated by the powerful and arresting tune, another example of essential folk music permeating the mass media. Warner Bros released an album called *Dueling Banjos* in 1973 with the implication that it was the soundtrack to *Deliverance*, but in fact it was the entire *New Dimensions* album with 'Dueling Banjos' bolted on. It was credited solely to Weissberg and Mandel – who played together only on 'Dueling Banjos'.

Washington Square continued to thrive during the 60s and was still the communal gathering place when The Even Dozen Jug Band came together in 1963. They rehearsed at Izzy Young's Folklore Center or in the warehouse space at the Elektra offices, but they all knew each other from playing and hanging out in Washington Square. John Sebastian explains how he met his fellow Even Dozen members Stefan Grossman and Maria D'Amato (later

Muldaur). "Stefan and I went to adjoining schools, and I had known Maria because the minute she hit the street every red-blooded male was going, 'Who is that girl?' She lived six blocks from my house. We started playing together in smaller groups, and because all of us lived around or could subway to Washington Square, we'd play in different combinations there on Sunday afternoons."

Dick Rosmini, one of the original Washington Square pickers, grew up in Greenwich Village and was a versatile banjoist, guitar player, photographer, and, later, a respected recording engineer. The proverbial guitarist's guitarist, he is all but unknown, but he did record one album for Elektra, *Adventures For 12 String, 6 String And Banjo*, and another for Imperial, *A Genuine Rosmini*. He can be heard on countless banjo and 12-string anthologies and demonstration records, as well as on albums by Bob Gibson, Theodore Bikel, Cyrus Faryar, Barbara Dane, Phil Ochs, Hoyt Axton, Doug Dillard, and Jackie DeShannon. He also recorded with Van Dyke Parks, who says, "*Adventures For 12 String* is an absolutely essential album. If you hear people like Leo Kottke or Jim McGuinn, you will hear how Dick Rosmini insinuated his style into so many other artists. He was a master." Rosmini died in 1995.

Cyrus Faryar, then with The Modern Folk Quartet, would record two charming solo albums for Elektra in the early 70s. He said, "Rosmini was so amazing you would have to look at his fingers to make sure he didn't have something hidden somewhere." Later, Jimmy Page said, "I had an album by Dick Rosmini, called *Adventures For 12 String, 6 String And Banjo*, and it had the best-recorded acoustic guitar sound I'd ever heard up until that point."[10]

Holzman's involvement with Rosmini was fleeting. "I love great instrumental music, and we just went and recorded it. But he never came back to make another record. It didn't particularly fit the evolving trajectory of Elektra Records in 1964. Rosmini was a throwback to the instrumental albums we used to do."

It wasn't until late in the 60s that Elektra finally recorded in Washington Square Park itself. And it was with David Peel, a true heir to the spirit of the Square. He was, and still is, a street musician and political activist from the Lower East Side. After two albums for Elektra, Peel would be produced by John Lennon and Yoko Ono.

Peel sets the scene. "I was playing all the time in [the Square], which was a hangout for radicals and bohemians in Greenwich Village. I'd improvise songs with guitar, harmonica, melodica, and percussion. One day, I had a big crowd around me, and this guy approached me and said, 'Hi, I'm Danny Fields from Elektra Records.' He bought me a steak dinner at Max's Kansas City and said he wanted to sign me. The Doors were on Elektra, so they had a credibility of reference. I was into the streets and revolution, but I had no problem with signing a record deal with Elektra."[11]

Even though it was recorded in 1968, *Have A Marijuana* by David Peel & The Lower East Side was made in old-style Elektra fashion, on a portable tape recorder. Peter Siegel, a former Even Dozen member, was dividing his time producing for Elektra and Nonesuch, and he was called in to capture Peel's particular brand of urban indigenous music.

"I didn't honestly believe it was the exact same thing as folk songs of East Kentucky," says Siegel, "but I modelled the production after that type of record. It was a documentary. It would be recorded on the street. I had a lot of nice ideas – like at the end of the record, David shouting out the credits to the crowd: 'Production supervisor Jac Holzman, yay!'"[12]

Have A Marijuana was an old-style protest album, and Holzman remembers it as fun to do. "David Peel was a phenomenon on the street, and we recorded it right out on the street. It was the spirit of Washington Square. Why not? Nobody was telling him or us what to do."

Today, you are more likely to see aspiring rappers or dancers in Washington Square performing to recorded music rather than an acoustic guitar. In the 50s, however, it was the prime breeding ground for young musicians – somewhere to play for fun, get girls, and learn the trade. The process continued in the 60s, by which time it was dominated by singer-songwriters, but in the 50s its benefits were unquestionable. It was where musicians could audition in the open for hungry record company entrepreneurs like Holzman and his rivals at Tradition, Riverside, and Vanguard. They were all looking for new talent to record for their labels or to help flesh out the sound for more established artists.

Remembering Elektra
Tom Paley

"When I went along to Elektra it was with Roger Sprung, and it was to accompany him for an audition with Jac Holzman. Roger was another banjo player – more bluegrass than old time – and a regular in Washington Square. As it turned out I ended up getting an offer from Jac but I don't think Roger ever did.*

The Appalachian songs I recorded were just a part of my repertoire, but that's what Jac wanted me to record. Jean Ritchie had already recorded an album of Appalachian music for him, and he saw that as a niche. I knew Jean and she must have put in a good word for me with Jac. Jean and I used to perform together on the Lower East Side but we never recorded together.†

Those songs are about something real – people singing from their own experiences – and that's what appealed to me. It is what drew me to folk music in the first place; it was straightforward in the way it was performed and it was saying things that I thought were important.

We recorded in the back of Jac's store and he engineered it.‡ It was very simply done, just my voice and guitar or banjo. When it came out [in 1953] it didn't make much difference to me at the time, or so I thought, but when people got to know who I was later through The New Lost City Ramblers, some said they had that record or that's where they first heard me and it was what got them into old-time music.

When I was 17, I joined an organisation called AYD [American Youth for Democracy], which was a left-wing youth group. It had branches everywhere; one of the groups ran square dances, and that's when I took up guitar, and then banjo. I was studying at the City College of New York [from 1945 to 1950] and took an undergraduate degree in mathematics before going up to Yale.

I was pretty hooked on music by then and began listening to New Jersey stations like WAAT, which had several country-music programmes; I liked The Carter Family, some Roy Acuff, Uncle Dave Macon, and I started buying old 78s in used record shops off 42nd street and 6th Avenue. Then, through the Library of Congress, I heard a lot more lot more terrific stuff recorded

---

* Elektra released *Off Beat Folk Songs* by The Shanty Boys in 1958.

† *Courting's A Pleasure*, although though credited to Paley, Ritchie, and Oscar Brand, simply combines tracks from Paley's 1953 Elektra album with Ritchie and Brand's *Courting Songs*.

‡ Ken Goldstein is also credited as producer.

during the Depression, and I was really taken with fiddle tunes and banjo tunes, which you didn't hear on the radio so much. So I was discovering the musicians who really influenced me: Clarence Ashley, Sam McGee, Wade Mainer, Roy Harvey, and some Doc Watson.

I ended up teaching mathematics at a number of colleges but I didn't stop doing the music. An awful lot of mathematicians are also musicians, mostly just amateur musicians. I was still mixing teaching and playing when The New Lost City Ramblers came to be.

I'd met John Cohen in New York before going up to Yale, after which I went to the University of Maryland, where I started playing with Mike Seeger, who I got to know through his sister, Peggy. When John came to Maryland one time in 1958, the local radio station asked if we'd like to do some numbers together. I suggested we get Mike along, too. It was the first time the three of us played together; it was pretty rough but it sounded pretty good.

To cut a long story short, we asked Izzy Young to put on a concert, because individually we knew our names could draw enough people in New York, and then John asked Moe Asch if he would like to record us. There was never any real plan it's just the way it came about. We wanted to stick closely to real traditional styles and have a string band sound, which offered a different aspect of the folk song revival. We didn't get rich from the records, but I was still teaching during that time, so what I made from the Ramblers was a little bit extra, not the other way round.

There was a guy who worked in the *People's Songs* office called Harvey Matusow; he was a volunteer worker, but it turned out he was an FBI plant. He started revealing how there all these really dangerous 'red' banjo players who were subverting America, but I didn't know I was one of them until at one point the Ramblers were playing a TV show; at the rehearsal, someone came round with a document for me to sign, but nothing for Mike or John. It turned out Harvey Matusow had named me as a member of the Communist Party. What I was told went something like this: "Tom Paley is a member of the Communist party, and as such he is part of the Soviet espionage apparatus in America."

The fact is, I was never a member of the Communist Party. I told the Network it was none of their business what my political connections were but we got dumped from the show. After that we didn't get any more TV work and gigs started to fall off; Mike and John were both upset about that and decided they wanted rid of me. So that was the secret behind the breakup of the original New Lost City Ramblers.*

It was one of the factors in my leaving America for Europe with my wife Claudia; we ended up living in Sweden for three years before moving to England toward the end of 1965. We found that Ewan MacColl and Peggy Seeger were able to fix tours for me pretty easily, so I knew there was work there. Peggy and I recorded an album for Topic records soon after.” †

Tom Paley was a member of The New Lost City Ramblers between 1958 and 1962, playing on the first eight Ramblers albums for Folkways. He is still working and living in Britain, where he has resided the same flat in North London for the last forty years.

* Matusow later wrote a book called *False Witness* in which he admitted he had been paid to lie about members of the American Communist Party. Before leaving for Europe, Paley recorded seven tunes for Elektra's *Folk Banjo Styles, 1962*, which also featured Eric Weissberg and Art Rosenbaum.

† *Who's Going To Shoe Your Pretty Little Foot? Who's Going To Glove Your Hand?*, released in 1965, was one of a handful of Topic albums also released by Elektra in North America, under the simplified title *Tom Paley & Peggy Seeger*.

CHAPTER

When Maidens Lost Their Heads

> "*Holzman's humor and ability to think outside the box would make Elektra the most forward-looking folk label as the revival peaked in the early 60s. And while not everyone appreciated his pragmatic approach – much less titillating songs with irreverent slants – it became increasingly difficult to argue with the results: The music confirmed his vision.*" **RONALD D. LANKFORD, JR., *FOLK MUSIC USA*[1]**

Perhaps the most trusted formula for folk labels in the 50s was to produce themed recordings and anthologies, although nothing else would have such impact as Harry Smith's monumental *Anthology Of American Folk Music*. Elektra had released its own share of anthologies early on: *Nova Scotia Folk Music*, recorded by Diane Hamilton in Cape Breton, was a favourite of Jac Holzman's. Even Cynthia Gooding's early albums followed a pattern of collecting international folk songs, with Turkish, Spanish, Mexican, and Italian titles.

The themed albums were blatantly opportunistic exercises on the part of the artists as well as the labels. They were a fad until well into the 60s, clearly meant for the expanding college market, and leaned especially on anything revelling in sexual innuendo. For Elektra, themed albums were vital to building a catalogue. "We didn't sign artists for long-term contracts," explains Holzman. "We were signing them for individual records. I didn't want the obligations of a long-term contract, and I didn't want to disappoint an artist by dropping them, which would hurt them. I'd say: when you have interesting material, let me know. I was seizing those openings and putting together thematic concepts, like *Bad Men And Heroes*, which was the first time I worked with Ed McCurdy and Oscar Brand. A title like that also made for a striking cover."

Bad Men And Heroes was a collection drawn from folk music of the far distant and more recent past, celebrating the lives in song of such characters as Robin Hood, Dick Turpin, and Captain Kidd, and American Western legends like Jesse James, Billy The Kid, and Woody Guthrie's Pretty Boy Floyd. The album features performances by McCurdy and Brand and is noteworthy for the first tracks by Ramblin' Jack Elliott before he left for Europe, where he was next heard recording for Topic Records in London.

The undisputed masters in the art of themed folk albums were Oscar Brand, Paul Clayton, and Ed McCurdy. Clayton recorded so many that, in later years, he described himself as "the word's most recorded young folk singer", inserting the word young to distinguish himself from Pete Seeger. All three were folklorists and collectors of songs but, unlike the Lomaxes or Carl Sandburg or Frank Warner, their livelihood also depended on performing and recording these songs. All three wrote songs of their own, too.

Clayton was more of a scholar-performer. He was a descendant of New England sailing families born in the great whaling port of New Bedford, Massachusetts, and he helped preserve much of the heritage of whaling songs from the region. After graduating from the University of Virginia with an MA, he became a serious collector of songs, eventually recording around 400 himself during the 50s and 60s for Folkways, Stinson, Riverside, and Tradition, plus two complete albums of irreverent bawdy material for Elektra, *Unholy Matrimony* and *Bobby Burns' Merry Muses Of Caledonia.* Clayton's most renowned recordings were whaling songs and sea shanties, notably on the album *Whaling And Sailing Songs From The Days Of Moby Dick*, recorded for Tradition in 1956, and the Folkways set *Foc'sle Songs And Shanties.* Clayton was a fixture in the Village, when not touring or travelling, and a Washington Square habitué. He committed suicide in New York in 1967 at the age of just 44.

Ed McCurdy's career first took hold in 1946 when, having failed in his attempt to become the next Sinatra, the Pennsylvania-born musician worked as a broadcaster and singer of folk songs for the Canadian Broadcasting Network. He cut his first album, *Sings Songs Of The Canadian Maritimes And Newfoundland*, in the early 50s for the Whitehall label.

By 1954, with a reputation for singing ballads and children's songs, McCurdy had moved to New York City where he recorded *The Ballad Record* for Riverside. Throughout the 50s he recorded simultaneously for Tradition, Riverside, and Elektra, following *Bad Men And Heroes* with two further anthologies whose titles flag up the content: *Sin Songs Pro/Con* and *Blood Booze 'N Bones*. Away from the folk world, he was an actor and announcer on children's television shows – he created and starred as Freddie The Fireman in 1956 for WABD Channel 5 – which was somewhat at odds with his songs about gambling, drinking, and loose women. McCurdy did voiceovers for L&M cigarette ads, the brand that boasted they were "just what the doctor ordered".

"Ed would often drop by the office to chat or cadge a local pizza," says Holzman. "One day, he asked if I knew *Wit And Mirth: Or, Pills To Purge Melancholy*, a collection of songs edited by Thomas D'Urfey and dating from the early 18th century. Ed described them as politely risqué Restoration folk music. I was totally fascinated but not sure how best to present this to an audience. Ed riffed, 'Why don't we say something about dalliance?' I countered, 'What about when dalliance was in flower?' Ed nodded his approval, then I added, 'And maidens lost their heads.' Ed cracked up. We had our title and our concept. We were in business. A week later he had the songs together and he came by and performed them in the office. It worked beautifully."

When Dalliance Was In Flower And Maidens Lost Their Heads was recorded in the New York apartment of Leonard Ripley (Holzman's friend from St John's College who had a slice of Elektra). Some distributors had reservations, but Holzman told them the songs had been sung for hundreds of years, in even more puritanical times. "The distributors were happy enough when college bookstores were ordering them by the box, with 25 to a box," Holzman recalls.

The original jacket for the album was based on line drawings by Bill Harvey, but Holzman later opted to redo the design using a photograph of men in tights – including Holzman himself in one of his Hitchcock-like cameos, wearing a red fez, alongside Leonard Ripley in green and Ed

McCurdy as court jester, frolicking with a couple of Playmates of the Month who showed appropriate cleavage.

"The *Dalliance* recordings were successful because of the respect we showed for the material," says Holzman. "The performances were light-hearted but seriously done, and Ed had a bravura way of delivering them. Adding Alan Arkin on recorder was Ed's idea, and we used Erik Darling playing banjo to simulate the sound of a harpsichord – it was important to have that post-Renaissance flavour. It was all mild innuendo, nothing smutty, and that's why it worked so well. The *Dalliance* series was much loved by college students, who would walk across campus singing the lyrics. We sold tens of thousands. It was the power of concept, although we didn't anticipate just how successful the *Dalliance* series would become."

Thomas D'Urfey's collections, published between 1698 and 1720, held over a thousand songs and poems, more than enough for two further volumes, plus a final one titled *Son Of Dalliance*. The second volume in particular maintained the same sense of deference to its gently ribald theme and the same rich accompaniments, this time with a real harpsichord played by Robert Abramson.

Ed McCurdy's final Elektra release came in 1961 with a double album, the far more respectful *A Treasure Chest Of American Folk Song*. Yet his serious work was overshadowed by the success of his bawdy songs. He continued to work in radio and television through the 50s and performed regularly, including three consecutive years at Newport.

McCurdy was sidelined by the next generation of singer-songwriters, although his sharpest and best-known composition, 'Last Night I Had The Strangest Dream', composed in 1950, became something of an anthem for the new performers. It was one of the earliest and most expressive anti-war songs and was covered by many, including Pete Seeger, Joan Baez, Carolyn Hester, and even Simon & Garfunkel (on their debut album, *Wednesday Morning 3AM*). It became McCurdy's signature song and the title track of his final album of new material, released in 1967. Toward the end of his life he returned to Canada, where he lived in Halifax, Nova Scotia, still singing folk songs and performing as a character actor on Canadian TV. He died of heart congestion, aged 81, in March 2000.

Oscar Brand says of his Elektra labelmate, "McCurdy was a trained singer who started singing folk songs; he could sing anything. Ed was a tough nut and when he'd had a couple of drinks could be nasty and bitter. When he was not in his cups, he was a doll. He was a funny, clever guy. Ed could make you laugh a thousand times with just five lines. And he had a gorgeous voice."[2]

McCurdy was less kind about Brand's vocal skills. "Oscar and I were strange friends. He's not my favourite singer; he knows that. He called me up once and said, 'Don't you think I'm singing better?' I said, 'I hope so.' But we owe Oscar a great deal. He has a filing system in his house and an additional one in his brain, and if ever I want to know anything about a song, I call Oscar."[3]

Brand is an elder statesman of American folk music, though some ten years junior to Pete Seeger. He was born in Winnipeg in 1920, and during the decades after the war he built a reputation in many fields, initially as a performer. He became a major force in folk music in the 50s and 60s, largely as the presenter of his *Folksong Festival* from New York on WNYC on Sunday evenings. It is now the longest-running radio show in history but was at a peak in its first 20 years, when Brand would play records and broadcast live performances by everyone from Woody Guthrie, Leadbelly, and Burl Ives to Harry Belafonte, Richard Dyer-Bennet, and Jean Ritchie. He also featured Bob Dylan's first radio appearance.

Brand's achievements are manifold: in broadcasting as NBC's director of children's programmes, as a documentary film-maker, as an adviser, presenter, narrator, scriptwriter, and an author of bestselling books, and even as the voice of the Cheerio ads. But in addition to all this activity, he found time to make over 90 albums and to write songs for movies, TV, and stage shows, including the Broadway and off-Broadway successes *A Joyful Noise*, *The Education Of Hyman Kaplan*, *In White America*, and *How To Steal An Election*.

Brand's best-known song outside of folk music is 'A Guy Is A Guy', a hit for Doris Day, which he cleaned up from a naughty World War II soldier's song, 'A Gob Is A Slob'. Brand's encyclopedic mind can summon up a song for any occasion or genre, and he's recorded for just about every known folk label. He made his recording reputation with a series of ribald songs for Audio Fidelity, *Bawdy Songs And Backroom Ballads*, in four volumes. All were performed to simple accompaniment directed toward the content of the song rather than Brand's breezy delivery. Having contributed to a handful of Elektra recordings with Ed McCurdy and Jean Ritchie, Brand eventually launched a string of albums for Holzman in 1959. He did not try straight bawdy songs – it was clear that Ed McCurdy had stolen his thunder there – but with *The Wild Blue Yonder* Brand made the first of a series of military-themed records.

"Brand has had the longest running folk-music programme on radio, for WNYC, so he had a fair amount of cachet in the New York area," explains Holzman. "He is a wonderful collector of material, in terms of searching and finding odd things, but in my opinion he is an indifferent performer. He was sort of a junior Pete Seeger without the political portfolio.

"He is a very nice, decent guy, well placed in folk circles and highly respected for his broad knowledge. You could go to him and say, I need ten great songs from the Revolutionary War, and he'd give them to you off the top of his head. He's a walking expert. He's the first person most people think of if they have a question in this area. He always returns your calls."

On his regular WNYC show, Brand honoured Armed Forces Day one year by playing a Navy song, an Army song, and a Marine Corps song, bemoaning the lack of an Air Force song. He was unprepared for what followed: one former flyer unloaded his entire collection of 238 songs on him, and plenty more aviators submitted their personal favourites. This gave Brand the idea for what became *The Wild Blue Yonder*. He bent Holzman's ear with the concept at Elektra's 10th Anniversary Party.

"I was a bit gruff with him," says Holzman. "Then later I realised it said something about who Oscar is. He is an encyclopedia of all kinds of songs, which are broadly modern folk songs. When Pete Seeger was asked to define a folk song, he said, 'If folks sing them, then they're folk songs.' I brought Freddy Hellerman in to maintain some discipline in the studio and give it a musical frame. We prided ourselves in making these records in no more than two evenings, and we just went through the set." Brand says, "We had a ball doing those songs. They reached a generation who were now able to be nostalgic about the war."[4]

The appeal of these songs was amazing, as Holzman recalls. "I just didn't think he was a very good singer, but if you want to record songs appealing to a bunch of hard-drinking pilots, Oscar was your man. A cultured trained voice would have seemed out of character with this material."

Elektra built an audience that was easily reached through the Army

& Air Force Exchange Service, effectively the US military's store. "One morning," says Holzman, "a bundle of papers arrived in a thick envelope from the AAFES containing an order for 10,000 units of *Wild Blue Yonder*. We had to ensure it wasn't an admin error for just 100 before breaking out the champagne. The orders just kept coming. We did a Navy version, *Every Inch A Sailor*, then *Tell It To The Marines*, then one of Army songs, then another Air Force one. They were all by degrees irreverent, anti-authority, and anti-bureaucracy, but always fiercely patriotic."

They kept on coming until *Cough! Army Songs Out Of The Barracks Bag*, Brand's final album for Elektra in 1964, a record somewhat against the grain of the new era that was unfolding. All the albums had wacky artwork featuring Brand at the centre, although the doctor on *Cough!* and the harsh drill instructor on *Tell It To The Marines* were both portrayed by Elektra's art director, William S. Harvey. "Eventually we ran it into a ditch," admits Holzman. "We moved on to civilian themes: golfers, skiers, boaters, sports car enthusiasts, doctors – you name it, we did it. With Oscar Brand, what you see is what you get – there's no artifice there. I like the man enormously. We had fun doing these records together, but my personal taste was shifting elsewhere."

Dave Van Ronk, another regular on Brand's radio show, does a good job putting Oscar Brand into perspective. "[He] always managed to tread a middle ground, both philosophically and in terms of musical approach. His own work was certainly in the cabaret style, without any of the guts and rawness that we demanded, but his repertoire was so huge that we had to respect it. Besides, he was always very supportive of what we were doing and had a genuine love for the more traditional styles."[5]

Brand was a long-standing member of the non-communist left, and he was often caught in the political crossfire as he criticised the communist cause, but was still chastised by the establishment. At times, he was blacklisted by both sides, but he held his ground. As Van Ronk recalls, after Brand outraged the left by staging a show with Burl Ives, who named names in front of the House Un-American Activities Committee, "Oscar just said quietly, 'Dave, we on the left do not blacklist.'"[6]

The other staple among folk labels was to record and document traditional and contemporary music from around the world. Elektra's first foray into world recordings came in 1953 with its fifth album, *Voices Of Haiti*, recorded by Maya Deren, an avant-garde filmmaker who had written *Divine Horsemen*, which was then considered the definitive book on Haitian Voodoo.

Paul Rickolt acquired the Deren recordings for Elektra. "Maya recorded these in Haiti with a wire recorder," he says, "for her own research into voodoo. Everything had to be transferred from wire to tape. And the sessions with Maya were absolutely horrendous. She had a very strong character and could be very difficult. The kitchen light often wouldn't go on and Maya would just snap her fingers and there it is: it would go on. She had all these voodoo tricks, supposedly."[7]

The album brought a welcome technical challenge for Holzman. He thought the material excellent, but its existence on fragile wire posed a problem. "I had to figure out how to transfer safely to tape and to re-equalise it simultaneously."

Voices Of Haiti outsold all Elektra's initial folk output, aside from Susan Reed's debut. Holzman continued to record or acquire further world-music titles, including *Festival In Haiti*, *Flamenco Guitar Solos* by Jim Fawcett (a US serviceman whose name didn't appear on the front jacket as Holzman felt it lacked authenticity), *Gold Coast Saturday Night* (highlife music), *Art Of The Koto*, and *The Pulsating Sounds Of Paraguay*. Well into the 60s there was a considerable range of flamenco, Jewish, Israeli, and Russian folk song. Music from around the globe and international folk music remained an integral part of Elektra's catalogue until 1967, when the cream of it was switched to the specialist Nonesuch Explorer series. There, these earlier recordings benefited from a retail price half that of Elektra.

Yet it was after he recorded two particular artists in 1955 – Josh White and Theodore Bikel – that Holzman realised that the artist's name could be as much the focus of attention as any musical style, theme, or concept might be. It was a major turning point in Elektra's future development.

CHAPTER 7

Spirituals & Blues

> *"Once Josh White decided to record for Elektra, we had a toe on the map of the folk world. Having an artist of Josh's stature was a seal of approval for Elektra."* **JAC HOLZMAN**

By 1955, Elektra had made considerable headway in just a few years and was establishing itself as a label that mirrored the disparate folk scene of the 50s. Folkways was still the leading label, and its boss Moe Asch had recorded the founding fathers of the movement: Woody Guthrie, Pete Seeger, Leadbelly, and Josh White, who more than warrants his place in such distinguished company. Yet folk music was being undermined by the anti-communist hysteria of the day.

Senator Joe McCarthy would lend his name to the era when the full power of the federal government was dedicated to the search for communists and subversives, which cast a pall over cultural life in the 50s. It's a measure of Elektra's increasing profile that Jac Holzman was approached by Josh White's manager with a view to recording the artist. "Josh did not have a recording contract," says Holzman, "and couldn't get one, because of his politics and some past connections that were suspect during the ugly years of the witch hunt by the House Un-American Activities Committee."

The HUAC had begun an investigation into the Hollywood motion-picture industry in 1947, epitomised by its action against the Hollywood Ten, but it soon cast the net wider to take in all branches of the entertainment industry, the media, and even the library system, removing around 30,000 so-called subversive titles from the shelves. *Red Channels* was a pamphlet listing the names of 151 writers, directors, and performers who, it claimed, had been members of subversive organisations before the war but had not so far been blacklisted. Its unfortunate array of talent included Larry Adler, Stella Adler, Charlie Chaplin, Leonard Bernstein, Aaron Copland, Joseph Losey, John Garfield, Arthur Miller, Paul Robeson, and folk performers Pete Seeger, Burl Ives, and Josh White.

Folk music may not have had the profile of the film industry, but the public knew Ives, White, and Seeger – and perhaps, to a lesser extent, others named from the folk world, like Richard Dyer-Bennet, Oscar Brand, and Alan Lomax. Journalist Gordon Friesen and Sis Cunningham, who later founded the folk-song magazine *Broadside*, were blacklisted in the 40s, as was *Sing Out* editor Irwin Sibler, who eventually appeared before the committee in 1956.

At the advent of the Red Scare, The Weavers had been forced to forgo their annual concert at Town Hall in December 1952, having lost their Decca contract. Their radio ties and bookings evaporated after Seeger and Lee Hays were named. Less politically active artists like Harry Belafonte, Susan Reed, and Cynthia Gooding were all tarred by association. As Gooding recalls, "I lived under the cloud of McCarthyism, very strongly, throughout the 50s. Just singing folk songs, you were probably considered far enough to the left, but I couldn't do anything about that. My husband was a Turk, not an American citizen. So I had to stay away from anyone whose politics were the least bit left-ish, because [my husband] could be thrown out of the country, leaving me and my daughter behind."[1]

Holzman's upbringing and his own sentiments were certainly liberal, and he was not about to allow the witch-hunt to affect his musical judgement. "I was impressed by Josh White the musician and performer: his compelling personality and terrific guitar chops. Elektra didn't have iconic figures like Guthrie, Seeger, and Leadbelly. Josh White had learned from Leadbelly, played alongside him, and started out leading blind singers around in the South, but had then become popular as a cabaret singer. He had the same cachet, the same roots, as a Sonny Terry or Big Bill Broonzy, but – quite wrongly in my opinion – was disdained by the blues purists because of his cabaret success."

Josh White was born in Greenville, South Carolina, in 1914. As a child he worked as a lead boy, or guide, for local street-singers Blind John Henry Arnold and Blind Joe Taggart. He described his early life during part of his testimony before the HUAC in 1950, explaining why he became involved with civil rights. "I was seven years old when I left my home in Greenville, South Carolina, to lead a blind man while playing the tambourine. Before I was eight years old I knew what it meant to be kicked and abused. Before I was nine years old I had seen two lynchings. I got to hate Jim Crow for what it did to me personally and because Jim Crow is an insult to God's creatures and a violation of the Christian beliefs taught by my father."[2]

By 1931, White had moved to New York City and settled in Harlem, performing blues and gospel songs and gaining a reputation as an outstanding guitarist. Over the decade, both his fame and his repertoire expanded beyond urban blues to embrace Tin Pan Alley songs, elements of gospel and jazz, folk songs from around the world, and hard-hitting political protest. In January 1940, he appeared with Paul Robeson in *John Henry*, a Broadway production that closed within a week but served to draw him further into the more sophisticated white entertainment world. Within months, he appeared at a Grapes of Wrath Evening on a bill that included Leadbelly, Aunt Molly Jackson, Woody Guthrie, and Pete Seeger. It was Seeger's concert debut. Alan Lomax called it the beginning of the American folk-song revival. White also became a regular on Lomax's CBS network radio show *Back Where I Come From.*

The 40s was the golden age of cabaret in New York City, where White honed his act first at the Village Vanguard, then at both Café Society venues, at the Blue Angel, and other nightspots. According to White's biographer, Elijah Wald, "By 1944, Josh was Café Society's top-billed act and rivalled Burl Ives as America's most popular folk singer."[3] He'd seen his fees rise from $75 a week to $500 by the middle of the decade. His appeal and notoriety deepened following a year-long partnership with the sultry Broadway musical comedy star and torch singer Libby Holman. She had seen White at the Vanguard and approached him to teach her the blues. Their interracial pairing raised eyebrows but was largely triumphant wherever they toured. White initially acted as her accompanist, playing guitar on Holman's 1942 Decca album, *Blues Till Dawn*, but two years later, when they teamed up again, he had equal billing on a nationwide concert tour.

Musically, White moved further away from the blues, crafting a more sophisticated style. When he opened at the Vanguard in 1941, Woody Guthrie wrote to the club's owner, Max Gordon: "Josh knows the blues ... from way back. He remembers that Joe Louis is the best boxer in the world ever and Josh White wants to be the Joe Louis of the blues guitar. After lots of years of hard playing and singing, Josh has got to be just that."[4]

His early New York recordings reflected White's blues pedigree, notably the records he made with the Carolinians for Columbia in 1940 and the Keynote album *Southern Exposure: An Album Of Jim Crow Blues.* For Keynote, he also recorded with The Almanac Singers, the loose collective that Guthrie once described as the only group who rehearsed on stage. Although they played songs steeped in social and political protest, "the accompaniment of Josh White's blues guitar on their Keynote recordings, alongside Seeger's eclectic banjo style, produced an ensemble sound not substantially different from, say, that of the Memphis Jug Band".[5]

White's earliest songs had been issued as "race records" intended for the black, rural population; he recorded early on for Banner, Conqueror, and ARC, a forerunner of Columbia and Commodore, the label for which Billie Holiday first recorded 'Strange Fruit'. White's most popular recordings came once he had crossed over to a predominantly white audience. 'One Meat Ball', for the Asch label, was a Depression-era song that became the first million-selling record by a black male artist. White even performed 'One Meat Ball' in the B-movie *The Crimson Canary*, and he acted in other low-budget Hollywood films – as a miner in the Randolph Scott western *The Walking Hills* – and starred in a Broadway play, *How Long Till Summer*.

White was in a unique position as a household name to both black and white audiences. He enjoyed further hits during the 40s like 'Jelly Jelly', a sexually risqué song composed by Earl Hines and Billy Eckstine, and 'The House I Live In', a fervently patriotic American song popular during World War II (also recorded by Frank Sinatra for a short film he made in 1945 to expose anti-Semitism and racial prejudice).

White had been a leading voice of black America and a voice that repeatedly reminded America of its social injustices, and also had become a major pop star and sex symbol. That didn't exactly endear him to his enemies, as Josh White Jr has observed. "He was the first black person to use sex appeal on white audiences. And he was lucky he didn't get killed for it."[6] He further alienated ultra-conservatives by the way he was accepted and befriended by white society, aristocracy, European royalty, and, notably, by America's ruling family, the Roosevelts. White's anti-segregationist stance, his support for international human rights, and the fact he would often speak on behalf of the Roosevelts at rallies – all this further fuelled McCarthyite opinion that he was a communist.

At the dawn of the 50s, McCarthy was given licence to investigate citizens about their political past. He made it clear to the witnesses called before the HUAC that the only way of showing that they had abandoned their left-wing views was by naming other members of the party. Those who did were dubbed 'friendly witnesses' by the right – and 'traitors' by the left. Like many, Josh White was caught completely off guard by the virulence of the anti-communist hunt, especially since one of the first targets was Café Society, the nightclub which had almost become White's second home.

After he was named in *Red Channels*, White was interrogated every week, and eventually he gave in to pressure and appeared before the HUAC on September 1 1950, without counsel, in an attempt to set the record straight. He defended his right and responsibility to bring social injustices to the attention of the public through his songs. Later he would also have to defend himself to the progressive left and explain his testimony as a friendly witness, although, unlike Burl Ives, he never gave the FBI or the HUAC names of party members. What also angered his more radical fans was that he spoke ambiguously against Paul Robeson's more hardline views.

All this effectively led to White being shunned by some folk festivals, clubs, concert promoters, and independent folk recording firms, who were caught in the crossfire between the right and the left. White's career declined. He was blacklisted in Hollywood and did not appear on radio or television from 1948 until 1963, when John Kennedy invited him to appear on the national CBS Television civil rights special *Dinner With The President.*

Once McCarthy began investigating communist infiltration into the military in October 1953, the senator's days were numbered. President Eisenhower was furious at the attack on the military and was determined to bring an end to McCarthy's activities. The Senate investigations into the Army were televised, which helped to expose the bullying tactics of McCarthy. He soon lost his power base when all America could see the proceedings. Jac Holzman followed these events avidly. "People were walking on cat feet, but that stopped the minute Joseph Welch so beautifully tied Joseph McCarthy in knots during the Army–McCarthy hearings. And then McCarthy was taken apart by Ed Murrow on television [on *See It Now*, March 1954]. It showed that things were changing for the better and it marked the beginning of the end of McCarthyism."

White spent much of this time, between 1950 and 1955, living and working in England and Sweden. He was particularly influential in Britain, where he became well known through tours and appearances on BBC radio and TV. Back home, he could barely support his family of five children; there were no more cabaret bookings in New York, just the odd engagement and college date around the country. That the blacklisted White recorded anything at all was entirely due to Jac Holzman and Elektra.

"Someone made an overture to me, essentially to find out if I would reject Josh White because of the political crap surrounding him," says Holzman. "But I said no, I would definitely want to record him. I said to him I can't pay you much money but I will pay you what you earn in royalties, and I think I know how to create a sound for you. You've been poorly recorded, but I'll give your voice and guitar an intimacy and presence. You'll hear the real Josh White coming out of the speakers. There won't be anything between the music and the listener. It was quite a pitch – and I was not sure I would get a yes."

Elektra slowly began revitalising White's career, in part by finding a new audience, but also by giving his original fans an opportunity to hear Josh White in high fidelity. Most of his early recordings were made as 78s and were almost impossible to find. White's debut for Elektra was both a departure and a return to his roots. It was Elektra's final ten-inch release, actually a double ten-inch LP. *The Story Of John Henry* was a 'musical narrative' punctuated by songs credited to Jacques Wolfe and Roark Bradford, authors of the flop *John Henry* Broadway show, but essentially White's own work, and ending with the traditional ballad, 'John Henry'.

"Most people now thought of Josh less as a blues singer and more a folk singer," says Holzman. "We met, he brought his guitar, and we hit it off. What so impressed me was that he could do so much on his guitar that I had never heard on record. And I knew what to do with that. We took advantage of the recent Neumann U-47 condenser microphone, which was easy to adjust for the right balance between voice and guitar. Josh learnt to paint with this microphone and instinctively knew how to emphasise his voice or guitar."

Holzman asked White what they could record that was special and that he hadn't done before, and White talked about the John Henry folk-song saga, which he had played in the Broadway show with Robeson. "But that was only part of it. He said: I can put all of this together and make a complete narrative of it. I trusted him to do that. Here I was, eight years after hearing him in my St John's dorm room, and now I have him recording for $100 advance plus $100 to his bass player.

"No one had ever heard the real Josh on records, until now," says Holzman. "He was a full partner in everything we did. I'd play the takes back over the big speakers, and he heard 100 percent of himself coming from those speakers – and he just said, 'Wow!' Then he asked if I was going to get that sound on the record, and I said sure. And then I prayed that I'd be able to do it! I worked very closely with Peter Bartók, who mastered these recordings to get the maximum level and frequency range on the disc. I wanted to preserve the air in the room, the bottom of his voice, and the depth and intricacy of his guitar work."

Elektra followed *The Story Of John Henry* with *Josh At Midnight*, both released in 1956 and both recorded at a converted old church in the East 20s owned by Esoteric Records, where Holzman appreciated the subtle acoustics. *Josh At Midnight* was Elektra's first 12-inch release and became the company's biggest seller so far. It drew on blues material, with new versions of 'One Meat Ball' and 'St James' Infirmary'. Like *The Story Of John Henry*, it emphasised White's pre-cabaret career.

Elektra would release a further five White albums by 1962, all emphasising blues and gospel material rather than the folk ballads that he'd become popularly associated with. "Many of his records were available in Europe," says Holzman, "but his earlier more blues-guitar material hadn't yet been issued on LP in America. I encouraged his vocal performance to be a bit more prominent and dramatic while bringing out the guitar. If you wanted to get a performance out of Josh, you invited a girl to the session or you suggested he invite a girl to the session. As long as he didn't chase her around the studio, he would sing his heart out. Most everything was done in two takes, three at most. Josh was a real pro and always prepared. I had never worked with anyone who had so much experience, and we learned from each other."

Oscar Brand, who knew White well, says that where Paul Robeson lectured his white audience from the stage on civil rights – which made them feel uncomfortable – White gave them the same message and expression of racial anger in his songs. "And then [he] would charm the pants off them when he got off the stage. The white men were fascinated by his unique mixture of southern charm, machismo, and smouldering energy, and the women – well, they were just blown over by his raw sexuality and wanted to taste the forbidden fruit."[7]

Holzman was after this atmosphere of an after-hours club for *Josh Sings Ballads And Blues*, released in 1956, where White was backed by jazz bass and drums and covered late-night standards such as 'One For My Baby' and Billie Holiday's dark 'Gloomy Sunday'.

Those first three albums were the best of the Elektra recordings and did well, enabling Holzman to help White through his financial difficulties, with occasional advances on royalties. He and Leonard Ripley even promoted a solo show at Town Hall in April 1956 – White's first solo appearance there in the 50s. White played month-long residencies at the hungry i in San Francisco and the Gate Of Horn in Chicago, and the college-campus circuit welcomed him. He even found himself back at the Café Society premises, although the old club had shut down ten years before. When the One Sheridan Square club opened in the same basement space in September 1959, White was its first headline act.

"I was never trying to make a political statement by signing Josh White," says Holzman. "I was only interested in the statement the records made. Signing Josh White and putting out *The Story Of John Henry* said: we are to be reckoned with. I took great pride in that record, and it started selling immediately. It was an early marker which said that Elektra was coming together. Not just for fans – it also meant that my distributors began to pay attention to me."

Holzman re-signed White in 1958, on completion of his customary three-album arrangement. *Chain Gang Songs* in that year went back to White's blues roots as he substantially re-recorded his Carolinians album, but with more of a work-gang holler than John Hammond's original production for Columbia. Like all White's seven albums on the Elektra label, it boasted an intimate, crystalline production that set it apart from previous recordings, repositioning his classic repertoire. The album's jacket showed a convict in stripes and chains and was, in itself, a statement in the era of civil rights.

His final album, *Empty Bed Blues*, sported risqué art on the jacket. The photo of a nude white woman sitting up in bed with her back to us was subversive, but it also tapped into White's former Café Society popularity. Holzman says that the jackets were special but that he wasn't trying to make any point. "Albums were sold on their covers and the reputation of the label. You just do what is right for the music."

The later albums were indicative of White's declining health, particularly the psoriasis on his nails that gave him great pain when playing guitar. "I don't think by the end he was able to play or sing to the best of his own standards," says Holzman, although White continued to make records for others, including two up-tempo blues albums for Mercury. He had never been entirely embraced by the new breed of 60s folk singers, who felt he had "whitened" the blues too much and preferred recently rediscovered country blues artists or the driving urban blues coming out of Chicago. Yet by 1963, at the height of the folk revival, a *Billboard* poll of college students ranked Josh White as America's third most popular folk singer, after Harry Belafonte (who was strongly influenced by White) and Pete Seeger, but ahead of Bob Dylan.

White was a featured performer at Martin Luther King's March On Washington in 1963. From that year on, White suffered a series of heart attacks and was in poor health until his death in New York in September 1969 during heart surgery. White's friend, Oscar Brand, remembered him as "tough, exacting, prickly, especially with white college boys. Jac handled him very nicely – not presumptuous, supercilious, all the kinds of things Josh despised. Jac wasn't political with Josh either. Josh had taken awful bites from both sides. All he wanted was recognition as a musician and as a man. To him, Jac did what he was supposed to do. And it was so great to find a record producer who paid you."[8]

In Britain, White had considerable impact. The first song Eric Clapton learnt on guitar was 'Scarlet Begonias' as recorded by White, while Keith Richards's introduction to blues came through White, even if he soon switched to the harder Chicago sound. John Renbourn, one of the British folk scene's finest folk-blues guitarists, said, "I was still in short trousers when I was first caught up by the blues after my mother took me to a Josh White concert. Josh's guitar instruction book was the only good one available and provided the basis for most of the players of my generation."

White's most far-reaching influence on British pop culture came with Lonnie Donegan, who launched the British skiffle craze in the 50s. Donegan said in 1999, "Josh White's 'House Of The Rising Sun' inspired me to go into music. This was the first American folk song I heard, and the experience kicked off my career, started me singing American blues and folk. I believe Josh started the British rock scene."[9]

America honoured White later by including him in the US Postal Service's 1998 'Legends Of American Music' set, where a painting of White, guitar in hand, was featured on one of a series of stamps, alongside Woody Guthrie, Leadbelly, and Sonny Terry. But as Elijah Wald observes, "Books on black entertainers rarely mention [Josh White], much less give him his due as a pioneer: the smart, cool man of the future."[10]

Elektra Records threw Josh White a lifeline in 1955 and recorded some of his best work. Holzman firmly believes that greater recognition is overdue, and that it was certainly not afforded White during the folk revival of the late 50s. "He suffered by comparison to the likes of Mississippi John Hurt, Skip James, or Son House, who had returned to the South and a level of obscurity again after recording in the 20s and 30s. They were idolised when they were rediscovered and unveiled for the first time in years. When they appeared at the early Newport folk festivals from 1959, they were playing to an audience of thousands who were just going to adore them. Josh White didn't have the luxury of being a rediscovered blues artist."

Many of the major figures who themselves helped shape music in America during the 60s and 70s acknowledge White as an influence, both as a singer and as an innovative guitarist. They include John Fahey, Ry Cooder, John Fogerty, Richie Havens, Fred Neil, and Ray Charles. As David Crosby put it in his 1988 autobiography, *Long Time Gone*, "Josh White put my head on 'tilt' at the age of ten, when [I heard] his recording of 'Strange Fruit'."[11]

Remembering Elektra
John Renbourn on Josh White

"I was obsessed with Josh White. My mother took me to see him when I was about 11 or 12; I was too young to go by myself. I had *The Josh White Guitar Method* book that was published in 1956. He played in England quite a few times in the 50s and toured regularly throughout Europe going into the 60s. He was actually living in London in the early 50s as a result of being blacklisted at home during the red scare. You'd often hear him on the radio. At one time he had his own BBC radio show, which was called *My Guitar Is Old As Father Time*. And he'd appear on TV too, on nightly magazine programmes like *Focus* or *Tonight*, as well as *The Josh White Show* [for Granada Television in 1961].

That's where my interest in blues recordings began, and I still love his blues playing. He had such a light touch and his voice was soulful. In the 60s there were some who thought he wasn't authentic enough and too smooth because he was a master of that sophisticated, cabaret blues style, but those old numbers he played are still powerful: 'Did You Ever Love A Woman', 'Jesus Gonna Make Up My Dying Bed', 'Red River'. I remember hearing *Jazz Greats Volume Four* featuring Josh White and Big Bill Broonzy [on the EmArcy label] and later, the *Chain Gang Songs* album, which was released here on Golden Guinea [as was *Empty Bed Blues*].

For others, the eye opener was when Chris Barber brought Big Bill Broonzy over here to play. He directly influenced a lot of home grown players, including Bert Jansch, who saw him in Edinburgh. Then Muddy Waters came over in 1958, and that came as a shock to people who had only heard acoustic blues as played by Josh White or Sonny Terry and Brownie McGhee. Skiffle was more or less over by then, so plenty of people had acoustic guitars and knew the basic chords, and it was Muddy Waters's visit that led to electric bands forming. I tried to play R&B for a while. Those Chess guys eclipsed Josh White in the end but he was a very influential figure, especially before groups like The Rolling Stones came along, after which blues and R&B records became less hard to find in Britain.”

John Renbourne (August 8 1944–March 26 2015)

CHAPTER

Those Were The Days

“Folk Songs Of Israel *really changed my way of thinking. Although the album only credits singer Theodore Bikel in small type, in a little over a year we sold about 15,000 copies – a big hit for us. He was a working actor just starting out in America and on Broadway, but he was the pivot point for Elektra: for the first time, the artist was as important as the material. That's when I realised that an artist could carry a folk record, which was a discovery for me.*” **JAC HOLZMAN**

Jewish music was one of the more self-contained strands of American folk music and was most prevalent in the major cities. It came with the early waves of immigration to the United States at the end of the 19th century as Jewish people brought with them their own distinct musical culture, a manifestation of life in the old country now heard in the tenements of New York City and other large urban areas.

There was no unified body of Jewish folk song, but instead one that reflected the many scattered Jewish communities around the world. These diverse traditions mingled Jewish trends with local forms. Yiddish folk song of Eastern Europe took on elements of character from each host culture – Russian, Polish, Romanian. By the 20s, some three million Jews had settled in America – well over a third in New York alone – and by 1914 they "had given the cultural life of New York a distinctive Yiddish and socialist colouring. Russian Jews particularly were moving directly from a medieval to a post-enlightenment condition, fiercely clinging to the past or fiercely abandoning it".[1]

This led to a vital Jewish theatre, which dominated New York City's Lower East Side and often rivalled Broadway for scale and quality. The repertoire ranged from nostalgic recreations of life in Eastern Europe, through translations of Ibsen, Shakespeare, and the classics, to romantic musical comedies. There were Jewish vaudeville theatres by the 20s and five Jewish radio stations in the New York area. Klezmer and Jewish music were essential to weddings, bar mitzvahs, and dances at political and social clubs.

The separate streams of American and Jewish music influenced one another. The opening clarinet solo from Gershwin's 'Rhapsody In Blue' is a reminder that, like so many of America's popular musicians, Gershwin was Jewish. Second-generation American Jews may have reacted against their parents' tastes and attitudes and embraced elements of American culture – Moe Asch's Americanisation in the 30s came with Western novels about Jesse James and Wild Bill Hickock and, later, through Alan Lomax's *Cowboy Songs* – but in the years after World War II, the Jewish population found solace in the old music, just as Anglo-Americans found comfort in the homely style of Burl Ives. By now, Yiddish theatre was declining, the radio stations were off the air, and many of the musicians were aging or had died.

On first hearing Theodore Bikel perform, Jac Holzman – who describes himself as a "cultural rather than a religious Jew" – thought it was a natural step to record an album of Israeli and Jewish folks songs with Bikel. "I first met Theo at a typical Village party, where he was passed the guitar," says Holzman. "I was struck by just how powerful a singer and performer he was. He would just suck all the air out of the room with a blazing performance, but I didn't know how much was sheer force of personality and whether it would transfer on to a record devoid of his physical presence."

Bikel was famous for performing this impressive act at parties, especially in London, and landed acting jobs as a result. "His personality burst through," says Holzman. "John Huston saw him at a party and immediately cast him in *The African Queen*. Theo was particularly good with Israeli, Yiddish, and Russian songs, and foreign-language songs in general. He agreed to come to my little railroad flat, and we taped a few of these songs to see how others would react, because I knew what he could do live."

The reaction was enthusiastic, so Holzman urged Bikel to make a record. They agreed it would consist of what Bikel knew best. "I knew there was a hunger and an audience," says Holzman. "It was a very simple and engaging record to make: just Theo's voice and his guitar." That first album was *Folk Songs Of Israel*, released in 1955. Bikel's best early albums for Elektra were steeped in both the Yiddish theatre and the rich folk-music traditions of Israel, Eastern Europe, and Russia.

Bikel's passionate and authentic interpretations meant that, even if the appeal was to a specific ethnic culture, his approach was still populist rather than scholarly. *Folk Songs Of Israel* was revamped in 1958 as a 12-inch album, adding a handful of songs, adapting the jacket, which now read *Theodore Bikel Sings Songs Of Israel*, and replacing the line drawing on the original with a photograph.

"It pictured a kibbutz girl in the kibbutz uniform of shorts and pert hat," explains Holzman, "her sun-bronzed legs marching happily across a field, with a hoe on her shoulder. This was an image of an energetic new Israel. Elektra received numerous enquires asking about the girl and the kibbutz she lived on. In fact, she was a model and the field was in Long Island." Also that year, Bikel released a complementary album, *Sings Jewish Folk Songs*, followed by further instalments: *A Harvest Of Israeli Folksongs* (1961) and *Yiddish Theatre And Folk Songs* (1964).

Holzman had no doubts that *Folk Songs Of Israel* would do well, because there were very few albums of Israeli folk songs and there was what he calls "a very big Israeli consciousness" in the United States. "You had a lot of Jews in the major cities where folk music was generally strong, and we were strong, and there was a freshened awareness of Jewish culture – it was only seven years since Israel had become a state."

He didn't expect the record to make a name for Bikel: it was all to do with the music and how the singer conveyed that music. "His next album in the same vein, *Sings Jewish Folk Songs*, had his name even bigger – and it did even better. Theo loved recording but never thought it would become an important factor in his career. He would have made the record for the joy of it, but he received $100 advance."

Bikel himself agreed. "I was an actor brought over to the US do a Broadway play, but I'd always sung in England, everywhere ... though I'd never recorded, and I never thought of doing so professionally. America's a strange place," he said. "They won't tolerate your doing anything well without forcing you to accept money for it. They were songs from my background. I only define myself as a folk singer when I sing songs in the idiom that relate to my own heritage. When I sing other people's songs, I'm a folk-song singer."[2]

Holzman thinks Bikel's acting background may have helped his sales a little. "He's someone who by virtue of his personality was able to make things happen for himself. When I met him, he was already doing theatre in New York, he had played the First Officer on the *Louisa*, the German ship that rescues Bogart and Hepburn in *The African Queen*, he had been in *Moulin Rouge* – none of them lead roles, but the fact that he was an actor and became more visible, that all made a difference."

Born in Vienna in 1924, Theodore Bikel was 13 when he and his parents left Austria for Palestine. He found his way to London after World War II to pursue an acting career, which he started at the Habima Theatre in Tel Aviv in 1943. After graduating from RADA, London's Royal Academy of Dramatic Art, Bikel was cast in West End productions such as *A Streetcar Named Desire* (1949), directed by Laurence Olivier, and *The Love Of Four Colonels* (1951), written by Peter Ustinov. He made his Broadway debut in *Tonight In Samarkand* in 1955. Aside from Tevye in *Fiddler On The Roof*, a role Bikel made his own in 1967, he had created the character of Captain Georg von Trapp for the Broadway production of *The Sound Of Music*, opposite Mary Martin, and it is in this role that he made a lasting impression on theatregoers.

Following his movie debut in *The African Queen*, Bikel found himself underwater as second-in-command to Curt Jürgens on a German U-boat in *The Enemy Below* (1957), playing cat-and-mouse with Robert Mitchum's destroyer commander. He earned an Oscar nomination as Best Supporting Actor for his portrayal of Sheriff Max Muller in Stanley Kramer's *The Defiant Ones* in 1958. Bikel was fluent in Yiddish, Hebrew, French, German, and English, which helped land many a role, and he was promoted to captain, this time of a Russian submarine, in the 1966 Cold War comedy *The Russians Are Coming, The Russians Are Coming*. In 1964, he appeared in the huge hit movie adaptation of *My Fair Lady*. "He asked me what I thought of him as Zoltan Karpathy," recalls Holzman, "and I said I thought he was suitably oleaginous."

Holzman knew a good thing once it came along. "It wasn't unusual to release two Theo Bikel records in a year, even when I signed The Doors – it was still a three-year agreement for two records a year. Theo had great versatility."

A Young Man And A Maid, recorded in collaboration with Cynthia Gooding, exploited Bikel's polyglot inclinations and his knowledge of international folk music. Testing his linguistic flexibility even further, *Folk Songs From Just About Everywhere* covered traditional folk tunes from ten countries and in eleven languages, and on this occasion saw him teamed with Geula Gill. She was a member of the Oranim Zabar Israeli Troupe, a trio completed by her then husband Dov Seltzer on accordion and Michael Kagan on the darabukka, an Arabian drum. They would later record a series of albums for Elektra. Here, though, Bikel and Gill romp through high-spirited versions of Bolivian, Argentinean, and Brazilian tunes. One Russian song on the album, 'Dorogoy Dalnoyu', was later given English lyrics by Gene Raskin, who re-titled it 'Those Were The Days', which became a Number One hit in Britain and a Number Two in the US for the Welsh singer Mary Hopkin. It was produced by Paul McCartney, who had discovered the song three years earlier.

By the end of the 50s, with such concerted exposure, Bikel's star was rising and, according to Holzman, by now all the elements of his career in films, in the theatre, and on records were working together, reinforcing each other and taking him beyond the broad American–Jewish community. "Within that community, some people knew Theo more as a singer than an actor," says Holzman. "That all-round visibility made him very attractive for concerts in large venues. He could play a big hall and make it seem like a living room."

Bikel's versatility made him one of the biggest-earning folk acts of the period, able to sell out concerts at New York's Carnegie Hall and Town Hall and Chicago's Orchestra Hall. He was also selling out colleges around the country on a touring schedule arranged by Albert Grossman (better known as the manager of Bob Dylan, Joan Baez, and, later, Peter Paul & Mary). Herb Cohen, who died in March 2010, was a friend and close associate of Holzman's and a business partner of Bikel's. Cohen, who had left the Bronx for Los Angeles, described Bikel's appeal. "Theo had a great voice," said Cohen. "He was a good guitar player, and he had a commanding presence as a performer. The records don't capture the dynamics of what he did, as an on-stage performer. He was very funny, very erudite, usually playing to a collegiate or an adult European-based cultural audience." Bikel carefully managed and maintained the various strands of his career: the recordings, the concerts, and the film and theatre work. He now had his own FM radio show, *At Home*, recorded in New York City and carried in Los Angeles, where he was now spending increasing amounts of time for his film and TV work. Bemoaning the lack of a folk club in Los Angeles, he went into partnership with Cohen to open the first local coffee house there, the Unicorn on Sunset Strip – so named because, until then, there was no such thing. Six months later, the two of them opened Cosmo Alley.

Herb Cohen described the scene in Los Angeles in 1957. "The Unicorn was just a coffee house that stayed open until two in the morning. We only had a restaurant licence, but it was the first coffee house in Los Angeles. The next year there must have been over 60 coffee houses in the greater Los Angeles area. We didn't have any entertainment whatsoever at the beginning – we'd have people come in and play guitar, but not on a real performance level. That didn't happen until a year later. Cosmo Alley was behind the Ivar Theatre in Hollywood. It was a nightclub where Lenny Bruce's first LA performances took place, Maya Angelou read poetry, and Theo performed when he was in town."

Cohen and Bikel paved the way for other folk venues in California, particularly the Ash Grove, which opened shortly afterward, while across country in New York City, Cambridge, Boston, Philadelphia, Chicago, and Denver, similar folk nightspots and coffee houses were springing up and ready for the commercial folk revival that was about to happen.

Bikel's all-round appeal only partly explains the unprecedented success of the two Russian albums he made next for Elektra, which sold more than everything else he recorded for the label. The 1958 album *Songs Of A Russian Gypsy* became Elektra's biggest seller so far. "It sold more than 35,000 copies in its first four months and ended up selling many thousands more over time," says Holzman. "For us that was big business. Especially when you take into account that there was little copyright. That was a bonus – it wasn't done for that reason. It was just one of the happy products of recording folk music. Bikel's Russian gypsy albums helped give Elektra a financial stability that we'd never experienced before.

"It was not just that there had been so little Russian material released. The success said a lot about Theo's performance. He was an actor with great energy, and this is where interpretations sometimes have it over the real thing. It was a carefully conceived and constructed record." As with his Hitchcock-like cameo on the first of the *Dalliance* albums, Holzman appeared as one of the instrumentalists on the jacket of *Russian Gypsy* when it was re-shot to give it more punch.

Bikel was backed by balalaika, accordion, violin, and bass balalaika, in settings arranged by balalaika player Sasha Polinoff and guitarist and arranger Fred Hellerman. His actor's timing emphasised both the emotion and the raw energy of the songs, which move from sadness to exuberance in a second. *Songs Of A Russian Gypsy* and the 1960 album *Songs Of Russia Old & New* are cut from the same cloth, using the same cast. For Bikel, these were songs that he loved and understood. "I spent part of my childhood in what was then Palestine, which is Israel now," he explained, "and there were quite a number of expatriates who performed that kind of music and those [Russian] songs."[3] Bikel was drawn to songs he already knew but also to the poetry behind the music.

He says the second album varied the theme somewhat. "*Songs Of A Russian Gypsy* was just that, but there were songs of new Russia that needed to be recorded, and there were songs of old Russia [which] are not gypsy songs that needed to be heard as well. The two needed to be juxtaposed, one to the other. So we came up with this notion of *Songs Of Russia Old & New*."[4] Although the wave of anti-communist feeling had lessened by the time these albums were released, America was still in the grip of the Cold War. The Cuban missile crisis would soon come as a terrifying reminder of that. Yet Bikel's Russian albums effectively spoke for the humanity of the Soviet proletariat rather than an enemy to be feared.

Bikel had fond memories of the songs from his student days. "I couldn't afford to go to Russia, but I could get to Paris, which is where the expatriate White Russians were and where the gypsies had opened nightclubs. They sang for the aristocrats, who also went to Paris, but where the aristocrats now drove taxicabs and would bemoan their fates into their vodkas and vow to take back Russia, if only Washington would give them the horses. I went to those nightclubs to listen to the same music they used to sing in Russia. I learned hundreds of songs while nursing one glass of champagne the whole evening."[5]

Bikel now had a reputation for interpreting a wide range of ethnic material, but his place in the broader scheme of the folk revival may seem a little tenuous. Certainly he was an important figure, but hardly a pivotal one. As one of the first batch of directors for the Newport Folk Festival, from 1960 onward, he assisted in its organisation year after year. Despite an early encounter with a drunken Bob Dylan, who gatecrashed a party he held in the summer of 1962, Bikel was one of the few among the so-called old guard to defend Dylan's famous performance at Newport in 1965. He told Pete Seeger and Alan Lomax that they couldn't hold back the future. In 1963, Bikel had travelled with Dylan to the Deep South (and paid for his air fare), joining Pete Seeger and Len Chandler to take part in a voter-registration rally in Greenwood, Mississippi.

At the same time, however, Bikel's appeal was diminishing, as Holzman could see. "Inevitably, the market cared less about him over time. Theo still had a cachet, but he was not consequential to Americans in the manner of a Woody Guthrie or a Leadbelly. His audience would always be limited, but it was very identifiable and most important to a small label like Elektra."

Having reached the age of 40, Bikel found himself surrounded by the new and youthful topical songwriters. In 1964, the same year as his final Jewish-themed album, *Yiddish Theatre And Folk Songs*, he released *A Folksinger's Choice*, a muddled collection of traditional and modern English material including 'Come Away Melinda', an anti-war song co-written by Fred Hellerman and Fran Minkoff. Despite the presence of guitarists Walter Raim and Dick Rosmini, and Jim McGuinn on banjo, Bikel sounds distinctly at odds with the material and out-of-touch.

"By the mid 60s," explains Holzman, "we had run out of material for him, and Theo felt that the label had moved in a much different direction. He saw that he was becoming less important to the label. I was always moving on, and I don't think he realised that about me. When I said I didn't see us making any further records together, he was in tears. I owed him that honesty, but I had changed course. We had a wonderful and productive relationship – I did 15 or so records with him. One fundamental problem was that Theo did not create material, and I was now working with people who wrote and performed songs from their own experience."

Bikel understood this. "Jac was practically out of the folk world," he said. "For several reasons – my own personal predilection musically, perhaps out of inertia – my musical taste didn't draw me toward that other world at all."[6]

His final album for Elektra was 1967's *Songs Of The Earth*, recorded with The Pennywhistlers, a pioneering vocal ensemble of seven young women who performed Balkan music. They would release an album of their own on Nonesuch Explorer a few years later. In the year that Elektra scored a Number One single with 'Light My Fire', all that linked Bikel and The Doors was a Joel Brodsky jacket photograph. Bikel's next album would be an unconvincing collection of contemporary songs recorded for Reprise.

He effectively bookended the folk era, since his final Elektra album was also the last of the 300 series in Elektra's catalogue: EKL-326. When Elektra released the first Love album, in 1966, it started a new numerical series for Elektra, known as the 4000 series, and signalled the label's freshened outlook and a shift away from folk music.

Holzman still feels indebted to his friend Theodore Bikel. "Theo's success was critical for us in so many ways. Besides Josh White, he was the first person whose name on an Elektra album would encourage someone to pick it up and look at it twice. I don't think he was particularly influential beyond bringing character to the sort of music he was recording, but boy, did he do that, particularly throughout the Jewish and Russian albums."

Songs Of A Russian Gypsy had come along at a time when Elektra was in a perilous financial state. Leonard Ripley, who had invested in Elektra in 1954, was now suing Holzman for control of the company. Holzman owed his suppliers $90,000, but the income from sales generated by Bikel's *Russian Gypsy* and the successful sampler series he pioneered and launched in 1954 encouraged him to borrow money and buy out Ripley. From that moment, Elektra was always fiscally sound and debt-free.

As a measure of gratitude, in 1959 Holzman offered Bikel – who died on July 21 2015 – a small part of Elektra. Bikel put in $20,000, commenting, "Five percent of Elektra was already worth more than the 20 grand. And Jac really didn't have to do that. But he did make the offer, and I accepted. The investment was later returned 25-fold."[7]

That same year, Elektra moved to new and bigger offices, located at 110 West 14th Street, still in the West Village. As Holzman recalls fondly, "Some wag called it The House That Theo Built."

CHAPTER 9

Folk Songs From Just About Everywhere

> "*This was a tough period, in the late 50s going into the early 60s, when I was desperately looking for stuff to do that was interesting. I didn't feel I knew where I was going, but I was very conscious that I had an operation to run and maintain. I wanted to be proud of everything that was in my catalogue, although I can see now that it doesn't necessarily all hold together for someone looking in from the outside. What it represents is one guy's adventure in record-land.*" **JAC HOLZMAN**

Thanks to Holzman's wily business sense and plenty of good will from his suppliers at vital times, he had managed to keep ahead of his creditors throughout the 50s, to keep ahead of the game. The days of recording in an artist's home, with recording costs just the price of the tape itself, were coming to an end. As Elektra Records approached its tenth anniversary, the label had achieved a financial stability boosted by sales of Theodore Bikel's two Russian albums. Throughout the decade, every release had broken even.

Elektra's titles repeatedly sold better than expected: the Josh White albums; Ed McCurdy's *Dalliance* series; three albums from flamenco-guitar maestro Sabicas; or the long-forgotten *Songs Of The Abbaye*. The *Abbaye* record had captured Gordon Heath and Lee Payant, who left a career in

Broadway behind them to open a bohemian nightclub in the St-Germain-des-Prés district in Paris. In 1954, *Songs Of The Abbaye* shifted a healthy 10,000 copies, three of four times more than any of Elektra's folk albums usually sold.

"I had built up a catalogue of recordings that were singular," Holzman explains. "Nobody else had *Songs Of The Abbaye,* and it was a tremendous seller. We had a real hit, with kids coming back from Paris having done the European tour and having seen Heath and Payant at the Abbaye. It was a basement club adjoining the police station, and the local gendarmes were very watchful of the audience disturbing nearby tenants. So instead of applauding, you snapped your fingers. It was that finger-snapping thing which showed up later in *Funny Face* with Fred Astaire and Audrey Hepburn. Leonard Ripley, who had just invested $10,000 in the company and helped keep us going when I really needed it, suggested Heath and Payant as Elektra artists."

Ripley knew little about the technological aspects of recording, says Holzman, but he had an excellent ear. "He went over to Europe with a portable Magnecord and did a great job. He was always hopping back and forth to Europe. Heath and Payant were so popular that people would return from France and, when the boat docked, would come directly to the office on Bleecker to buy their commemorative copies of *Songs Of The Abbaye.* It sold so well we did a second one, *Encores From The Abbaye.* The Abbaye records also appealed to Americans remembering a war-time visit to Paris only a dozen years before."

Gordon Heath and Lee Payant met in 1947, when Payant appeared in an off-Broadway Shakespeare production that Heath directed. Both wanted to work in Europe and focus on their passion for folk song. They became lovers, moving to Paris in 1949 and opening the Abbaye there. It was a taste of Greenwich Village on the Paris Left Bank, but with its own flavour. Each table had a candle, and everyone was entitled to a request before the end of the evening. After each request was granted, the appropriate candle was snuffed out, and once all the candles were out, the Abbaye was closed for the night. This was the scene that Ripley captured. By the end of the decade, however, Heath and Payant were releasing albums on their own Abbaye label. The two were major figures on the Parisian cabaret scene until 1976, when Payant died.

With his diverse and distinctive catalogue falling into place, Holzman was looking for a way to reach more people. He had no budget for advertising, and there were few appropriate outlets. As an inveterate moviegoer, he hit upon an idea to adapt the film trailer to suit the needs of the record business. "My concept – and I have always been big on concepts – was a sampler LP, which would be a collection of musical trailers, a compendium of carefully assembled material. It would have lyric extracts and notes, all on a ten-inch LP to sell for a bargain price of $2, which was unheard of in 1954."

The first such Elektra compilation, *The Folk Music Sampler*, sold mostly through the mail, and Holzman immediately realised its potential. He inserted a sampler clause in all new artists' agreements, which allowed him to use one track from any album, royalty-free. That first sampler bragged that it contained "outstanding folk & ethnic recordings" and sported a new logo designed by Bill Harvey: a drawing of a musician seated on a conga-shaped barrel, playing a guitar.

Aside from the sampler spreading the word, Holzman knew it was important simply as something new, and that it showed how creative Elektra was in reaching for its audience. He followed it in 1956 with Elektra's first 12-inch sampler, also sold through retail outlets as well as mail order. The sampler or compilation became commonplace in the record business, but in 1954 it was an enterprising notion. "It may seem obvious now," says Holzman, "but it presented the best of all possible worlds. We were actively promoting our records, the public was getting a full LP for $2, and Elektra was being nurtured by the profits."

The second Elektra *Folk Sampler* had notes by Holzman's wife (and the label's first employee), Nina Merrick, announcing that the songs derived "from cultures startlingly different, from lands across the sea, and from the wealth of traditionally American music". It clearly identified Elektra's watchwords: "True high fidelity, attractive jackets, fully documented notes, and complete lyrics printed in an accompanying booklet."

Holzman today says he never considered that he made fillers and that every release seemed right to him at the time, even if some decisions he now feels were misguided. One such LP, Alan Arkin's *Once Over Lightly*, just wasn't a serious enough record. It was made when Arkin was still a struggling young actor. Arkin later formed The Tarriers with Erik Darling, in which he sang lead and played guitar. He co-wrote the 1956 hit 'The Banana Boat Song', better known through Harry Belafonte's version. Next, The Tarriers teamed up with future Elektra artist Vince Martin, scoring a second pop hit with 'Cindy Oh Cindy'. Arkin recorded *Folk Songs (And 2 1/2 That Aren't) – Once Over Lightly* for Elektra in 1954, its levity confirmed by that bracketed subtitle.

Holzman cannot disguise the enthusiasm he still feels for one or two of the label's more idiosyncratic releases that reflected his love of technology: the *Elektra Playback System Calibration Record* in 1955, for fine-tuning audio equipment; and, a few years later, the *Morse Code Course*, for acquiring and sharpening skills in sending and receiving international Morse code. These releases might raise a chuckle today, but they made sound economic sense, at least to Holzman, who knew exactly who would buy them: people like himself.

"Folk music was our musical base," says Holzman, "but I always had a broader view than that. The calibration record was for serious audiophiles – because I was a serious audiophile. RCA had put one out, which I considered inferior, so we just did our own. We sold only 700 copies, but the idea was to help set up your playback equipment. Whether people bought it or not, here we are contributing to an audio standard, which I wanted Elektra to be known for. It was important to me that we do it, because it said something about Elektra: we were strange, and inside our own muse."

Holzman would grab ideas that interested him personally, his more bizarre choices laying him open to accusations that he would release anything. But he did the *Morse Code Course* record because he was an active ham-radio operator and saw the need for it. A quick financial turnaround was hardly his motivation. "The Lafayette radio catalogue carried it, and we sold a hundred a month for years. Predictably profitable. *Authentic Sound Effects* came about in a similar way. That series was crucial when we released it in the 60s, because the sound effects were inexpensive to produce, but they really put the fat on the chequebook. We invested in meticulous production for each of the sound effects albums, which in aggregate sold almost a million copies. Even though I couldn't have told you what the money might be for, I knew it was needed."

Elektra continued to issue a steady flow of world-music titles, including a regular stream of flamenco albums. Leonard Ripley had a particular

RIGHT Jean Ritchie, whose 1952 album was Elektra's first folk LP. **BELOW** Elektra's first LP, produced by Jac Holzman while he was still attending St John's College and released in March 1951.
BELOW RIGHT The Record Loft, which Holzman opened in New York City in late 1951.

ΣLΣKTRA

e. e. cummings
rainer maria rilke
franz kafka
friederich hölderlin

New Songs
by
john gruen

georgiana bannister
soprano
john gruen
piano

Holzman in his home electronics lab in the 50s. Post-war technological advances in audio engineering inspired Holzman at St Johns to think he could one day record music himself.

TOP Hally Wood's 1953 LP *O' Lovely Appearance Of Death*, the first jacket designed for Elektra by Bill Harvey. **ABOVE** Tom Paley and Peggy Seeger. **FAR LEFT** Early Elektra albums by Josh White and Theodore Bikel. **LEFT** Cynthia Gooding, whose recordings for Elektra between 1953 and 1962 explored songs from around the world.

RIGHT The Limeliters – Glenn Yarbrough, Lou Gottlieb, and Alex Hassilev – whose 1960 debut gave Elektra its first chart album.

BELOW The 'folk mafia' relaxing at the Newport Folk Festival in 1965: Jac Holzman, Theodore Bikel, Pete and Toshi Seeger, Harold Leventhal, Fred Hellerman, and Maynard Solomon.

TOP Three Elektra artists: Dick Rosmini (left, with guitar), Fred Neil, and Bob Gibson. **ABOVE** Holzman recording on location in 1955. **RIGHT** Judy Collins's breakthrough album, *Judy Collins 3*, and *Tell It To The Marines*, with Bill Harvey as the drill instructor on the cover.

LEFT AND BELOW Nonesuch's initial foundation was baroque classics but the label soon broke new ground with Beaver & Krause's electronic music manual. **BOTTOM** The Elektra gang celebrate Judy's first Gold album, *Judy Collins 3*. Back row, left to right: Bill Harvey, producer Mark Abramson, Jac Holzman, Larry Harris, Mel Posner, Keith Holzman. Front row, left to right: Steve Harris, Paul Rothchild, Nina Holzman.

TOP Tom Rush, who developed a highly individual 12-string and bottleneck technique in Boston and Cambridge clubs before signing to Elektra in 1965. **ABOVE LEFT** The *Zodiac Cosmic Sounds* LP. **BELOW LEFT** Tom Paxton. **ABOVE** Phil Ochs, who like Paxton was signed by Elektra in 1964.

LEFT The the original line-up of Love. **BELOW** The Nonesuch team in the 60s, left to right: Jac Holzman, Bill Harvey, Joshua Rifkin, and Tracey Sterne. **BELOW LEFT** The Paul Butterfield Blues Band's influential 1965 debut LP. **BOTTOM** Paul Rothchild recording the Butterfield Blues Band.

passion for flamenco. In 1957, Elektra released its first album by one of the most renowned flamenco guitarists of the day, Sabicas.

"He was an amazing flamenco guitarist," says Holzman, "known worldwide as one of the best, and very highly rated in Spain. He did not trust record companies to pay royalties and insisted on a flat fee, up front, which was not something we usually did. So we paid him his requested $1,000, easily the largest advance we had paid in Elektra's history so far. If Sabicas had elected to take royalties, he would have made a lot more money." Holzman says Elektra explored these special markets. "We did three albums in all with Sabicas and, later, three with Juan Serrano, the first of which was *Olé La Mano*, in 1962. Juan was brought over from Spain to do the *Ed Sullivan* TV show and ended up living in America."

Serrano was described in *The New York Times* as having "ten dextrous fingers that often sound like twenty". The same could be said of Sabicas, and the effect was brilliantly illustrated by a freeze-frame photograph on the jacket of his second Elektra album. Aside from his fee, Sabicas's only other stipulation was that he have final say over which takes were used. Since a key aspect of his art was improvisation, the pieces were recorded three or more times for him to choose from, with the sessions engineered and produced by Ripley. Elektra released three volumes of Sabicas recordings through 1957 and 1958, each with liner notes by Cynthia Gooding.

The Theodore Bikel albums had already proved to be something of a cash cow for Elektra. While Holzman was still hunting around for something to inspire him, he unleashed a torrent of Israeli and Russian material. There were six albums from the Oranim Zabar Israeli Troupe; the second, *On The Road To Elath*, gave Elektra's latest recruit, Mark Abramson, his first production credit. Abramson had joined Elektra in 1958 as an assistant to the in-house engineer David A. Jones and would become one of the label's most successful producers, best known for his association with Judy Collins. He died in 2007.

In a similar vein were albums from husband-and-wife Hillel And Aviva, who had achieved some fame in the early 50s as the first authentic team of folk singers to come out of Israel. In 1958, Ed Sullivan scouted Israel looking for young performers for a special TV show celebrating ten years of the State of Israel, and he came across another duo, Ran Eliran and Nechama Hendel. They became known as Ron & Nama and were introduced to American audiences by Sullivan, performing 'Tzena Tzena Tzena', which The Weavers had recorded as the flipside to 'Goodnight Irene'. Elektra released two albums of their Hebrew recordings and two by Sasha Polinoff And His Russian Gypsy Orchestra. Polinoff came fresh from Theodore Bikel's Russian gypsy albums, and his new records were *Balalaika* and *Fastest Balalaika In The West*, presenting a Russian equivalent of the equally dextrous US bluegrass music.

Another twist in the Israeli series was *The Dudaim* by Dudaim, a duo comprising Benny Amdurski and Adam Guryon, who performed contemporary Israeli folk music. By 1958, two years after the Suez crisis, the dominant songs of the time were militant, up-tempo, and patriotic, but Dudaim offered an alternative, with acoustic guitar and soft ballads, and they became stars in Israel for several decades. While Holzman may have been guilty of milking a good thing, this was, nonetheless, music that he admired and understood.

"There was very little world music at that time," he says. "We had done a certain amount, but our biggest focus had been on Theodore Bikel and on the Oranim Zabar group. Ron and Nama fleshed out a category of music that I thought was really important, influenced by the cultures these people had come from, most particularly Russian and Eastern Europe. That was fascinating to me. We knew we had a decent Israeli audience, so it was always a safe bet."

Holzman found the contemporary Israeli material exciting. "It was like watching a planet being born – because we always thought that this music continued a tradition and was something evolving again. Israel was an incubator for new Israeli songs that preserved a cultural identity and yet moved forward. The material was fascinating: it was a group voice, not just in the vocals and the choruses but in the way that everything was so well integrated. The Oranim Zabar group sometimes had five people all playing instruments. It was another aspect, the kibbutz influence on music, although I didn't always say that to people. We stopped by the mid 60s because there was no place to take it, and by then I was more excited by the complexities and promise of rock. At that point I could get an adrenalin hit from Israeli material, but it took stronger stuff later."

Another tributary of world music came through artists brought to America by impresario Sol Hurok. Holzman describes him as a remarkable man, one who, despite opposition, succeeded in importing the Bolshoi Ballet to America during the Cuban missile crisis. In the 30s, 40s, and 50s, Hurok organised international tours and brought theatrical companies and artists over from Europe, Russia, and Israel, and he made it possible for American artists to tour the Soviet Union throughout the cold war period.

"He would bring in artists," says Holzman, "I would be informed, and while they were here for their Sol Hurok engagements, I would put them into a hall and record their show in a single evening. I recorded Kimio Eto, a blind Japanese koto player, for *Art Of The Koto*, there was Hillel And Aviva, and classical guitarists Presti & Lagoya – all as a result of the Sol Hurok connection. One of the Hurok-generated albums that I loved is *Gold Coast Saturday Night*, by Saka Acquaye And His African Ensemble, which was highlife music, originating in Ghana." The Acquaye record incorporated rhythmic styles and instruments from Cuba and the Caribbean, jazz styles from America, and traditional music from West Africa – a revolutionary sound in 1959 (and later reissued on Nonesuch).

Holzman also nominates a record that had a significant influence on him, *A Treasury Of Music Of The Renaissance*, which was a double-LP that Elektra released during 1962. It didn't sell well – he estimates about a thousand copies – but it was sold for the price of a single album. "That sowed the seed for Nonesuch," says Holzman. "It stayed in my mind. I knew there was an audience for it, but I realised that it didn't make sense to people at the time as an Elektra recording."

One experiment Holzman would not return to in the future was Elektra's brief foray into jazz, in 1957, when he released half a dozen albums, including records by the New York Jazz Quartet, Teddy Charles, and The Jazz Messengers led by Art Blakey. "I was simply trying to find another genre I could build catalogue around," he explains.

The recordings were mostly blowing sessions, with the musicians arriving at the Carl Fischer Concert Hall in New York City and jamming. Holzman found it all too unfocussed. He put together the New York Jazz Quartet, for example, because he admired the individual players – hot Blue Note musicians including Herbie Mann – and thought that putting them together would create something special. But other labels already did this better. "I was too far behind to catch up with Riverside and Bethlehem. Elektra was never going to be anybody's first choice for a jazz record. Other genres interested me more. I respected jazz, but I didn't love it enough."

Holzman preferred to make records that stimulated him or often that just appealed to him personally. There were many avid collectors of show albums, and *The Golden Apple* – an early-50s musical based on the legend of Helen Of Troy – was an original stage soundtrack that he loved. The album was out of print, so he went and leased it. "It didn't matter how much it looked out of place among the rest of the catalogue. There was *Spook Along With Zacherley*, which was just fun to do, and *Presenting Joyce Grenfell*. She was another brought to America by Sol Hurok. It really appealed to me that she is so quintessentially English."

John Zacherley was a DJ and radio personality in Philadelphia who hosted a regular horror-movie show on TV. His album came out on Elektra in 1960 and then in 1963 moved to Crestview, a shortlived offshoot catering for more pop-based material. Holzman knew Riverside named itself after a local phone exchange, and Crestview was his exchange in California when he went there in 1962 to try for the first time to establish a West Coast base for Elektra.

Comedy records were a staple of the period. Alongside eccentric British comedienne Joyce Grenfell, Elektra released records with roots in America's comedy counter-culture, for example *Jean Shepherd And Other Foibles* (1959) and *Will Failure Spoil Jean Shepherd?*, the latter recorded at the Greenwich Village nightclub One Sheridan Square during the last week of 1960. Shepherd was a gentle political and social satirist with a broad hipster perspective, well known for his radio monologues broadcast on WOR in New York City. He also provided liner notes for the first album by Shel Silverstein, then known for his writings and drawings for *Playboy* magazine. Silverstein returned the favour, contributing liner notes to a number of Elektra albums, including *Jean Shepherd And Other Foibles* and *Gibson & Camp At The Gate Of Horn*. He later became Bob Gibson's most regular collaborator and, of course, wrote 'A Boy Named Sue' for Johnny Cash and many of the early breakthrough hits for Dr. Hook.

But in 1957, Silverstein recorded a boozy-sounding ragtime knockabout album with the seven-piece Red Onion Jazz Band, where he hollered and cavorted through a bunch of customised standard songs and a couple of originals. It's another anomaly in Elektra's catalogue. Here, perversely, was an established folk label releasing indulgent and decidedly off-the-wall material – just as, elsewhere, The Kingston Trio became the first real folk-pop phenomenon. "I felt that folk music wasn't really going anywhere," says Holzman, "I thought The Kingston Trio was glib. They legitimised folk music as a broader genre, and that was fine by me. Others acted as if it was against traditional roots and should be stamped out, but I thought it was good that a much larger audience was now aware of folk music."

The Kingston Trio were inspired in equal parts by The Weavers and by the smooth harmonies of The Four Freshmen, and they took much of their immediate style from The Tarriers and The Gateway Singers, with their well-rehearsed choreographed act and a wholesome look with peppermint-striped button-down shirts. It was only after 'Tom Dooley' was lifted as a single from their debut Capitol album that things picked up – a choice inspired by Frank Warner's original version of the song on his early Elektra album. By October of 1958, the Trio crashed the *Billboard* Top Ten, where they remained for the next four months. Within a year they had four albums in the chart and eventually became the first group to sell more albums than singles.

The Kingston Trio had a defining collegiate appeal, and they were perfect for the proliferating college concert circuit. Plenty of others followed in their wake over the next few years, and all of them consisted of variations on the Trio's basic style and bright folk appeal. They included The Brothers Four, The Highwaymen, The Cumberland Three, The Journeymen (with John Phillips and Scott McKenzie), the more topical Chad Mitchell Trio, The New Christy Minstrels, briefly including Gene Clark but fronted by the gruff-voiced Barry McGuire, and The Serendipity Singers, like the Christy Minstrels a nine-strong combo of singers and musicians.

Gene Clark wasn't the only future member of The Byrds to tread the boards in a hootenanny-style folk outfit. David Crosby had been in Les Baxter's Balladeers, while Jim McGuinn toured with The Chad Mitchell Trio. At the same time, two founder members of Buffalo Springfield, Richie Furay and Stephen Stills, started out together in The Au-Go-Go Singers. If nothing else, these groups provided a useful apprenticeship.

Despite any reservations about The Kingston Trio, Elektra pitched in by signing the more sophisticated Limeliters for one album before they moved to a major label, RCA, and later recorded The Travelers 3. The Travelers 3 had a fuller sound than The Kingston Trio and looked different, with a Japanese–American banjo player and a Hawaiian guitarist. But the diverse background and cultural mix barely contributed to their originality. Holzman considers The Travelers 3 an enthusiastic and unashamed Kingston Trio knockoff, whereas he found The Limeliters more authentic interpreters of folk and in possession of a good theatrical presence.

The singer in The Limeliters, Glenn Yarbrough, had been at St John's College with Holzman, and among their fellow students they were voted as the two least likely to succeed. Yarbrough had made one of Holzman's first recordings, while still at St John's, singing 'Follow The Drinking Gourd'. It was released as one of five 78s in 1951, between *New Songs* and Jean Ritchie's debut album.

After serving in Korea for three years, Yarbrough returned to his studies in classical Greek and pre-Socratic society, ending up at New York's School For Social Research and playing folk music to help pay his way. Family commitments took him to Aspen, Colorado, where he began performing at the Limelite club with Alex Hassilev. They teamed up with musicologist and bass player Lou Gottlieb, one of the original Gateway Singers, and debuted at Cosmo Alley as The Limeliters.

Elektra had already released two albums by Yarbrough: *Here We Go Baby!* in 1957 (later renamed *Glenn Yarbrough*); and, with Marilyn Child, *English And American Folksongs*. His debut had surprisingly commercial overtones for an Elektra record, with Yarbrough's clear, high tenor voice accompanied by a chorus, an orchestra, and The Shanty Boys (the Washington Square instrumentalists).

Holzman was impressed by The Limeliters. They were smart – Gottlieb had a musicology PhD from UCLA – and funny on stage, and they were first-rate professional players. "I really wanted to get a Limeliters record. The problem was Glenn, who did not want to sign to Elektra. The Limeliters had pop ambitions, and Glenn didn't think Elektra could deliver. Eventually, he agreed to waive his objection. I released their first record and it charted, though only in the lower reaches. We did release a single, 'The Hammer Song', which was rare for us, but that went nowhere – so maybe Glenn was right. But at least I had a chart album, for the first time ever. It went to Number 72."

Fittingly, The Limeliters' album had been recorded in December 1959, its minor success some consolation for Holzman at a moment when not only Elektra but also folk music was in a curious period of transition. Overnight, one bowdlerised branch of folk music had become mainstream thanks to the success of The Kingston Trio.

However, a more accurate reflection of the co-existing strands in folk music can be found in the wide range of performers at the inaugural Newport folk festival in July 1959. There was something for everyone: Odetta, Pete Seeger, Jean Ritchie, Frank Warner, Sonny Terry & Brownie McGhee, John Jacob Niles, Ed McCurdy, Oscar Brand, Cynthia Gooding, Earl Scruggs, and The New Lost City Ramblers. It was if someone had turned the clock back at least five years, aside from the presence of The Kingston Trio.

Folk was still a mix of traditionalist and revivalist styles, although the most significant appearance came when Bob Gibson brought Joan Baez on stage during his set. She would soon become the first folk superstar of the 60s, with a repertoire that, while entirely traditional, made an impact that was revolutionary.

CHAPTER 10

Where I'm Bound

> *"In 1959, Bob Gibson introduced Joan Baez to the world at the Newport folk festival, not long after Paul Rothchild had seen her in Cambridge at Club 47. His one-line take was 'Bare feet, three chords, and a terrified attitude.' At Newport she was an instant sensation. Albert Grossman snapped her up for representation and made a swift deal with Maynard Solomon at Vanguard. Once the record was released, Vanguard couldn't press them fast enough. In 1960, when she returned to Newport, she was a star. It rankled me that we didn't have an artist as exquisite as Joan."* **JAC HOLZMAN**

One of the major changes at Elektra in the 60s was a shift from releasing a miscellany of material that encompassed the various strands of folk music to become a more artist-based label. Theodore Bikel and Josh White had shown the potential of the artist's name above the title, but neither offered a gateway to the 60s. At the end of the 50s, however, Holzman signed two artists who would help the transition to the new era.

Bob Gibson was firmly at the cusp of 50s and 60s folk styles. Judy Collins, whom Gibson brought to Holzman's attention, began an association with Elektra in 1961 that lasted until 1984. She epitomised one of Holzman's underlining principles: that Elektra wasn't necessarily looking for groundbreaking changes but for evolutionary changes.

Gibson was something of a conundrum. He was a clean-cut professional who at the same time had all the demons normally associated with a Fred Neil or a Phil Ochs – both of whom he influenced. In a rare interview with *Hit Parader* in 1966, Fred Neil was unusually forthcoming. "Almost all the folk groups, when they started out, had nothing but Bob Gibson's chord progressions," he says. "Whether there were three or five in the group, they all sounded like Bob Gibson. He never got credit for this, which is ridiculous because he's one of the biggest influences in folk music.

"I'd been in New York doing blues for a long time, and I'd had it. But Gibson said I was doing folk music and should stick around because something was going to happen – and he was right: Gibson is far ahead of his times. He should be getting a lot more recognition. Gibson was one of my influences."

It's something that John Sebastian, who played on the sessions for Fred Neil's Elektra recordings, substantiates. "Bob Gibson's guitar style was a big influence on a lot of people early on: Fred Neil, for sure; Richie Havens was another. Gibson was the first guy to take a 12-string, taking what Leadbelly had done with it but jazzing it up."

Gibson is a grossly overlooked figure whose neat-and-tidy stance belies his contribution to the folk revival. "Other artists really respected Bob Gibson," explains Holzman. "First of all, he was a great player – very important. He had superb instrumental technique and would fill Town Hall, accompanying himself on banjo and guitar, with enormous authority and charm. When he was loaded … boy, that was a problem. He cleaned himself up several times. He had a very fine eye for other artists. He was the one who told me about Judy Collins, and I went out to Colorado to see her. I didn't think she was ready yet – but he was right about her. He was right about Hamilton Camp, and I was thrilled to record and release the *Gate Of Horn* album they did together. Hamilton Camp was a joy to work with – wonderful technique, full of fun – and the two of them together were magic." The *Gate Of Horn* album is credited to Bob Gibson and Bob Camp, who had changed his name to Hamilton Camp by the time he recorded a solo album for Elektra, *Paths Of Victory*, in 1964.

Born in New York City in 1931, Bob Gibson was a salesman before he was inspired to take up folk music after he heard Guthrie, Ives, and Leadbelly on the radio and saw Pete Seeger perform. He took up the guitar and banjo, another player indebted to Seeger's trusty manual. He got his break by winning on Arthur Godfrey's *Talent Scouts* programme. He learned to play Jamaican music when he worked cruise boats off Florida, passing a couple of tunes on to Alan Arkin and Erik Darling who, as The Tarriers, wrote and recorded 'The Banana Boat Song' based on something they learned from Gibson.

He recorded four albums for Riverside between 1956 and 1958, and on his first recordings for them he set out a style from which he rarely wavered. He played light but strident banjo and 12-string guitar, sang with a warm tenor voice, and offered a wide assortment of traditional folk tunes, often reworking them with new words and coming up with the occasional original song himself, such as 'Mighty Day' and the oft-recorded 'Well Well Well'.

He struggled with lyrics and collaborated over the years with Shel Silverstein, Hamilton Camp, Tom Paxton, and, very early on, Phil Ochs. Ochs's brother Michael says that Gibson was Phil's biggest inspiration. "Bob Gibson was the most melodic of the folk singers, and both Phil and Bob had a great sense of melody. And Phil actually had a better sense of lyrics. Gibson had three great melodies that he had no words for. So, within a few days, Phil put lyrics to them. One was 'One More Parade', another 'That's The Way It's Gonna Be'. So, for an amateur, Phil got to co-write with a major singer very soon in his career."[1] Both songs appeared on Phil Och's 1964 Elektra debut *All The News That's Fit To Sing.*

Gibson even went out of his way to offer advice to Ochs about the risks of topical songwriting, outlining his own problems in finding work on television and radio as a result of the House Un-American Activities Committee investigations. Their first encounter lasted only a few days but made a real impression on Ochs. "I don't think Gibson gets nearly the credit he should for being the seminal influence on Phil," says Dave Van Ronk. "It was like Bob collaborating with his political self, or Phil collaborating with his non-political self. It was perfect."[2]

Holzman wanted to do an album with Gibson and Camp, but the first record Gibson made for him was the unlikely *Ski Songs*, in 1959. Despite its title, this was not an Oscar Brand-style themed album but a new collaboration with two women who were writing for *The Denver Post.* At the time, Gibson was living in Aspen, Colorado, and was an enthusiastic skier. He explained in his biography, *I Come For To Sing*, that he decided to write a musical about skiing. "It was fun to do and it produced entirely new songs rather that being rewrites or rearrangements."[3] Out of it came songs like 'In This White World' (a hit for Glenn Yarbrough as 'In This Wide World') and 'Super Skier' (made popular by The Chad Mitchell Trio).

"I don't know why nothing ever happened with the ski [musical]," says Gibson. "But it was never produced. All that was ever produced was the album, *Ski Songs*. It was the biggest-selling album I ever cut. It seems a little isolated, subject-wise, but there are a lot of skiers and I made a lot of money from that album. I recorded it backed by an electric guitar, a bass, a banjo, plus background singers. This was happening stuff. It may not have been a major change, but it was the next logical step."[4] The most unusual aspect of the arrangements was the presence of jazzman Joe Puma and his electric guitar, which marked a rare and early use of that instrument by a folk performer.

When it came to his next Elektra album, *Yes I See*, Gibson went even further down that road. It was recorded in RCA's studios in Hollywood and, while not entirely explicit, Gibson credits Specialty A&R man Bumps Blackwell in helping to put the record together. It was part pop and part folk, as Gibson explains. "Jac Holzman couldn't believe it, because we spent $1,600 to produce it. He told me he was outraged, and I thought, well, that's not so very much. You got all the instruments and all those voices and everything."[5] The line-up included The Gospel Pearls singers and the ubiquitous guitarist Tommy Tedesco. "It was one of the first instances where a white artist sang with black women," Gibson adds.

Yes I See was released in 1961. That same year, Roy Silver, Gibson, and his brother Jim opened an agency in New York City on Sullivan Street, in the Village. It was called New Concepts, and it had a roster that included Fred Neil, David Crosby, Bob Dylan, and Richie Havens. After Albert Grossman took over Dylan's representation, he bought out Roy Silver for a reported $10,000. Gibson, who had started out with Grossman at the Gate Of Horn and was *the* folk star in the Midwest, returned to Grossman's management company. Grossman considered putting Gibson and Camp together with a female singer as a new kind of folk trio, an idea he eventually brought to fruition with Peter Paul & Mary.

Gibson's final solo release for Elektra, in 1964, was *Where I'm Bound*. Here he took a more contained approach, and it was his first to feature wholly original material, some written with Shel Silverstein while another has a co-writing credit for Fred Neil. It was hardly a singer-songwriter record, but by Gibson's standards it was far more sombre, with songs like the fatalistic 'The Waves Roll Out' and the poignant 'The Town Crier's Song', co-written with Hamilton Camp (and covered by Judy Collins on her third album).

Holzman says that Gibson was a facile writer. "I don't think he wrote memorably, but when you put what he did with the performance he gave to those songs, it became memorable. Tom Paxton wrote songs every day; so did Dylan. Gibson was the best of what Paul Rothchild called the 'sports jacket and open collar' folk singers, which was how you presented yourself on stage."

Gibson's most revered album was made with Hamilton (then still Bob) Camp, recorded live *At The Gate Of Horn* – a club considered by many artists as ground zero in the critical Midwest. Gordon Lightfoot says that the album was the one that got him interested in folk music. "When I think back, it's [Gibson] and it's Dylan, and that's about as far as it goes."[6]

Perhaps Gibson's greatest champion is Roger McGuinn, who later would revolutionise the 12-string Rickenbacker sound with The Byrds. "Gibson & Camp were always pushing the envelope, trying to take folk more into a pop realm," says McGuinn. "*At The Gate Of Horn* was an incredible musical experience. I was in the audience when they recorded that album. Bob was very influential: he was the reason I got into folk. He came to my high school when I was 15 and performed. It was so inspiring that I immediately enrolled at the Old Town School of Folk Music. I bought a banjo and a guitar and became a folk singer, just based on Bob's performance at my school. He also influenced Peter Paul & Mary, The Kingston Trio, The Limeliters, just about everybody … even Bob Dylan."

At The Gate Of Horn featured material mostly written or rewritten by Gibson. He would take snatches of music from different songs and put them together. The duo tore up the rulebook on two-part singing, and McGuinn still marvels at their "almost-Beatles harmonies". Simon & Garfunkel opened their debut album with Gibson's 'You Can Tell The World' and took a lot from Gibson & Camp's adventurous vocalising.

Despite re-energising the folk world, Gibson & Camp never recorded for Elektra again. Camp says: "We only lasted for about a year-and-a-half, maybe two years. I had my family, and travelling got old to me. We were kind of unruly guys; we broke up through drugs and strong drink."[7]

It was Gibson's dependency on drugs that derailed his career. "Drugs were all over the place," he admits in his autobiography. "The business I was in condoned it. But I had no sooner gotten in, than I wanted out. I spent from 1960 to 1978 trying to get out, quitting for two or three years at a time, but I always went back. I remember looking at my arm and saying, why did I do that? Why? So in 1966, I left the business. I thought if I got away from that, everything would be fine. I had decided to try the geographic cure. I moved out of New York City to upstate New York."[8] He finally cleaned up in 1978 when he began attending AA meetings, but by this time the public's interest in folk music had peaked and left him behind.

Following *Where I'm Bound*, Gibson didn't record again until 1970, after which he produced a steady flow of fine records for his own Legend Enterprises label until his death in 1996. The recordings included a live reunion with Hamilton Camp and a studio release by the pair, produced by Dick Rosmini.

Bob Gibson is not well remembered today and is most commonly cited simply for introducing Joan Baez to the world at Newport. "He never got the widespread recognition he deserved," McGuinn says. "That's true. He was an unsung hero, probably because he got into heroin and fell out of favour. Very sad. Everybody on the scene assumed he was going to be as big as Bob Dylan. He was that talented."

Holzman says that the folk people of Bob Gibson's generation tended to work on a more fundamental level. "It was licks and integration, and Gibson was always one for perfection, almost to the point of slick. He was so good and made it look easy. Of course, that makes everybody jealous, and when you get to the 60s, his manner of performance was no longer of the moment. But he had a tremendous impact on other musicians on the way up."

None more so than Tom Paxton. Gibson produced a number of Paxton's post-Elektra albums in the 80s. "Many coffee-house folk singers had the wrong impression about what Gibson was doing," says Paxton. "They took the fact that he was a sophisticated urban performer without bothering to understand that he had roots, really knew his instrument, really knew folk music, and knew damn well how to perform. Those things had become passé, but no one had a greater sense of time: absolutely flawless. I learned from watching him. In a musical field that often glorifies amateurism, Gibson was pure pro. Nothing wrong with that."

At the end of 1964, Bob Camp released a solo album for Elektra, *Paths Of Victory*. By then, he'd made the change to Hamilton Camp, after associating with Subud, the Eastern spiritual movement (as did Jim McGuinn, who became Roger McGuinn). Camp was working in San Francisco as a member of the improvisational theatre group The Committee. His album was recorded in California by Jim Dickson, who produced a handful of albums for Elektra, and *Paths Of Victory* is best remembered for including seven Bob Dylan songs, many unreleased at the time, including 'Paths Of Victory' and 'Guess I'm Doin' Fine'.

Camp's own impassioned and apocalyptic 'Pride Of Man' is the highlight of *Paths Of Victory*. It's a song he traded with Dino Valente and which figures on the first Quicksilver Messenger Service album thanks to the Valente connection. In return, Camp recorded one of the first versions of Valente's evergreen hippie anthem 'Get Together'.

In 1973, Camp returned to Elektra, with less distinction, fronting the group Skymonters. Camp had recorded sporadically through the 60s but mostly concentrated on his acting career. He had been a child actor and made his Broadway debut in 1964, working continuously in theatre, TV, and films. His movie credits include *Bird*, *Heaven Can Wait*, *Eating Raoul*, and *Dick Tracy*, and he made appearances in TV series such as *ER*, *M*A*S*H*, *Hill Street Blues*, and *Cheers*. Camp had just completed a new original album shortly before his death in October 2005.

* * *

Judy Collins was one of Elektra's most innovative artists, and her work has been as consistently challenging as anything the label has released. Her eventual commercial success, most notably with 'Amazing Grace', has somewhat stifled appreciation for the bold recordings she made throughout the 60s.

Born May 1 1939 in Seattle, Washington, Collins got her early musical influences from her father, Chuck Collins, a singer, composer, and radio personality. By age ten, she was a child prodigy, studying classical piano and singing in opera productions in Denver with famed orchestral conductor Antonia Brico. In 1974, Collins co-directed an Academy Award-nominated documentary, *Antonia: A Portrait Of The Woman*, about her classical mentor. Then, when she was 16, Collins discovered folk music and dropped out of MacMurray College in Jacksonville, Illinois, switched her Steinway for a guitar, and was soon singing in folk clubs.

"I never thought of making a career out of my singing until I was living in Boulder with my husband," she says, "after my son had been born and I needed a job. I was 19, and I began singing at a local lodge in the Rocky Mountain National Park, about 30 miles northwest of Denver. Then, in the fall of 1959, I found myself with two choices. I had broken my leg skiing and it was in a cast from my ankle to my hip – just as I had been offered a six-week engagement at the Gate Of Horn. We had been offered a job at a Forest Fire Lookout at the Twin Sisters Peaks in Colorado, but because I was on crutches that wasn't a safe choice, so I took up the Gate Of Horn engagement."

The Gate Of Horn residency put Collins on the map, she says. She was offered opportunities to play at places like the Exodus in Denver and the Gilded Garter in Colorado. "After that, we moved east, so I was able to take up offers from the Golden Vanity in Boston, the Gilded Cage in Philadelphia, and Gerdes Folk City and other clubs in the Village. I had a good way to make a living, but I didn't think I was ready for the next level, which was to make a record." Nor did Jac Holzman, initially. "I didn't think she was totally committed," he remembers. "She had a family and a kid, and I didn't know if she could balance that with her music."

Once Holzman felt she was ready, he moved quickly, as Collins recalls. "Jac approached me with a firm offer to make a record for Elektra at the Village Gate, where I was filming a TV show with Theodore Bikel and The Clancy Brothers. John Hammond came to me one week later and said: I'd like you to make an album for Columbia. I said you're too late, because I have a gentlemen's agreement with Holzman. I know now that Jac was looking for another Baez to do for Elektra what she had done for Vanguard. Hammond responded, saying, 'You're with Jac; he'll do right by you.' He was right. I lucked out so much with Jac."

Collins already knew Elektra because she'd bought a lot of their records, by Josh White, Ed McCurdy, and so on, and she was already friendly with Bikel and knew Jean Ritchie's records. Ritchie recalls, "I was very excited when Judy Collins came along, because she was more pop than the rest of us. Somebody asked Jac about her, and he said: oh, she's just great – she's Jean Ritchie with balls. That got back to me, and I was so mad. But Jac was always thinking ahead."[9]

Collins's first album, *A Maid Of Constant Sorrow*, was released by Elektra in the fall of 1961. It was blessed with a natural acoustic feel, with augmentation on second guitar by Fred Hellerman (who had played on Joan Baez's debut) and on banjo by Erik Darling. It consisted entirely of traditional material, highlighted by the sad title track, a timely lament in 'Wars Of Germany', and several songs of Irish rebellion, like 'Rising Of The Moon', reflecting her friendship with The Clancy Brothers and the Irish traditional songs she had learnt from her father.

Golden Apples Of The Sun followed swiftly, a companion piece that relied on literate and traditional material but had a more confident, purer, and intensified vocal delivery. Collins was now living in New York and had immersed herself in Greenwich Village life, which exposed her to the new city songwriters whose work would dominate her next three albums.

The first evidence of this came on *Judy Collins 3*, released in December 1963 and with arrangements provided by McGuinn. It had covers of two Bob Dylan songs, plus Fred Hellerman and Fran Minkoff's anti-war 'Come Away Melinda', and a thrilling reading of Pete Seeger's 'Turn Turn Turn'. The assured *Judy Collins Concert* followed, recorded at Town Hall in March 1964, with more songs provided by contemporary Village writers: Dylan again, Fred Neil, and three apiece from Tom Paxton and Billy Edd Wheeler.

By the *Fifth Album*, released in 1965, Collins further consolidated her position as the most accomplished interpreter of outstanding new songs, performing material by Phil Ochs, Eric Andersen, Gordon Lightfoot, and Richard Fariña. Mark Abramson, who became Collins's regular producer, said, "Before that, if you were a folk singer you did folk music. If you happened to write stuff, you would do that. But only your own. Judy was the first to make the transition to being an interpreter of contemporary folk-tinged songs."

After a spell with The Chad Mitchell Trio, McGuinn was playing with Bobby Darin when, at guitarist Walter Raim's suggestion, Judy Collins went to the Flamingo in Las Vegas to check him out. McGuinn was invited to play on the sessions for *Judy Collins 3*. "I used to hang around with Paul Rothchild, and he introduced me to John Sebastian, and we both started doing sessions at around the same time," recalls McGuinn. "I was on Judy's third album, and I gave her a lot of ideas for arrangements. We worked on 'Turn Turn Turn' – everybody in the folk world knew the song because we all followed Pete Seeger. Judy ended up giving me a credit on the record as musical director, which sounded a lot grander than just being a session musician. I'm not sure if I was altogether worthy of the title, because mostly I was just saying things like: this would sound great with a cello. The main difference in my arrangement of 'Turn! Turn! Turn!' was that I made it into more of a melodic thing. The way Judy sang it was very similar to the way we did it with the Byrds."

Collins is intellectually curious by nature, and her approach to music reflected that, distinguishing her from Joan Baez. But it was soon clear to Holzman that she was far more than a Joan clone. "Once Joan Baez had arrived, people asked if I was looking for my Joan Baez," he says. "Judy's first album was a bit too close to Baez, but by *Golden Apples Of The Moon*, I could see the seeds growing. By the third album, Judy was a more complete artist. If ever there's an example of a cover selling a record, that was it. When I initially saw the photograph, I was just knocked out, and I said to Bill Harvey, 'Can you make it life size?' He said, 'Sure, that's what I intend to do.' There were those piercing blue eyes. By then she had completed two albums and was beginning to build her own audience."

Holzman recalls the *3* album breaking out first in the Boston/Cambridge area, which had several college radio stations. "That cover and her choice of material – a terrific, edgy, unsettling interpretation of 'Masters Of War', and very little traditional material – it just clicked. It began selling immediately at the Harvard Co-op, which was the record Mecca for every college student within a ten-mile range of Cambridge, just the best audience concentration for someone like Judy and Elektra. The Co-op was re-ordering almost daily. A box of 25 one day, two boxes the next. That's when we were sure that something important was happening."

Holzman's estimation is that Baez was on a narrower path than Collins. Collins understood that she would eventually have to write some of her own material, but for now she had a treasure trove from all the writers in the Village. She heard new songs before anyone else recorded them, often before the writer had recorded them. Songwriters were thrilled to see their material recorded by her, says Holzman. Collins confirms the idea.

"I was very aware of the songwriters, because they were in my own circle," she says. "It was inescapable: all these wonderful writers. I had made two albums that were basically traditional, and my third album was a first step in the water – which also raised the awareness of people like Bob Dylan and Tom Paxton. I wanted to do an album of songs of the city singers. Of course, I knew Pete Seeger. Harold Leventhal was my manager at this point, and he managed Pete. Often, when I'd come up to the office, there'd be Pete stretched out on the couch, sleeping, trying to recover from his chaotic schedule.

"I remember Dylan when he was a funky rough-and-ready Woody Guthrie-type singer and, at the time, no great shakes," Collins continues. "There were others on the scene you'd have said were more likely to make it. And then I read the lyrics to 'Blowin' In the Wind' in *Broadside*, and I was just knocked out, like everyone else. 'Tomorrow Is A Long Time' I just had to record. He epitomised what was so strong about the Village scene. It was a coming-together and a synchronicity of writing and music and theatre and performance, a way of nature shaking everything up and redirecting it, and we were all part of it."

On *Fifth Album*, Collins carefully embellished her original acoustic sound with delicate contributions from such fine musicians as Bill Lee, known for his work with Odetta (and today as the father of Spike Lee), Eric Weissberg, John Sebastian, and her close friend Richard Fariña. Fariña not only played dulcimer on two songs but also composed the haunting opening track, 'Pack Up Your Sorrows', as well as the poem on the album's jacket. Just as Dylan's songs were about to be reconfigured as folk-rock, Collins recorded one of the earliest covers of 'Mr Tambourine Man', which she'd heard Dylan singing at Albert Grossman's house. She showed that Dylan songs could be no less powerful when delivered in a gentler, more considered manner.

She recalls that Holzman and her producer, Mark Abramson, believed in taking risks and not playing it safe. "They never told me that I was crazy for wanting to expand my style and move away from what I had done previously, which is how I came to do Brecht & Weill's 'Pirate Jenny' and adapt songs from Peter Weiss's stage production of *Marat/Sade*."

Taking its title from John Lennon's most poignant early song, her 1966 album *In My Life* is sweeping in its range. "I was captivated by those songs and the depth and passion of *Marat/Sade*," she explains. "I got hold of a tape of the *Marat/Sade* music, and I sat down in my New York apartment in front of my tape recorder and began to rearrange the songs into a single cohesive piece. In those days I had to cut together the pieces of tape, physically, until I had exactly what I wanted."

Holzman believes it marked another stage in her development. "Judy is naturally curious and was always open to experiment, and *Marat/Sade* is a perfect example. She chose to do that, and in so doing became another kind of singer – not a folk interpreter. Judy would search out songs that would touch you, and the context of their origination was relevant but not overriding."

Collins felt uncomfortable doing anything that sounded folk-rock and still has a dislike of rock instrumentation. But when Dylan presented her with another new song, 'I'll Keep It With Mine', she was persuaded to record it with many of Dylan's regular studio musicians. "That was the most electric recording I made, and one of the worst," is how she still views that cut. "It's not a success, it's not a particularly good Dylan song, and I never allowed it to get on to an album. I recorded it primarily because Dylan said he'd written it for me. There was some contention about this, but on the *Bootleg Series* he says he wrote it for me, so I guess he must have," she says. 'I'll Keep It With Mine' surfaced only briefly, as an Elektra single in 1965.

Collins heard the material she recorded first-hand from the people who wrote the songs. "That was certainly the case with Dylan, and with Tom Paxton, who lived just down the street from me. Gordon Lightfoot played 'Early Morning Rain' for me in person. Richard Fariña used to send me everything he wrote. Eric Andersen was another friend. One day he was heading up to see me on 96th Street, and he was carrying a notebook with him on the subway. He started jotting down some ideas for a song. Then when he turned up at my place, he asked if I'd excuse him for a few minutes. He went into my bathroom and finished writing the song." The result was 'Thirsty Boots', which became the flipside of 'I'll Keep It With Mine' and earned a place on her *Fifth Album*.

Eschewing any further forays into folk-rock, *In My Life* was a bold step toward a more baroque style. Collins remembers that she and Abramson and Holzman would turn to each other and ask: what's next? They knew it was important to keep changing. "*In My Life* was a particularly dramatic shift," she says, "because we were all eager to break free of the folk mould. We wanted to move laterally into other kinds of material, and because I had been a concert pianist, because I'd studied and been exposed to all kinds of music from childhood, I had an eclectic sense of music. So it was perfect to be allowed to make more oddball and dramatic choices. I had a good ear for a good song, which I inherited from my father. Jac would always say that choosing songs that would last forever to put into my repertoire was something I excelled at."

The *In My Life* album did just that, featuring a broader mixture of songs and a richer baroque flavour that reflected the style heard on some of the recordings on Elektra's highly successful sister label, Nonesuch. The lush, delicate arrangements were by Joshua Rifkin, then on the payroll of Nonesuch. "From the first meeting at Jac's apartment that led to *In My Life*," says Rifkin, "Judy, Jac, and Mark Abramson made it clear to me that they were looking for a fuller musical frame, and they invited me onto the project for that very reason. Beyond that, my brief was indeed entirely open – basically, to do whatever I wished. In retrospect, it was pretty gutsy of them."

In My Life, which was recorded in London at Sound Techniques studio, is now celebrated as the first album to feature songs by Leonard Cohen. It began a long association between Collins and Cohen. "Leonard Cohen brought me his first songs," she says. "He played me 'Dress Rehearsal Rag' and 'Suzanne', and I said I have to record those. But he didn't see himself as a songwriter. He was a poet and a novelist, but as a songwriter, and certainly as a performer, he was totally lacking in confidence. I was able to record his first songs and, literally, push him on to the stage the first time – he didn't know how good he was and would freeze up. He came to see me at the suggestion of a mutual friend, and he had just written three songs, not just to find out if I would record them, but to find out if they were even songs."

Holzman says the Cohen songs were the missing element to the *In My Life* album. "When I listened to an in-progress version of that record," he says, "I just didn't think it was there yet, and I told Judy we needed a couple more songs. She said, 'Where am I going to find more?' and I just said ask around. That's when she discovered the Leonard Cohen material."

Significantly, *In My Life* was released in November 1966 simultaneously with Love's *Da Capo* and Tim Buckley's debut, and barely a month ahead of the Doors' debut album, effectively positioning Judy Collins alongside the artists who would drive Elektra in a new direction.

Baez and Collins will always be compared, but it's Collins's work that is more enduring, certainly in Holzman's opinion. "Baez was successful very quickly, whereas Judy had the luxury of developing herself over more years. Joan Baez became a star overnight, and that makes you less willing to adapt. Judy would take risks and felt no need to define herself, and she was always going to be an album-developed artist. We just released a few singles as calling cards for her albums, and whether she would have a hit single one day was never an issue. " By the time she did, says Holzman, referring to 'Both Sides Now' in 1968, she was already established through her albums. "The *3* album was the breakthrough record for Judy and for Elektra. The emergence of Judy Collins marked the start of the next phase for the label."

He recalls an occasion some years ago when he was having lunch with Maynard Solomon, once chairman of Vanguard Records, the major label on which Baez first recorded. "He said that Joan was usually limited in what she was prepared to try, whereas Judy, influenced by her classical background, had the capability to do anything. I don't think Joan worked to the level of mastery that Judy did," Holzman concludes. "Maynard Solomon had thought I was signing another Joan Baez, but it was only later that he realised he had failed to see that adventuresome streak in Judy."

Judy Collins's artistic audacity and eventual commercial breakthrough in the late 60s helped keep her with Elektra until long after Holzman left the label in 1973. Yet in 1961, when her first recordings appeared, he had no inkling of Collins's true potential, and he was far from sure where Elektra records was heading.

High Flying Bird

> *"Elektra hadn't made much impact in the 50s the way it did later. There were remarkable artists and some great successes, but it was also about building a platform upon which to improve and grow. We stayed afloat for ten years, and I threw a party at the swanky St. Regis Hotel to mark the anniversary in October 1960. But I woke up the next morning and thought: great party – but what's next? We had covered the broad scope of folk music and its tributaries better than any other label, because we worked at it harder. I now wanted to do something more lasting. It was the end of one phase in anticipation of another."* **JAC HOLZMAN**

Once Holzman bought out his partner Leonard Ripley and took full control of Elektra in 1958, he moved his now seven-strong company to larger offices at 110 West 14th Street. It allowed him to build a small studio that could easily handle spoken word, voice-overs, sound effects, overdubbing, and mixing, and also meant he could hire his first full-time engineer, David A. Jones. In turn, Jones was given an assistant, Mark Abramson. With sufficient space, Bill Harvey was also able to take on a full-time role as art director. Mel Posner had joined in the summer of 1957, after discharge from the Army, and, to Holzman's relief, took over packing and shipping records to the distributors. Posner originally intended to go back to college but stayed and eventually became president of Elektra/Asylum in 1974, after Holzman had moved on.

This was the team that carried Elektra forward into the 60s. The next pivotal recruit, in 1963, was Paul Rothchild. Elektra's first full-time staffer had been Nina Merrick, by now Holzman's wife. "It was a captivating business by the end of the 50s," says Holzman, "in that it kept me engaged from the moment I arose until I went to bed. All I thought about was Elektra. I would talk about Elektra to Nina, who I met in 1955 and married that same year. Throughout the years of our marriage, Nina shared this passion. We discussed every opportunity and problem. I ran everything by Nina, and she loved the music business, whereas most wives wished their husbands would shut up about it. This was our life – all my soul-searching was done with Nina's support. It made for a real bond. It looked and felt like a family operation, and we took some flak for that, but make no mistake about Nina's importance to Elektra – plus the bonus that she lightened me up. People thought that if Nina's hanging out with Jac, he's OK – because I was competitive, even with the labels I was friendly with."

Running an independent label was always a stretch financially, and so the other labels couldn't fathom why Elektra needed an art director. Holzman admits he was kidded for hiring Bill Harvey. But he knew it was important that Elektra records caught the fan's eye in the display racks. He thought Vanguard, for instance, failed to produce jackets that were the equal of their records. Bill Harvey, however, had flair and could create images in many different styles. "Elektra graphics," says Holzman, "by intention and hard work, were a key part of our identity."

It was after Harvey drew the famous guitar-player logo for the first sampler album that Holzman insisted he work only for Elektra. Harvey was an accomplished illustrator and photographer with an unerring eye for the finer points of typography. His designs would fill the entire space of the 12-inch vinyl jacket, with no better example than the jacket for *Judy Collins 3*. The images are expertly cropped, the lettering positioned with uncanny precision, and the familiar Elektra logo always present.

In an era where word-of-mouth was so important, where there was little radio play, and no expansive marketplace for album reviews or advertising, Harvey's vision helped to establish and consolidate Elektra's identity. Holzman and Harvey fought constantly, as Bill Harvey Jr recalls.

"The counterpoint between my father and Jac helped make great things happen," says Bill Jr. "It was a creative conflict that sustained itself for over 20 years. When you have relationships which are too comfortable, amazing things don't happen. Jac opened a door which allowed my father to be at the cutting edge of record-cover design and the evolution of the idea of using a record cover as a statement. Those covers became statements about the label in a 12-by-12 format: they conveyed something about the music itself or the artist."

Holzman was now managing Theodore Bikel, who was increasingly busy in television and films, most of which were shot in Los Angeles, so Holzman was travelling to the West Coast about every six weeks. He shared a duplex apartment just south of the Sunset Strip with Bikel. Holzman says that in 60s New York City, everyone was crawling over the music like a bunch of maggots and no one was paying much attention to California. "Generally, albums and artists that were successful in the East tended to travel West, but not the reverse. Especially in folk music. But I felt we were missing something. There was no arc to it, and the music I was hearing in the clubs, on audition tapes, and on the radio yielded no clues."

Holzman could see or hear nothing that was going to make the difference, so he decided to act on a hunch. In the summer of 1962, leaving the main business responsibilities in New York to be handled by Bill Harvey and Mel Posner, he opened a small Elektra office in Los Angeles, intended as a West Coast A&R and marketing outpost.

Los Angeles may have worked its sun-drenched charm, but Holzman soon realised that all anyone talked or cared about there was movies. Records weren't taken seriously. Through a connection with Jim Dickson, who acted as a freelance A&R man for Elektra in Los Angeles, the label released a handful of albums that Dickson produced, usually using downtime at World Pacific studio. Dickson was a studio veteran who in the 50s had recorded the hipster's hipster, Lord Buckley, originally releasing the material on the Vaya label in 1951. Holzman leased the Buckley tapes and released them first on Elektra and then on his offshoot Crestview label, in 1963, as *The Best Of Lord Buckley*. "Lord Buckley was one of a kind," says Holzman, "and he represented the pseudo hipness that was typical of what I saw every day dealing with artists and managers in California."

Dickson teamed Los Angeles singer Dián James with The Greenbriar

Boys: John Herald, Bob Yellin, and Ralph Rinzler (who replaced founder member Eric Weissberg). They had formed in 1958 out of informal jam sessions in Washington Square, signed to Vanguard, and sang and played backup on several songs on Joan Baez's second album. Banjo-player Yellin sought Vanguard founder Maynard Solomon's permission to record a one-off album as *Dián & The Greenbriar Boys* for the rival Elektra label.

Dickson also brought The Dillards to Elektra, and the first of five albums for the label, *Pickin' And Fiddlin'*, appeared in 1963. While The Greenbriar Boys or The New Lost City Ramblers were Village-based old-time and bluegrass bands, The Dillards were the real deal, straight out of Missouri but pitched toward the same urban-folk market. Purists sometimes bemoaned the band's onstage self-mocking comic monologues, derived from their days as The Darling Family when they were regular guests on TV on the popular network *Andy Griffith Show*.

The Dillards, featuring brothers Rodney on guitar and dobro and Doug on banjo, released two more relatively routine bluegrass records for Elektra before moving briefly to Capitol in 1965. "The Dillards were highly respected among musicians," explains Holzman. "A couple of them looked like they came out of the *Deliverance* movie, but they were a very smart bunch. When the deal was over after three albums, we let them go, but I heard some of the songs they were doing that ended up on *Wheatstraw Suite*, released in 1968, that went beyond bluegrass. A couple of years later, *Copperfields* was a great summing-up, with their musicianship stretching the conventions of the genre. They are both terrific albums, but they didn't have a Gram Parsons figure: someone to bring them along. They were all about the music, with no nonsense whatsoever. I valued my relationship with them."

Holzman's California sojourn wasn't working out – there were indifferent recordings by singer-songwriter Bob Grossman and Travelers 3 – aside from one jewel of a signing. "Judy Henske was the most interesting artist I found in California," he says. "She stood apart from anyone else around, anywhere. There was no pretence about Judy Henske. She was totally authentic and herself. Cass Elliot admitted that she took whole hunks of stage business from Judy. She was skilled at ingesting new material and making it work for her. Since it helped if you saw her perform, we recorded her first album in front of a studio audience. I wanted there to be people present so she could play to them. It was an expensive session, at RCA's studios in Hollywood, but I thought it was the only way to capture her."

Henske had arrived in Hollywood in 1960 and played with Kingston Trio founder Dave Guard as a member of The Whiskeyhill Singers, releasing a rather stiff eponymous album for Capitol in 1962. Herb Cohen saw her and signed her up for management immediately, after she played his Cosmo Alley nightclub. She regularly opened for Lenny Bruce – a tough audience for any girl with just a banjo to hide behind – but she won them over by developing a snappy patter between songs.

"Some people sing the song and they are defined by the song. In Judy's case, the song was defined by her," said Cohen. "She validated the material rather than being subservient to it. God knows what she was. When Judy Henske signed to Elektra, it was still a folk label, though more esoteric. But Judy was in a class of one. She was not a commercial folk artist by any means."

Henske picks up the story. "Herb Cohen was managing me – in that strange phrase, he was the man who 'discovered' me. And he was a friend of Jac's. So he invited Jac to see me perform at the Unicorn. Picture me there: a total beatnik, clad in a rubber duck-hunting jacket, with hair down to my waist. I sat there, on top of a piano, and sang my entire repertoire of jazz songs, or what I called jazz, for people who had come to hear the outrageous Lenny Bruce.

"Jac spent tons of money on my first album. He found this African-American disgruntled jazz guy [Onzy Matthews] and got him to arrange a whole bunch of cuts, all my funky songs – 'Low Down Alligator' and 'Good Old Wagon' – but with a big band. A really big studio, with a big audience invited."[1]

Michael Ochs witnessed the power of seeing-is-believing with Henske. "Judy was probably the first superstar in the whole movement," he says. "She was the first to make *Newsweek*, in a big article about this six-foot-one singer. She'd stomp her feet so heavy on the floor that she'd go through the floorboards. She was this real Bessie Smith-type gutsy singer, but white. It only added to the confusion that on the first album cover she was all dressed up in pearls with a beautiful white dress and wearing a Louise Brooks wig. No one knew quite what to make of her."[1]

Despite good notices, *Judy Henske*, her stylistically confusing debut, unsurprisingly failed to find an audience. After all, she was the queen of the beatniks, but here she was belting out songs like Ethel Merman on what was ostensibly a folk label. "They had brought me out one way and then they went, 'Whoa! We'd better cut back.' So *High Flying Bird* was a better album," she says of the second record, released in 1964. "It was a smaller band: more banjo and guitar stuff. It sounded more like a human being than, you know, a chanteuse. Somebody at Elektra attempted to find songs that nobody else had done. Billy Edd Wheeler had written this song called 'High Flying Bird', which wasn't actually a folk song, but I loved the imagery, and it made for a wonderful title for that album."[2]

Henske gives the track its definitive performance. Her bluesy, gutsy vocal is supported by a full backup band, with electric guitar by Jack Marshall and drums by veteran session man Earl Palmer. It was one of the first examples of what would come to be called folk-rock. Thanks to her version, the song would be covered by Richie Havens, Jefferson Airplane, and Stephen Stills.

Henske was sharing a bill at the Village Gate in New York with Woody Allen when *High Flying Bird* was released in 1964. Years later, Allen drew upon Judy's life and personality for the character of Annie Hall, who, like Judy, hailed from Chippewa Falls, Wisconsin.

Henske left Elektra to the regret of everyone involved. It just wasn't working out. She later recorded albums for Mercury and Reprise, but her finest hour was *Farewell Aldebaran*, where she was teamed with her then husband, Jerry Yester, released on Herb Cohen's Bizarre label. Always slightly out of step with the times, she was never the star she should have been, as Cohen lamented. "She became successful, but not on record. She did *The Judy Garland Show*, which was a big deal on TV in those days, and she headlined all the major clubs. Bette Midler modelled herself on Judy, with much of her early stage show influenced by Judy's act. Judy is one of the most intelligent people you could ever meet: really smart, erudite, and witty."

Holzman's California trip simply wasn't delivering the music he'd hoped to find there. When he looks back on that time now, he recalls most of the music on the West Coast, with the exception of Henske, being simply insubstantial. "I hoped that at some point the West Coast would be allowed to incubate something worthwhile. It did so later, in part out of the folk movement, in groups like The Byrds, but that hadn't happened yet. So after a year in California, I was very disappointed. Even more because Dylan had happened back in New York and I had missed that, and I didn't know what the hell else I was missing. In fact, I never heard about Dylan until I bought his first record in Wallach's Music City in Los Angeles. I found it in the remainder bins – hardly anyone had bought it – but that made no difference. Clearly he was astonishing."

Despite the California lifestyle, Holzman concluded that he was a much duller person in Los Angeles. He felt he wasn't challenged, and he thought Elektra was still lacking a clear sense of direction. "I was paying bills and salaries – four people in LA, seven back in New York – but I didn't have my arms around anything solid on the West Coast to get excited about. Plus, I was obsessed that my competitors in New York, such as the Solomon brothers at Vanguard and John Hammond at Columbia, were getting ahead of me."

In the summer of 1963, Holzman shut down the LA office and moved back to New York. After a year away, the city rejuvenated him, and for the first time he decided to move Elektra away from the Village. He relocated the office to an uptown location, in the Sperry-Rand building, at 51 West 51st Street.

When Elektra started out, there were few other predominantly folk-based labels. Folkways was just about it, and was unquestionably the front runner. Even though California hadn't gone as planned, Holzman could see his label moving forward once he had returned to New York. "As Elektra grew, my competition changed. In size and presence, we had moved beyond Folkways, Tradition, and Riverside, and by the late 50s, we were nosing level with Vanguard."

Folkways always had the kudos. It was firmly associated with the principal recordings of the founding fathers of the folk revival and released Harry Smith's monumental *Anthology Of American Folk Music.* Dylan voiced a common feeling when he said Folkways was the label he wanted to be on – although legend has it that he couldn't get past the door to see the label's boss, Moe Asch. While the Folkways legacy in American ethnic and international folk music is unimpeachable, its only direct link to the new folk was in distributing *Broadside* magazine's collections of recordings by the up-and-coming topical singer-songwriters.

"Moe thought I was in competition with him," says Holzman, "but I never felt I was. I was more like a nephew he admired but wished he didn't have any pretensions for his business. Folkways had the iconic names – Guthrie,

Seeger, Leadbelly – and released a series of great Josh White records ahead of me. Moe was a documenter, and we worked in different segments. I was always looking for a broader audience. He would cater to narrow segments: very specific. If you wanted *Wedding Songs Of The Sudan*, he had such a title, and he could do very well selling just four or five hundred copies."

Folkways did good business through mail order, says Holzman, and to specialist shops. They would press records in quantities of 100 – and jackets in quantities of one. "He had a standard jacket, with a pebbled surface to which he would glue the appropriate label. Notes came in an accompanying booklet. They'd open the mail and cheques would fall out. Except for Woody Guthrie or Pete Seeger, they would press small quantities as they needed them, but of hundreds and hundreds of titles."

Musicians came to accept that if they wanted to record for Folkways, they could not expect high quality. Ed McCurdy explains, "They used to say that Moe mastered through a gravel filter. Jac was the first person who put folk songs and folk music on records of good quality."[3] Later, Moe Asch would dismiss stereo recordings, insisting that they "never gave you an accurate sense of the original sound".[4] If there was an Elektra sound, it was always one of great intimacy. The voices didn't sound as if they were coming from the speakers, but more as if they were in front of the speakers.

Asch was renowned for his caution about paying royalties to his artists. But as Dave Van Ronk observes, at least Asch gave you the chance to record. It provided Asch with the upper hand when it came to payments.

"[He] could be an exasperating man," says Van Ronk, "and he would never pay you ten cents if he could get away with five."[5] According to Holzman, musicians would come by, and Asch would push some boxes aside, record direct onto his Presto disc recorder or his tape machine, pay them a very modest fee, and off they would go. "Or they'd sell him an idea for a collection and he'd send them off with a small advance that would barely cover recording costs. Collectors would send him unsolicited tapes or field recordings, and sometimes he would send back a cheque, knowing he intended to release it. He didn't worry too much about contracts or how it sounded on disc. In Moe's mind, business was simple, and he never worried about anyone suing him."

Holzman thought Asch saw him as some upstart kid, but they got to know each other because Asch's offices were across from Holzman's favourite Mexican restaurant. "He and I would lunch there, and I helped bring him into the network of independent labels. There was an informal communications network where we would help each other. I found out about section 3484(H) of the Postal Laws & Regulations, because I took the time to read them. There was a loophole I discovered where I could ship records, label them as soundtracks, and be able to mail them at the very low book rate. After I had been doing this for six months, I shared the strategy with Vanguard and with Caedmon. We would talk to each other about distributors and manufacturing, but we were more guarded over artists. I was disappointed when Tradition snagged Odetta. Was I jealous of Vanguard getting The Rooftop Singers? Damn right I was! And I thought we could have done it better. But I loved that they had a Number One hit single, which meant that I, too, could have a Number One without drifting too far from my centre of gravity."

The Clancy Brothers started the Tradition label with little more ambition than to record themselves and some of their friends. Of the brothers, Patrick was most heavily involved, helping Diane Hamilton to run the label. The first Tradition release was *The Lark In The Morning*, in 1955, a collection of Irish folk songs sung by Irish singers and recorded in Ireland. Liam, Paddy, and Tom soon formed The Clancy Brothers And Tommy Makem, one of the most successful groups in Irish music history. Tradition released their definitive early recording, *The Rising Of The Moon*, and many of their other albums.

There were other notable releases by Tradition: Seamus Ennis's *The Bonny Bunch Of Roses*; Odetta's towering *Sings Ballads And Blues* and *At The Gate Of Horn*; recordings by Etta Baker, Lightnin' Hopkins, Barbara Dane, The Kossoy Sisters With Erik Darling, Ed McCurdy, Paul Clayton; and a series of ballads from the British Isles recorded by Ewan MacColl, A.L. Lloyd and Peggy Seeger, among others, brought to the label by Ken Goldstein. Once The Clancy Brothers signed to Columbia Records in 1961, their involvement with Tradition diminished and, in 1966, the label was sold to Bernard Solomon at Everest, who kept the catalogue barely alive.

Meanwhile, in 1955, the omnipresent Ken Goldstein had gone to Bill Grauer and Orin Keepnews, who had founded Riverside Records two years earlier as a progressive jazz label. Goldstein offered to produce a folklore series for them. Initially, he licensed ten albums from the Workers' Music

Association in London (later to become Topic Records), but he went on to record Oscar Brand, Billy Faier, Bob Gibson, Jean Ritchie, and Paul Clayton for the label. Riverside's folk sideline subsided once Goldstein left to supervise blues recordings for Prestige in 1960.

For a decade, Goldstein is said to have produced over 500 albums for 13 labels. At first, he wrote liner notes for Folkways and Stinson, then went on to produce albums for those labels and for Elektra, Riverside, Tradition, Prestige, and Folk-Lyric, among others, in order to fund his PhD in Folklore at the University of Pennsylvania. Once he'd achieved that, he began teaching at the University in 1963, retiring from record production.

"The reason we outstayed Tradition and Riverside," says Holzman, "was that I never let up. My competition was always changing. Tradition didn't last that long, and a lot of that was because the Clancys were becoming busier themselves, and Riverside was always first and foremost a jazz label, whereas for me it was only about Elektra."

The only significant label to turn its sights toward folk music at the start of the 60s was Prestige, the New York-based jazz label run by Bob Weinstock. His attention was drawn to the Cambridge folk scene centred on Club 47 following the success of Joan Baez. Weinstock saw a ready market and thought folk records would be cheap to produce – and the ideal man to run his label was already in place in Cambridge. Paul Rothchild, then a salesman for Dumont Record Distributors, had already recorded the Charles River Valley Boys bluegrass band, pressing 1,000 copies on his own Mount Auburn label – its sole release.

Under Rothchild's supervision, Prestige/Folklore gave Elektra and Vanguard a run for their money, until Prestige returned exclusively to jazz soon after Rothchild jumped ship to Elektra. Rothchild had produced an impressive series of folk records for close on three years for Prestige: albums by Tom Rush, Ramblin' Jack Elliott, Eric Von Schmidt, Bill Keith & Jim Rooney, and Geoff Muldaur, soon to become a key player in The Jim Kweskin Jug Band. Holzman, meanwhile, always kept a close watch on the scene around Boston and Cambridge, which he could see did not just mirror but was often ahead of what was coming out of New York City.

Vanguard's classical division was the cornerstone of the label, and so it had only dabbled in folk music until releasing *The Weavers At Carnegie Hall* in 1957. But it had become Elektra's only serious competitor and at the start of the 60s was more than a few inches ahead, after a series of coups: signing Joan Baez; acquiring the rights to the Newport Folk Festival; and scoring a Number One hit with The Rooftop Singers' single 'Walk Right In'.

This was a spur to Holzman. "Given the Weavers' political leanings, Vanguard was the right choice for them after their comeback, and Vanguard was a hell of a label. Not having the Newport Folk Festival recordings didn't mean anything to me – those recordings were just a snapshot in time, even though there were some wonderfully iconic performances. Joan Baez was another matter. She was somebody I really liked. I thought she was somewhat limited, but she was a gorgeous ballads singer."

Holzman says that Maynard Solomon's success at Vanguard goaded him into action. He knew he had to give Elektra a greater presence. "Maynard and I were always cautious of one another. We had a slightly guarded relationship. I think he viewed me as a parvenu, because he grasped the size of my ambition. I admired Maynard: he had taste, intellect, and focus. I envied the scope of his abilities. And Maynard might have wished for more of my energy and willingness to take risks."

When Baez signed to Vanguard, Holzman saw that it was a simple, straightforward record for them to make. Later, when it shifted to music they were not fully tuned in to, they were a little hesitant. The Rooftop Singers hit was, according to Holzman, a happy accident – Vanguard was very good at recording self-contained artists. "You just have to capture the performance of a Joan Baez or Rooftop Singers, where the arrangements and performance are key. They didn't require any fancy production. But I had a hunch that there would come a time when we would have to support the artist and the album with richer production."

That, says Holzman, was one of the attractions of Paul Rothchild. Holzman thought that Rothchild knew how to do that better than he did. "In many ways, my skills and Maynard Solomon's were alike. Now I had someone in Rothchild who was different, who could do what I didn't know how to do. Rothchild had the ability to bring more than their live performance out of an artist. And that gave us an edge, because Vanguard was never able to capture electric music as well as we did."

Vanguard still recorded with the same equipment and in rooms with acoustics that were better suited to classical recording. As Holzman soon discovered, electric music demanded something different. "You had to draw out stronger performances, to blend them with a more complex palette, using highly sophisticated new techniques."

Vanguard did not sign a contemporary rock group until 1967, when they released the exquisitely trippy *Electric Music For The Mind And Body* by Country Joe & The Fish. By then, even Folkways had given way to the rising tide, exploring commercial folk recordings on its Verve/Folkways imprint, distributed by MGM. The first Verve/Folkways releases were titles by Seeger, Guthrie, and The New Lost City Ramblers, before the label signed the likes of Richie Havens, Tim Hardin, Janis Ian, and The Blues Project, which featured Al Kooper and Danny Kalb and took its name from the Elektra anthology on which Kalb had appeared.

Everything fell into place almost immediately after Holzman returned from California in the summer of 1963. "Luckily, the minute I got back, the scene that Dylan would throw the spotlight on was evolving rapidly, and singer-songwriters like Tom Paxton and Phil Ochs had now arrived in Greenwich Village. The *Hootenanny* TV show finished what The Kingston Trio had begun, transforming folk music into something slick. People clapped and were encouraged to sing along to everything – which sent me right over the wall. *Hootenanny* and the changing public attitude to folk music told me it was time to move on. John Sebastian made a very telling comment. He said: we're running out of folk songs, so we'd better write some. Paul Rothchild and I realised the truth of that."

By the end of 1963, Elektra was back on course and Holzman had found his sense of direction. "If there was something that turned me around," he admits, "it was Koerner Ray & Glover. It was as if I'd found my legs again: I felt I was back on solid ground. Some of the more critical folkies forgave me for every perceived slight because I had recently released the Koerner Ray & Glover album. They were pleasantly surprised to find it on Elektra. And we had Paul Rothchild now."

The timing could not have been better. Although Elektra had moved uptown, its roots were still in Greenwich Village, and there – no question about it – something was happening.

CHAPTER 12

All The News That's Fit To Sing

> *"Dylan made it look easy, and it wasn't. Many of the Village writers tried to outdo Dylan, and they couldn't. Tom Paxton wasn't one of them. Paxton was very comfortable with the level of his craft, but it was Phil Ochs who was most driven by Dylan's presence. For almost every singer-songwriter, it comes back to Bob Dylan and the Village scene, which in the 60s was greater than they were individually. They were Greenwich Village songwriters, and it was the Village that defined them."* **JAC HOLZMAN**

The first coffee houses in New York City opened in the Italian quarter in the late 40s, following a recent European tradition. Hangouts like the Rienzi, or the Figaro, where the playwright Edward Albee is said to have found the title for *Who's Afraid Of Virginia Woolf?* written on the bathroom wall, established a trend for caffeinated lounging well before folk musicians and the beats moved in.

One of the best-known coffee houses was Gerde's Folk City, at 11 West 4th Street. It had opened in 1952 but only became a folk club eight years later. Its Monday-night hootenanny showcases were key launch pads for many a career. Dylan first played there in February 1961, and it was after his show at Gerde's on September 29 that he was ecstatically reviewed by Robert Shelton in *The New York Times*, which trumpeted his precocious talent to a world outside the Village.

The foundation for committed folk clubs had been laid in Chicago, at the Gate Of Horn, opened in 1956 by Albert Grossman and his partners. Historically, San Francisco's hungry i was among the first nightspots to book folk musicians, back in 1954, and the Gate Of Horn became the most celebrated magnet for folk in the Midwest. It wasn't until 1958 that New York City's first dedicated folk venue opened, at the Village Gate.

Folk festivals were on the horizon, an indication of a rapidly bourgeoning folk boom. The biggest and most influential was held at Newport as an offshoot of the annual jazz festival. The first Newport folk festival took place in 1959, produced by George Wein from the jazz festival board with Albert Grossman. It was held for a second time in 1960, but following a riot at the jazz festival, the folk festival skipped a year until the summer of 1962, by which time there was much more interest. Attendance at Newport rose from 17,000 at the start to 70,000 by the folk festival's peak in the mid 60s.

Similar events followed at the University of Chicago, at UCLA in Los Angeles, and at Monterey, all held for the first time in 1963, plus the Berkeley festival and, on the opposite coast, the Philadelphia folk festival – all evidence that a national infrastructure for folk music was in place. It's no coincidence that many of these were held on university campuses or in college towns. This was the bedrock of the folk audience. College enrolments had increased from two-and-a-half million in the late 50s to nearly four million by 1962. The post-war babies were coming of age.

All kinds of folk co-existed happily, side by side – traditional, or topical, or the more mainstream popular folk, epitomised by Peter Paul & Mary in the early 60s. They appealed to the waning audience for The Kingston Trio as well as the more radical student body. Peter Paul & Mary, Joan Baez, and Bob Dylan were all shrewdly managed by Albert Grossman. Peter Paul & Mary took Dylan songs like 'Blowin' In the Wind' into the charts, but it was Dylan's second album, *Freewheelin'*, released in April 1963, that provided the generative spark for the era of topical singers and songwriters.

"I always thought Peter Paul & Mary were really 'Puff The Magic Dragon' but lucked into 'Blowin' in the Wind' because Al Grossman was their fabricator and manager,' Jac Holzman says. 'To me, Peter Paul & Mary were an extension of The Kingston Trio, and just as much a confection. They were perfect for the hootenanny audience, although they were positioned better in the way they also tapped into the civil rights movement. It was very tastefully done, and whipped into shape by their producer, Milt Okum. They sold a ton of records, but they didn't do anything for my heart."

Oscar Brand once quipped that you could walk from New York to California by just stepping from one coffee house to another and never touching the ground. The coffee-house phenomenon and the spread of folk music even made the cover of *Time* magazine in November 1962, with an image of Joan Baez, and a piece inside headlined 'From Sybil With Guitar', which took a slightly irreverent stance. "Everywhere, there are bearded fop singers and clean-cut dilettantes. There are gifted amateurs and serious musicians. New York, Boston, Chicago, Minneapolis, Denver, and San Francisco all have shoals of tiny coffee shops, all loud with basic sound. Indiana has a place called The Fourth Shadow where people squat on the floor and sip espresso by candlelight over doors that have been made into tables. Strings are jumping at The Jolly Coachman in Council Bluffs, Iowa. Incredibly, Omaha, just across the river from Council Bluffs, has two places, The Third Man and The Crooked Ear, where queues sometimes run to a hundred head. When something is that big in Omaha, Daddy, it can be said to have arrived."

But Greenwich Village was America's bohemian heartland, bristling with so much raw talent and energy, and that was indeed echoed in Chicago, San Francisco, and Los Angeles. It was in coffee houses that Bob Dylan and Joan Baez began performing, in Minneapolis and Boston respectively, and this was the arena for those who wanted to follow them.

Holzman knew the Village inside out. "It was a few square blocks of clubs and bars, red-sauce Italian restaurants that had been family-run for generations, and, of course, the coffee houses. The Kettle Of Fish was the hub, and from there you fanned out and sampled the action. The Gaslight was directly downstairs, just a short walk to Gerde's Folk City, the Village Gate, and the Bitter End. Izzy Young's Folklore Center, a few steps above MacDougal Street, was a storefront that carried records, sheet music, instruments, strings, capos, and just about everything else for the urban folk singer."

Holzman remembers Izzy Young as a man with a big heart and very open ears. "When we released *Music From Bulgaria*, an out-of-print album we licensed from EMI, Izzy put a big poster in his window saying god bless Elektra for this re-release. Vanguard and Elektra kept him alive." Izzy would sell records and not pay for them, Holzman recalls with a smile. With Izzy, the rent came first and everybody else was secondary. His importance was his willingness to listen. "He was a big part of the support mechanism in the Village. His place was a place where you would hang out."

Michael Ochs, who would later manage his brother Phil, witnessed the transition from one era to the next. "Everybody was in this ten-block radius. It was dirt cheap. Almost any kid could afford it. Most places, there was no cover charge, maybe a two-drink minimum. The Pete Seegers, the Oscar Brands, the Ed McCurdys would still be playing, and it would usually be a mixture [of the old guard and new arrivals on the scene]. Ed McCurdy would be the headliner and Patrick Sky would open for him, or Oscar Brand would be the headliner and have Phil Ochs opening for him."[1]

Being part of the scene was no guarantee of success. Tom Paxton, for one, had to wait his turn. "I came to New York City in 1960," he says. "Dylan arrived in '61, Ochs in '62, Eric Andersen in '63. I was performing professionally for three-and-a-half years before I got a contract with Elektra. It seemed like it was never going to happen until I finally got an audition for Jac. There was a scene at the Gaslight, and I was there every night, whether I was working or not. If I went to a movie, I went in the afternoon – in the evenings I was always hanging out in the Village. You didn't dare miss out on anything. You might end up being impressed or envious if someone played a new song that blew you away or, maybe, an opportunity might come up which you could grab. You had to be there every night."

As Ronald Lankford observes in his book *Folk Music USA*, "The fine art of hanging out, or being seen on the scene, was also an artist's ticket to a piece of the pie. Everyone dreamed of getting a gig at Gerde's or the Village Vanguard, followed by a write-up in the *New York Times* by folk scribe Robert Shelton (whose rave critiques boosted the careers of Dylan, Baez, and Buffy Sainte Marie, among many). This chain of events culminated when you signed with Vanguard, Tradition, Riverside, or Elektra, because a recording contract was the end of the Village road."

Buffy Sainte-Marie, who recorded for Vanguard, was on her way to study in India but got no further than New York City. She was sucked in. "It was a very special time for students and for performers. Every city, every campus had somewhere to play, somewhere where you'd feel at home. It wouldn't have happened without the special convergence during the

Kennedy years: the empowerment of students, their pressure to end the war, and songwriters taking music into their own hands despite Tin Pan Alley. The 60s was a perfect time for me, coming from an outsider perspective and having something to say. It was an incredible time for people of the student generation. And we were all talking to each other – it was so international, in terms of music and the radio and what the folk labels were doing. You'd hear flamenco next to delta blues next to songwriters and Celtic music."

In this more open, optimistic Kennedy era, as Dave Van Ronk observes, it was much easier than during the McCarthy years. "We were very open about our radicalism, and when the civil rights movement and the anti-war movement came along in the 60s, we jumped in with both feet. Had we gone through what the older generation went through in the 50s, I wonder if we would have been quite so gung-ho."[2]

Tom Paxton and Phil Ochs, both signed to Elektra, were two contrasting personalities. "Much depended on the individual," says Holzman. "Watching the process that artists went through to create the material was fascinating: how flexible they were, and how this interacted with their different personalities and different talents."

Tom Paxton, with his cosy, almost avuncular presence, seemed like part of the furniture at Elektra, just like Judy Collins. Never one to rely solely on topical material, he showed a rare diversity on his 1964 debut, *Ramblin' Boy*, and provided hits for Peter Paul & Mary, The Chad Mitchell Trio (for whom he had flunked an audition to join years earlier), and Julie Felix. He expertly mixed protest and romance, satirical songs and children's songs. He was one of the strongest voices against the electrification of folk and the commercial exploitation of protest songs, most notably in a *Sing Out* jeremiad where he dismissed the new movements as "folk-rot", saying: "Nothing could be more ridiculous than to suppose that while frugging, the kids are going to be contemplating Red China."

Paxton wasn't convinced at first that he would be signed. "My start with Elektra was a little shaky. It was early 1964, and I had been in New York for about four years, doing nothing but singing folk music. I was beginning to wonder if it would ever happen. So my manager, Harold Leventhal, called up Jac Holzman and said, 'Look, this is ridiculous, you have to give Tom a deal.'"

Holzman invited Paxton to his house to sing. They lived a block apart, says Paxton, but he considered it a universe away in terms of style. "Jac had this wonderful new apartment filled with bookshelves and so on. I sat with him in his study and sang three or four songs for him – during which time he did not look at me at all. When I'd finished, he sat there for a minute, which seemed like an eternity. Then he finally said, 'I certainly hope you can sing with a little more energy in the studio.'"

Holzman offered Paxton his standard deal. "I could do one session," says Paxton, "which would be a three-hour session – and not a minute more under the musicians union rules. If it went well, he would sign me to a contract for three albums. If it didn't go well, I could have the tapes to do whatever I wanted with. Well, fortunately, it did go well, and we did seven albums together."

Ramblin' Boy was a strong debut littered with many of Paxton's signature songs, such as 'I Can't Help But Wonder Where I'm Bound' and 'What Did You Learn In School Today', although the most accomplished, 'The Last Thing On My Mind', only just made the cut. "The whole song came very quickly," he says. "I sang it that night at the Gaslight for the first time. Paul Rothchild was there, so I performed it for him in the stairwell at the club, and he had some excessively nice things to say about it. So we added it to the album. It became something special because it communicated very straightforwardly. The verse tells the story; the chorus is the emotional response to the story."[3]

Paxton's second album, *Ain't That News!*, included among its tracks his most effective topical song, 'Lyndon Johnson Told The Nation'. This song showed that protest didn't have to be served up with vinegar. "Tom confronted using his own best weapons," observes Holzman, "which were intellect, irony, the well-wrought phrase – and the truth. His lyrics, aside from the melodies, were corrosive without being venal. When they were matched to a lilting tune, those lyrics became even more devastating." The sing-along 'Lyndon Johnson' is the perfect example.

Having quickly established a reputation as one of America's foremost folk singers and most imaginative yet adaptable songwriters, Paxton extended his range on the third album, *Outward Bound*, by writing what he calls "songs that were more observational, where I would think myself into other people's shoes".

Paxton had become the consummate folk singer-songwriter, and one with a broader appeal than, say, Fred Neil or Phil Ochs. For John Sebastian, he was the complete opposite of someone like Neil. "He came from a different tradition, which fed from the songs of Woody Guthrie and Pete Seeger," says Sebastian. "With him, his strength was always in the writing, although he had a warm presence and an 'in your living room' singing style."

Paxton is nothing less than an old-school all-round artist. "For me," he says, "politics in song was important, but it was only part of what was important to me. My metabolism was changed by hearing *The Weavers At Carnegie Hall.* My whole career since then is almost a commentary on that album, just the breadth of repertoire in that one concert. That's what I strove to achieve after hearing that one stupefying concert: political songs, children's songs, love songs like 'Kisses Sweeter Than Wine', fine old American folk songs. That album was my benchmark."

He had no desire to go electric. Paxton says he was never seriously tempted to plug in and didn't think he would be very good at it. "I knew that what I was good at was simple storytelling in songs. To me, the most beautiful sound is still an acoustic guitar." His approach is well summed up by Eric Andersen, on whom Paxton kept a watchful eye after he arrived in the Village. "You could just get up with your guitar and sing," says Andersen. "The power of the instrument superseded the need to have a band. One person with a guitar could spread a lot of joy or do a lot of mental damage by exposing some truths."[3] But no one gets to the essence of Paxton's songs better than Bob Gibson. "They just try to tell a story," says Gibson, "and let the idea form in the ear of the listener."[4]

Paxton's first three albums were produced by Paul Rothchild, but on the eve of recording *Morning Again* in 1966, Rothchild took Paxton to one side to explain that he was heading for California to produce Elektra's new signing, The Doors. Peter Siegel was brought in, and he provided the right environment for the transition to a fuller sound on Paxton's recordings. "I hated to lose Paul," says Paxton, "but Peter dragged me kicking and screaming into the second half of the 20th century. Without asking me to change myself at all, he showed me a different way of working in a recording studio. He brought in interesting people to work on that album. It was really fun for me to hear my songs fleshed out, without turning me into something I was not."[5]

He remained true to his artistry and his humanitarian ideals. "Paxton wrote so damn well," says Holzman. "He was prolific, great on nuance, and uncanny with children's material. He is certainly of one of Seeger's children, more than Guthrie's. But it's interesting: Seeger, Guthrie, and Paxton all had a fondness and strength when composing children's material. That's the thread that links the three of them."

Children's songs mark out a strong vein in Paxton's work, with classic songs in 'Jennifer's Rabbit' or 'Going To The Zoo'. He says that writing a children's song employs the same skills and techniques as adult songwriting. "The big difference is the vocabulary – not just the actual words, but the special universe which children occupy. It's smaller than the rest of the world, but every bit as engrossing and as full of imagination."[5]

The Elektra years are unquestionably Paxton's most memorable, and he now regrets leaving the label too soon, in 1971. He subsequently recorded an album every year or two for a sequence of labels, including Reprise, a number of labels in Britain, where he settled for time, and Vanguard, Flying Fish, Appleseed, and his own mail-order outlet Pax, among many others. The material is no less bittersweet and assured, sympathetically addressing the human condition, but it is overlooked these days. No one can ever accuse Tom Paxton of trying to be fashionable.

Greenwich Village in the 60s was a bustling, hustling hotbed of raw talent. Holzman says you might sit down in, say, the Kettle Of Fish and the table would be filled with characters, each one trying to look different, each one trying to sound different, each one trying to carve out his own persona. And everybody was looking for their own style. "There was very little backbiting," he says, "until Dylan came along. He raised the bar, because he was so facile that he could do in a moment what others would spend days on, and they would still get a less good result."

Almost everyone in the Village was in Dylan's shadow. But where others accepted Dylan's ability, Phil Ochs was always more competitive. Dylan would bait him mercilessly, singling out Ochs ahead of the other Village singer-songwriters. Paxton was close to Ochs, hanging at places like the Kettle Of Fish, Gerde's, or the Gaslight. "Phil was funny, he was edgy, he was very bright, he loved arguing," Paxton recalls. "He liked putting his two cents in, and he could be very dogmatic about it, but he was a good-humoured guy, no question. It was a band-of-brothers kind of thing in the Village. When Dylan became a 'spokesman for his generation' you couldn't help but wish this might happen to you as well."

Arthur Gorson was Ochs's manager and a fellow activist. He describes Ochs as the toughest of the lot, in that he was the surest of his own talent, had the biggest ego, and was the most prolific. "Even though Dylan's presence hurt Phil at times," says Gorson, "it didn't damage him and prevent him from growing as a creative artist."[6] Holzman, too, saw how Dylan's presence affected Ochs. "Phil was close to being bi-polar in his relationship to Dylan. He admired Dylan's extraordinary imagination and choice of words but was incredibly angry that he couldn't match it. Equally annoying was that Dylan felt no rivalry toward anyone. Dylan knew he was on a cloud, floating above the pettiness, but Dylan energised Ochs. I don't think Ochs would have written as well but for the eight-hundred-pound gorilla that was Bob Dylan's talent."

When Phil Ochs committed suicide in 1976, he was best remembered for the series of acoustic protest songs he recorded for Elektra in the mid 60s and for one song above all, the anti-war rallying call 'I Ain't Marching Anymore'. Only his 1966 *In Concert* had made even the slightest impression on the charts, because it featured 'There But For Fortune', which had been a hit for Joan Baez, reaching the Top Ten in Britain. Today, we can see that Ochs, alongside Dylan, was arguably the best of the topical Village songwriters, a true political agitator who wrote passionate songs about real people and events. His writing never diminished in quality, despite the way he abandoned the simple folk form in 1967 to make four extraordinary, iconoclastic, experimental pop albums for A&M, which, like Ochs himself, simply did not fit into the surrounding world. By the late 60s, Ochs's directness was passé. Music had become more of a soundtrack to change, and rock music, by its very nature, needed to be rebellious and high on shock value, even if essentially a popular entertainment medium.

Phil Ochs was born in 1940 in El Paso, Texas, in comfortable middle-class surroundings. He began performing at Ohio State University after he was turned on to folk music and left-wing politics by his friend Jim Glover (who later recorded a number of Ochs songs with the duo Jim & Jean). Ochs found a natural home in the Village when he arrived there in 1962. As with Dylan, Woody Guthrie was an early influence: Ochs's rousing march tune 'Power And The Glory' is a direct descendant of Guthrie's 'This Land Is Your Land'. Holzman recognised the connection. "I saw him as a lineal descendant of Woody Guthrie in two ways: he wrote political songs, and he was prolific. I liked the fact that he had more acid to what he was singing, and for Elektra he was the perfect counterpart to Tom Paxton."

The political nature of Ochs's songs led him to become heavily involved with *Broadside* magazine, which published many of his early songs, all bearing the hallmarks of a crusading journalist. His first two Elektra albums, *All The News That's Fit To Sing* (1964) and *I Ain't Marching Anymore* (1965), also reflected this passionate topicality. 'I Ain't Marching Anymore' was one of the most striking songs written against the war in Vietnam and became a staple of the anti-war movement. The song almost defined Phil Ochs. It tapped into the mood of the era but also trapped him there. It was the clarion call for a generation living under the spectre of the draft and fighting a war for a purpose not clear to anyone.

"Look at his posthumous reputation," says Van Dyke Parks, who produced Ochs later in his career. "It's odd to think that there was a lack of success in his own lifetime. 'I Ain't Marching Anymore' is his most famous song, but he had so many songs that people co-opted and put into their own shows. Phil was revered by everyone, and there was a long-held sibling-like rivalry between him and Bob Dylan. If you watch the Martin Scorsese documentary on Dylan, there's not one mention of Phil Ochs. I know Bob had final editorial approval, and I don't doubt that he just didn't want to see that man's face on screen. I have the highest regard for Bob Dylan, but quite frankly he's an archly competitive man. It's clear to me that Phil had an absolute influence on Bob: he had a sense of rage and courage that was immediately apparent."

By 1966, most of Ochs's peers had, like Dylan, moved away from finger-pointing, but he was still addressing political and social issues with his usual logic and clarity. His final Elektra album, *In Concert*, was claimed to be recorded at Carnegie Hall; it includes the wry 'Love Me I'm A Liberal' but also sees him shifting away from political issues to quite touching effect, as on 'There But For Fortune', and 'Changes', his most reflective song.

"The power of Phil's material was its provocative nature," says his manager Arthur Gorson. "In Phil's eyes, if the songs he was writing weren't dangerous – if they weren't going to annoy someone so much that they might threaten his life – then he didn't think they were important. But then one day he came back from a trip to Canada with a song that was totally apart. And that was 'Changes'. It was a breakthrough for him, as it proved that Phil could tackle subjects other than burning political issues and which affected the music he would make for the rest of the decade."[7]

In Concert was Ochs's final acoustic album before he tried to cast off the shackles of his image as the folk troubadour. He left Elektra, which he felt hadn't done enough for him, and New York City, moving to Los Angeles. He browbeat Holzman about poor sales, saying that Elektra was focussing on its new signings, Love and The Doors, while simultaneously making outrageous demands for a new deal. "He wanted to try something in a pop vein," Holzman remembers, "but I wasn't convinced that Phil had the voice or the ability to write and carry a really good album in that genre. He owed me two more records but asked if I would release him, and I said certainly, if that's what you want."

Signing to A&M, Ochs debuted with *Pleasures Of The Harbor* at the close of 1967. It was a wonderful mix of baroque folk and melodic pop, including the jaunty 'Outside Of A Small Circle Of Friends'. It was the closest Ochs ever came to a hit, but the line "smoking marijuana is more fun than drinking beer" cut short its radio life. His later recordings for A&M presented an artist even less sure of his context or of any consistent musical direction.

The A&M years are, nonetheless, littered with exceptional Ochs songs. He was still writing prolifically in 1968, when he released *Tape From California*, which reverted to a simpler approach and included the ironically exuberant 'The War Is Over'. Ochs's most outlandish notion was that the only hope for America was a revolution and, for that revolution to happen, Elvis had to become Che Guevara. Tom Paxton recalls Ochs expressing this in the Kettle Of Fish, years before. Ochs transformed himself into Elvis-as-Che, requesting Nudie the rodeo tailor to make him the gold lamé suit that he wears on the jacket of 1970's *Greatest Hits*. The title was deliberately misleading: here were ten new songs, some great, but none hits. The portentous 'No More Songs' found Ochs worrying that he was running out of things to say, a fear that soon took on deeper significance.

The *Greatest Hits* record was produced by the mercurial Van Dyke Parks. The sarcastic intention of the title and the spoof claim on the back that "50 Phil Ochs fans can't be wrong!" were completely misunderstood and simply seen as further evidence that Ochs had lost his way. Parks never doubted Ochs's integrity. "He was one of a kind," says Parks, "but I think he also might have alienated anyone who might have considered being his patron, because if there was one thing that Phil didn't like it was patronage. He made that clear: he could not be bought. They say every man has his price, but they could never find one for Phil. To me, he was a pole star for the counter-culture, because he was completely incorruptible and beyond purchase."

Greatest Hits was Ochs's final studio album. For the remainder of his life he suffered serious writer's block. He spent much of 1975 in New York City, often living on the streets, with the occasional trip back to LA. His few remaining friends did not know how to help him.

Ed Sanders of The Fugs was one of the co-founders of the Youth International Party, known as the Yippies, along with Phil Ochs and others who helped plan the Yippies' *Festival Of Life*, which was to take place in Chicago to coincide with the Democratic National Convention in August 1968. "Chicago was meant to be a united front against the war and a celebration of the underground, but few of the rock stars turned up, aside from Phil. We were there with the thousands, chanting 'the whole world is watching' while the police bashed their clubs on undeserving heads."

Sanders charts the Chicago riots and Ochs's disillusionment as the beginning of his downward spiral. A further catalogue of disasters and disappointments culminated in him adopting the alternative personality of John Butler Train; Ochs publicly announced that Train had murdered Phil Ochs and replaced him. "He moved back to New York and even owned a bar there, called Che," says Sanders, "and I watched him get more and more alcoholic and more fearful. One time he was so drunk he started breaking his own windows. This was when he had slipped into becoming John Train. Even in those lowest moments during the 70s, Phil was always 'have voice, will sing'. He never turned down any benefits but he increasingly felt defeated and he ran out of confidence and storylines."

Tom Paxton recalls two different meetings toward the end of Ochs's life. "The last time I saw Phil happy was at the rally in Central Park after the fall of Saigon," he says, referring to the War Is Over event that took place in May 1975. "It was a mass celebration, and Phil was there, smoking a huge cigar with a beaming smile on his face. Some time later, I met him on the stoop outside the Bitter End. He called out to me, and he was drunk, and I had to go put my guitar away. I said to him I'd come back, but I didn't. He was in terrible shape, and when he was drunk he was difficult to be around. I don't subscribe to the view that the end of the war deprived him of his windmill or that it gave him some kind of closure."

Joan Baez sang 'There But For Fortune' with Ochs at the rally. It turned out to be his final public performance. She feels that his greatest contribution was that he lived his life according to his music. "Some may say that was his downfall. His songs, more than his death, still speak to us all."

For Holzman, Ochs simply lost the fight with his inner demons. "The anger that he had within him made him the best of the topical songwriters we had recording for Elektra, but his anger gnawed away at him. Had he been less self-destructive, and had he lived, I'd like to think his voice would have been heard again." Tom Paxton agrees. "I've often said, a little facetiously, that if Phil could have lasted until Ronald Reagan became president, he'd have gone on forever."

Ochs's career had been spiralling steadily downward during the 70s. In January 1976, afflicted by what would today be diagnosed as clinical depression, he moved in with his sister Sonny in the suburban Far Rockaway neighbourhood of New York. It was there on April 9 that his nephew David found Ochs hanging from his belt in the bathroom.

Ochs was one of a number of troubled writers who found a home at Elektra for part of their careers, and he was haunted by a line from his song 'Chords Of Fame': "God help the troubadour who wants to be a star." That, says Holzman, was the kernel. "It starts as a small cancer and then it grows into a big one. I saw very little of him after he'd left the label, and perhaps I should have picked up the phone and tried to help him. People who knew Tim Buckley and Phil Ochs were shocked by Tim's death, but I don't think they were surprised by Phil's suicide."

* * *

Missouri-born Mark Spoelstra is one of the forgotten singer-songwriters on Elektra's books. His style was closer to that of the folk-blues interpreter Tom Rush, but his lyrics, no less topical, tended to be more philosophical and open-ended than Ochs's or Paxton's. Like Paxton, Spoelstra was one of the early arrivals in New York City in the autumn of 1959. Then he became friends with Bob Dylan when he blew into the city over a year later.

Spoelstra was recommended to Folkways by John Cohen of The New Lost City Ramblers; he recorded two albums for the label, *The Songs Of*

Mark Spoelstra, released in 1963, and the live *Recorded At Club 47*, made after he moved to Cambridge. Dylan was, by all accounts, irritated that Spoelstra got a deal with Folkways when he'd been summarily dismissed by Moe Asch, the label's boss. Soon afterward Spoelstra was called up by the draft, but as a Quaker he instead worked alongside migrant black workers in West Fresno, California, and his experiences inspired him to write his own material.

Through Paul Rothchild, Spoelstra switched labels to Elektra, and his debut appeared in 1965, *Five & Twenty Questions*, with liner notes provided by Richard Fariña. The title song was Spoelstra's own 'Blowin' In The Wind', a questioning song that pointed to the need for social change. Musically, he accompanied himself skilfully on the 12-string guitar, and he included three impressive John Fahey-like instrumentals. Unusually for Elektra, *Five & Twenty Questions* was recorded in Los Angeles, after Spoelstra and Rothchild attended a festival in Big Sur during Spolestra's two-week break from alternative service. While it was not exactly a prison camp, attendance there was compulsory, which prevented Spoelstra from any touring to promote the record.

State Of Mind in 1966 was in much the same vein, with songs such as 'Sacred Life', 'Too Late', and 'Soulless Blues' castigating the war. Perhaps it was the album's dated simplicity, but it made far less impact than his debut, and Spoelstra was dropped. Holzman says: "Paxton and Ochs had a hunger; Spolestra didn't. We were moving on to other things by 1966, so we let him go." Spoelstra resurfaced in 1969 with an album for Columbia, produced by James Guercio, then the hotshot producer of the band Chicago, and two tracks were featured in the movie *Electra Glide In Blue.* Spoelstra made several albums for smaller labels before his death in Pioneer, California, in February 2007.

It was Spoelstra who recommend Kathy Larisch and Carol McComb to Paul Rothchild. When Rothchild was asked later to single out some of his favourite Elektra work, he cited *Tom Rush*, the first two Paul Butterfield albums, and the first two Doors albums plus *Morrison Hotel.* But he also picked a couple of albums that sold next to nothing at the time: Joseph Spence's *Happy All The Time* was one, *Kathy & Carol* the other. Rothchild describes *Kathy & Carol* as the most beautiful Renaissance-style record he ever heard. "It's just perfect. If you like Joan Baez, here's Joan Baez times two, with gorgeous harmony singing – like angels. And they meant it: it was real for them."[8]

Carol McComb confirms their dedication. "We played traditional folk tunes, but we would go out of our way to make sure that our interpretations were different to anyone else's. We would often spend a whole day working out the parts for a single song. We loved to think of it as creating a picture in sound. Kathy is a visual artist, so she definitely sees things that way. Paul Rothchild took real good care of us in the studio. It was an excellent first experience. He taught us microphone techniques that I still use today. The best thing was that he didn't try to impose anything on us: he let us be ourselves. It wasn't long after we made our album that Paul was arrested and out of action for a year, and somehow we never did a second album for Elektra."[9]

Holzman was happy with the balance of music that was emerging from Elektra, with songwriters and with interpreters, as well as what he describes as the more ethnic releases. He felt it was important that Elektra remained in contact with its folk roots. In line with this, Holzman recorded Jean Carignan, the French-Canadian fiddling sensation from Newport in 1964, and from Britain he licensed The Ian Campbell Folk Group, from the Transatlantic label, and two monumental and important albums from Topic, The Watersons' *Frost And Fire*, and *The Iron Muse*, an anthology of songs from the industrial revolution compiled and arranged by A.L. Lloyd. "I admired the Topic label," says Holzman. "Albums they released had that coal-under-the-fingernails British tradition – which did not run in my DNA, but I could recognise and appreciate it when I heard it. The Watersons I just loved. I wasn't hearing that combination of voices anywhere in America."

Jean Redpath is another artist of purity, says Holzman, and one with a unique sense of tradition. "Jean conveys the heart in the Scottish ballad tradition. There's no artifice about her. She was a pure singer in the tradition of Jean Ritchie, and you don't tamper with an artist like that. If no one bought unaccompanied songs, I didn't care."

Jean Redpath was born in Edinburgh, Scotland, where she attended university and discovered the School of Scottish Studies and its rich folk heritage. Redpath arrived in the United States in 1961 with $11 in her pocket and wound up in Greenwich Village. An appearance at Gerde's Folk

City won her further bookings and a rave review in *The New York Times*, and she soon came to the attention of Holzman. She would record three exquisite, untainted albums for Elektra between 1962 and 1964: *Scottish Ballad Book*; *Songs Of Love, Lilt, Laughter*; and *Laddie Lie Near Me*.

During the period from 1963 into '64, Elektra had the financial strength to do whatever it wanted, says Holzman. The label could make records that didn't sell a lot but were worth doing irrespective of sales. Elektra had a solid cachet and knew its audience would take a chance on buying records they hadn't heard.

Peter Siegel – who would later record Joseph Spence for Nonesuch – made an album with Oliver Smith, a blind street singer Siegel discovered singing on a downtown corner. "I could hear him a block away," Siegel wrote in the album's liner notes. "I asked him if he'd ever been recorded. 'No,' he said. Would he record tonight, I wondered? 'Well, I'm doing pretty well here tonight,' he said. 'I might make ten or fifteen dollars.' I told him the recording fees would be more than that. He said in that case, he'd be interested."

Thirty minutes after Siegel heard him, Smith was in the studio recording a two-hour session that provided 13 first-take songs. "It took several days for it to sink in how good he was," Siegel continued in the liner notes. *Oliver Smith* is one of many unsung Elektra albums. At least people eventually discovered Spence's *Happy All The Time*, even if it was not soon enough for Rothchild. "We went on a hunt to find Joseph Spence," he says, "and that is one of the most fun records I ever made. It was done in Spence's living room. Total production costs were under $1,000, including airfare for two people, a cheap hotel, tape stock, paying Joseph Spence, and buying guitar strings. It was probably the best, the purest record I ever made, and its history on Elektra Records … it sold 93 copies."[10] This is a figure that Holzman notes as definitely underestimated.

Fritz Richmond, then best known as the washtub-bass player in The Jim Kweskin Jug Band, had been a devotee of Spence since hearing his first recordings, made by Sam Charters in 1958. In January 1964, Richmond was instructed to set off for the Bahamas himself, and on only his second day there he managed to track down Spence, asking if he would consider recording again. Spence admitted that he'd never heard the first record, but that he'd love to make another one. Richmond sent a terse cable back to

Rothchild: "Spence lives. Will record. Bring 12 sets of heavy bronze guitar strings." The New York folkies went nuts. Izzy Young obtained Rothchild's copy of the cable and hung it on the wall of the Folklore Center. Rothchild was soon in Nassau, where they recorded *Happy All The Time* on a battery-operated but high-quality portable Nagra tape recorder, along with two microphones.

Spence's recordings have had an influence on the music of the Grateful Dead, Ry Cooder, The Incredible String Band, Davy Graham, David Byrne, Kate & Anna McGarrigle, Van Dyke Parks, and Taj Mahal, among others. "I hadn't even heard of Joseph Spence until Fritz or Rothchild brought him to my attention," admits Holzman. "Now, I appreciate he is one of the great natural guitar geniuses of the last 50 years. Spence had such a dynamic effect on so many people."

Holzman thought that Elektra, in doing so well, had a responsibility to invest back into the roots of folk music. "We could record an album of Negro spirituals, or one with Maxwell Street Jimmie Davis, and if it made an impression as to the breadth and passion of the label, that was reason enough for me. If it was quality and if it could pin a few ears back, it had done its job, and I was proud to support it."

It was in March 1940 that Alan Lomax had taken Woody Guthrie into a recording studio at the Department of the Interior in Washington, DC. What emerged from three days of sessions was a collection of songs and conversations featuring many Guthrie classics, including 'Do Re Mi', 'Pretty Boy Floyd', and 'I Ain't Got No Home'. These sessions first appeared as a three-LP boxed set on Elektra in 1964. Supervising and releasing this and the equally historic Leadbelly *Library Of Congress Recordings* set that followed amounted to some of Holzman's proudest achievements.

It was an eye-opening experience for Holzman. "Elektra had been chosen to issue this incredibly important Library of Congress effort. An engineer was assigned to guide me through the Library's intricate restoration process, which began with the time-consuming and exacting transfer to tape of the acetate originals, requiring precise matching of a stylus to the width of the groove of each disk.

"In order to delete annoying clicks and impulse noises, we dubbed them to high-speed master tapes, which I then took to my home studio and doggedly excised every click with a razor blade and editing block. There were at least a thousand clicks on the Woody Guthrie recordings, and it was absolutely worth the effort.

"The set was bolstered by phenomenal notes from Alan Lomax. He was so late delivering them that he ended up dictating them, in their entirety, to my secretary, Pearl, while waiting to board a flight to Europe. They were perfect: I didn't need to change a word.

"Those recordings caught Guthrie at the beginning of his real maturity, and they were universally praised. The Leadbelly recordings were easier to do. Both sets were emotionally important to me as documents entrusted to Elektra."

Holzman notes one further factor in the affair. "Both Guthrie and Leadbelly were singer-songwriters. That's where Elektra was focused – and here I am going back to two of the best. Guthrie and Leadbelly were providing a contextual floor for the upcoming generation of singer-songwriters. Those boxed sets connected us to our folk antecedents and to the folk world that 'was', just as we were heading in a fresh direction."

Remembering Elektra
Sonny Ochs on Phil Ochs

"Phil lived in his own world; [he was] extremely shy. It was difficult for him to make friends. Growing up we moved an awful lot as a family and that was devastating for him. I was outgoing, and could make friends easily but for Phil it was excruciating, because it would take least a year to find a friend, then next thing you know we'd move and he'd have to start over again. That's why he was so wrapped up in himself and in movies, he loved movies.

He loved John Wayne and Audie Murphy, absurdly; it's what you wouldn't expect of Phil, because they made such gung-ho patriotic movies. But Phil was very patriotic. People didn't realise that. They thought he was certified left wing. Thing was, he loved his country. He had no time for the people who said "love it or leave it". He believed, "My country is great so let's fix the flaws. We need to right the wrongs."

You know the expression that converts are the worst. When somebody discovers a new *ism*, whatever it is, they just become totally consumed by it. That's what happened to Phil, and that's what happened when he became part of that scene in Greenwich Village. This was a whole new world that he loved and he always the defender of the underdog.

Phil looked at things differently to most of the other songwriters; he always saw the plight of individual. He has a song called 'Lou Marsh' on his first album, *All The News That's Fit To Sing*, which is one of my favourites that you hardly hear; it's about a social worker who was killed trying to break up a gang fight. That was the journalist in Phil. He wrote a song about William Worthy, who was arrested coming back into US after he went down to Cuba. I think his strength was he saw the human side of things. 'Changes' was another powerfully compassionate, deeply personal song.

Phil's writing became subtler; it was less folk-based when he left New York and Elektra Records and went to A&M in California. 'Flower Lady' is such a beautiful song about a woman who goes out to sell flowers and in end hobbles home without a sale. Another song, 'The Party', has the line "the wallflower is waiting, she hides behind composure, she'd love to dance but prays no one asks her".* He could paint incredible pictures with beautiful, poetic words; to me those are snapshots of human beings.

That didn't mean he abandoned his political commitment to the civil rights movement and the anti-war movement. In 1967 he organised two huge rallies to declare *The War Is Over* when Vietnam was at its height – it was an absurdist theatre of protest – and thousands joined him on the streets of LA and New York in support.

The Chicago riots were the death knell for his generation of extreme idealists who thought they were going to change the world. They really thought they could elect somebody through the system – Eugene McCarthy opposed Lyndon B. Johnson in the Democratic Convention running on an anti-Vietnam war platform – who could bring about the end of the war. It was such a slap in the face. Nothing could stop the war. That was the point when Phil really got disheartened. He really died emotionally in Chicago. When Phil put out his next album, *Rehearsals For Retirement*, he said, "This is my first themed album, and that theme is the death of America." It was death of idealism and everything he had believed in.†

He started to go downhill and his career followed the same path. He spent

* Both songs are on Och's A&M debut, *Pleasures Of The Harbour*.

† The cover shows a tombstone with Phil's name on it, indicating that he was born in Texas in 1940 and died in Chicago in 1968.

a lot of time travelling in the 70s. He spent some time in Chile, where he became friends with Victor Jara; then both Jara and Allende were murdered following the coup there in 1973. So he put together a benefit for Chilean refugees called *An Evening with Salvador Allende*. The following year he went to South Africa, where he was mugged in Dar-el-Salam. His attackers choked him, which permanently injured his vocal chords. As a result he lost his three top notes and he couldn't sing as well anymore. He must have felt everything was going against him, and his mood swings became even more exaggerated after that; he would get extremely high, then crash down to amazing lows.

Phil was insanely manic when he was putting together the *War Is Over* concert in 1975, where over 100,000 people gathered in Central Park and he sang 'The War Is Over' for real. That was one of those highs; it was a great moment and a tremendous success though he was not in great shape. After that he crashed.

During the John Train period he was frightening.* I wouldn't let him come to my house. It was like in Jekyll and Hyde when the Hyde character has come out and won't go back. Afterward, he was very apologetic; he was humiliated by his behaviour as John Train. In the winter of 1975, he came to visit for a few days and stayed until he killed himself. We knew it was coming. I would come home from school, and if I didn't see him sitting in the living room – or at the piano – I would go through the whole house looking for the body. I finally got him to see a psychiatrist, who gave him lithium. I would come home each evening from teaching and say, "Did you take your medicine?" He would say yes but, after he had killed himself, I found the bottle, and he hadn't taken anything.

In the end he was just so down. He said, "People don't want to hear those old songs any more. All I have is old songs." Nothing would motivate him. He felt he'd lost the muse; it wasn't coming. Yet here we are, 40 years later, and his songs still hold up, these 'supposed to be' topical songs. Topical songs should be throwaway songs. It's absolutely amazing that his songs are still relevant. ”

* The name John Train was an amalgam of Ochs's movie heroes John Wayne and John Ford (or possibly John F. Kennedy) and poet William Butler Yeats. 'Train' is often attributed to Coltrane, but in an unreleased Ochs's song he sings, "Train stands for hobos at the missed silver gates."

CHAPTER 13

Blues, Rags & Hollers

> *"During my first serious conversation with Paul Rothchild, we got to the point where I intended to go, and Paul felt comfortable enough to complain about his boss at Prestige. So I was able to ask him what he was earning, and I said I'll double that. Plus royalties and a car allowance. He walked out with almost everything he asked for. He turned into a highly skilled producer and a lifelong friend."* **JAC HOLZMAN**

By the early 60s, the folk audience was particularly knowledgeable about the blues, fuelled by the rediscovery of country-blues singers such as Skip James, Bukka White, Mississippi John Hurt, Fred McDowell, Lightnin' Hopkins, and Son House, who were now working at festivals, clubs, and coffee houses. There was also an increasing awareness of the great urban bluesmen like Muddy Waters and John Lee Hooker. Such was the impact of blues music that a growing school of young acoustic players were now striving to emulate their heroes, whether it was fearless enthusiasts such as Dave Van Ronk and Koerner Ray & Glover or stylish interpreters like Tom Rush and Stefan Grossman.

When Jac Holzman returned from California in 1963, he had fortuitously picked up on the Minneapolis trio Koerner Ray & Glover's debut *Blues Rags And Hollers*, first released on the local Audiophile label, who pressed only 300 copies, almost entirely sold at gigs. Holzman acquired the original masters, patched up a few technical faults, and reissued *Blues Rags And Hollers* on Elektra before the year was out.

Holzman was aware that he needed someone within Elektra to attract the new breed of musicians drifting into the Village every week. He needed someone who spoke their language and knew exactly who to recruit. "Paul Rothchild was on the street more than me," he says, "because of my intense workload. Paul would do better than me with raw talent. I was unable to go in the studio as often as I wanted or the label needed. We had Mark Abramson producing, but Mark couldn't do it all himself. Paul came from the Boston area, had broad and deep music smarts, smoked dope, and was exactly the right guy at the right time. He was the perfect choice to attract artists – he was one of them. He carried himself well: the borsalino hat, the leather coat, stuff like that. I was perceived as being a little bit more conventional, and I was more sound oriented, more business oriented. Paul was more the real deal."

Rothchild had first met Holzman in the 50s when he was running a small classical and jazz collectors shop on MacDougal Street that stocked some of the early Elektra 10-inch LPs. Rothchild recalled that "those records were delivered by Jac Holzman, across the eight blocks in between, on the back of his Vespa motor scooter". They had much in common. Rothchild, brought up in Teaneck, New Jersey, had also been raised on classical music: his mother was a singer at the Metropolitan Opera. At first he was captivated by jazz, then roots blues records. After moving to Cambridge, he remained in contact with Holzman as a salesman for the Boston distribution company that handled Elektra, even winning an Elektra national sales-incentive competition. Rothchild accumulated enough books of trading stamps to exchange for a refrigerator.

It was when Rothchild began running the Prestige folk division that Holzman knew he'd found his man. Holzman had an ulterior motive, too. "One of the factors in bringing Rothchild to Elektra was that I wanted Tom Rush and needed to get a commitment from him. I knew what I was going to get from Tom, and that was terrific. It was also important to us because Tom was part of the Boston scene, and it was good for Elektra to have a presence in that scene, which was not just a mirror image of what was happening in New York. New England had a cachet of its own."

If Elektra eventually became renowned as the label that signed The

Doors, then Paul Rothchild would became famous as the man who produced them. Rothchild's output during his first three years at Elektra was little short of phenomenal, although his activities were curtailed for eight months after he was busted in 1965 for possession of dope. He was a guest of the New Jersey State Prison from November 1965 until July the following year. Holzman kept him on salary.

Once paroled, Rothchild went straight back to the studio to produce Tom Paxton's third album, *Outward Bound*, and complete the work begun by Holzman and Mark Abramson on the second Butterfield Blues Band album, *East-West*. Before he was incarcerated, Rothchild had produced all of Phil Ochs's Elektra albums, the first two by Tom Paxton, two with Fred Neil, as well as records with Tom Rush, Mark Spoelstra, Koerner Ray & Glover, Joseph Spence, Kathy & Carol, the Project series, and The Even Dozen Jug Band, and he signed The Paul Butterfield Blues Band and produced their pivotal debut album.

No less important to Holzman in positioning Elektra at the heart of what was happening in Greenwich Village by 1963 was the arrival in the mail of the rough-and-tumble first album by Koerner Ray & Glover. It would later be a factor in The Doors' decision to sign with Elektra, particularly for self-confessed Elektra nut and Doors guitarist Robby Krieger.

"John Koerner, Dave Ray, and Tony Glover were three white guys from Minnesota, like Bob Dylan," says Krieger, "and somehow they'd got into the blues – they loved country-blues, blues rags and hollers, and they really put their own twist on it. They tried to sound black but really had their own sound. It had a great energy. Koerner played a National seven-string guitar, Glover was a harmonica player, and Dave Ray played the 12-string Leadbelly-style. He did a great job; he was really into Leadbelly. And they did their own stuff, too. It had a real beat, even though they didn't have drums or bass."

Koerner Ray & Glover were recommended to Elektra from an unlikely source. Paul Nelson, who had produced the trio's Audiophile album, ran a music fanzine in Minneapolis called *The Little Sandy Review,* which was influential in the folk world, and often critical of Elektra, particularly the Josh White recordings. "There were always these arguments about what was or wasn't genuine folk music," recalls Holzman. "*Little Sandy Review* was big on authenticity, and they always chided me for not being authentic enough.

I would send them funny notes in return, so we had a dialogue, and there was a respect there. They suggested Koerner Ray & Glover get the record to me, and that record changed things for me." At the outset, Tony Glover wasn't entirely convinced. "I thought this was kind of dubious, because at that time [Elektra] had people like Josh White and Oscar Brand, and to me, [these were] kind of ersatz people."[1]

After a few days, *Blues Rags And Hollers* floated to the top of Holzman's listen-to pile. "I put it on, and I absolutely fell in love with it. It was gutsy and totally unselfconscious roots music. Those guys could stomp and play their asses off. When I listened to the opening cut, 'Linin' Track', I was riveted – I knew what I was hearing. These are white kids, yet they sound like Leadbelly's offspring."

Holzman booked a flight to Minneapolis to meet the trio and, as he puts it, to take their temperature. "They thought I was a very strange dude. By that time, I had accumulated a little money, and they always thought anybody with money tended toward being weird and arrogant. Glover eventually capitulated, saying I was the only rich guy he ever met who wasn't an asshole. He would have been uncomfortable giving a straight compliment. It was a positive expressed negatively – he was one of those good people for whom things never happened the way he wanted. And Dave 'Snaker' Ray would become an insurance salesman. That's tough when you have this fire burning inside of you."

Tony 'Little Sun' Glover recalls, "One time I was giving Jac some shit about Oscar Brand, and he got uppity and said, 'It's guys like those that give me the money and the time to record you,' which I thought was a pretty good comeback. When Jac signed us, he expected to lose money. He was really surprised when we sold enough records to earn back his investment and our advance."[2]

Elektra made three full albums with Koerner Ray & Glover, all produced by Paul Rothchild. The second, *Lots More Blues Rags And Hollers*, was released in July 1964 and was a typical 50-50 mix of full-on shamelessly derivative originals and blues classics learnt from Leadbelly, Bukka White, and Memphis Minnie. The group was much influenced early on by the Sam Charters anthology *The Country Blues*, in its own way as important as the Folkways *Anthology Of American Folk Music* set. For Glover, *Country Blues* was an invaluable collection of "jug bands, back porch music, all sorts of stuff".

"In the beginning," explains 'Spider' John Koerner, "we were trying to copy the blues guys whose music we loved – and I think we probably overdid it, the way young people overdo. What held us together was our common interests. We were just folk musicians, really. It certainly surprised me when it turned into a career – I was supposed to be becoming an aeronautical engineer. When Jac Holzman took us East to record our second album, and we played at the Philadelphia Folk Festival, that's when we discovered all these other people out there, working in a similar kind of area – although none of them sounded exactly the way we did."[3]

After Koerner Ray & Glover completed the sessions for their intended third album, Holzman and Rothchild noted that there weren't any numbers featuring all three playing together. The resulting tapes were split into two 'solo' albums: *Snaker's Here!* featured Dave Ray and *Spider Blues* featured John Koerner, while both had Tony Glover's harp on some tracks. Uncannily, combined sales of the two albums almost exactly matched those for *Lots More Blues Rags And Hollers*.

The final group album, *The Return Of Koerner Ray & Glover*, consisted almost entirely of original songs, aside from four trademark Leadbelly songs performed by Dave Ray. It hit the streets around the same time as Dylan's *Highway 61 Revisited*, a pointer that things were changing. The trio drifted apart, having taken their collaborations as far as they could. Afterward, Tony Glover's name became the most visible, as a rock journalist – he wrote for *Crawdaddy*, *Creem*, and *Rolling Stone* in the 60s and 70s. The group also played the occasional reunion show together, especially in the 90s, and even recorded together again, for the 1996 album *One Foot In The Groove*. Dave Ray died in 2002, since when Koerner and Glover appear as a duo from time to time. They released a new album in 2008, 45 years after their Elektra debut.

Koerner Ray & Glover played country-blues like young punks, fast and furious, but they were always aware of the integrity and history of the music, and they found favour everywhere. When Holzman visited The Beatles to ask for their blessing for *The Baroque Beatles Book* album in 1965, George Harrison and John Lennon both eagerly declared they were fans of Koerner Ray & Glover. Holzman was taken to meet them by publisher Dick James, who drove them there in his Rolls Royce. "George Harrison chirped up immediately that he loved the record," says Holzman, "and then John Lennon commented, 'Anyone who records Koerner Ray & Glover is OK with me.'" The British folk-pop femme fatale Marianne Faithfull namechecked Koerner Ray & Glover, too, in an interview with the British magazine *Folk Scene.*

Closer to home, John Sebastian, then Paul Rothchild's nightly on-the-street companion, was a first-hand admirer. "It was raggy, it was bluesy," says Sebastian. "It was goodtime music. Played a little bit faster than the original guys, but that was because they were excitable young white boys who sped up. It was a step along the path toward what became a style that The Lovin' Spoonful drew upon."

Robby Krieger even copped a lick or two, as Tony Glover recounts. "Elektra lifted five tunes from our first recordings with them for a collection called *The Blues Project.* One of them, 'Southbound Train', had an infectious little riff that turned up several years later, slightly mutated, as the basis for The Doors' 'Love Me Two Times'. I figured it must have been a coincidence. Some four or five years later, I interviewed The Doors for an article and Robby Krieger asked, 'How'd you like that song we stole from you guys?'"[4]

The Blues Project (1964) was the first in a series culled from various strands of music emerging from the Village, aimed at giving artists their first shots at recording. Paul Rothchild conceived it as "simply documenting all the people I could possibly get on record in small pockets of folk and writing exploration". For *The Blues Project*, he gathered everyone he knew who was a good blues singer. "These were interpreters, not the originators. Jac included detailed booklets accompanying the discs, explaining the styles, the songs, and the players. Then I did the *Old Time Banjo Project*, the *String Band Project*, and the *Singer Songwriter Project.* They gave something Elektra needed badly, which was an association with not just the commercial aspects of folk music but the roots of it and the people who were current progenitors."[5]

Holzman saw it also as a way of inducting Rothchild into the scene. "I knew Paul could pull that series together: he was good at getting everyone to commit. It also gave him high visibility. He was greatly respected for his work in Boston, but it helped his career to be respected for his work in New York, and for a larger label."

Rothchild captured a true cross-section of Village life and music. "There was so much talent out there, but I knew we couldn't justify a whole album for each artist. For *The Blues Project*, I brought in the best white urban blues interpreters. Spider John Koerner and Dave Ray, of course, Geoff Muldaur, Dave Van Ronk, Eric von Schmidt, Ian Buchanan, Danny Kalb, Mark Spoelstra, John Sebastian. They were sitting waiting to go on next, barbershop style. I got Bob Dylan to come down and play piano – we wrote him in on the liner notes as Bob Landy. I did all the tracks in a single 12-hour session at Mastertone."

The Blues Project was ready to roll immediately and set the tone for the series. The *Old Time Banjo Project* was co-produced by John Cohen and featured Allan Block (from The Sandal Shop) and his daughter Rory, and gifted pickers like Bill Vanaver, Julian 'Winnie' Winston, and Bob Siggins from The Charles River Valley Boys. Rothchild later took the entire Valley Boys group down to Nashville to record the entertaining bluegrass-style *Beatle Country* album in 1966.

The *String Band Project* gathered together players from further afield, enlisting Peter Siegel and Dave Grisman from The Even Dozen Jug Band, Peter Rowan, who plays mandolin on the album with The Mother Bay State Entertainers and who, with Grisman, would later record as Earth Opera, and The Dry City Scat Band, which included Richard Greene on fiddle and mandolin and David Lindley on banjo and fiddle. The album had one of Elektra's finest early jackets, with an illustration by Bob Pepper, who later created the *Forever Changes* jacket art.

Surprisingly, the *Singer Songwriter Project* was the weakest of the series. It featured Richard Fariña and Patrick Sky, both signed to Vanguard, David Cohen, soon to re-emerge under the name David Blue, and the young Canadian singer Bruce Murdoch, whom many thought would make a lasting impact. "Bruce was underage and without relatives in the United States," Richie Havens wrote in his autobiography. "He had outstayed his visa and could not get an extension. Suddenly, he lost all the momentum he had built up, went back to Canada, and was so disappointed that he stopped singing and writing."[6] The four gently touching songs on *Singer Songwriter Project* were all that Murdoch recorded during his sojourn in Greenwich Village.

An almost natural outgrowth of the scene in New York City and Cambridge and on the West Coast was the formation of a number of jug bands. The first, and best, was The Jim Kweskin Jug Band, drawn from the Club 47 nexus of musicians – Fritz Richmond, Geoff Muldaur, Bill Keith, Mel Lyman – and inspired by a popular form of music from the South in the 20s and 30s that reached its apogee in Memphis, headed by Gus Cannon's Jug Stompers and the Memphis Jug Band. The appeal of the Kweskin band was its loose instrumentation using a lot of homemade instruments.

For Holzman, The Even Dozen Jug Band almost became another Project album. "That record did the same thing as the Projects: it gathered people from different musical disciplines and put them in a group context. Jug bands were real; they didn't feel like a confection to me, because the musicians came together organically, and there weren't that many opportunities to play together outside of the bluegrass bands. I think it strengthened folk music, although not a lot was recorded. Kweskin did three albums for Vanguard, and his was the grandfather jug band of it all. There was also Dave Van Ronk's Hudson Dusters, and we had the Even Dozens."

True to their name, The Even Dozen Jug Band were 12 in number and boasted a remarkable array of talent in the making. Among the line-up was Joshua Rifkin, who during a ten-year association with Elektra worked on arrangements for Judy Collins and edged his way onto the Nonesuch Records team. Today, he is one of America's most renowned musicologists and conductors.

The Even Dozens would become more famous individually than collectively, as Rifkin explains as he introduces them. "John Sebastian, credited as John Benson, played harmonica and went on to form The Lovin' Spoonful. Steve Katz became a member of Blood Sweat & Tears. Dave Grisman is well known as a mandolin player. Stefan Grossman had an interesting career, mainly in Europe. Peter Siegel became a producer at Elektra, specialising in world music. And we had a singer named Maria D'Amato who later achieved fame as Maria Muldaur."

John Sebastian says the Even Dozens didn't form for fun. "The real impetus was Paul Rothchild, who was interested in producing a jug band if we could get it together. Eventually, we lost Maria to the Kweskin band, who were in fact much better, so there wasn't much to keep us going."

Peter Siegel remembers it differently, but adds, "If you ask anyone in that group, they'll tell you they were the driving force. My version is that

Stefan Grossman and I were the driving force. There was a suggestion that The Even Dozen Jug Band, which already existed in that name, would record for the Spivey label; Stefan had been working with Victoria Spivey. Our manager was Izzy Young; Jac told Izzy he wanted to record us, and Izzy steered us toward Elektra."

Rifkin recalls that the sessions for their sole album, released on Elektra in 1964, were pretty chaotic. "As you would almost inevitably expect from any group of our age and size, there were surely some tensions, even if details now escape me. We were not, after all, a band that grew 'naturally' but were purpose-assembled, and we came from a sufficient variety of backgrounds to ensure something less than complete unanimity in everything, musical and otherwise." He recalls doing a lot of the work to shape the arrangements. "I even 'conducted' some of the bigger numbers. Paul oversaw everything, and, of course, did much to shape things himself. It was a complex collective process, and Paul was indeed masterful in creating order out of chaos."

"We were all excited and thought the record might be a big hit," says Siegel. "What did we know? We were young and we thought it might be a fad that would take off which was something Jac felt. There was some division within the band because everybody was of college age, and whereas I wanted to go on tour, other members didn't want to quit school. We made that one album, played a few gigs and then people went their separate ways."

It was a shortlived affair, with sheer numbers on stage also preventing them from touring, because costs would have been prohibitive. As Sebastian recalls, "The first two shows we did were New York Town Hall and Carnegie Hall. My father, who was a classical musician, howled with laughter at this, but there was an enthusiasm within the group that was really supportive, so you never felt too exposed."

"The Even Dozen Jug Band was like a soup base," says Holzman. "Sometimes you toss in a different ingredient. These were young and serious musicians, but not taking themselves too seriously, and every one of them went on to do something bigger."

Compared to the organised chaos of the Even Dozens, Tom Rush was the consummate stylist. As Rush explains, his repertoire was more expansive than most. "I came out of the Cambridge scene, which was more purist than it was in New York. I was more omnivorous than many of my contemporaries. Most folkies on the Cambridge scene homed in on Woody Guthrie, Delta blues, and the Carter Family. My taste was broader than that, which did lead sometimes to a kind of artistic schizophrenia."

Holzman was particularly enthralled by Rush. "He had a style, a compelling voice, a relaxed feeling about him, and he could play his ass off. He was the best of those stylists. He could source good material and play the shit out of it. Just listen to his skilful amalgam of several Bukka White songs, 'The Panama Limited', on his Elektra debut, *Tom Rush*. He's one of the most entertaining performers you'd want to see, even to this day. He was a gifted interpreter of great songs, yet in his early days he was not confident enough of his own writing skills."

Making the transition from Prestige to Elektra was not without its complications for Rush. "I wanted to go with Paul, so I went to Prestige with a compromise deal." Rothchild was working with Prestige at this stage. "I told them I'd give them one more album, and if they didn't like it I was willing to quit showbiz, I didn't really care. Actually, I was bluffing, but I didn't really want the aggravation. Prestige said OK, probably because I wasn't very high on their list of priorities and they didn't want to invest a lot of legal time in me."

He added one last proviso: that Paul Rothchild should produce his last album with the label. "They didn't like that a bit, because Paul had walked out on them. But they eventually agreed, and I went to Jac to explain what I wanted, and he was fine with it. So we recorded that second album for Prestige, me and Paul, with Fritz Richmond playing bass. We delivered the master to them, and then headed back into the studio the very next week to record the first album for Elektra. The Elektra record actually got into the stores first, within 30 days of the session."

Tom Rush's eponymous debut appeared in 1965, and it even pleased Paul Nelson of the *Little Sandy Review*. "I don't think I've yet heard a city singer so completely at home in the entire depth and breadth of American folk music," Nelson wrote.

Rush had to dig deeper when he came to record his second Elektra LP, *Take A Little Walk With Me*, released in 1966. After making albums back-to-back, he'd used up much of his repertoire. Side one rested on familiar ground, containing a couple of performances that epitomise his class: the way he lives every nuance of Eric von Schmidt's 'Joshua Gone Barbados', for example, or his yearning reading of the traditional blues 'Galveston Flood'. Side two featured Al Kooper leading a full electric band through a set of Chuck Berry, Bo Diddley, and Buddy Holly songs.

As Rush explains, it was a case of needs must. "I'd kind of run out of traditional stuff that excited me. I couldn't come up with an album's worth of tunes, so I embarked on a more schizophrenic project. I turned to the music that had excited me in my teens, like The Everly Brothers, Fats Domino, Chuck Berry, all these incredibly charismatic and energetic artists who were nothing like one another. Rock'n'roll was the first music that moved me, so I decided I'd pay tribute to it." Despite the fact that he used many of the same players as Dylan, he denies he was following that path. "I was just looking for songs I liked and knew. I needed to make an album and the clock was ticking."

Tom Rush provided a bridge between folk and the singer-songwriters of the 70s with his final Elektra album, *The Circle Game*, released in 1968, where he showed himself to be a thoughtful, immaculate interpreter of material by others, whether drawing from the past or from contemporary song.

Elektra had its share of troubled artists, and artists who were trouble – including Phil Ochs, Tim Buckley, and Delaney Bramlett. But Fred Neil ruffled the most feathers. These days, Neil is revered, although in Holzman's eyes, while "he is certainly highly regarded today, it isn't for his humanity".

Paul Rothchild produced both of Neil's albums for Elektra, one of which paired him with Vince Martin. The other is the classic *Bleecker & MacDougal*. Rothchild clearly didn't enjoy the experience. "For my sins, I had to produce him. He was a brilliant songwriter and a total scumbag. The forerunner of the unreliable performer; the original rock flake. We'd book recording sessions and he'd show up or not show up."[7]

Cyrus Faryar, once a member of The Modern Folk Quartet, played on a number of sessions with Neil. He explains why Neil wasn't easy to work with. "I think Freddie was as much of a mystery to himself as he was to others. He is hard to describe. Everyone you spoke to about him would give you a different perspective, a different facet. Freddie could and would have been a hard person to do business with. When you recorded with him he never played anything the same way twice, because he couldn't remember what he had played on the prior take. A producer would say, 'Take two' – and he'd ask, 'What happened?'"

For all his distaste, Rothchild still brought out the best in Fred Neil. John Sebastian, who with Felix Pappalardi played on the sessions for both Neil's Elektra albums, talks of how they would "babysit" Neil, pushing him to do another take or maybe come up with another verse. Sebastian also sat in with Rothchild when he edited the recordings, sometimes splicing the best takes together.

On their first session together, for the Vince Martin and Fred Neil collaboration *Tear Down The Walls*, Sebastian says that Martin was the driving force. "Fred was very lazy, and it took Vince to break him out of that. I took over that role. But even more, Felix Pappalardi would be the one to push Fred. He would nail Freddie down, to make sure he would finish the job. Freddie had such a fine talent but he only seemed to record under duress." The ever-reasonable Tom Rush could see both sides. "Fred was a pretty intense guy who didn't like to feel cornered or be told what to do. So I can only think that Paul was trying to 'produce' Fred too much, and that Fred might have seemed difficult to Paul."[8]

Herb Cohen knew Neil better than most, as his longest-serving manager, seeing him through his association with Elektra and then Capitol. Cohen's view is that Neil had no work ethic. "His work ethic was not to work. He hated everything to do with performing, recording, writing songs – everything he was so good at. And yet his whole persona was based on music and performing. He was a nice guy, and he could be aloof with people he didn't know. But we had a lot of fun. He got on best with other musicians, but to work with Fred, you'd have to fit yourself around him. He got stoned a lot but it didn't affect his singing – the voice was always magnificent. Listen to his version of 'The Water Is Wide'. Nobody gets that low. He was brilliant."

Cohen stressed how influential Neil was. "Every folk musician in New York, if they heard that Fred Neil was going to do a set at the Night Owl or Café Wha?, they'd come running, because he didn't perform that often. To hear him singing was amazing. Of course he was impossible to produce, but he was so good that you couldn't help trying to get him to do something, just because you wanted to see it done.

"The biggest song he ever wrote and recorded was 'Everybody's Talkin'', done in one take," Cohen continued. "The song was written in five minutes, in the toilet, because I wouldn't let him out of the studio. He had recorded nine songs [for his 1966 Capitol debut, *Fred Neil*] and we really needed one more. But Fred said that he didn't have any more, that he just wanted to leave. I said I had his bags in the car, but we needed one more song. He went to the toilet, got loaded, and about five minutes later came back and said: I'm just going to do this once. That's it – he sang the song one time, and we took him to the airport. About three years later, Nilsson recorded it, and Fred made enough money on that one song alone to retire."

Fred Neil was born in Ohio in 1936. Before he arrived in Greenwich Village, in 1960, he had released a handful of singles in a rockabilly pop style, and his songs had been covered by Roy Orbison and Buddy Holly. He played sessions for Paul Anka and Bobby Darin and was eking out a living as a Brill Building staff writer. Herb Cohen: "He wrote a lot of stuff that you'll never know he wrote, because he never put his name on it – he would write something, sell it for $50, and leave."

Once in the Village, Neil hung out as much with jazz musicians as early folkies like Hoyt Axton, Bob Gibson, Dino Valente, and Len Chandler. He befriended Lenny Bruce and often opened for him. Neil quickly developed a style and a presence all his own, taking the authenticity of the great forefathers of folk music and assimilating it – from Josh White, Leadbelly, and Lonnie Johnson to Ray Charles. It was one of his crowd, Dino Valente, who introduced Neil to Vince Martin.

Martin was a perfect foil to the deep-voiced Fred Neil. Their voices and 12-string guitars combined to create a brand of pop folk that brings to mind Gibson & Camp's *Live At The Gate Of Horn*. Neil deeply admired Gibson, whom he thanks for assistance on *Bleecker & MacDougal* and who helped mix Neil's last official release, *Other Side Of This Life*, in 1971. Martin & Neil made just one album together for Elektra, *Tear Down The Walls*, heavy on covers and traditional material but spiced by such Neil originals as 'Wild Child In A World Of Trouble'.

John Sebastian says that what made the duo so special was their link to commercial folk music. "When you put two singers and two guitarists together, it will sound like folk music – but they also had a pop connection. Vince was really well known because of 'Cindy Oh Cindy', a big hit record.

And Fred had a wildly diverse background: he was in a gospel group, we know now he was hanging out with Buddy Holly and Roy Orbison back in Texas, and his father was a jukebox distributor in the South."

They were scheduled to record a live album at the Bitter End, but Neil broke a string, walked off stage, and vanished. Vince Martin didn't record again for Elektra, or too many other labels. He later led the exodus of New York folk graduates to Florida, where Neil eventually followed. Neil's next recording was his own *Bleeker & MacDougal* album, an undisputed classic. It's an album of absolutely classic songs and performances from one of folk's most important and individual voices. It's intense, deeply personal, introspective, bluesy, and melodic.

The album includes Neil's own version of 'Candy Man', which had been the B-side to Roy Orbison's 'Crying' single in 1961, 'Other Side To This Life', which would be covered by The Lovin' Spoonful, The Youngbloods, and Jefferson Airplane, and the breathtakingly resonant 'Little Bit Of Rain', which deserves to be as well known as his later songs 'The Dolphins' or 'Everybody's Talkin''. With 'Blues On The Ceiling', Holzman has said "you could almost forgive him his irresponsibility as a human being".[9] The album stretches the bounds of folk or folk-blues as Neil fuses blues, pop, folk, gospel, and jazz, and all blessed with that voice which Odetta once said "no microphone can possibly capture. [Fred's] voice is a healing instrument".[10]

Judy Henske knew him well. "I was a fan of Fred Neil," she says, "and, most of all, of his voice. He was a wonderful singer and had a thrilling way of going way down to a note and bouncing off it. I can't think of anybody else who could do that in that way, except maybe Merle Haggard. He was a great writer, too, but he was a beautiful singer – matchless, peerless. He was also very bashful, and he was very withdrawn, and he was, of course, a heroin addict.

"One time Herb Cohen asked me if I could talk him round from calling somebody to get a fix. It was at Herb's house, and I was on speed. So I was sitting there, speeding away, and I spent about six hours talking non-stop, telling Fred what a great artist he was, and about the evils of heroin, and how the drugs were going to rob him of what was most special about him, how they made him depressed and fragile, and on and on and on and on, until eventually I ran down, and I finally stopped talking. Throughout this time, Fred had not said a word – I mean, not one single word. There was silence. Then he looked up at me, and said, 'But do you know anyone you could *call*?'"[11]

Neil's drug addiction didn't make him any easier to work with. Holzman clearly subscribes to this view. "Fred Neil was an artist's artist," he says. "He wrote very well, and he was possessed with a wonderful voice, but he was a pain to deal with. He tried to bully people though his manager, Herbie Cohen. Other artists envied him that natural voice, and because he didn't play much it always became an event to see him when he did. But he was lazy and he didn't put out a great body of work – in quality, yes, but he recorded very little. We cut him loose after *Bleecker & MacDougal*."

Fred Neil recorded little after leaving Elektra, and *Bleecker & MacDougal* is only rivalled by his first Capitol album, produced by Nik Venet, who captured a different sound, almost a smoky, jazz, late-night cocktail feeling. Venet revealed a more contemplative side on *Fred Neil*, much more laidback than the *Bleecker* album and one of the definitive recordings of the classic Greenwich Village era. Its jacket measures up to the record: just Neil, guitar case in hand, brilliantly photographed by Mort Schuman on the chilly streets of New York City and every bit as iconic as Dylan's *Freewheelin'* jacket.

John Sebastian tries to explain Neil's allure. "He was pretty much the wellspring, as far as Greenwich Village goes, in the beginning – it was between him and Timmy Hardin. He was mercurial, he was difficult, he was what astrological types would call very Piscean. Whenever an obstacle approached, he'd swim around it. If the obstacle hit, Freddie would be long gone. He was beyond anything we could understand. He had such specific musical skills, an unbelievable voice, and a rhythmic guitar style based on everything he had learned in rock'n'roll – but combined with jazz, bossa nova styles. He could hear music in anything, in street noises, the humming of an elevator, and he brought all this into his music."

Fred Neil influenced so many: Gram Parsons, Stephen Stills, Paul Kantner, Tim Buckley, David Crosby. It's been said that Crosby Stills & Nash considered calling themselves The Sons Of Neil, although Stills doesn't entirely confirm this.

"Fred was my original mentor in New York when I was trying to establish myself on the folk scene in the mid 60s," says Stills. "He ended up hating that scene, so he moved to Coconut Grove and Key West in Florida – as far away as possible from Greenwich Village. I only have fond memories of him. I love that guy: he was a very funny man, really amusing. And what a great friggin' singer. It took me, literally, years to understand his delivery – that lower voice phrasing he had. Remarkable. I was 40 before I really got it. Do people say we were originally called The Sons Of Fred Neil? That I don't recall. But it's possible, because he was such a huge influence."[12]

David Crosby is of the same mind as Stills. "Freddie taught me a lot. He was an amazing folk singer, probably one of the best voices any of us ever had. He was crazy and self destructive, but, oh man, could he sing. He was an amazingly talented guy who didn't fit the commercial world at all. The more commercial the world became, the more Freddie would disappear. Until he completely disappeared."[13]

When Fred Neil died in July 2001, the first line of most obituaries remembered him as the author of 'Everybody's Talkin'', the theme to *Midnight Cowboy.* "As a result," said Herb Cohen, "he never wrote anything again, because he didn't have to. It was good for him, but not for the rest of the world. We all lost something."

CHAPTER 14

Quality Recordings At The Price Of A Quality Paperback

> "*In 1963, pop culture had no real standing. Classical and jazz had kudos and were venerated. My decision to move in a more pop direction with Elektra presented an opportunity to rapidly develop a very different repertoire. So the concept for Nonesuch was quite simple: the music was proven and attractive to a college audience, the notes were musically authoritative and not pompous, and the jackets reflected a down-to-earth whimsy that said: these are not elitist records.*" **JAC HOLZMAN**

Jac Holzman's love of technology is something that can never be underestimated in the way he shaped Elektra Records. It manifested itself from the very beginning, when he made it clear that he was committed to making records with the best possible sound quality. His fondness for baroque and classical music was, by contrast, reflected nowhere in Elektra's output during the 50s.

He had shied away from classical recordings in the beginning because he knew each title could always be surpassed by another, better interpretation. It was an area where the major labels excelled, along with some independents such as Vanguard and Westminster, but at a significantly higher price than pop music. By 1963, Holzman was able to pursue his aptitude for technology and his classical leanings in ways that left an indelible mark on Elektra, as well as yielding a level of income that ensured the stability of his record company. It provided significant funds to carry Elektra forward in new directions.

Holzman began work on what became the *Authentic Sound Effects* series in 1961, and it provided the ultimate cash injection for Elektra. It also epitomised Holzman's foresight. Few would have understood the potential, let alone the need for these records to be made with such precision and expertise. Why sound effects? Holzman knew why, although even he was surprised at just how well they sold.

"During that time in the early 60s, when I couldn't find enough music I respected sufficiently to record, I had an idea," he recalls. "I was watching TV one night and fastened on to sound effects. I thought, has anyone ever created a library of stereo sound effects? And the answer was no. This led to my commitment to record an entire series containing a broad selection for a basic library."

Holzman hired a young engineer, Mike Scott, who did most of the recordings around New York City, and together they figured out how to produce and record them. For the complicated effects, such as a car crash, they spent more time and money. That recording alone was so effective that it was frequently licensed for films and television shows.

"For two weeks I spent my evenings watching dramatic TV, writing down every effect and prioritising them," says Holzman. "I had seen listings of sound effects in audio journals, which gave me a sense of how the effects should be organised. I listed about 500 sounds to start with, from door buzzers and railroad crossing bells to heartbeats, whip cracks, avalanches, and buildings being demolished. I wanted to have the entire series recorded before we released the first volume. The effects were not done randomly and were spread over quite a long period. We were doing this between other projects."

The series was immediately successfully. By 1964, Elektra had released a collection of 13 albums, the first stereo sound effects in high fidelity and the first commercially available encyclopaedic library. In time, Elektra sold nearly a million copies – and did not have to pay mechanical or artist royalties. Costs were limited to pressing the discs and printing the jackets. That left $1.40 per record going straight into the bank.

The series was intended to be the very best of its kind. "We kept the jackets very simple," says Holzman, "just saying what they were – no fancy distracting graphics. Those were the guidelines I gave to designer Bill Harvey, to keep it very professional." Holzman came up with new special features. "With some, we provided a special ruler, which went on to the turntable's centre spindle and guided you to the track you needed. We had additional features that had never been done before. This wasn't me being fussy: it had to be precise, because some sound effects were quieter or louder, and the problem was how to capture the essence of the sound without distortion. We had strict rules regarding the transfer to disc. One person was selected to do this because they were experienced in getting high levels on to the disc while maintaining sufficient 'land' between the grooves to make track selection easy."

Elektra released three *Authentic Sound Effects* albums initially, to show they were serious about the project, after which they issued them every two months. Once they had a basic series of ten, they marketed them all over again as boxed sets in slipcases. At first the series was pitched to the public, but soon it reached rabid professionals. The whole thing was carefully planned. "This wasn't a novelty release," says Holzman. "We took small ads in the *Journal Of The Audio Engineering Society* that gave them an aura of professional distinction. And they were inexpensive: $5 each, and we sold the basic package of ten for $50. They became real must-have items for audio fans."

Each one of the *Authentic Sound Effects* series declared, "Ideal for theatre groups, home-movie enthusiasts, radio and TV stations, slide shows, industrial presentations, parties, sound buffs, and many others." They were indeed a licence to print money and became the backbone of Elektra's financial stability during the label's singer-songwriter and blues-interpreter period. What for some might have been a throwaway idea became a testament to Holzman's attention to sonic fidelity and his marketing savvy.

Some of the individual sound effects were featured on Elektra's own recordings: the champagne-cork pop at the start of Love's 'Que Vida'; the thunderstorm on The Doors' 'Riders On The Storm'; or the atomic-bomb conclusion of Love's 'Seven And Seven Is'.

The success of *Authentic Sound Effects* encouraged Holzman to develop another idea, which had been marinating for a few years. "I had been producing records long enough now to trust my own judgement, even if it seemed wacky to others," he says. "The sound effects had certainly been spectacularly correct. I saw that series as a way to fund Nonesuch, although Nonesuch never needed money. We had $25,000 invested, but after the first six weeks waiting to see how Nonesuch would be received, multiple re-orders poured in. They were selling in boxes of 25 – unheard-of in classical music. We were on to something new."

Nonesuch was officially launched on February 14 1964, releasing its first ten records – with a simple ad campaign in the monthly *Schwann Long Playing Record Catalog* and *High Fidelity* magazine. The copy read, "Quality Recordings (not Records) At The Price Of A Quality Paperback." In Nonesuch's first year, sixty titles were issued, selling almost a million units and netting over half a million dollars. Those initial records included *The Baroque Trumpet*, Albinoni's *Adagio For Strings & Organ*, Bach Cantatas, and *Masterpieces Of The Early French & Italian Renaissance*.

Holzman says it was one of the rare instances in the record business where success in classical music was so great that it could underwrite popular music. As Keith Holzman, Jac's younger brother, who now worked at Elektra, wryly observed, "Nonesuch was the tail wagging the Elektra dog."

Holzman began to focus on Nonesuch in November 1963 and had the label up and running within three months. "But the seed of the idea was once again born from personal experience while I was attending college at St John's. I remembered trying to decide which of two Westminster records I would buy. The Westminster label recorded classical titles with care and that matched my taste in music, but their albums were $5.98 each, and I would drive myself nuts choosing."

The key to Nonesuch came when he was sitting in a restaurant opposite Carnegie Hall, waiting for his distributor, Harry Lew, who was running late. Holzman began to reflect on his school years and that choice he had been forced to make. "I wondered if I could devise a series so you could afford to buy both. That was the wow factor. When I explained the idea to Harry, he told me I was crazy to go up against the major labels and Vanguard. I knew the majors had the catalogue, but I didn't think they had the will to adopt my pricing. At $2.50 each, there was sufficient margin to give retailers an incentive, with an extra ten percent for themselves. Then I thought about the packaging, and then about where the music was going to come from."

Holzman's plan was to license existing albums from small European labels and repackage them for his targeted American audience, commissioning artfully enticing jackets. And he had a ready-made list, compiled in three loose-leaf books where he'd clipped reviews of many of the baroque records issued in Europe, divided into label, genre of music, and country (mostly France, Germany, the UK, and Scandinavia). "I had no idea why I was keeping this information," he says, "until the Nonesuch concept became real for me."

His approach was contrary to the way the major labels worked. "Classical music was rarely profitable for them, so they would need to defend the high price they charged. One thing I'd learned in the music business is that old habits and practices die hard. Their recordings were pointed toward an audience who could afford $4.98 or $5.98 a record. I thought that if you made them to sell at half that price, you might sell twice as many. And you would be able to experiment with repertoire, so the music fan could, in turn, afford to take a chance on your experimentation. Entrepreneurship begins with a passion, and you learn to adopt the process to fit the task. Nonesuch was a passion-driven enterprise with logic underpinning it. Passion always wins over process if you do it with rigour."

Holzman knew that those who produced classical recordings thought that they appealed to people who went to classical concerts. "My reading," he says, "was that you were surrounded by music at all times, and music was easily integrated into people's lives. You just have to draw them in. Take a look at the covers. We gave them all a common frame, although we changed the colours. But we printed the logo very, very large – big up front, and big at the back. It was instant recognition. Bill Harvey and I fought all the time about everything, yet frequently I'd walk in and just say wow! He had it so right."

Many of the Nonesuch jackets are now collectable. Harvey had drawn from his Madison Avenue ad-agency experience to devise a fresh and appealing look. "My main idea was to get a multi-range of illustration styles," he says, "but to keep it within a single format that would stamp Nonesuch as Nonesuch. And it really worked."[1]

One doubter was Holzman's friend and rival, Vanguard's Maynard Solomon. He couldn't believe that anyone would try such a crazy stunt, especially a folkie like Holzman. He tried to convince Holzman that he was in over his head. Yet, within nine months, reports were coming in from the field that Nonesuch was a winner, as other labels began releasing similar low-priced classical lines, including Vanguard's Everyman series. They were all scrambling to catch up.

Nonesuch was shooting for a very particular audience at the beginning, but had managed to bring a new audience along, too. It confirmed Holzman's belief that the audiences for both Elektra and Nonesuch were similar. He personally guided the label through its first year, with Joshua Rifkin and Ed Tatnall Canby as primary consultants, but by late 1965 he needed someone to take over the daily management. Tracey Sterne had recently left Vanguard, and she was soon given substantial autonomy at Nonesuch. She brought a formidable range of contacts to Nonesuch, including musicians, music publications, reviewers, and university music departments. Once Sterne was established, she was putting out 40 to 50 albums a year, freeing Holzman to concentrate on Elektra once again.

"In the first year of Nonesuch I did everything," says Holzman. "I made all the selections, typed the label copy, and worked with Bill on the jacket concepts. Josh Rifkin was my on-hand musicologist and I asked Ed Canby to write the notes. Once I had Tracey Sterne join us, she proved to be invaluable. When I hired her, she said she didn't know anything about running a label, and I said don't worry, I'll teach you. She was wonderful. She was a terrific magnet for musicians, and I had wanted to broaden the catalogue, which she facilitated. She amplified my ability – she had tastes I didn't have. We would sit down for an hour or two every week and Tracey would present the new projects she was considering. We'd discuss the budgets and talk about the core idea, the raison d'etre of each project. At the end of the meeting, we'd give each other a hug. I never said no to her."

Brooklyn-born Tracey Sterne, a child prodigy, continued her career as a concert pianist before shifting focus to the production side of classical music, first as a publicity assistant with impresario Sol Hurok, then with Columbia Records, before landing at Vanguard.

Rifkin had come to Nonesuch by an unlikely route: as the kazoo-player of The Even Dozen Jug Band. Their recording had taken place in the summer of 1963, between Rifkin completing Juilliard, as a composition major, and starting at New York University. Nonesuch used his wider abilities and expertise to the full. "Before long, I was overseeing most of the printed copy on Nonesuch," says Rifkin. "I edited people's notes, I wrote notes, I did the research on the titling, I helped work out details on the covers. It was at

Nonesuch that I learnt my musicology, my music history, and where I learnt to write well. So there I was, at 21, helping to run a record company."

Everyone was excited about the new musical impulses coming at them, says Rifkin. "I still recall Mark Abramson and Paul Rothchild bringing in the earliest Frank Zappa albums and all of us joining together in the small editing studio to hear Dylan's first electric discs. We sampled the new Elektra artists: the first edits of Love and the earliest Doors recordings, which I didn't care for half so much as I liked Love. Everybody was young, too. I was a baby barely over 20, but my elders either hadn't reached 30 or were not far past it themselves. It was fun, and fun brought success."

In Nonesuch's second year, the Explorer series was launched, initially by deleting all the flamenco, Japanese, Indian, and African music from the Elektra catalogue and switching it to Nonesuch with new jackets, a little re-editing, better mastering, and at half the price. Holzman knew there was an overlap. "I could transfer *Art Of The Koto* or Saka Acquaye or *Music Of Bulgaria* to Nonesuch, records that would have been lost in the rapidly evolving new Elektra catalogue."

The Explorer International Series is where Tracey Sterne's talents really flowered as she set out to enrich and expand the label with newly commissioned titles produced in-house. She had substantial help from Peter Siegel, who had joined Elektra as a producer the same day that she started. Siegel turned out 15 to 20 albums over the next few years for Nonesuch and also produced albums for Elektra – including Pat Kilroy's *Light Of Day,* a bold, early venture into psychedelic folk, Tom Paxton's *Morning Again,* the unreleased Stalk-Forrest Group (later to become Blue Öyster Cult), and records by Oliver Smith, Paul Siebel, and David Peel, among others.

Stefan Grossman was the conduit to the Pat Kilroy album being recorded. He recalls first meeting Kilroy in Berkeley in the summer of 1963. "He was singing Jimmy Reed tunes, including 'Big Boss Man' as well as Child Ballads and some pop tunes like 'Garden Of Eden' [a one-off pop hit for Joe Valino in 1957]. I was impressed with his vocal intensity whether he was singing blues, ballads, or the telephone book." Two years later, Kilroy and flautist Susan Graubard arrived in New York. "They stayed at my place on East 8th Street between A and B Avenues before heading to Europe, and I introduced him to Peter Siegel, who was very impressed with Pat's singing, particularly the blues material."

On returning from Europe, Kilroy had come up with a batch of new songs he wanted to record inspired by a glockenspiel he'd picked up in London. "Peter wasn't impressed by Pat's original tunes although they were still recorded but it was a case of give and take in the end. It wasn't the acoustic blues album Peter had envisioned. He asked me, Marc Silber [bass], and Eric Kaz to do a blues oriented session with Pat, which included 'Mississippi Blues' and 'Canned Heat'; we didn't play on the other songs, which used Susan playing flute and the glockenspiel and tabla player Bob Amacker."

A disagreement over recording 'Garden Of Eden' only increased the tension between Kilroy and Siegel, who feels that the mix of the blues material with Kilroy's more experimental songs failed to hang together meaningfully. *Light Of Day* is now seen as something of a milestone, as an early foray into Eastern music or 'acid folk', as it's termed today – an album to be applauded for its intent rather than its uneven results. "Sometimes those off-the-wall ideas work," says Holzman. "Pat Kilroy was heading in a direction that, to some extent, I would say Tim Buckley perfected. Pat Kilroy prepared me for Tim Buckley; he had a good voice, but he didn't have the voice that Tim Buckley had."

Another band Siegel produced was Earth Opera, whose two albums, *Earth Opera* and *The Great American Eagle Tragedy*, were ultimately too self-conscious and unclassifiable to succeed commercially. "But when the Red Sox were actually winning the World Series in 2004," says Holzman, "the single 'The Red Sox Are Winning', taken from Earth Opera's debut album, was played all over Boston radio. Nobody knew who the hell Earth Opera was, though."

It was Siegel who made another pilgrimage to record Joseph Spence on his home turf in the summer of 1965. The two had first met when Spence played a handful of shows in New York City soon after the release of his Elektra album *Happy All The Time*. Spence invited him back to the Bahamas, where Siegel (who travelled there with fellow old-time music enthusiast Jody Stecher) was able to record Spence's extended family, including the Pinders. On Siegel's return, he took the tapes to Moe Asch, with whom they sat gathering dust, until Siegel, now working for Elektra, retrieved them for the first of two breathtaking volumes, released as *The Real Bahamas* on Nonesuch Explorer. When Brian Wilson heard the harmonies of the Pinder family, he fashioned his own Bahamian hymn, 'He Come Down', which appeared on the Beach Boys album *Carl & The Passions.*

During Sterne's tenure, Nonesuch began the most ambitious series of world music recordings in the commercial music business, rising to more than 100 releases in the Explorer Series, including those made under the supervision of her successors, Keith Holzman and Bob Hurwitz. The records presented indigenous music from around the world. Among the very first and most successful were remarkable field recordings captured by the inveterate traveller-musicologist David Lewiston and produced for disc by Peter Siegel.

This was world music at its purest and most engaging, with much of it, like the Lewiston-recorded Balinese sounds on *Music From The Morning Of The World* and *Golden Rain*, hitherto unheard in the West. Lewiston made the connection to Nonesuch simply by looking in the racks of a Sam Goody record store on his return to New York City from his Balinese field trip. He wrote a pitch letter, simply addressed to Nonesuch and, dutifully, heard back. When Peter Siegel listened to the tapes he came rushing out of the studio moments later, saying, "Hey, this you've got to hear!"

Tracey Sterne did the same thing when she heard Lewiston's Indonesian recordings, calling out to Holzman over the intercom to come and hear this remarkable music. "I agreed that we had to have *Music From The Morning Of The World*," says Holzman. "We made the deal on the spot, and David did nothing but make these kinds of records for us. He would receive commissions for over a dozen projects and had the comfort of knowing that everything he recorded would be released … even if we didn't understand *Monkey Music* – which sold well too. I was delighted and honoured to work with and support people like David. He had ears I didn't possess. Once you hear and understand something far from your experience, you fill in between the furthest point out from your angle of acceptance and your normal angle of acceptance. You expand, you exercise, you stretch. It's like Pilates for the ears."

Nonesuch Explorer would achieve immortality though the inclusion of one of its recordings on the Voyager Golden Record launched into space aboard the Voyager spacecraft in 1977 by President Jimmy Carter. It represented "a present from a small, distant world, a token of our sounds, our science, our images, our music, our thoughts, and our feelings." Preserved on the gold-plated phonograph record is a track from a 1969 Nonesuch recording, *A Bell Ringing In The Empty Sky*, performed on shakuhachi (notched flute) by Goro Yamaguchi. The record nests in a protective container which, if Voyager One can survive meteors, black holes, and a host of other threats, is expected to last over a billion years. For Holzman, the interstellar disc is a tip of the hat to the excellence of the Nonesuch Explorer series and the people who caused it to happen. "The music deserved to be recorded," he says, "and the homogenisation of cultures would leach and intermix and create a new gumbo of music devoid of its local singularity. Nonesuch Explorer became the Folkways for another generation, people wishing to sonically immerse themselves in music discovery."

Given Nonesuch's penchant for embracing new directions, Joshua Rifkin suggested that the label should record Scott Joplin. Everyone went for the idea. Rifkin: "We did with the Joplin record what we did with every Nonesuch record, which was to put it in the stores and see what happens. Within a few weeks, we began to sense that something was afoot. Journalists started writing about it and radio stations played it."

Nonesuch's revival of Joplin and ragtime piano came straight from Rifkin's own piano recordings and inspired Marvin Hamlisch's Academy Award-winning score for *The Sting.* Nonesuch's musically authentic 1970 and 1972 volumes – both called *Piano Rags* and later repackaged as a double album – and Rifkin's third in the series, issued in September 1974, put Nonesuch on the *Billboard* album charts.

Holzman wanted to look even further into Nonesuch's future. "I knew once we had stabilised, with our firm roots in baroque music, we could move towards contemporary music. We could bring our audience with us, because we were never directing this to a musical aristocracy. We could do world music and electronic music, if the guiding principles for the making of each album remained the same: appreciation for detail, sumptuous sound, a proper tonality with the notes, and arresting covers. We could then issue anything we wanted except contemporary pop music – because we had Elektra for that."

Holzman says it was inevitable that Nonesuch began to record almost all its new releases. "That process began soon after Tracey Sterne joined us. The European licences would expire in just a few years, and we had already siphoned off the top level of repertoire that existed in Europe."

Sterne was officially the label's coordinator, but she preferred the title of editor. She continued to skim the best material from those European sources

Holzman had originally cultivated, but she began to build her own roster of artists, drawing talent from the contemporary classical and new-music circles of New York. Projects she developed at Nonesuch steadily won critical plaudits and even sold unexpectedly high numbers. Composer George Crumb's *Ancient Voices Of Children*, inspired by the poems of Federico García Lorca, sold more than 70,000 copies, an extraordinary achievement for a modern piece from an avant-garde source. Aside from Crumb, Sterne remained to the fore of contemporary classical music, with further commissions to Elliott Carter and William Bolcom.

* * *

Nonesuch was the first American label to address electronic music, putting together two of its most renowned pioneers. Bernie Krause remembers that it was Holzman who introduced him to Paul Beaver. "Paul had a place in LA," says Krause, "a one-storey redbrick warehouse, pretty funky, falling apart more with each earthquake. Inside he had the largest collection of Novachords, the first synthesizer, built by Hammond in the 30s."[2] Krause had been a banjo player in The Weavers, the final replacement for Pete Seeger, and was already exploring early prototypes of modular synthesizers, excited about the potential of the instrument and the medium of electronic music. He and Beaver bought a synthesizer but couldn't get anyone in Hollywood or any record companies interested in recording electronic music until Tracey Sterne gave them the opportunity for Nonesuch at the instigation of Holzman.

Krause: "Jac took the risk and offered us a contract to record *The Nonesuch Guide To Electronic Music* as two LPs and a detailed booklet. The album remained on the *Billboard* classical charts for 26 weeks, one of Nonesuch's bestselling packages of the time. It was the key to introducing the synthesizer into pop music and film, something that broke down all the walls in the music business. Jac's vision gave a voice in the world to a new musical instrument, in effect the first to be successfully introduced since the saxophone a century before."[3]

Originally issued as a double album in 1966, the *Guide* contained 68 short tracks over four LP sides. It was revolutionary because the pieces demonstrated each module of the synthesizer, without accompaniment, rather than deploying it as an atmospheric instrument to enhance other instruments, as would become the norm. Beaver and Krause became a highly visible team. They demonstrated their capabilities in their booth at the Monterey pop festival, turning on The Byrds, George Harrison, and Micky Dolenz of The Monkees to the synthesizer's possibilities. The duo eventually recorded in their own right, and their two best-remembered LPs were made for Warners: *In A Wild Sanctuary* in 1970 and, a year later, *Gandharva*, recorded live in San Francisco's Grace Cathedral. Their partnership ended with Paul Beaver's death in 1975.

Beaver made a telling contribution to Elektra's wonderful astrological concept album of 1967, *The Zodiac Cosmic Sounds*, arguably the first time the pioneering Moog keyboard synthesizer was used on a pop record. The 12 tracks were each inspired by the 12 astrological signs, smoothly narrated by Cyrus Faryar and with a soundtrack using sitars and exotic percussion, flutes, harpsichord, psychedelic guitar licks, and the Moog. It was a collaboration between composer and arranger Mort Garson, poet Jacques Wilson, and co-producer (with Holzman) Alex Hassilev, formerly with The Limeliters.

Canadian arranger Mort Garson, a graduate of the Juilliard School, began writing musical scores in the 1940s. During the 60s he worked for several popular singers, including Doris Day and Mel Torme, and co-wrote Ruby & The Romantics' hit 'Our Day Will Come' as well as arranging hits for The Lettermen and The Sandpipers. By the time he came to orchestrate *Zodiac Cosmic Sounds*, Garson (born in 1924) was already middle-aged. His passion for the Moog and astrology took him to extend Holzman's idea and compose an entire album of music for each zodiacal sign, as released by A&M Records. Garson continued to seize the moment and engaged in other off-the-wall projects all set to Moog music, including *The Wozard Of Iz*, produced by Bernie Krause, a socio-political satire built around the children's classic, narrated by Nancy Sinatra; *Electronic Hair Pieces*; *Lucifer – Black Mass*, *Music For Sensuous Lovers*, and *Plantasia*, an album of music to make plants grow faster. His first work for Elektra had been an orchestral mood music concept, *The Sea*, for which he adopted the name the Dusk 'Til Dawn Orchestra and recorded in London. It was only given a limited release after the project was upstaged by Warner Bros and another easy listening album also entitled *The Sea*, credited to Anita Kerr, Rod McKeuen, and The San Sebastian Strings.

"*Sea Drift* was an idea which somebody ripped off," says Holzman, "but I was committed to Mort Garson. At the time asking your star sign was supposed to be a failsafe pick up line and although it's a corny concept it worked on many levels not least because no-one had used electronic instruments like that before. Although people bought *Zodiac Cosmic Sounds* for the electronics as much as the concept, I knew we were on to something when we when we played it our distributors who were completely enwrapped because they were listening for their sign."

Zodiac Cosmic Sounds also benefited from an A-list team of LA session musicians such as Carol Kaye, Hal Blaine, Bud Shank, Mike Melvoin, and percussionist Emil Richards. It was tightly rehearsed but everyone had a ball, and the album turned out to be much more than just a Summer of Love period piece that drew on all things fashionably new age and mystical. It was perfectly contextualised by Abe Gurvin's vividly brilliant psychedelic sleeve art depicting each of the participants star signs; Holzman's was Virgo. The finishing touch was the instruction 'MUST BE PLAYED IN THE DARK.'

Delivering such lines as "nine times the colour red explodes like heated blood" and "incendiary diamonds scorch the earth" in an effortlessly smooth baritone voice, narrator Cyrus Faryar found it hard at times to keep a straight face. "Astrology was so pervasive at this time," he fondly recalls. "In everyday life you'd meet people and almost the next words out of their mouth after 'hello' were, 'What's your star sign?' There were some remarkable people involved in that project, such as Paul Beaver. That was one of the earliest uses of the Moog, and Alex had quite a time taping it. It may have been a frivolous idea but the execution of it was taken very seriously. We all had a grand time doing it."

In the wake of his success with *The Nonesuch Guide To Electronic Music*, Holzman next took a leaf from patrons of the arts from the 17th and 18th centuries. He commissioned an entirely new electronic music composition. "Recordings are the perfect medium for commissions of music that cannot easily be played live," he says. "You could give a commission to a composer, and he would create for the medium. That was a radical idea, since electronic music could not effectively be done live in the 60s and early 70s."

Holzman and Sterne approached Morton Subotnick to undertake the first ever piece to be created for the medium of home stereo. Subotnick was not only a gifted composer, he also helped design the Buchla touch-pad synthesizer on which the album was created. *Silver Apples Of The Moon* was the result. The record featured exotic timbres and dance-inspiring rhythms –

commonplace today but unusual then – and was a surprising entrant to the classical-music charts.

Elektra, including Nonesuch, merged with Atlantic and Warners in 1970 to form the Warner Music Group, after which Nonesuch continued unchanged in scope and direction and without interference. Holzman maintained his regular meetings with Tracey Sterne, who remained in charge after Holzman departed in 1973 to become Chief Technologist at Warner Communications. Leadership of Nonesuch has been remarkably stable: two people, Tracey Sterne and, since 1984, Bob Hurwitz have been at the helm. In the years between, from 1978 to 1984, Keith Holzman ran the company with great skill after Sterne left. When Bob Krasnow took over the chairmanship of Elektra Records in 1984, he brought in Hurwitz, then head of operations for ECM. Hurwitz in turn brought in David Bither, and the two have helped Nonesuch develop an impressive contemporary roster since the 90s, which has included Wilco, Emmylou Harris, Youssou N'Dour, Laurie Anderson, Ry Cooder, and Randy Newman. In 1997, Cooder put together an ensemble of unknown Havana musicians, which resulted in unexpected success for The Buena Vista Social Club and their hit Nonesuch album.

Nonesuch also continued its relationship with the leading contemporary musicians and composers Philip Glass, John Adams, Steve Reich, and Kronos Quartet, all of whom made their first recordings with the label over 20 years ago. Nonesuch today maintains the same artist-driven principles as did its original parent label, Elektra, and the same forward-thinking vision it has always had, inspired first by Jac Holzman and then Tracey Sterne.

In 2008, Nonesuch once again delved back into the Elektra catalogue, this time to re-release the *Baroque Beatles Book* album, first issued in 1965. It had originally been another out-of-the-box idea from Holzman, who realised that the influence of the Beatles songbook had become so widespread that it even spilled over into MOR and easy listening. It was in elevators; it was everywhere.

From this sprang the concept of baroque interpretations of Lennon & McCartney songs as a serious musical exploration, packaged with humour and an eye toward the Christmas season. On release, it received unprecedented radio play for an Elektra album and made Number 83 in the charts. Holzman was even granted permission to proceed by The Beatles themselves.

The album operated on a simple premise: to arrange Lennon &

McCartney melodies – nothing beyond 1965 – in the style of Handel, Bach, and Telemann. The liner notes and titles were knowing – 'Epstein Variations, MBE 69a' and 'Cantata For The Third Saturday After Shea Stadium' – but musically the album was both accomplished and inventive.

Joshua Rifkin "rediscovered and edited" the pieces. The now-famed conductor remembers, "We were absolutely crazy about The Beatles' music. Even if we had fun with it, it was fun in a way that took it seriously, giving it its due. And we weren't looking to do only their hits: we did do our share, but we were just looking to do the tunes that mattered most. I only recall positive reactions to the album from colleagues in the classical world – those of my age, at least, were all passionate Beatles fans themselves and were amused both by the project itself and by my success."

The Baroque Beatles Book could only have arisen through the confluence of Elektra and Nonesuch and the ability of Jac Holzman to think laterally. Rifkin pays tribute to his former boss's approach. "I don't think Jac ever tried to figure out 'where the market would go'. Indeed, those for whom this is the chief motivation usually fail to produce anything particularly good. In putting his finger on his own pulse, you might say, he was also putting his finger on the pulse of his time. Not many people have this gift."

Holzman lived for movies, watching them closely and taking lessons from what he saw. "In the film *Sergeant York*, the title character is played by Gary Cooper, a religious pacifist later decorated for his skill at killing. A flock of geese fly overhead and York instructs his fellow doughboys not to aim directly at them but to sight ahead of them. He explains that if you aimed at the geese you'd never hit one, because the bullet would pass behind them. Instead, aim ahead of them and the bullet and geese will meet. That scene stuck with me, and I applied that lesson to Elektra. Never aim for any point where the crowd is. Always aim for a place where no one else has yet arrived."

Remembering Elektra
Peter K. Siegel

"I knew Paul Rothchild's name through records I'd bought that he'd produced for the Prestige label, and he was introduced to me by Jac Holzman as the person who was going to produce The Even Dozen Jug Band. That was the first time I really observed what a record producer does. The A&R department at Elektra was made up of producer-engineers, and I used to hang around Elektra and talk to Paul Rothchild and Mark Abramson. Mark was just a little older and came out of a more classical engineering tradition, which often [meant] recording in concert halls rather than studios; I learned different things from each of them and a lot from them both.

There were other smaller labels where I could do work even with minimal, self-taught skills. So I was able to work for County Records;* I did remastering work for them, including the very first album they released, which was compiled from old 78s by Charlie Poole. I was also doing work for Alan Lomax, and for Folkways, where Ralph Rinzler would hire me to assist him in producing; I would do a little editing, clean things up, do the sequencing, and take the tapes to Moe Asch to get them mastered. Moe never cared about the sound; he only cared about the music.

One of the things I did just a few months before I went to work for Elektra while I was working for Folkways was to go to the Bahamas with Jody Stecher [in June 1965]. We recorded the album that became known as *The Real Bahamas*. Recording Joseph Spence and the other great Bahamian singers was a big deal for me, and we eventually gave that album to Jac for the Nonesuch Explorer series. To begin with I worked on a lot of singer-songwriters for Elektra, but at the same time I was producing, supervising, and originating albums for Nonesuch Explorer, all based on original recordings with high-quality production values and good engineering.

I was still learning on the job when I went to Elektra, and I was hired initially as assistant engineer. Among my tasks [was to] clean the magnetisers and align the tape heads, splice tapes – those kind of tasks. I'd also make the LEDO, which was a term Jac used that stood for Leveled Equalised Duplicate Original: it was a protection copy that included level changes and some EQ and compression, if necessary. Jac ran a very tight ship in all aspects. The way he ran Elektra Records, very little was left to chance. Everything went through Jac. He gave the label an identifiable sound, an identifiable look, an identifiable artist roster.

Elektra Records had a sound which was already established by the time

* Founded in 1963.

I became involved. Jac liked recordings with a lot of presence, which meant that you would feel the artist was right up close to you and hear the crisp sounds of the instruments. So there was a balance between the classical mic position and the mic position required to capture that presence. That Elektra sound didn't come from nowhere; it came from those different roots that Paul and Mark represented – and from Jac himself.

I was hired toward the end of 1965, when Paul Rothchild was on hiatus for about six months.* My first job was working on Mark Spoelstra's *State Of Mind*, which Paul had been recording. Steve Noonan's self-titled album was another where I picked up the pieces from Paul, and I worked on Dave Ray's *Fine Soft Land*, which was produced by Paul Nelson who wasn't an engineer. I recorded the Neil Young Elektra demos that eventually came out on the *Archive Volume 1* big boxed set. I wasn't particularly proactive about it; Jac would have said there's somebody coming in to record some demos, and I would produce them. I did the same thing with Jackson Browne. I would go over the songs with them, record and pick the takes, and hand them over to Jac. Later on, both those jobs became significant, even though neither of them recorded for Elektra.

Jac would usually assign me to work on projects but I would also go to him if I wanted to make a case for recording something. The Oliver Smith album was a personal project but it turned out Jac wanted it and he released it. Another project came through Stefan Grossman and his then girlfriend, Rory Block. They both learned to play guitar in the styles of old Mississippi bluesmen, the way Charlie Patton or Willie Brown played – they didn't sing but they could perform quite beautifully. I recorded tapes of Stefan and Rory playing duets on a Nagra mono tape recorder in my bedroom. Jac said he didn't want to put it out as an artistic work but would do it as an instruction album, so it became *How To Play Blues Guitar*.† Rory didn't like the idea so she took her name off it and used the pseudonym Sunshine Kate – a reference to Moonshine Kate, who appeared on Fiddlin' John Carson's records.

Stefan introduced me to Pat Kilroy, but that was an album I was ill prepared to produce; it was more than just one guy with a guitar. Pat Kilroy

* Rothchild was serving eight months of a two-year prison sentence in New Jersey for possession of a suitcase full of marijuana which he maintained was delivered to his home one morning without his knowledge.

† Eventually released in 1967.

could play slide guitar and sing a very pristine version of delta blues; my idea was an album of Pat Kilroy and his guitar playing traditional blues and that's how I sold it to Jac, but Pat wanted to explore different kinds of music: what became known as early psychedelic music with an Eastern feel. It's acquired a reputation for being groundbreaking since.

Pat brought in Bob Amacker who played tabla and Susan Graubard to play flute, mostly on tracks he'd written. In the end, Stefan played electric guitar, Mark Silber played bass, and Eric Kaz played harmonica on a few blues things, so the album ended up being a series of compromises. I didn't have the experience to deal with a situation where the artist wanted something different, and I don't know if I was [being] reactionary, wanting him to stick with the blues, but I felt the two styles didn't go with each other.

Tom Paxton was great to work with. I produced *Morning Again* and *Things I Notice Now*, released 1968 and '69. Jac wanted him to record in a certain way, using a process I had not done before – nor since – where I'd make demo tapes of Tom singing songs with just the guitar, then I would go figure out what I thought would be good accompaniment. [I'd work out] the right arrangements and then we'd go back into the studio. I used musicians that I knew, including some great jazz players who were also pit musicians for the theatre group The Negro Ensemble Company.* We produced some beautiful tracks; I love 'Victoria Dines Alone', where I just brought in a cello player.

It was Danny Fields who came across David Peel & The Lower East Side. These were street kids, and I recorded them outdoors. We got a permit to tap into the power lines in Washington Square that were at the base of the street lamps. It was fun. There was a story there, and I like albums that tell a story. It sold well, probably because of the title, *Have A Marijuana*. By the second album, *The American Revolution*, David had started playing with drums and bass and it wouldn't have worked to record that ensemble on the street. They were not the most accomplished bunch of musicians; I brought in a bass player, Herb Bushler from The Negro Ensemble Company, because it needed some grounding. So I produced a rock album of sorts, and then I walked around the East Village with a tape recorder at night and recorded street sounds and people talking and I put those into the crossovers; we

* Seigel also used members of Earth Opera and Soft White Underbelly.

also had Marshall Efron play the role of a cop. So there was a little horsing around, which helped give it an identity. I've heard people say it's a punk record. After he finished with Elektra he meets John Lennon and the next record he makes is for Apple. David Peel was who he was and it was fun working with him. I don't think he ever took any drugs at all by the way. He just had that image. That was his schtick.”

Born in Brooklyn, New York, Peter K. Siegel was introduced to folk music at a very young age; his parents had 78s by Woody Guthrie and Leadbelly, and they knew the Almanac Singers. He witnessed Guthrie and Leadbelly live and was playing guitar and banjo by the time he was in his teens. As a musician, he recorded for Elektra with The Even Dozen Jug Band, and is featured on both the String Band Project and the Old Time Banjo Project. Siegel's final album for Elektra as a staff producer was 1969's Woodsmoke And Oranges *by Paul Siebel, after which he took up a job at Polydor. In more recent years he produced, compiled, and annotated the* Friends Of Old Time Music *boxed set in 2009, having personally recorded many of the 14 concerts between 1961 and 1965 that brought dozens of legendary traditional musicians to New York for the first time, including Doc Watson, Roscoe Holcomb, Clarence Ashley, and Joseph Spence. As a musician, he has recorded two albums with Eli Smith since 2009,* Twleve Tunes For Two Banjos *and* The Union Makes Us Strong.

Remembering Elektra
Bernie Krause

“After I graduated from the University of Michigan in 1960, I went to grad school in Boston, at MIT. As a musician I was more interested in jazz but capable in folk music playing guitar and banjo; I got a job working for Manny Greenhill [a promoter-manager whose Folklore Productions operated in the Boston area for decades]. He was a terrific boss; I spent most of 1961 and '62 setting up an annual folk concert series around Boston, booking a lot of major folk acts. That's when I first met Jac; everybody knew Jac and Jac knew everybody because he was hanging out at the clubs looking for talent.

We booked The Weavers in October 1962. I thought they weren't progressive enough so I was doing a satirical take on Weavers songs at Club

47, where Lee Hays caught the end of my set. He said, "If you're such a wiseass, why don't you audition for the Pete Seeger chair?" They needed somebody to play banjo and sing tenor for a reunion tour that was coming up. So I went along; I was one of 300 who did the audition, and I got the job.

I never contributed much to The Weavers. It was a time when folk music was in transition, and The Weavers were old hat. They officially broke up at the end of 1963, but the last concerts spilled into 1964.*

Soon after that I went home to Detroit and worked as a contract musician at Motown for a while before heading to California in 1965. I attended a series of lectures by Stockhausen, and I began working with some of the newly developed modular instruments at the Tape Music Centre at Mills College in San Francisco.

My mind was made up that I wanted to study electronic music; there were only two analogue synthesizers on the market: Mills College had the Buchla, but I'd seen Robert Moog's first prototype in operation in New York and I couldn't take my eyes of it.

It was around this time I met Paul Beaver through Jac Holzman, who called me because he'd heard I was working with synthesizers.† He had just hired Paul for this piece of astrological nonsense where he wanted to combine the synthesiser with and an orchestra and rock instrumentation – and this became *Zodiac Cosmic Sounds.* Paul and I just hit it off. We were able to come up with enough money to buy one of Robert Moog's early models for $15,000, which was delivered to Paul's warehouse [in downtown Los Angeles] in the spring of 1967. We'd already agreed to become Moog's sales reps on the West Coast and had secured a small space at the Monterey Pop Festival, where we were going to demonstrate the Moog.

Paul and I were really good friends; our albums together were a reflection of that musical partnership. He was 13 years older than me, politically conservative, and bisexual – I was neither of these – yet we were close, and we loved working together. Paul was more the technical wizard, and he was also very good on keyboard; he'd been a successful jazz organist. I'm terrible at the keyboard but I had very good musical ideas, so together it worked. Paul

---

* Krause can be heard on *The Weavers Reunion At Carnegie Hall 1963*, released by Vanguard.

† Beaver was an experienced keyboardist and special-effects man on countless B-movie soundtracks and television shows, and was already an established session man.

was able to realise my ideas on the Moog in ways that I could not have done.

I wasn't credited for *Zodiac Cosmic Sounds* because I was at the sessions more as an observer. We had sold Mort Garson a Moog and we taught him how to use it; he was a very fast learner and one of the very few musicians who really understood the technology. Mort Garson went on to do all the other signs of the zodiac as separate albums, and a lot of other themed, conceptual stuff that was hip at the time. He was very prolific, and he cottoned on to something straight away.

Mort was a hustler, and he was working more at the novelty end of electronic music. His approach was very opportunistic. His albums were great examples of a kind of early new-age music. He was the first to explore and exploit that budding new-age genre, which was very much an extension of the popular San Francisco, hippie flower scene of the late 60s.

Paul Beaver was ahead of me; we spent months tirelessly exploring how to fully operate the Moog, because there was no detailed manual. We were teaching people the basics, and at the same time Paul was explaining the technical aspects to me. I was recording all the sessions to learn from and making extensive notes.

When we were on the plane to Monterey, I happened to sit next to Jac Holzman; I was telling him this and he said, "Why don't you guys put together an album?" That was how the *Nonesuch Guide To Electronic Music* came about. I transcribed all my notes from the learning sessions, which became the basis for the 16-page booklet, and we compiled the music for the *Nonesuch Guide*, which it is still the standard reference in the industry. It was on the *Billboard* charts for 26 weeks; that was our debut album, and it certainly got our names out there.

We were certainly surprised how well it did; even Jac didn't see it as being a big seller, but he was the last of the great risk takers of that era. Nobody has come close to what he did. He always trusted his instincts, and that was why the sound-effects series did so well. He had created Nonesuch as a spin-off from Elektra. Our guide to electronic music, still in its infancy, succeeded in a similar way. It fulfilled a need and Jac's extraordinary level of credibility at the time, and Elektra's standing was a factor in that. Jac had such insight into areas where nobody else really saw the possibilities.

Paul and I were both working about 80 hours a week at double scale for sessions and making good money, but not for our own work. We were the go-to guys in that field, and we were still representing Moog, selling synthesizers, and teaching people how to use them, but by 1972 the bloom was off the rose, and our career as studio musicians was declining rapidly. We sowed the seeds of our own decline because people were now using the Moog themselves; the Minimoog was more adaptable, and we had a lot of competition with ARP.

Paul and I did 135 features and probably worked on some 250 albums.* If pushed, the *Performance* soundtrack is my favourite; it really complements what's on screen. I'm proud of all the albums we made together. *In A Wild Sanctuary* was the first album on the theme of ecology and the first album that used natural soundscapes as a component of orchestration. One of us had to go out into the field and do the recording. Paul didn't want to it, so it was left to me, and it made such an impression that it changed my life: it gave me something to really aim for when Paul died.”

Paul Beaver died suddenly on January 16 1975, at the age of 49. Bernie Krause pursued the new direction inspired by his field work for In A Wild Sanctuary, *earning a PhD in bioacoustics from Union Institute in Cincinnati in 1981. It was a field he was already in the process of defining, travelling around the world and adventurously recording eco-systems. He has recorded and produced a series of environmental recordings for the Nature Company and his own Wild Sanctuary label.*

* Beaver & Krause released three albums for Warner Bros, and are best known for *In A Wild Sanctuary* (1970) and *Ghandarva* (1971). They were also doing film work together, starting with *The Graduate*.

CHAPTER 15

East-West

"Hell man, I'm Jewish, I've been Jewish for years. I'm not Son House. I haven't been pissed on, stepped on, shit on. But Butterfield was something else. There's no white bullshit with him. It wouldn't matter if he was green, if he was a planaria, a tuna fish sandwich … Butterfield would still be the blues." **MIKE BLOOMFIELD**[1]

The year of 1965 marked a watershed for popular music. Dylan released *Highway 61 Revisited*, soon afterward followed by 'Like A Rolling Stone' and just a month before his electrifying appearance at Newport, folk music's very own civil war. The Byrds had just topped the charts with 'Mr Tambourine Man' and, in December, The Beatles unleashed *Rubber Soul*. No less significant was the arrival of the first album by The Paul Butterfield Blues Band.

Bob Dylan and The Beatles are the twin pillars holding up the 60s. When 'I Wanna Hold Your Hand' made *Billboard*'s Number One spot in January 1964, it was the first of nine Top Three singles by The Beatles that year, six of which went all the way to the top. Such was the impact of The Beatles that they helped shake America out of its malaise and sadness following President Kennedy's assassination in November 1963.

"It was so traumatic for the country," Holzman recalls. "And unlike most events in history, both adults and kids were equally devastated. The Beatles' breakthrough came in the immediate aftermath. Their music required no brains at the beginning, and it was a good way for the country to let off steam."

For many folk musicians, seeing the *Hard Day's Night* movie was the prime catalyst for change – not least for Jim McGuinn. "I noticed that The Beatles were doing folk-music chord changes in their songs, probably because of their skiffle background. They were also doing lots of fourths and fifths harmonies, which up to that point in time had been exclusively Appalachian. There was so much going on in those songs that sounded so simple on the surface, but it was the folk-music chord changes that inspired me. I started doing traditional folk songs in Greenwich Village, but with a Beatles backbeat."

Rubber Soul was the result of The Beatles' first extended stretch in the studio. It opened them up on so many levels, including their lyrics, which reflected an awareness of Dylan's writing. Dylan's influence is clear, especially on John Lennon's contributions to the album: 'Norwegian Wood', 'Nowhere Man', and 'In My Life'. For Holzman, this was their coming of age. "*Rubber Soul* is the reset button. This was a body of work unlike their previous albums. People who took music seriously could relate to their thoughtful and very human approach. *Rubber Soul* turned people's heads – and it certainly made me realise that this was something more than I had been hearing and recording."

Holzman loved the singer-songwriters because they injected new life and a freshness, a perspective, into folk-slanted music. "But it was clear that this was still not enough. Bands were on the horizon. You might have someone playing second guitar or harmonica or bass, but the next evolutionary step was to create and perform within the framework of a band. It was the next natural step."

That natural step is usually perceived as folk-rock, which became the catchall phrase for every folk musician now forming a band and plugging in. It didn't always manifest itself as folk-rock. Another strain, garage-rock, drew inspiration from the British Invasion groups – Them, The Kinks, The Yardbirds – while others, including The Doors, fed off The Animals or The Zombies, where keyboards and Vox organs came into the mix.

Elektra is often mentioned as a label that pioneered folk-rock: Judy Henske's use of electric guitar and drums; the ensemble playing of Fred Neil's recordings; or Bob Gibson using electric guitars on *Ski Songs*. These have all been cited as precursors of folk-rock … but not by Jac Holzman. "I always thought that folk-rock was a bastard thing, unleavened," he says. "I had no objection to folk music with a beat, but folk-rock was neither one thing nor another. We tried a few tracks – 'One Time And One Time Only', a Tom Paxton single released only in the UK, and Phil Ochs's version of 'I Ain't Marching Anymore' recorded with The Blues Project – both terrible and unreleased in America. Folk-rock always seemed to be two extremes trying to reach a centre of agreement, trying to find its core."

Arguably the only out-and-out folk-rock record on Elektra is David Blue's eponymous debut. "The *David Blue* album was trying too hard for something," says Holzman. "He had been around for a long time before anyone gave him a chance to make a record, and we went ahead, but the finished result was less than stellar, and I seriously considered not releasing it. Unfortunately, everybody knew he had made the record and people in his circle would have said, what's wrong with it? David Blue was part of the Village scene, and I thought we owed him that much."

Holzman describes the record as an attempt to emulate the sound and dynamic that Dylan achieved on *Highway 61 Revisited*. "Which was definitely not folk-rock. There was a great deal of improvisation, as in the way the Hammond B3 was used, and it came together in the epiphany that was 'Like A Rolling Stone', a sensational piece of material that no one could have predicted. John Hammond once told me, 'I thought Dylan was honest and interesting and of the moment, just like I thought Billie Holiday was. I didn't know it was going to turn into this.' I never thought The Byrds were folk-rock, either. They were not artificial, and it came from deep within them. McGuinn always knew what he was about. I saw that when he worked with Judy Collins – he was full of ideas and overflowing with taste."

Tom Paxton, one of the lone voices in the Village who resisted going electric, has a similar perspective. "If Dylan had not plugged in, would folk music have gone electric? Absolutely, although Dylan plugging-in accelerated that process immensely."

In truth, Dylan's abandonment of topical songs was as radical as his going electric, and when both The Beatles and Dylan became more introspective, that instigated a sudden turn lyrically. Pop music could be about anything, as could folk music. No longer welded to a tradition or bound to topicality, the commercial folk boom died of its own obsolescence.

Most of the folk singers who had emerged in the early 60s had, to one degree or another, released albums, so their music took on a more permanent aspect. They were no longer scuffling on the street; they had all more or less become established and comfortable. Phil Ochs observed this process with wry vitriol when he wrote the notes for his friend Jim Glover's album *Changes* in 1966 (by Jim & Jean). "The folk boom has come and gone like a plague," said Ochs. "Many grew their hair down to their wallets and jumped on the Beatle bandwagon in true hands-across-the-sea spirit. Palms upwards as usual."

Jim McGuinn, David Crosby, and Gene Clark had been among the first of America's folk musicians to take serious note of The Beatles. Only these three of the embryonic Byrds line-up played on the single that Holzman agreed to release on Elektra, choosing the name The Beefeaters for its quintessentially English connotation. Featuring Beatles harmonies and simple chord structures, 'Please Let Me Love You' coupled with 'Don't Be Long' was issued as a rare single for Elektra in 1964. The label was poorly equipped to promote 45s, and the record slipped into oblivion. "We were just fledglings," is how McGuinn sees it today. "We hadn't discovered our sound yet. David Crosby knew Brian Wilson and took 'Please Let Me Love You' over to him. He was very encouraging. He said, 'You're almost there – keep working at it.' As The Beefeaters, we had a one-off single deal with Elektra. The deal with Columbia was also for a one-off single – 'Mr Tambourine Man', it transpired – with the option of an album if it was a success. It was Miles Davis who got us on Columbia. We performed for his agent, Benny Shapiro, at his home. Benny had a teenage daughter, who came running down the stairs all excited about what she heard. The next day, Miles came over and Benny told him what had happened, and Miles picked up the phone and recommended us to Columbia, where he carried a lot of weight."

Elektra was first in line to sign The Lovin' Spoonful, who had come together early in 1965. John Sebastian assembled the group with Canadian Zal Yanovsky, from The Mugwumps, and two members of Long Island rock group The Sell-Outs, Steve Boone and Joe Butler. They began rehearsing at the Night Owl. Holzman thought them better than 20 jug bands, and he wanted them badly for Elektra.

Although the group made a series of demos, their management demanded a hefty advance and had already signed away their publishing to a company with its own record-label connection. With neither Holzman nor Sebastian wanting to ruin a good friendship over a deal turning sour, both backed away.

Sebastian later confessed that it "was the worst decision I ever made in my life". But not before recording a handful of songs for Elektra, which the group allowed the label to have for the 1966 compilation *What's Shakin'*. The four Spoonful tracks are three rudimentary and familiar rock'n'roll covers, including The Coasters' 'Searchin'' and Chuck Berry's 'Almost Grown', with only the fourth, John Sebastian's 'Good Time Music', conveying the Spoonful's ebullient good-time spirit.

What's Shakin' was never intended as an 'electric' entry in Elektra's Project series. "It was simply unreleased material that was available to us," explains Holzman. Alongside the four Spoonful tracks were five fiery leftovers from The Paul Butterfield Blues Band's early recordings, one each from Al Kooper and Tom Rush, plus the only recordings by Eric Clapton & The Powerhouse. This was a blues-based group put together by Joe Boyd who was then running Elektra's London office.

The Powerhouse was, in hindsight, arguably the first supergroup and featured Eric Clapton, Jack Bruce, Steve Winwood (credited as Steve Anglo), Manfred Mann's Paul Jones, and Spencer Davis drummer Pete York, who had stepped in because Ginger Baker was unavailable. However mouth-watering the ensemble looks on paper the impromptu sessions in 1966 yielded indifferent results, but it didn't matter, because toward the close of 1964, Elektra had signed the real thing. "One of Paul Rothchild's earliest independent signings was the Butterfield Blues Band," recalls Holzman. "This was yet another beginning, and we could never have imagined at the time where it would take us."

Paul Butterfield was a white boy from Chicago and a mean harmonica player who had worked all the city's dives and bars. He was a great bandleader who assembled a series of extraordinarily great Paul Butterfield Bands, even though his later outfits tend to be overlooked when compared to the classic line-up on his first two Elektra albums. Featured were the twin guitars of Michael Bloomfield and Elvin Bishop, keyboardist Mark Naftalin, and the solid, grinding rhythm section of Sam Lay and Jerome Arnold. Paul Rothchild had first seen Butterfield playing with Nick Gravenites in a Berkeley club, the Creamery, back in 1963. Two years later, at a party in Cambridge, Fritz

TOP Bruce Botnick, Paul Rothchild, and Jim Morrison in a still from the film *When You're Strange*. **ABOVE** Rothchild (left) and Botnick at the console at Elektra Studio B, mixing *The Soft Parade*. **RIGHT** The Doors' monumental debut, released in January 1967.

RIGHT Always at the forefront of technology, Jac Holzman endorses the Dolby noise-reduction system, which Elektra began using in 1967. **BELOW** Bruce Botnick, engineer on innumerable classic Elektra albums, at the controls in Sunset Sound studios.

"Elektra was first in recognizing the value of the Dolby System for multi-track rock recording,"

says Jac Holzman, President of Elektra Records. *"Since early 1967, we have used Dolby units on most of our recordings of The Doors, Judy Collins, Tim Buckley, Tom Paxton, The Incredible String Band, Roxy, and many others. The New Music can have a surprising dynamic range, and we find that the Dolby System not only gives a really low-noise background during quiet passages, but it helps to preserve the clarity and definition of complex musical textures. A related advantage is that the mixdown is faster and less tedious. In working out the final mix, we no longer have to resort to intricate equalization schemes to retain crucial nuances and subtleties of the performance."*

LEFT Tim Buckley. **BELOW LEFT** *A Cold Wind Blows*, Elektra's first original collection of British folk songs. **BELOW** Mike Heron and Robin Williamson of The Incredible String Band, the only Elektra UK signing of any note in the 60s.

ABOVE Landmark debut LPs by MC5 and The Stooges. **RIGHT** Judy Collins with David Anderle, who produced her *Who Knows Where The Time Goes* album and headed Elektra's West Coast office.

ABOVE David Peel recording live in Washington Square, New York City, in 1968. Producer Paul Siegel is at the front, looking up. **LEFT** Jac Holzman with Mickey Newbury, a Nashville songwriter who made four atmospheric albums for Elektra in the 70s.

TOP Harry Chapin, whose songs struck a chord with American audiences during the 70s. **ABOVE** Holzman with Mo Ostin and Joe Smith, who guided Warner Bros so successfully through the 60s. **LEFT** LPs by Earth Opera and Swamp Dogg – the latter a contender for 'worst cover ever'.

Jac Holzman and Judy Collins, who re-signed to Elektra in the early 70s, by which time most of the label's key 60s acts had moved on.

TOP Jac Holzman demonstrating a Panavision camera in 1984. **ABOVE** Queen were Holzman's last major signing, the ultimate glam-rock band. Left to right: Brian May, Roger Taylor, John Deacon, Freddie Mercury. **RIGHT** Carly Simon's *No Secrets*, one of Elektra's biggest successes of the early 70s.

Richmond strongly urged Rothchild to check out Butterfield again. He was now fronting a full-on electric blues band playing at a bar in Chicago. There, at Big John's, where the band had been playing nightly for almost two years, Rothchild was blown away.

After his set, Butterfield took Rothchild to a different club to hear another local band, this time featuring an explosive young white guitarist, Mike Bloomfield. Before the night was out, with the carrot of a deal on the table, Rothchild persuaded Bloomfield to join the Butterfield Band. Butterfield's current guitarist, Elvin Bishop, wasn't upset. "I didn't resent him coming in," says Bishop. "With Bloomfield and me, it was a very odd couple. I was from the country and I couldn't even think as fast as he could play. No one was as good as Bloomfield. Technically, he was a monster. He started out as a blues freak, pure and simple, but we went through a period in the middle 60s when all of us were wide open to everything we could lay our hands on."

Paul Rothchild's first recordings of the Butterfield Blues Band, in December 1964, marked his first stab at recording electric music, and they were abandoned, even though thousands of copies had already been pressed as a first album. Mark Abramson, assisting Rothchild, remembered: "They were loud. Nobody on Elektra had ever been that loud before. We were a folk-music label: if there were drums, it was somebody going tchk, tchk, tchk. In the Butterfield Band, the way Sam Lay laid into the drums scared the daylights out of us, technically. We had to figure out how to record loud by trial and error."[2] The sessions did provide one track, 'Born In Chicago', for an Elektra sampler, *Folksong '65*. Within a month, sales of the sampler were booming, exceeding 60,000, because people were asking for the Elektra sampler with 'Born In Chicago' on it.

In 1987, while trolling through storage facilities hunting for Doors masters, Rothchild unearthed the original tracks from those first sessions, later released on Rhino, in 1995, as *The Original Lost Elektra Sessions.* "They have just about the right amount of grit," says Holzman. "When I first heard them, I couldn't imagine what Paul was worried about. It was earthy and ragged, but Paul insisted it wasn't right. If someone insists, I trust them."

It had taken three attempts at recording the Butterfield Blues Band before Rothchild was happy with the result. A second series of live recordings at the newly opened Café Au Go Go in New York yielded nothing. Third time around, back in the studio in New York City and using four-track for the first time, Rothchild knew he had nailed it. Much to Holzman's relief, because it had cost $50,000. "There was a buzz that worked in our favour when *The Paul Butterfield Blues Band* album was released in 1965," says Holzman. "That was the year they played at Newport and caused a real stir."

The controversy surrounding that appearance added to public interest and curiosity. For Rothchild, "Bottom line, the Butterfield Band opened another door to American musicianship. It made the electric blues a viable form for popular music, made it possible for hundreds of American performers to play electric music."[3]

Elvin Bishop understood the impact the band made. "The greatest thing about it was the intensity and consistency. Sam and Jerome had been playing with Howlin' Wolf before Butter. To say he was a hard taskmaster is a nice way to put it – he was an awesome presence, but Butter didn't take prisoners either. Have no doubts, Butter was the bandleader – he was a tough guy." Rothchild, too, had no doubts. "Butterfield was the genuine article: feeling the blues. I believe he was one of the greatest bandleaders this country has ever had. He's right up there with Benny Goodman or Nelson Riddle."[4]

In the space of a year, the Butterfield Blues Band made a remarkable transition from the powerful, frenzied blues of their first album to the mind-and-genre-bending possibilities of *East-West*. 'Walkin' Blues' and 'I Got A Mind To Give Up Living' kept their feet on familiar ground, but not the two long focal tracks, Nat Adderley's 'Work Song' and the 13-minute instrumental 'East-West'. Its futuristic improvised mix of blues and jazz would later be termed raga rock, and the modal experimentation owed more to Ravi Shankar and John Coltrane than Muddy Waters. So integrated is the twin-guitar interplay of Bishop and Bloomfield that Elektra cleverly credits the order of the solos on the jacket. It was just as smart as the instruction on their debut: "We suggest that you play this record at the highest possible volume to fully appreciate the sound of The Paul Butterfield Blues Band."

The criminally unrecognised guitarist Glenn Phillips, who was once described by Little Feat's Lowell George as the most amazing guitarist he'd ever seen and who once gave Frank Zappa some backstage guitar lessons, was an impressionable 15-year-old when the first Butterfield Blues Band album was released. He cites Michael Bloomfield as the most influential guitarist on his generation. "The first Butterfield album opened up a whole new world to middle class suburban white kids," he says. "The intensity of the band's music drew us in like moths to a light, and once we were drawn in, we kept going deeper and deeper into the history of the blues. That led not only to the discovery of a world of great music, but also to a social awareness of how sheltered our lives had been.

"The improvisational 13-minute title cut on *East West* was the blueprint for the entire jam-rock movement. Go back and listen to the debut album of just about any California psychedelic bands of the era and you'll hear [Bloomfield's] influence on their lead guitarists: Jerry Garcia with the Grateful Dead, John Cipollina with Quicksilver, Barry Melton with Country Joe & The Fish, even Carlos Santana. They were all great guitarists who evolved into unique players, but Bloomfield was undeniably their touchstone."

Jorma Kaukonen of Jefferson Airplane was one of those California-based musicians indebted to Bloomfield once he began making the transition from acoustic to electric guitar. "The first Butterfield Blues Band record I was turned onto was *East West*, which I still consider to be really important. I was an acoustic player and had the Airplane not hijacked me I probably would never have picked up the electric guitar. When I did start playing electric guitar, Bloomfield was my first mentor. I also listened to Buddy Guy, T-Bone Walker, and B.B. King, but I went to see the Butterfield Blues Band play many times. They were incredibly powerful in a 'modern' way without losing any of their blues 'authenticity'. I always found Mike to be brilliant. In the long term it's hard to say how influential he was, but we all listened to him back then, and when he first came to San Francisco we become friends and played together quite a bit. The story of how his life evolved is tragic."

When the Butterfield Band performed 'East-West' live, they would jam on it for up to an hour. They played regularly in the burgeoning San Francisco ballroom scene, at venues like the Fillmore and Winterland, and were a huge influence on the city's jam bands. Elvin Bishop shrugs them off today. "Quicksilver, Big Brother, and the Dead – those guys were just chopping chords. They had been folk musicians and weren't particularly proficient playing electric guitar – folk is where they were coming from. Then along comes Bloomfield, and he could play all these scales and arpeggios and fast time signatures. Bloomfield would do a fire-eating act during 'East-West'. He'd wait until the middle section, they'd bring the lights down, we'd be playing the groove, and he would bend back and put the thing in his mouth and blow it out. And I'd ask, 'How d'you do that, man?' And he'd say, 'All you have do is to remember not to inhale.' He just destroyed them."

Within a year of the release of *East-West*, Bloomfield (along with the group's original rhythm section) had departed. Butterfield would add a horn section by 1967's *The Resurrection Of Pigboy Crabshaw*, just as Bloomfield's new band, The Electric Flag, added horns to enrich the impact of their sound. A year later came *In My Own Dream*, after which first Mark Naftalin and then Elvin Bishop departed, leaving only Butterfield himself from the original line-up.

Butterfield had signed a management deal for the band with Albert Grossman in the summer of 1965, just ahead of their historic appearance at Newport that year. Grossman also owned a production company, GrosCourt, with John Court, who was brought in to produce the two subsequent albums after *East-West* and, in the process, ousted Rothchild, who felt both were disasters, "one right after another". Elvin Bishop agrees. "The further Butter moved away from the blues, the more he was moving away from what suited him best. The other stuff just splattered out: too much formlessness. It no longer had the same shape or intensity."

It was Bishop who suggested the 19-year-old guitarist Buzz Feiten to Butterfield, and, despite having some big shoes to fill, Feiten brought a youthful exuberance that energised the band, especially onstage. The performance at Woodstock was a memorable example. Trumpeter Steve Madaio was added to a formidable horn section, with tenor and alto sax players Gene Dinwiddie and David Sanborn already in place since 1967. For the next album, *Keep On Moving*, it was Holzman who arranged for Jerry Ragovoy to handle the production. Ragovoy had an impressive track record, as the writer of 'Piece Of My Heart' and 'Try' as well as 'Time Is On My Side', The Rolling Stones' first US Top Ten single. A producer for United Artists and Loma, Ragovoy was known for his skills at combining soul, blues, and jazz arrangements.

If the intention was to try to create a more commercial R&B sound to revive interest, then the band had other ideas. They wanted a jazzier reflection of their live performances. Ragovoy didn't feel that the end result lived up to their talent. He cites Sanborn and Feiten as two of the best players he worked with – listen, for example, to Feiten's solo on 'Where Did My Baby Go'. *Keep On Moving* remains the best of the post-Bloomfield albums, and *Rolling*

Stone considering that "they have evolved through the cataclysmic past few years with as clear and coherent a musical statement as their first album in 1965".[5] A live album produced by Todd Rundgren followed in 1970. A year later, with Feiten and Sanborn gone and despite Rothchild's return as producer, they were unable to summon up the old magic on *Sometimes I Just Feel Like Smilin'*, Butterfield's last for Elektra. The group disbanded soon after, Butterfield settling in Woodstock and forming the more rock-centred Better Days. He was by then a heroin addict, and years of heavy drinking caused problems that resulted in peritonitis. Paul Butterfield died of heart failure in May 1987.

Bloomfield never fulfilled the promise of his early career, enjoying his greatest commercial success with Al Kooper on various underwhelming Super Session projects. He, too, was a heroin addict, and he died from an overdose, aged only 36, in 1980. Elvin Bishop proved far more resilient, with a string of successful albums for Capricorn in the 70s and even a Number Three hit in the US charts with 'Fooled Around And Fell In Love'.

Looking back, Holzman says, "There's something primary in them that the music spoke to. The first two albums are definitely the most important, but we stayed with the Butterfield Band. Paul had an audience, and a hold on that audience, although it began to diminish later. I was prepared to follow wherever they wanted to take it. They put us on the map in so many ways."

The Butterfield Band's participation at the Newport folk festival in 1965 foretold that times were changing. It was the core of Butterfield's band who backed Dylan when he famously plugged in on that Sunday evening, July 25th, but it's often overlooked that the Butterfield Blues Band caused as much of a furore when they played the blues workshop hosted by folk-music traditionalist Alan Lomax that afternoon.

Paul Rothchild sets the scene. "Lomax was loaded for bear. After the traditionalists, and ahead of Butterfield's set, he got up and said, 'Today you've been hearing music by the great blues players. Now you're going to hear a group of young boys from Chicago with electric instruments. Let's see if they can play this hardware at all.'"[6] Manager Al Grossman and Lomax came to blows, to the astonishment and amusement of all present – including Holzman. He recalls the incident and the sight of "two overweight and out-of-shape growlers rolling in the dirt. Hilarious!"

That evening, Dylan's performance went down in history, although not for Elvin Bishop. "I met Dylan. Nice guy, but I was ambivalent. I thought he couldn't sing, couldn't play harmonica – but then I'd played with Little Walter. But he didn't need my sympathy. What I remember about Newport was hanging out with Mississippi John Hurt and Mance Lipscomb and splitting a half pint of whiskey with them – that was the high point for me.

"When we played in the afternoon," Bishop continues, "people weren't sure. Some of the older guys were wondering how to respond, but we didn't get booed. They weren't there to see us in the way they were to see Bob Dylan."

If Dylan's evening performance split the folk world into two camps, plenty agreed with Paul Rothchild's opinion. "To me," he says, "that night at Newport was as clear as crystal. It's the end of one era and the beginning of another."[7]

His Elektra boss felt the same. "Dylan and folk music and Elektra were never the same again," says Holzman. "It was enormously exciting. It was of such intensity that it almost lifted me off the ground. I started tingling all over. To me, the question had been answered as to where I was going. We had recorded the Butterfield Blues Band, done well with the singer-songwriters. Now we were going to marry the two into something unique. Bands can have an impact that a solo artist rarely achieves. I saw the future for Elektra. And I knew exactly where I was heading – back to California."

CHAPTER 16

Maybe The People Should Be The Times

"Eclectic is a tired word, but if it should be applied to anyone in the business of music then Jac Holzman would be that man. I was included in the Elektra orbit, which was extremely flattering. Elektra was one of the hot spots in town. You could feel so much musical energy in Los Angeles, but Elektra brought something from New York to the party. LA musicians and New York musicians were colliding in a place where anything seemed possible, and Jac was instrumental in that. He had an influence all over town, not just at Elektra." **VAN DYKE PARKS**

The shift of musicians and much of the recording industry to the West Coast had gathered momentum by the mid 60s. Historically, New York City had always been the musical centre, but by 1965 the charts reflected that records produced in Los Angeles were becoming dominant. LA boasted Number One successes with The Byrds, Gary Lewis & The Playboys, Sonny & Cher, The Beach Boys, and Barry McGuire, compared to New York's sole success with The McCoys and 'Hang On Sloopy'. By 1967, even more bands originating in LA were topping the charts: the rejuvenated Beach Boys, The Association, The Mamas & The Papas, The Monkees, The Turtles, and The Doors.

New York City was becoming tired and used up. As the writer and critic Ellen Sander observed: "The heavies evacuated the Village and split to California. Folk had become too commercial to be comfortable, tourists jamming every coffee house were degenerating the scene, cover charges and two drink minimums popped up everywhere we used to hang – for free."[1]

"I was drawn to California," explains Holzman. "New York was overrun by the usual suspects. The fact that nobody had signed Love signalled a vacuum of passionate A&R men. I could see what was going on out there. New groups were coming together, mostly Easterners who had moved to California. Jim McGuinn, John Phillips, Phil Ochs – you didn't miss any of your friends in LA, because they were there." McGuinn confirms this. "LA became more energised, mostly because so many people from New York settled there."

Holzman had tried to establish a West Coast presence prematurely in 1962, but this time his decision to focus more heavily there was an informed choice. "The music in New York was corseted, whereas in California, artists were finding each other naturally rather than being cobbled together by managers. Big, big difference. You'd hang out there, you could get loaded, you'd bond – it was a lot more fun for me. New York was too cut and dried. I still spent a lot of time in New York, but I found my life and work in LA to be more relaxed and more productive. In LA, everyone came in late and worked very late. The lifestyle was so appealing."

By 1965, Holzman saw bands forming around singer-songwriters. He knew that protest songs had run their course. "We're no longer talking about bands that were subservient to a frontman. What was apparent about California bands was that if you took even one person out, they no longer sounded the same. The best groups had the balance just right of solo vocals, harmonies, and instrumentation – The Mamas & The Papas or Buffalo Springfield are perfect examples."

In 1963, Jim McGuinn had been in front of the exodus that headed west, and he quickly recognised that among New York labels, Elektra had a more contemporary attitude. So it was no surprise to him that they should operate on both coasts after 1965. "I give full credit to Jac Holzman for being alert to changes in the music world," says McGuinn, "for having his finger on the pulse of what was happening out there, and for being willing to move quickly and respond to the scene. Elektra was a small label, so it was easier for them to react swiftly, but moving swiftly only works if you have the right creative instincts, and Jac's were second to none. He's a pretty sharp guy. Also a pilot. I always had a lot of respect for that."

Record labels were always slower on the uptake than musicians. Many of the biggest Los Angeles-based artists were signed to East Coast labels – The Byrds, Sonny & Cher, and soon Buffalo Springfield, Love, and The Doors. Love was exactly the type of band that could take Elektra into the future, and Jac Holzman knew it from the moment he saw them at Bido Lito's in Hollywood.

"I saw Arthur Lee on stage," says Holzman, "and I knew this was 'my band' and that I was going to do whatever it took to sign them. I try to understand each band within their own context, and if the hairs on the back of my neck go up, I pay close attention. Bido Lito's was a scene from one of the more amiable rings of Dante's Inferno: bodies crushing into each other; silken-clad girls with ironed blonde hair. Love was cranking out 'Hey Joe' and 'My Little Red Book'. Inwardly, I smiled. 'My Little Red Book' was by Bacharach & David and featured in the Woody Allen movie *What's New Pussycat?*. Hip but straight. And here was Arthur Lee and Love going at it with manic intensity."

The Byrds had set the tone and raised the stakes for all the other LA bands. The music scene there was swarming with clubs lining the Strip or in Hollywood. Most famous was the Whisky A Go Go, and there was Ciro's, Gazzarri's, Pandora's Box, the London Fog, Bido Lito's, and the Trip. With The Byrds touring much of the time, Love had become top dogs.

Michael Stuart, then drumming with local rivals The Sons Of Adam, sets the scene. "On stage, Arthur was decked out in his signature multi-coloured sunglasses, combat boot – one only, and scowl, and he was banging the hell out of his tambourine. John Echols had a lead-guitar style like no other. Loud and frantic, soft and melodic. Jazz, rock, classic, flamenco … he could do it all. Played a double-necked Gibson 12-string and six-string – he was equally accomplished on either neck. Bryan MacLean, eyes closed, his head tilted down almost to his chest, appeared to be fighting from falling off while he played."[2]

"Arthur's custom-made multi-coloured glasses looked like they were cut from precious stones," says Holzman, "and the faceting presented him with a view of a world no one else saw – like looking through the eye of an insect. Arthur must have seen multiple images – everything coming in from all sides. It says so much about Arthur, and then of course you add that to him being loaded … ."

Holzman was surprised at the opportunities so open to him in LA. "Nobody else was reaching out to sign Love. Columbia had dropped The Doors in 1966 before I went after them. That was the beautiful thing about coming out to the West Coast: everybody was on top of everything in New York, but the West Coast was a little sleepy. So you put an aggressive New Yorker in there, who is both very selective and competitive – and I pulled out two of the first-line acts."

Holzman found Love fresh, exotic, and deliciously weird. "Arthur Lee's background was Memphis R&B, but Love also understood and embraced traditional pop values. After all, here was a band playing 'My Little Red Book'. Love was nothing more or less than Arthur's conception of what it should be – a terrific band with tons of energy and crazy as loons. That appealed to me. When there's an element of danger, when you don't know what a band is going to do next – that attracts me. Bland bands need not apply."

It was Holzman's long-time West Coast friend and associate Herb Cohen who acted as the intermediary on the deal that the label made with Love. As Cohen recounted, "I was, for a minute, managing Love, and I helped sign them to Elektra. Then I stopped, because they were unmanageable. Love were a bit bizarre, even for me, and they were stoned all the time. Elektra offered us a deal, and at the time the band were all living together in this tiny hotel room, hungry and wasted."

Arthur wanted a $5,000 advance, says Cohen, and so they arranged to meet Holzman at the bank. "Holzman cashed the cheque and counted out the $5,000 in $50 bills, after which Arthur tells the other guys to wait at the hotel. He has to get 'something'. So they do as they are told and head back. Arthur returns a few hours later and shows them a two-door gull-wing Mercedes, telling them that this was for the band and their equipment. They all stare at the car – no one says a word. Then he hands each guy $100, as that's all that's left of the advance. They look at him, and still no one says anything." Holzman: "Arthur had a curious sense of cubic capacity. That car was just big enough for him, his girlfriend, and his brand new harmonica."

Love began recording their debut album at Sunset Sound Studios on

January 24 1966. The line-up was Arthur Lee, lead singer, Bryan MacLean, guitar and vocals, John Echols, guitar, Ken Forrsi, bass, and Snoopy Pfisterer, who had replaced original drummer Don Conka. Conka's descent into drugs was the inspiration behind the album's harrowing song 'Signed D.C.'.

Holzman produced the album with Mark Abramson, and both were novices at recording rock. Also, it was Bruce Botnick's first job for Elektra as engineer (he would play a vital part in future recordings for the label, not least his involvement in every Doors album). Love's debut was completed in just a week and marked Elektra's entrance into the rock album era.

Abramson was well aware of their inexperience. "At Elektra, we didn't know anything about recording intense electric music. We did folk music as well or better than anybody; Butterfield-type blues we learnt from scratch. When rock'n'roll came in, it was back to school again, and Bruce Botnick was our professor. A mic here, a mic there; all these baffles around the drummer; people in the studios with earphones. We watched Bruce with our mouths open. He saved our collective asses."[3]

The *Love* album never fully overcame the sum of its parts: too many Jaggerisms, too many other Anglophile leanings, especially toward The Who's brash sound. And they were beholden to The Byrds, for whom MacLean had once been a roadie. It's a compelling, underrated debut, nonetheless, and was a solid marker for Elektra to put down as its first ever rock album.

The chosen single was 'My Little Red Book', which John Echols once said they played from memory after hearing Manfred Mann's version in *What's New Pussycat?*. It provided a particularly satisfying and memorable moment in Holzman's life. "I was driving to Annapolis, to St John's College, where, 15 years after being tossed out at the end of my junior year, I was now a member of the Board of Visitors and Governors. I was tuned to a local Baltimore station, and from out of the Mercedes speakers blew 'My Little Red Book'. It was the first time I ever heard an Elektra single on Top 40 radio, and it was a small but sweet triumph, a validation."

Love initiated a new numerical series for Elektra – the 4000 series – and the company pioneered a radically new kind of LP jacket. It was printed in colour directly onto smooth stiff board, and now both the front and back of the jacket were in full colour. Love was also the first Elektra band to have their own custom-designed band logo. Bill Harvey devised an elaborate psychedelic design with male and female symbols. Aside from its own distinctive Elektra logos, no other graphic identifies Elektra more than the Love logo.

Love's debut made an impact. Steve Harris had just joined the label as its bi-coastal radio promotion supervisor. He says: "Love was considered too weird for a lot of other companies to have signed. It was an extension of folk – the weirdness of folk into the weirdness of the new LA psychedelia. The audience that had moved on from folk would pick up on this. At college co-ops, Love sold very well."[4]

Bruce Botnick remembers how LA's jazz community reacted. "In Hollywood, that album really set the jazz world on its ear. Artists I was recording for Pacific Jazz Records and Contemporary all bought the album. They were interested in what Arthur Lee was doing – Arthur was an admired and recognisable figure on the Hollywood music scene."

In the summer of 1966, Love had their second and biggest hit, reaching Number 33, the intensely ferocious '7 And 7 Is', recorded by the first album line-up and with free-form, almost unfathomable lyrics about Lee's childhood. It was a full-on raging garage-punk classic and mirrored the crazy extreme of its 12-hour studio session.

John Echols recalls '7 And 7 Is' as "without doubt the most difficult song we ever did, as far as the actual recording process was concerned. We wanted controlled chaos, with lots of compression, a distorted bass, and over-the-top high end. We also needed to have the mic bleed on the bass track, but not on the guitar tracks. Add to that the drums needed to perfectly match the tempo of the vibrato, which gave poor Snoopy fits, though I must admit he surprised me, by actually pulling it off. The blues tune that we play after the explosion was a song I had written as a standalone instrumental."[5]

Holzman, who produced the track, remembers tensions running high: Arthur beating up the band, demonstrating to each member how they should play their parts, and saying how he was a better musician than anyone – except, perhaps, Echols. "Even after the band went home it wasn't over," says Holzman, "because Bruce and I had yet to create the atomic explosion that was the inevitable ending of that song."

Drummer Michael Stuart took over after Snoopy had struggled with the breakneck drumming on '7 And 7 Is' and Tjay Cantrelli, a flute and reed man, further embellished the band's sound on Love's second album, *Da Capo*, produced by Paul Rothchild. "The line-up changes allowed us to move in a new direction," says Michael Stuart, "away from the folk-rock genre into what would have to be characterized as jazz rock. With Arthur, diversity was of paramount importance, and the first three Love albums were a study in diversity: a trilogy of folk rock, jazz rock and baroque-influenced symphonic rock."[6]

On side one of *Da Capo*, Love fashioned a collage of songs, with the Latin-flavoured 'Que Vida', the Spanish acoustic shadings of 'The Castle', and the intricate 'She Comes In Colors'. Side two was given over to 'Revelation', a sprawling epic-styled jam that never quite took flight and lacked in spontaneity. *Da Capo* is one half a genuine classic album: the gentler, more acoustic mood-shifting songs of side one, and Lee's veiled autobiographical lyrics, a preface of what was to come on *Forever Changes*. "I thought 'Revelation' was a little overdone," says Holzman today, "but Arthur always tended towards experimentation and liked the idea of using the 12-inch LP's playing time to try something new."

John Echols says, "'Que Vida' and 'The Castle' were both worked out in the studio, with Paul Rothchild breathing down our necks. He had expected to be producing an album much like the first Love album; he was rather taken aback by the abrupt change in musical direction and was not sure where we were going with *Da Capo*. He was also less than pleased with our habit of writing the songs in the studio, rather than having them completed beforehand. [Engineer] Dave Hassinger told Paul, 'This is great material, cut them some slack.' Paul came around and did indeed cut us some slack."[7]

The group would run through many of the songs at Arthur's place, although nothing except 'Revelation' was played live before going into the studio. Echols recalls how Arthur, Bryan, or whoever was writing something they thought was interesting would usually show the others an outline. "Most times, in a very informal manner, we started to work out our individual parts. After a lot of back and forth, and a whole lot of changes, a song would emerge. Contrary to popular misconception, [all of the] Love songs were very much a group effort."

One outcome of the all-day session for the '7 And 7 Is' single was a conversation between Holzman and Lee where Lee made a rare admission that a suggestion by Holzman "wasn't a bad idea after all". Holzman remembers the session as an endurance test. "It was a hundred decibels beyond loud, and I was accustomed to recording singers who accompany themselves on guitar with a single microphone. I had, over the years, developed a deep appreciation for the sonority of the solo acoustic guitar. I suggested to Arthur that I thought there was a quieter tonality which might be a winning context for the band. What would happen if you advanced backwards? What would it sound like if their rock'n'roll sensibility was applied to songs accompanied by acoustic instruments? I also suggested using words as drones, and he liked that: to experiment with sustaining vocal notes." Lee listened and, as Sandy Pearlman observed, *Forever Changes* finished what *Da Capo* began. Pearlman called it "Arthur Lee's insane mutation of Mick Jagger into Johnny Mathis".[8]

Forever Changes was produced by Arthur Lee and Bruce Botnick. While the album is essentially a product of Lee's vision and his preoccupation with death and the war in Vietnam, over the years, Lee typically sent out mixed signals about the recording of the album. He talked it up, he put it down, and, at times, he took complete credit for the end result. Before his death, he acknowledged and praised the orchestral arrangements and orchestrations by David Angel, which, in the past, he had often dismissed. While *Da Capo* represented a more collaborative process within the group, all the evidence is that *Forever Changes* was driven by Lee to a far greater extent, though not without some group input.

With Rothchild unavailable and unwilling to work with Lee again, Botnick was originally scheduled to produce *Forever Changes* with Neil Young (one of *the* might-have-been moments in rock history). After Young withdrew, Holzman gave Botnick the nod to proceed by himself. Botnick picks up the story. "That album had a life of its own. From the start, there was a problem with the band, who were so overwhelmed by Arthur. They were beaten down: no enthusiasm; no desire on their part to stand up. At the first session, I realised that they were too uninvolved, and some of them just too stoned. I called Jac and said I wanted to do another session, but we should bring in the Wrecking Crew [Phil Spector's legendary session players]. So Arthur worked out the arrangements for two songs, 'Andmoreagain' and 'The Daily Planet'. The rest of the band was in the control room, literally in tears, and they came to me at the end and said, 'Look, we can do this,' and I said OK, show me."

Michael Stuart maintains that the group were not mere observers during the Wrecking Crew sessions. "We all walk in and there are strangers in our chairs, [including] this middle-aged woman wearing glasses, sitting in the middle of the room thoughtfully studying a chart and holding a Fender bass. Carol Kaye. She was Kenny's replacement.

"Then I looked over at Carol Kaye and Kenny, and Kenny is showing her what to play on 'The Daily Planet', and the moment was overwhelming. All of a sudden, Arthur walks by Kenny and Carol and he pauses for a moment and listens and says, 'That sounds pretty good what you're playing, Kenny. Why don't you go ahead and play the bass on this cut, and she can play something else, like rhythm guitar.' And he walked away. So Kenny played the bass on 'The Daily Planet' and Carol played rhythm guitar."[9]

A few weeks later, during August and September of 1967, the re-focussed and re-invigorated Love completed the rest of the album. "I really wanted to go back and re-record those two tracks with them," says Botnick today, "but there was no time. By then, Arthur had distanced himself from his own band. He was dictatorial, and intellectually he had moved beyond them. Arthur was a super-bright person who had all this energy, plus he could play their instruments better than they did. At the time, I didn't totally understand but, looking back to the first album, you could see it coming. Arthur was never just 'one of the guys in the band'. He was always the leader, the supernova, and the main songwriter. He was the arranger, the one who dictated how, where, and what they would play."

Echols denies that the band was quite so strung out as is often portrayed and there is absolutely no denying that his lead guitar parts clearly stand out amidst the textures and arrangements. Botnick agrees. "Johnny played some great leads, but it took Arthur to get Johnny to do more than Johnny would do – whatever it took, he got the best out of Echols."

Echols feels that his and Bryan MacLean's playing was an integral part of Love's distinctive sound and that they effectively "put Love's stamp on the words Arthur was writing. That sound, the guitar interplay, was recognisable no matter the direction the music took. I'm more of a jazz/R&B player, with a touch of Spanish thrown in to round out the mix. So I would describe my style of playing as being rather eclectic. I loved Johnny 'Guitar' Watson, Django Reinhardt, Luther Allison, Kenny Burrell, Wes Mongomery, and Gabor Szabo. Bryan was deeply influenced by bluegrass music. He liked fingerpickers like J.E. Mainer & The Mountaineers, Jimmie Rodgers, Maybelle Carter, and Alton Delmore. He developed a style that was truly his own. He knew just how to move in and around the chords I was playing – it was great timing."[10]

What propels and establishes *Forever Changes* as a transcendent album are David Angel's spellbinding orchestral arrangements, which grace seven of the eleven tracks. "Arthur and I were talking about adding strings," says Botnick, "so I called my mother, who was a music copyist for Frank Sinatra and Nat King Cole, and asked her if she knew anyone fresh and talented. She suggested David Angel. He did a superlative job. Arthur would sing the parts to David, who would write the charts. You'll notice there's a big influence of the Tijuana Brass. I was also recording them for A&M at the time. Of course, that influence was more apparent on 'Alone Again Or', which has an authentic Spanish flavour."

John Echols presents a different picture. "'Alone Again Or' began life as a bluegrass-y tune – it was little more than an instrumental intro, with a catchy vocal hook. Since neither myself or Bryan played banjo, we really didn't know what to do with the song. It almost didn't make the cut. I was warming up near the piano, noodling Spanish riffs, when David Angel walked by. He listened for a few minutes before asking me to 'play that for Bryan, this would go great in his song.' When I returned, David and Bryan were sitting at the piano writing a trumpet part that would mirror my Spanish guitar noodling."[11]

While *Forever Changes* is dominated by Arthur Lee's songs, it is 'Alone Again Or', one of two composed by Bryan MacLean, that sets up the entire album, almost surpassing the songs that follow. Holzman sequenced the album, as he did nearly all Elektra recordings. "*Forever Changes* would not have worked without 'Alone Again Or', which is a portal song," he says. "You choose to enter, and if you didn't get it after that, you would never be ready. If you surrendered to the song, the entire trip that followed was simply stunning. 'Alone Again Or' was the only song with which you could begin, because *Forever Changes* demanded that the listener cast aside judgement and surrender to it."

Noting the underlying conflict within the band, particularly between Lee and MacLean, Holzman says that we would not have *Forever Changes* had it not been for Botnick. "From the vantage point of time, Bruce would today be credited as 'album saviour', not just producer. When Arthur finally realised that *Forever Changes* was the apogee of his career, he wanted all the credit, even for those elements of the album he was dragged into kicking and screaming. Arthur could not share credit: he had to be the author. Author and Arthur are not too distant."

Despite the tension, Botnick says he loved working with Lee. "I loved his wicked sense of humour, but during the final mixes he said some hurtful things to me that I wasn't mature enough to deal with. It was an intellectual put down, pursued from his viewpoint, which I wasn't smart enough to handle. I called Jac and said, 'Take my name off the album,' and that's why the LP says produced by Arthur Lee. But I really produced that album."

"Arthur was very difficult to work with," says Holzman with a sigh. "He was a downer, so super-critical of those he dealt with. He rarely had a complimentary word, because he considered himself better. But he couldn't keep it together to show the world his true talent. Arthur is one of the few geniuses I've met. But genius needs focus and intent, otherwise it just discharges into the ground."

Forever Changes is Love's masterwork, wrapped in its own web of intrigue and contradictions. David Anderle, who ran Elektra's West Coast outpost and studio, once described it as "punk with strings". The end result is a record that's both claustrophobic and gloriously uplifting, with lyrics we still puzzle over. 'Alone Again Or' is superficially plaintive compared to Lee's alienated philosophical lyricism, and it made an obvious single, becoming a minor hit in the UK, where the album, too, charted, at Number 24. In America it flopped, the album reaching only 154 on the *Billboard* chart and the single only 'bubbling under'. Describing the background orchestrations as "pleasant", *Rolling Stone*'s misguided verdict was that "its weakest point is the material. Some of the songs meander and lack real melodic substance".[12]

The album was heralded by a billboard on the Strip that suggested you "watch for the third coming of Love", but *Forever Changes* failed to live up to that expectation. To compound matters, it was totally trumped by The Doors' second LP, *Strange Days*, released earlier. David Anderle saw the tide turn. "When I came to Elektra," he says, "it was Love-land. Very quickly it became Doors-land."[13]

Love's experimental nature meant that there was no identifiably signature sound, no doorway through which to enter their world. Nor did Love co-operate in the promotion of their records, much to Holzman's exasperation. "Arthur would have loved for everything to happen the way it did for The

Doors. He was envious. He had originally introduced me to The Doors, and they would eclipse Love. The Doors had the first billboard on the Sunset Strip. Arthur felt betrayed, but The Doors gave us more to work with. Love was not a functioning touring band that would play outside of California. The Doors came to New York for a month after the first album and the New York scene adopted them."

Doors keyboardist Ray Manzarek agreed. "Arthur didn't want to tour. Love were the quintessential California stoners, to the hilt. Arthur said, 'What do I want to go to New York for? Everything is going great here on the West Coast. I'm fine right here.' So they never really broke nationally, because you had to go to New York. It was the national media centre."

Unlike Love, explains Holzman, The Doors shared everything as equals. "They were better organised," he says, "and willing to do what it took. The Doors had a sound and an attitude. That's a huge difference. Arthur was never trying to achieve a predominant Love sound, because his ideas were always changing. And while that was negative commercially, I found it musically appealing. His voice identified Love."

Holzman concludes that people did not have a clear idea of what to expect from Love, and Arthur did not like that what happened to The Doors did not happen to him. He thought The Doors were very good but he thought Love was better. "The Doors hit within four months of the release of the first album, and everything fell into place," says Holzman. "Love never achieved the same national consensus – except in California and in England, where his appeal was mysterious. Arthur wanted the ride but not the responsibility of driving the bus."

Herb Cohen has a similar perspective. "The reason Arthur never had a career was because he was so far ahead of it that there was no way he was ever going to do anything logical. There are artists who succeed in failing. It's the will to fail. No matter what he did that was positive, he managed to do something negative. This has nothing to do with how brilliant he was or that group. People tend to confuse the music with the musician – but in fact the music is one thing, the person something else. God knows there were enough weird things going on around him, but he would create situations that undermined what he could have achieved."

In January 1968, Love recorded a new single, the blistering 'Your Mind And We Belong Together', coupled with 'Laughing Stock', a song that illustrated how dysfunctional Love had become. This single, too, went nowhere. A new line-up was assembled only days after the old band had fallen apart during a brief, disastrous American tour. In later interviews, Lee branded his former group as junkies, thieves, and murderers who couldn't play. "There hadn't been a whole lot of communication between members of the band for a while," says Michael Stuart, of the sessions for that final single. "We were drifting in different directions, and there was just an inescapable feeling that, all things considered, things were coming to an end." Looking back, however, Stuart still feels that Arthur "richly deserves all the good things people have said about him and his creations, and no doubt he deserves almost all the credit for the success of *Forever Changes*. After all, it was his brainchild. He wrote and sang most of the tunes. He was the engine that pulled the train."[14]

Love Four Sail featured the new recruits, including another fine guitarist in Jay Donnellan, whom Lee quickly decided wasn't good enough, so he was replaced by the more flamboyant Gary Rowles. The record was produced entirely by Lee and is a fascinating and overlooked record. Songs like 'Nothing', 'Always See Your Face', 'Robert Montgomery', or 'Dream' could have made the cut on previous albums, and 'August', a one-take torrent of ringing guitars, is vintage Love. Released in August 1969, for all its flaws *Four Sail* is Arthur's Lee's last truly consistent piece of work.

Remarkably, the new four-man Love actually set out on the first of many European tours by Lee during the 70s, arriving in the UK for the first time in February 1970. Lee had already signed to Blue Thumb, a label modelled on Elektra and run by a future Elektra president, Bob Krasnow. For Holzman, *Four Sail* was Lee's exit strategy. "It was heading in a direction I didn't think served him very well. He burned through people very quickly. He had severed all ties with the original band and he was doing the same with Elektra."

Released by Blue Thumb within eight months, the double LP *Out Here* was drawn from the same sessions as *Four Sail*, after Holzman had taken first pick. Sadly, little of Lee's output during the 70s measured up to those final Elektra sessions. *False Start*, *Vindicator* (released as Arthur Lee & Band Aid), and 1975's *Reel To Real* are chequered affairs, though his singing, as ever, transcended the material. The 70s albums reveal Lee abandoning the complex textures of Love's Elektra recordings for harder rock and a Hendrix-inspired R&B approach. His output into the mid 70s was certainly prodigious, but other period recordings, including *Black Beauty*, recorded for Hair producer Michael Butler and Paul Rothchild's shortlived Buffalo label, and an album for Columbia, *Dear You*, went unreleased.

The problem for Arthur Lee was that, while he wanted to move on, his fans were resistant to his harder-edged change of style. Aside from a piecemeal second solo album in 1981, it wasn't until 1992 that another full studio album appeared, *Arthur Lee And Love*. Released by two respected European independent labels, New Rose in France and Creation in the UK, it was subsequently reissued as *Five String Serenade*, renamed after the one classic track that hinted at the old Love sound.

More than a decade after its release, *Forever Changes* began to pop up in critics' polls as among the greatest rock albums ever recorded. By the 80s it had diminished in importance, finding it hard to compete among a new generation embracing The Velvet Underground and The Stooges. Ten years later, *Forever Changes* was back on everyone's radar. Coinciding with the well-received 1992 studio album, Arthur Lee finally began touring again with makeshift versions of the Love band, using local LA musicians and, in the UK and Europe, young groups like Shack and The High Llamas as Chuck Berry-style off-the-shelf backup.

At the end of the 90s, Lee was jailed in California's Pleasant Valley State Prison, serving half of a 12-year sentence for firing a handgun outside his LA apartment. *Forever Changes* was repackaged, remastered, and re-released in 2001 by Rhino Records, just as Lee emerged from prison. The following year, he began performing *Forever Changes* live with a full orchestra to awestruck audiences. He could do no wrong, and at long last had achieved the universal acceptance that had always eluded him.

Only John Echols and Michael Stuart survive from the group which recorded that album. Bryan MacLean died on Christmas Day 1998; Arthur Lee on August 3 2006. Just days later, Holzman commented, "He had given me, Elektra, and music so much, and that he had chosen to live his life so carelessly was the ultimate sadness."

More than any other act, Love was responsible for the huge cult interest in the Elektra label in the UK after 1966. Love was a bigger group in Britain than back home, certainly outside of California. Others, like David Ackles, and even Tim Buckley during his more 'difficult'-album era, also found greater favour in Britain.

It wasn't until November 1965 that Elektra first opened a UK office. Joe Boyd, who ran the London outpost, was born in Boston and graduated from Harvard in 1964, where he once roomed with Tom Rush and became friends with Paul Rothchild. It was Rothchild who brought him to Jac Holzman's attention, eventually leading to the job in London. Boyd had already spent time as a production and tour manager for George Wein in Europe, where he travelled with Muddy Waters, Coleman Hawkins, Stan Getz, and others. Becoming heavily involved in different aspects of the bourgeoning London underground scene, Boyd and John Hopkins – a leading figure in London's counter-culture of the 60s – opened London's first psychedelic ballroom, UFO, in 1966, while he was holding down his Elektra position.

Boyd's most visible act during his tenure at Elektra was in signing the Edinburgh-based Incredible String Band. Not only did he produce the group but he also took over management, prefacing a remarkable four years between January 1967 and January 1971 when, under the auspices of his newly formed Witchseason Productions, he oversaw the careers of an extraordinary range of brilliant artists, including Nick Drake, John Martyn, Fairport Convention, Sandy Denny, and Richard and Linda Thompson.

The Incredible String Band were the only British act of any real significance signed by Elektra until Queen in 1973. "The UK was always a fertile source for new artists," says Holzman. "I had no expectations about The Incredible String Band, but they had a mystique and a quirkiness which made it easy to build an audience. They stood out in America and would sell out the Fillmores on both coasts."

Boyd recalls playing Holzman a demo of 'October Song' and 'When The Music Starts To Play'. "The Incredible String Band were something he had never heard before," says Boyd, "and he authorised an extra £50 to chase Transatlantic Records out of the picture." The Incredible String Band recorded their self-titled debut one day in May 1966 at Sound Techniques Studio. It was released in late June. Within months, the three members had drifted apart. Clive Palmer travelled to Afghanistan; Robin Williamson took the hippie trail to Morocco; Mike Heron remained behind. When Williamson returned, he reunited with Heron, and the duo overflowed with ideas and highly imaginative songs, not to mention a collection of bizarre and exotic instruments: finger cymbals, hand drums, sitar, oud, gimbri, flutes, and tamboura. Boyd produced the resulting record (as he did all their

Elektra output), and *The 5000 Spirits Or The Layers Of The Onion* proved to be a defining moment.

The album went beyond folk, shifting away from their debut's blend of original songs and traditional material with a more jug-band style. The inspired duo's deceptively original, innocent songs bordered on the bizarre: sometimes mystical, often childlike, they were held together in a hybrid of Indian and Scottish traditional folk styles. *5000 Spirits* came in a jacket no less distinctive as its predecessor after Boyd commissioned The Fool to design one of the great psychedelic jackets. In both look and content, it was effectively the *Sgt Pepper* of the folk world. "The cover was just wonderful," says Holzman. "It suited the trippy audience likely to be attracted to their music. There was a huge hippie element, particularly in California, and much dope being smoked throughout America, and those people became their new audience."

Mike Heron explains that the band's first album grew out of music they'd heard back in Edinburgh. "We'd sit around, smoke a few joints, listen to Ravi Shankar, jazz albums, and American folk. It was quite insular. When we recorded *5000 Spirits*, our horizons, our influences had expanded. Also, the times had changed. From the moment Joe Boyd signed us, he didn't think of us as a folk band but as an 'underground' band. It was to our advantage that we were not seen in the folk category. People no longer really cared about musical categories, and we'd play alongside Pink Floyd or The Move at underground clubs like UFO."

The prolific Incredible String Band maintained the delirious heights of experimentation on their 1968 album *The Hangman's Beautiful Daughter*, which delved deeper into eclecticism and spirituality, particularly the long, epic centrepiece, 'A Very Cellular Song'. With celebrity fans like Mick Jagger, Marianne Faithfull, and Paul McCartney, and avid support from DJ John Peel, it became an essential hip album, even reaching Number Five in the UK charts – considerably better than any Elektra release to date – and was nominated for a Grammy in the folk category.

That same year came *Wee Tam And The Big Huge*, further establishing the band in America, helped by a broader scope and style and a wonderfully jumbled ensemble sound that moved them beyond weird folk to something approaching rock.

Having played the Newport Folk Festival in 1967 as a duo, the expanded Incredible String Band line-up, which added girlfriends Rose and Licorice, was now sharing the bill at the Fillmore West for a week with the Grateful Dead. "We were very keen on Elektra," says Heron, "because we loved their Nonesuch albums. They let us raid the shelves and we came back with all we could carry – things like *Tahiti: The Gauguin Years.* These records were prime influences. I did a straight pinch on 'A Very Cellular Song': the beginning part is from Joseph Spence's *The Real Bahamas,* which includes the original version of 'I Bid You Goodnight', and the Grateful Dead would end their concerts with it, too. Joseph Spence certainly influenced my guitar playing."

Holzman remembers that when The Incredible String Band later came to America with a dance troupe, Stone Monkey, to coincide with the release of their seventh album *U,* it was reminiscent of today's Cirque du Soleil. "Just without muscles, and much less rehearsed. It was a very different style, but still singular, and that's what Elektra was about. The early albums did tremendously well in Britain and helped launch Elektra there, but I think the later albums found more of an audience in the US."

Boyd recorded four further Incredible String Band albums for Elektra, until 1971, when they switched to Island Records. Their later conversion to a rock-oriented approach, and to Scientology, divided their fans. Boyd was not always convinced by the new direction. Heron and Williamson, always a volatile pairing, were increasingly at odds with each other, and the band formally split up in 1974.

The group's influence on British folk-rock in the late 60s and through the 70s was profound. It had a discernable impact upon recordings by The Beatles, The Rolling Stones, and David Bowie, all of whom kept a close watch on the provocative underground scene. Both Jimmy Page and Robert Plant were admirers, and Led Zeppelin's shift toward a more acoustic approach and mystical lyricism on their third album was confirmed by *Led Zeppelin IV,* which denotes a definite influence of The Incredible String Band alongside the two other major British folk rock groups of the day, Pentangle and Fairport Convention. When Mike Heron released *Smiling Men With Bad Reputations* in 1971, Pete Townshend and Keith Moon of The Who (credited as Tommy and the Bijoux), John Cale, and Steve Winwood lined up alongside the expected Witchseason folk-rockers.

The Incredible String Band came to embody the notion of the hippie ideal in Britain. They made some extraordinary records, incorporating Indian and African instrumentation and traditions and effectively presenting 'world music' some 25 years before the term was coined. They also fully anticipated new age sensibilities if not with their music but in their philosophy and outlook. Despite their singularity, The Incredible String Band begat a number of imitators in the early 70s. Groups adopting their template to one degree or another included Dr. Strangely Strange, Forest, Comus, and Jan Dukes De Grey; Clive Palmer would return from his travels in 1969, picking up where he left off by joining the Cornwall-based Famous Jug Band before recording two wonderful albums with Clive's Original Band (COB), *Spirit of Love* (1971) and the gloriously titled *Moyshe McStiff & The Tartan Lancers Of The Sacred Heart* (1972).

Thirty years after The Incredible String Band split up, folk music was going through one of its sporadic revivals (which unusually has sustained itself to this day) and the group became hip once again under the umbrellas of nu-folk, alt-folk, and twisted folk – mercifully now simply described as folk. The Incredible String Band were perceived as founding fathers of this new scene, especially when Heron and Williamson began performing again in 1999 together with Clive Palmer. Williamson left in 2003, but despite an understanding that neither would use the name without the other's involvement, Heron and Palmer continued to tour the UK, Europe, and the US before disbanding again in 2006. Clive Palmer died on November 23 2013, aged 71.

CHAPTER 17

Extracts From A Continuous Performance

> *"Jac was a little apprehensive about someone three thousand miles away with an Elektra chequebook in his hand, and although I didn't see it that way at the time it was quite possibly for good reason."* **JOE BOYD**

When Joe Boyd was tentatively sounded out by Jac Holzman for a job with Elektra, he came away wondering if he'd blown the opportunity. As he later explained to British writer Ken Hunt, he met Holzman at a festival taking place in a ski resort in Connecticut in August 1965. "There was a reception backstage after the first concert. I'd had a hard day, swallowed a glass of cheap red wine quickly and found myself in conversation with Holzman. He said, 'So tell me, you've been to England a few times, what's Elektra's presence over there?' I answered, 'Oh, it's crap.'

"I said, 'Well, first of all, the records cost too much. There's no good promotion. You're not a serious presence.' I said it all in rather blunt and undiplomatic manner because I'd had a few drinks. Afterwards I said to myself, 'What am I doing? I've insulted Jac Holzman.' To the contrary, I think. Paul Rothchild had already been pushing him to see if there might be a job of some kind at Elektra. So, rather than insulting him, Holzman quite liked my attitude and my aggression about what ought to be done about Elektra in England. At the end of September I was invited to come up to a meeting with him and Rothchild and they asked if I wanted to go to London and open an Elektra office."[1]

Joe Boyd duly arrived in London in November 1965 to set up and run Elektra's first UK-based operation, employed by Elektra under a joint venture with Record Imports Ltd, whose main focus was on the Nonesuch catalogue. The company already managed an impressive classical catalogue and handled the revered Blue Note label; Elektra had an office above its basement warehouse at 7 Poland Street in Soho.

As early as 1960, Elektra had begun issuing LPs in the UK through Audio Fidelity, including both local pressings and distribution of American product. LPs were also licensed through and released on Pye's budget label Golden Guinea, launched in 1957. It was a catch-all brand – classical, jazz, Latin, pop, folk, comedy, even Bertrand Russell talking about nuclear disarmament, religion, education and Cold War paranoia – with LPs selling for 21 shillings, – 10 shillings (50 pence) less than a regular UK album. By contrast, imported Elektra albums sold for 10 shillings more, at roughly two pounds. Holzman preferred to export US product rather than risk poor mastering and impaired packaging, but this wasn't cost effective. The added problem with the Golden Guinea releases was that despite carrying the Elektra logo in the top right-hand corner, the back cover always carried a half-page advertorial that read: 'Ask Our Dealer For These Popular L.P.s.' There, the Elektra titles – which included albums by Theodore Bikel, Oscar Brand, The Limeliters, flamenco guitarist Juan Serrano, and Josh White – were in company with the likes of *Rolf And Tino's Mediterranean Holiday*, *Ottilie Patterson's Irish Night*, *Mexican Fiesta*, and comedy albums by Tony Hancock and Steptoe & Son. Elektra, as Joe Boyd had rightly pointed out, had no presence in Britain.

In January 1966, Elektra in Britain was still very much a folk label. Tom Paxton and Judy Collins were its best-known ambassadors, although Phil Ochs, Tom Rush, and Spider John Koerner had all played on the booming folk circuit, and even The Paul Butterfield Blues Band came over for a handful of dates. By 1965, folk music in Britain had finally made a commercial breakthrough. The *NME* even declared it the year folk went pop: Dylan had enjoyed five major UK pop hits, including 'Subterranean Homesick Blues', 'Like A Rolling Stone', and 'Positively Fourth Street'; both *Joan Baez 5* and *Farewell Angelina* were UK Top Ten albums in 1965, while her cover of Phil Ochs's 'There But For Fortune' was also a Top Ten single in June. British artists as disparate as Donovan, The Seekers, Marianne Faithfull, The Searchers, and The Silkie – all embracing folk to one degree or another – were having hits and following in the footsteps of The Byrds, and Manfred Mann were successfully covering Bob Dylan songs. Given its folk credentials, if Elektra was ever going to get a toehold in the UK, 1966 was the year to do it.

While Record Imports Ltd continued to take care of Nonesuch, a shortlived pressing and distribution deal was made with Decca, purely for 45s, which resulted in four now ultra-rare singles being released on the London American label in 1966: two by Love, 'My Little Red Book' and '7 And 7 Is'; Judy Collins's 'I'll Keep It With Mine' and the Butterfield Blues Band's 'Come On In', a non-LP single that featured Mike Bloomfield. The Decca arrangement lapsed when Polydor took over manufacture and distribution of Elektra in August, and the following year Elektra moved two streets across Soho to 2 Dean Street.

As it turned out, the deal with Polydor was fortuitous. Originally formed to compliment Deutsche Gramophon Geselleshaft's operation in Britain, Polydor had opened its own manufacturing plant, and by 1966 had signed production deals with Robert Stigwood, which resulted in him bringing The Bee Gees and Cream (on the Reaction label) to Polydor, as well as Kit Lambert and Terence Stamp's Track Records (home to The Who, Hendrix, and Arthur Brown) and Georgio's Gomelskyi's Marmalade label (which scored with Julie Driscoll), and making licensing agreements with Atlantic and Stax. These acquisitions placed Polydor at the heart of some of the most vital and original music of the mid-60s.

According to Paul Rothchild, rock'n'roll was still "new stuff to Jac" during that year of transition, which is why Holzman started up a secondary label in Britain named Bounty, which, said Rothchild, "was designed to keep Elektra's nose clean."[2] Bounty's first release was Josh White's *Josh At Midnight*, followed by a series of folk titles (including albums by Bob Gibson, The Even Dozen Jug Band, and *Folk Banjo Styles*) and more ethnic titles (*The Koto Music Of Japan, Sabicas*, *Balalaika* by Serge Polinoff) from the US catalogue that conserved the label's heritage. Bounty also picked up a number of blues albums from Testament Records, an American independent founded by *Downbeat* editor and blues authority Pete Welding in 1963 (including titles by Muddy Waters,

Otis Spann, and Fred MacDowell). It was a sound move to appeal to the new generation in Britain that was discovering blues music through John Mayall's Bluesbreakers, whose popularity had risen massively since Eric Clapton joined the group in 1965. Bounty was a shortlived exercise. It ceased to be part of Elektra in 1967, when it was taken over by Polydor.

Holzman had begun licencing folk albums from independent UK labels as early as 1964, among them The Ian Campbell Folk Group's self-titled debut and *The Rights Of Man*, Topic's groundbreaking *The Iron Muse* and *Tom Paley & Peggy Seeger*, as well as two albums by The Corrie Folk Trio, leased from Waverly Records in Scotland. *A Cold Wind Blows*, however, was the British first folk album recorded specifically for Elektra, and it was produced by Joe Boyd following what he later described as a personal voyage of discovery of British folk music that had begun on his earlier visits.

Like Holzman, Boyd was attracted to the kind of unique folk music that wasn't to be found in America. "I was a terrible snob coming into the folk world," he says, "because I had cut my teeth on old Sleepy John Estes records, Louis Armstrong and the Hot Five, and Jelly Roll Morton's Library of Congress recordings, so I was judging everything against that.

"Then what I found in a lot of folk clubs in London, places like Les Cousins, tended to be singer-songwriters strumming guitars and I just thought, 'Oh God, this American disease is spreading.' What appealed to me was more intrinsically English folk music; I loved The Ian Campbell Folk Group because of Dave Swarbrick's playing, but I also loved Ian's singing, and I loved the Watersons, Anne Briggs, Martin Carthy, Jeannie Robertson, Cyril Tawney, and Louis Killen – that was the revelation for me in going into a British folk club, and particularly clubs outside of London."

Travelling round Britain in his new role, Boyd began recording in Edinburgh at the start of the year for what became *A Cold Wind Blows*. There he taped one of the disregarded yet defining figures of Scottish folk music, Matt McGinn, who was something of a precursor to Billy Connolly, a fellow Glaswegian with an ear for local dialect and a witty and humane take on everyday life. His next port of call was Newcastle, where he recorded Geordie singer Johnny Handle (Eric Burdon of The Animals is on record as saying it was through Handle that he first heard 'The House Of The Rising Sun'). Handle went down the pits when he left school, later becoming a teacher, and 'Dust' is an impassioned miner's lament about one of its greatest and most life-threatening hazards: sucking in lungful's of coal dust. Back in London, Boyd recorded the more cerebral Alasdair Clayre, and a couple of months later the wonderfully idiosyncratic Cyril Tawney, the best known of the contributors, who already had a reputation for singing maritime songs and West Country folk, usually delivered in a warm, affecting melodic style.

Tawney's four contributions should all have been absorbed as folk standards. 'Monday Morning' is a timeless song about getting up for work "at the wrong end of the week"; the touching, beautifully sung, shanty-style 'Ballad Of Sammy's Bar' is a unique take on unrequited love; those and his much loved seaman's song 'The Oggie Man' all appear on *A Cold Wind Blows,* which was released at the same time as the Incredible String Band's debut in June 1966. It's an album of original songs in traditional styles, with one of Alasdair Clayre's songs providing the title; Peggy Seeger and Martin Carthy play on certain tracks, and the cover photo is by Boyd's friend and UFO partner John Hopkins. Elevated by Tawney's songs, *A Cold Wind Blows* remains an interesting snapshot of British folk music caught between traditional and original material. It was a worthy enough release but, by comparison, the original material on The Incredible String Band's debut was nothing less than radical and forward-looking. It was, as Boyd described it, "influenced by American folk and Scottish ballads but full of flavours from the Balkans, ragtime, North Africa, music hall and William Blake".[3]

In May – the same month he would record the debut album by The Incredible String Band – Boyd also recorded a 7-inch EP by critic and poet Sydney Carter, featuring Martin Carthy on guitar and with vocals by light-entertainment radio stalwarts The Mike Sammes Singers on Carter's most famous song, 'Lord Of The Dance'. Today it is gleefully sung by what Boyd describes as "happy-clappy liberal Christians the world over." Boyd had met Carter when he first came to London in 1964 and was entranced by his odd, offbeat songs. "Sydney Carter was eccentric, middle-class, donnish, kind, off-hand, and idealistic – he had worked in the ambulance corps during World War II rather than fight. He wrote poetry and did a little teaching, but his primary source of income seemed to be fees and royalties from writing songs with Donald Swann of the Flanders & Swann comic duo.

"I wish the God-botherers had been quicker off the mark with the title song; the EP might have sold better and not been a black mark against my track record with the Elektra bosses back in New York."[4]

Boyd's final 'folk' recording a few months later was Alasdair Clayre's self-titled debut. Clayre was a fellow of All Souls' College Oxford, a philosophy scholar whose LP had the distinction of a set of liner notes by Iris Murdoch. His career in folk music took second place to his other achievements as poet, novelist, critic, broadcaster, director, and producer for the BBC. Singing wasn't his strongest suit, his voice too clipped and polite when he was being serious and sometimes reminiscent of Jake Thackray.

Clayre had met Vashti Bunyan in Oxford in 1965 and provided the words to her single 'Train Song'. Boyd would later say that one his reasons for recording Alasdair Clayre was because of his friendship with Bunyan, whom he wanted to sign. Clayre released a further album, *Adam & The Beasts*, this time for Folkways. He committed suicide in 1984. Judy Collins recorded his translation of Jacques Brel's 'La Colombe' ('The Dove') on *In My Life*. "We had mutual friends," she says, "and I was told that he was depressed because he felt he had compromised himself by doing a TV documentary version of his book (*The Heart Of The Dragon*, a study of Chinese culture) which was a serious work that he had spent years researching."

One of Boyd's first quests on arrival in London had been to find a decent, unsigned British blues band for the putative Elektra 'electric blues project' album that had already been discussed before he'd left New York. What transpired instead was an 'all-star' line-up put together with Paul Jones (then still the singer with Manfred Mann) featuring Jones, Eric Clapton, Jack Bruce, Steve Winwood (under the name Steve Anglo), Spencer Davis Group drummer Pete York, and piano player Ben Palmer. Boyd produced the one-off recordings at Olympic Studios in late January – still smarting that he was never credited – resulting in the three pre-Cream tracks that were included on the *What's Shakin'* LP under the name Eric Clapton & The Powerhouse. The tracks are highlighted by Winwood singing 'Crossroads', with Clapton providing the soon-to-be ubiquitous Cream guitar lick. By the time *What's Shakin'* was released later in the summer, Clapton had already formed Cream with Bruce and Ginger Baker. Cream was announced to the world in *Melody Maker* on June 11, the inner booklet for *What's Shakin'* merely noting that Clapton had been an easy winner in a musician's poll in *Melody Maker* as the best lead guitarist in the country. Like the rest of the all-star group, aside from Paul Jones, Clapton was unknown in the US.

Talking about the Elektra job, Boyd told Ken Hunt that he felt his job description was "slightly fudged" because he really wanted to be a producer, rather than undertake the day to day running of the UK outpost. He was frustrated that Holzman wasn't keen on him scouting for new artists and has often contended that Holzman turned down Eric Clapton, as well as Pink Floyd and The Move, during 1966. Holzman has no recollection of rejecting any of them, or certainly of their being any realistic offers on the table, adding that such was the feeding frenzy to sign acts in Britain that Elektra was unlikely to have been in the running or have the necessary scale of operation to handle them. In any event, Holzman's priority was taking care of business in his own back yard, not least the label's commitment to "new stuff" during the months when Paul Rothchild was serving time which was just as Love broke into the pop charts and Holzman was negotiating to sign The Doors.

Ultimately Boyd felt restricted. "It was a difficult situation. There was a personality difference with Jac, who was very hands-on. I was clearly listening more to Rothchild encouraging my A&R side than to Holzman, who wanted a marketing and promo guy to concentrate on Elektra's American output. I enjoyed the business side but saw A&R as part of developing a UK image for Elektra. That proved too radical for Jac, who wanted tight control on A&R – and I certainly made some bad choices – Alasdair Clayre, for example. That was a good early lesson to never make a record you aren't passionate about. And that, in itself, was an Elektra maxim."

Boyd left Elektra toward the end of 1966, just as advance copies of Love's *Da Capo* and Tim Buckley's debut were arriving. He had already set up his own production company, Witchseason Productions, initially to produce The Incredible String Band and Pink Floyd (he would produce their debut single, 'Arnold Layne', in February 1967). One significant and lasting corollary to Boyd's tenure at Elektra was his discovering Sound Techniques studio where, early in 1966, Mort Garson was producing the orchestral concept album *The Sea* using English string players. "So Jac authorised that I should get £200 out of the bank, and go down to this studio to pay the musicians in cash at the end of the session. I went to the studio where they were doing this stuff, and it was Sound Techniques in Chelsea, and the engineer was John Wood."[5] Boyd's partnership with engineer John Wood usually operating out of Sound Techniques was responsible for a series of extraordinary recordings by The Incredible String Band, Sandy Denny, Nick Drake, John Martyn, Fairport

Convention, Fotheringay, Richard Thompson, and countless others. The pair continued to work together after Boyd returned to America in 1971 and the studio became one of the most important independent studios in the UK.

Reflecting on his year at Elektra, Boyd feels indebted to Paul Rothchild. "I learned the studio from Rothchild. He gave me confidence and demystified the process. Elektra's transformation – with Tim Buckley, The Doors, and Love – was remarkable. Bill Harvey was a great art director. I continued working with the company after I left, and relations were always good, with Jac very supportive of my new independent producer role with The Incredible String Band. We went way beyond boss-and-employee." In 1985, Paul Rothchild said of his old boss, "Jac truly did allow freedom. He created an environment which allowed people with new ideas to come in and try them out."[6] Just as Rothchild himself flourished in that environment and eventually moved on, Boyd was definitely a beneficiary of that freedom, and his career flourished rapidly in the immediate aftermath of his year working for Elektra.

One of the most extraordinary and, in hindsight, significant albums that Boyd brought to Elektra was *AMM Music*. Subtitled *Extracts From A Continuous Performance*, the album was recorded over two nights at Sound Techniques, on June 8 and 27 1966 by AMM. The intent of the musicians – Cornelius Cardew, piano and cello; Keith Rowe, guitar; Lawrence Sheaff, bass and cello; Lou Gare, tenor saxophone; and Eddie Prevost, percussion – was to avoid harmony and rhythm in an attempt to create one indistinguishable ensemble sound. Its two tracks were determined by the space available on each side of an LP. 'Later During A Flaming Riviera Sunset' and 'After Rapidly Circling The Plaza' both stop at around the 21-minute mark.

In the years since, *AMM Music* has been variously been described as having been produced by Joe Boyd with John Hopkins or self-produced for DNA Productions, which was run by Hopkins and Peter Jenner, who was also co-managing Pink Floyd. Jac Holzman certainly attended one of the sessions and is even pictured on the original 1967 jacket, where he is co-credited as producer. "I didn't produce it," he says, "although I was there some of the time. I was always interested in the avant-garde so I thought it was a good thing to do. It was certainly Joe Boyd who brought it to my attention."

AMM were attempting to create a new form of music altogether that didn't adhere to the principles of traditional free improvisation – it's more a controlled wall of sound than free jazz, and it was one of the first albums of its kind to appear on a mainstream label. As such, it's a fascinating example of early underground music. John Stevens's Spontaneous Music Ensemble just beat it into the stores with their album *Challenge*, but as Joe Boyd has noted, "One of the formative things in the creation of what we now think of as Pink Floyd, the long extended solos, the abstract ventures into space with the guitar, it all comes from here." Guitarist Keith Rowe has recalled Syd Barrett observing the recording from the control room as they improvised 'Later During A Flaming Riviera Sunset', and Peter Jenner certainly gave Barrett an advance copy. Thus it can be seen as the bridge between Barrett's quirky, nursery rhyme-like songs and the long drawn-out improvisational pieces Pink Floyd began performing live from October 1966. The song 'Flaming' on Pink Floyd's debut album, *The Piper At The Gates Of Dawn*, clearly references the AMM session which Barrett attended.

Peter Jenner recalled another coincidental link between Pink Floyd and Elektra involving Love's single 'My Little Red Book'. "I thought it was a terrific record," he said. "I don't think it was available in England. Maybe Joe Boyd had given it to me. I was talking about it to Syd, and I hummed it to him. I'm not the world's most musical person, and my mishearing of it led to Syd writing 'Interstellar Overdrive'." It became one of Pink Floyd's defining songs. "I really do think musicians channel the culture."[7]

Joe Boyd's replacement in the UK office was Clive Selwood, who had started out as UK Elektra's sales manager. "It was still essentially a folk label," says Selwood, "and the leading lights were Judy Collins and Tom Paxton. They could each fill the Royal Albert Hall without any hits. Someone like Spider John Koerner would arrive with his guitar and spend three months in Europe playing folk clubs. That was the basis of the label, which was beginning to change as I took over from Joe because albums by Love, Tim Buckley, The Doors and the second Incredible String Band album were all suddenly very hip."

Selwood had actually left Elektra's employ and was working for Polydor on Elektra products when Boyd left. He remembers meeting with Jac in London. "We went off for a drink and he said, 'I'd like you to come back and work directly for me.' We were crossing Oxford Street at the time, so we were standing on the island in the middle of Oxford Street, and he said, 'What are they paying you?' I told him and he said, 'OK, we'll double that.'"[8]

By now Selwood had become friends with John Peel, who was working as a DJ for the offshore pirate radio station Radio London. Peel's influential late night show *The Perfumed Garden* had been almost the sole outlet for Elektra records in the UK. After the closedown of Radio London, Selwood became Peel's agent; the irrefutably impartial Peel didn't see there being any conflict, and he continued to champion Elektra releases once he resurfaced on the BBC's new pop station, Radio 1, where Peel presented *Night Ride* and *Top Gear* to a discerning listenership. "Clive always represented the label," says Holzman, "whereas I think there were times when Joe was representing himself first and the label second. I was out of sight, so I needed confidence in whoever was running the label over there. Clive was a whiz on marketing, which I don't think, and I'm sure he'd admit this, was what Joe Boyd wanted to focus on."

Aside from The Incredible String Band, only one other group signed to Elektra in the 60s is remembered at all widely. That group came together by series of chance meetings in West London's Bayswater area and was called Eclection, but they were more an international convention, comprising one Brit, two Australians, a Canadian, and a Norwegian. By August 1967, Michael Rosen (guitar), Georg Hultgreen (guitar), and Trevor Lucas (bass) had added singer Kerrilee Male on a stopover visit from Australia. She had been recruited by fellow Australian Lucas, who had been on the folk circuit in the UK since arriving from Melbourne at the beginning of 1965.

Georg Hultgreen, who wrote most of the songs on the group's sole album, was born in Norway, the son of a Russian father of royal blood and a Finnish mother, respected sculptor Johanna Kajanus, whose surname he later adopted. "Everything did happen quite quickly. Michael Rosen heard that Jac Holzman was over in London, and we somehow managed to persuade him to come and see us rehearse. He liked our sound, which he described as mid-Atlantic folk-rock. When he offered us a deal, we were stunned, because we were all in awe of the label."

Eclection's first gig was at the Royal Festival Hall, where they supported new labelmate Tom Paxton. Drummer Gerry Conway joined soon after, on the recommendation of British blues pioneer Alexis Korner. Holzman says he was also impressed by the band's three strong vocal harmonies and the "slight out-of-world aspect of their lyrics" which, says Conway, were mostly a consequence of "Georg's bizarre command of the English language as a result of such a multi-lingual upbringing".

The group's name, Eclection, was coined by none other than Joni Mitchell. Michael Rosen's girlfriend Marcie was a close friend of Mitchell's – she is immortalised in the song 'Marcie' on *Song To A Seagull*. "Michael told Joni about the band's far-flung origins," says Kajanus, "and she exclaimed, 'What an eclectic bunch of people you are. Why don't you call yourselves Eclection?' Of course, we all knew that this wasn't a real word, but Eclection did seem to reflect the sum total of the band and its influences rather well."

Eclection's self-titled album was released in August 1968. It's something of a mixed bag: an uneasy hybrid of psychedelic, muted folk-rock and California sunshine pop that never scales the sum of its parts. 'Nevertheless', the breezy first single from the album, was chosen as the launch song for the opening of Harrods' new 'swinging' department, The Way In; it was a turntable hit but nothing more. Kajanus says it was Elektra that edged the group toward a more commercial direction by hiring Bee Gees producer Ossie Byrne. Byrne had produced The Bee Gees' first international hits in 1967, 'New York Mining Disaster 1941' and 'Massachusetts'. "I seem to remember Jac Holzman being very keen on the idea," says Kajanus, "as Ossie Byrne was known for his nurturing and encouraging attitudes when working with new bands – which indeed turned out to be the case with us."

Kajanus feels Election were "premature with the recording of our album", which suffers from the excesses of post-*Sgt Pepper* pop ambition, attempting an ornate, baroque-pop style while following a direction that was more an American folk-pop sound. "It was very harmony vocal-based," says Gerry Conway. "The opportunity to record happened so quickly that it didn't reflect what the group was really like once we went on the road. Some of the orchestral arrangements distanced it from our true sound."

Within three months of the album's release, singer Kerrilee Male decided to leave, disappointed that she was underused as a lead vocalist. "After Kerri left," says Conway, "people were regularly coming and going. The last line-up of the group was with Dorris Henderson (a charismatic American performer), who Trevor and Michael knew from the folk clubs; Poli Palmer – later in Family – who played vibes and keyboards; and we even had Gary Boyle on guitar. All fantastic players, but it was a million miles away from that Elektra album." The line-up with Dorris Henderson cut only one single, 'Please (Mark II)', a cover of a song originally recorded by California band Kaleidoscope.

"As a whole, I find it impossible to judge the Eclection album," says Kajanus, "because of all the emotions, good and bad, that it evokes when listening to it. There is a prevailing sense of something special that emanates from the album that could have been nurtured into something greater, had we found more common ground artistically." Eclection petered out naturally toward the end of 1969, by which time Kajanus says he "had lost all emotional and musical connection with the group" and its "hopelessly jazz direction". The timing was fortuitous for Trevor Lucas. He and drummer Gerry Conway resurfaced with Lucas's girlfriend Sandy Denny (they married in 1973) in Fotheringay, the group they formed in January 1970. Eclection's demise had come about just as Denny had left Fairport Convention on the eve of the release of their milestone *Liege & Lief* album.

Speaking in 2006, Holzman said he thought Eclection were a fascinating group of individuals and the album they made was wonderful. "I think our mistake was in not bringing them to the States, because they would have benefited from getting out of England. There was such stiff competition there at the time and in the States they might have found things easier. They needed some work doing but they had a sound that could have travelled anywhere." Kajanus also bemoans the fact that "a lot of opportunities for Eclection were probably lost back then. It's like cracking a safe: you have to have the right combination before you can open the door to success". In an interview before his death in 1989, Lucas expressed regret that Eclection didn't record a second album in 1969, adding that Elektra had showed no interest in recording another one anyway. As it was, the label recorded two albums by British groups that year but neither survived on the label too long.

Leviathan evolved out of The Mike Stuart Span, a group that had formed in Brighton on the south coast of England in the mid 60s. The Span recorded a handful of singles, including one widely acknowledged British psych classic, 'Children Of Tomorrow'. On signing to Elektra, at Jac Holzman's suggestion, they changed their name to Leviathan. Elektra launched Leviathan's recording career in April 1969 by issuing two singles simultaneously, 'Remember The Times' and 'The War Machine', mounting a campaign with the tag line 'The Four Faces Of Leviathan'. A third single,

'Flames', was released in October soon after the group had completed an album at Trident Studios; at one point there was talk of them recording as part of Elektra's notorious, misguided Paxton Lodge experiment. "Elektra was a highly respected label, and we couldn't have asked for more," says the group's former singer, Stuart Hobday. "I guess that we all felt confidence in what we were doing and to have that recognised by Elektra was a bit like winning the Lottery."

The group was, however, struggling to survive financially, as they were unable to sustain themselves through gigs, and when Holzman decided against releasing the album, they called it quits, just as a documentary, *A Year In The Life*, was shown on UK television. Clive Selwood had organised a fly-on-the-wall documentary about the making of the Leviathan album for the BBC. "I'm quoted as saying, 'In a few months, girls will be writing in, asking what colour pyjamas they wear.' It was cruel, but this line was used over the closing shot, which showed one of the guys going to work on a building site. The Mike Stuart Span, they were more of a pop band but they wanted to be more inventive, more progressive. I signed them and produced the record. It wasn't unknown for Jac to scrap an album. Some would say he had more taste than sense. You have to take risks and you have to be ruthless and it's a fine line, but Jac always knew where to draw that line."

"I can't recall exactly why we shelved the album," says Holzman. "We had wanted to expand into the rock market in the UK but I didn't think the Leviathan album was strong enough to make an impact."

Surprisingly, Methuselah's *Matthew, Mark, Luke & John* – a stodgy brew of overwrought, gospel-infused heavy rock – was at least released in North America, but the group were let go within months. They tinkered with the personnel, switched names to Amazing Blondel, and remodelled their sound, taking a more acoustic approach and adopting medieval/Elizabethan instrumentation. It won them a deal with Bell for one album in 1970 before Amazing Blondel moved on to Island Records.

Clive Selwood remained at Elektra after the Polydor deal came to end and Elektra became part of the Kinney Group. He was crucial in nurturing Elektra in Britain, and he fondly recalls Tim Buckley and David Ackles making their first trips there. Selwood was certainly instrumental in The Doors finally breaking in the UK, where it took three albums and seven singles before 'Hello I Love You' hit the charts ahead of their first European tour in 1968. It was Selwood who organised the filming of The Doors on that visit that resulted in the classic documentary *The Doors Are Open* being aired on Granada Television.

"It was a real coup and almost unheard to get such coverage, especially when you consider that The Doors were not that big a group in England at the time," he says. "It was very traumatic at the Roundhouse. The Doors were due to do an early set each night to accommodate the filming, but inside the Roundhouse they were trying to keep the crowd quiet while the group were driving round in a limo because they refused to go on first. They were saying, 'We're not going on unless we top the bill,' and Jefferson Airplane were winding them up by saying, 'No, we are topping the bill.'

"I managed to resolve it. Jim was as charming a man as you could ever wish to meet, very slow speaking so he took his time considering and answering questions which would annoy the cameramen but he wasn't doing it to be difficult. People assumed he was stoned but we weren't used to his laid-back American cool. When we were at the airport the day they left, the group apologised and said they'd been terrified coming to London as they'd heard there was a lot of negativity toward them; they were quite paranoid, especially about the filming."

CHAPTER 18

Take A Journey To The Bright Midnight

> *I liked the Doors, every one of them. They were good guys and they were smart. Their problems had nothing to do with their music. It was just what they were going through. I would be there to support them, and they knew that. Elektra wouldn't have the reputation it now enjoys but for The Doors, and I know they will figure prominently in the opening sentence of my obituary – which is fine with me. They trusted me and Elektra, a small label who needed and wanted them, and we knocked ourselves out to make it happen.* **JAC HOLZMAN**

After Holzman saw The Doors at the Whisky in May 1966, it took until July before he was able to sign the group that would change the course of Elektra. Within a month, they were in Sunset Sound recording one of the great debut albums of all time. But first, Holzman had to convince Paul Rothchild to produce the band. Rothchild was enamoured with The Paupers, a Canadian group who would eventually sign to Verve/Forecast. Despite the backing of impresario Albert Grossman, they flopped miserably. Rothchild was still on parole, and it took some convincing to get permission for him to leave the New Jersey area to work in sinful California. Holzman had to guarantee Rothchild's good behaviour to his parole officer before he could leave for California.

"Rothchild rehearsed The Doors for two solid weeks," recalls Holzman, "running the material so as to make it second nature when the band got into the studio. They could lay down just a few takes and not drain their enthusiasm or energy. You take the song to 80 percent of where it has to be, and the extra 20 percent comes from the excitement and pressure of recording. When the album was completed, I took the tapes home and listened to them through headphones. I grinned the whole way through. Neither I nor anyone else had heard its like before."

Rothchild knew exactly how to capture their unconventional sound. "I didn't want a Doors record to sound like any other. If you have something special, the best you can do is to keep it as pure as possible."

Engineer Bruce Botnick says: "We nailed the sound on the first day. And after that, no one touched a knob, an amplifier, or a microphone. It was all recorded live. Even tape delays on the voice were done in the moment."

The band's work in the clubs had given them enough prepared material for two albums. Guitarist Robby Krieger knew his band was ready. "All they had to do in the studio was turn on the tape recorder. We knew those songs so well: we'd been playing them three sets a night for a year at least. That album came naturally. What else would open the album but 'Break On Through'? What else would close but 'The End'?"

"The joy of that first album comes from the whole point of putting a rock'n'roll band together, which is to make a record," said keyboard player Ray Manzarek. "To actually be in a recording studio for that first time is an existential moment. It only happens once in your life, and if that doesn't energise you nothing will. You've got a beat Southern gothic French symbolist poet who joins with a classical jazz-blues keyboard player, a jazz marching-band drummer, and a bottleneck American-folk-blues flamenco guitarist. Take those four disparate types and play Bertolt Brecht and Kurt Weill, Willie Dixon, plus our own songs. *The Doors* combines all those elements."

The Doors was a devastating debut with a new, dramatic sound and confrontational, controversial lyrics about sex and death, all of which introduced America's first adult rock band. There were outstanding songs, knife-edge drama, and inspired performances from all four members of the band.

"One day, Jim said, 'We don't have enough material, so why don't you guys write something?'" Krieger recalls. "I went home, and the first thing I came up with was 'Light My Fire'. It's been downhill ever since. Jim admired songs rooted in universal subjects. So I figured I would write about the base elements. I loved the Stones' 'Play With Fire', so I chose to write about fire, using folk-rock chords. There was a version of 'Hey Joe' by The Leaves and I was drawn to the chord sequence. On the solo I wanted my guitar to sound like Coltrane's 'My Favorite Things'."

Krieger also wrote the songs 'You're Lost Little Girl' and 'Love Me Two Times' for the first two albums, and these marked him out as the only regular songwriter in the group apart from Jim Morrison.

Holzman discovered immediately that they were instinctively smart about issues that had broken up other groups. "All monies from performing, writing, and publishing were split equally," he says, "and all copyrights were listed in the name of the entire band. When it came to their visual image, The Doors knew what needed to be done – they put their personal egos aside and Jim up front. During the photo shoot for the first album cover they said to Bill Harvey, 'Let's make Jim a little bit bigger.' They knew he was the draw."

Holzman had committed to releasing the album in November 1966, but he was afraid it might get lost during the Christmas holidays. He convinced the band to wait, releasing *The Doors* on January 4 1967 and having pledged to release no other album that month and focus exclusively on The Doors. It was a strategy he would come to repeat. "I knew this album would catapult Elektra to another level," says Holzman. "The record seethed with incredible power and internal strength, all powered by a conventional line-up of musicians. It did not sound of its time: it was a timeless sound."

Holzman backed his faith with the first-ever billboard on the Strip to launch a pop album and a band. The billboard simply said 'Break On Through With An Electrifying Album' and featured the jacket photo, with Jim Morrison's head floating above Sunset Strip. "Because no one had even used a billboard to promote music before," says Holzman, "people in music knew we were serious. The DJs, who still picked what they played, were driving to and from their station offices and were impressed by it. When I took that billboard I reserved it for a year in advance. All new Elektra artists wanted to be on the billboard."

The Doors upped the ante on everything, says Holzman, and their debut record was better than their live performance. "You only have to listen to the

Matrix tapes done after *The Doors* was released," he says, referring to tapes of two renowned shows recorded at San Francisco's intimate Matrix club in March 1967. "Rothchild and Botnick vested time, care, and experience into that first album. It was lovingly nursed into existence."

Love had achieved reasonable airplay with 'My Little Red Book', but Holzman knew Elektra must address AM radio for The Doors. "In the past, we had released singles with the hope that they would be played and become a calling-card for the album. The impetus given to alternative music by FM radio, starting in the mid 60s, was introducing new acts and selling records. We had very large Doors sales just on the strength of FM in Los Angeles."

To give them a national push, Holzman relied on Steve Harris, who knew who to talk to DJs and how to work with programme directors. Holzman spoke firmly to local distributors throughout the country, tying their future distribution of Elektra to their success with AM radio. He advised them: "We must have your local radio support to launch this band." It was 'Break On Through' that conveyed the essence of the first album. The title was a statement in itself and it was the obvious introductory single. Holzman says the philosophy was simple. He knew they were going to lose the first single and wanted to see what the 'consensus' single was – and that would most likely come from what was played on FM. "When we were convinced that it was 'Light My Fire' and that we could cut it to the required length for AM radio, we went with it. Suddenly, the album was selling 250,000 a month and the single even more. We couldn't press them fast enough. That blew our sandals off."

At first, the band couldn't believe the severity of Rothchild's radio edit of 'Light My Fire'. He had simply removed all the solos. Ray Manzarek seethed. "Robby and I looked at each other and we both hated it. Then Paul said to just imagine you're a kid in Minneapolis, Minnesota, you are 17 years old, and you've never heard of The Doors. You love rock'n'roll – and this comes on the radio. We thought about that, and Morrison presciently says, well, if you hear it on the radio like this, and you like it, and go out and buy the album, then you get the bonus of a seven-minute 'Light My Fire' that you never expected. And we all said, 'Call New York and tell Jac it's a go!'"

'Light My Fire' is a tour de force. The song spirals out of Manzarek's flowing organ line into a perfectly timed and executed guitar solo from

Robby Krieger. All this, plus hooks and choruses. It was a pop hit that defined the year, as much as Jefferson Airplane's 'White Rabbit' or even *Sgt Pepper*. 'Light My Fire' topped the chart for the first three weeks in July 1967, selling over one million copies. Elektra was 16 years old, and this was its first Number One single.

"After 'Light My Fire'," said Manzarek, "everything just exploded, two years from the day that Jim and I sat on the beach and he sang 'Moonlight Drive'. That was the middle of July 1965, and in mid-July 1967 The Doors were the number one band in America." Bruce Botnick adds a cooler perspective to the oft-told tale of the beginnings of The Doors. "Jim wasn't a musician. Zip. As has been told through the ages, he sat on the beach and sang some songs, quietly, to Ray. When Ray said let's start a band, Jim didn't really understand what that meant. This wasn't his world." It would become his world, and eventually it swallowed him. But from day one, The Doors were utterly distinctive, and they still are.

Bruce Botnick has the longest and closest relationship with the group, and he pinpoints what was so different about them. There were no peace-and-love vibes and nothing beyond their improvisation to link them to the acid-rock movement in San Francisco that built around groups such as the Grateful Dead and Quicksilver Messenger Service. In Los Angeles, they were far removed from The Byrds or The Mamas & The Papas.

"Melodically, they were very strong, and lyrically they were amazing," says Botnick. "The Doors paid no attention to any prevailing sound, although the folk-rock style was dominant in LA. Robby has that flamenco background, and Butterfield and blues music were an influence on him. But they had none of the identifiable 60s crutches, no electric 12-string guitars, harpsichords, nor even a bass player. That really set them apart."

That, and Jim Morrison's talent for poetry, his lived-in voice, and his brooding, towering presence. "Jim was a huge Elvis fan," explains Botnick, "and an even bigger Sinatra fan. When I first met Jim and showed him where he was going to sing in the vocal booth at Sunset Sound, I had a Telfunken U-47 microphone up, and he froze. He looked at it and he said 'Frank Sinatra'. And I said right. On Sinatra's *Swinging Session* there's pictures of a U-47 with a Capitol logo on, and that's when I knew he was a Sinatra fan. Jim had this enormous vocal range and could go from a whisper to a scream, from zero to sixty in two seconds. He could croon and then scream. I'd marvel – how do you do that?" Paul Rothchild, too, realised that Morrison was blessed with a magnificent vocal instrument. "His was one of the greatest voices I've ever had the delight to work with," said the producer. "He talked about being a crooner, admiring Sinatra's phrasing enormously, and he could do a mean Elvis. But he was really an accidental musician."[1]

"When we hit, we were ready," Manzarek confirmed. "'The End' was originally three minutes long, a farewell to Jim's UCLA girlfriend, but we had so much time, and we chose to experiment and stretch it. We were playing an Indian modal style, and it just went on and on, and Jim improvised – like a jazz band. I don't want to be in a band that plays the same songs the same damn way every night. And no jazz group had a singer who could do what Jim did. Wasn't that amazing? We had Jim Morrison, a poetic improviser with words."

Holzman says The Doors were the result of natural selection: they found each other. "Robby's guitar-playing looked so deceptively simple. Mike Bloomfield would eke out an E-minor chord and go into an orgasm on stage with the sheer bravado of his own technique. Robby would be spinning incredible riffs, and he might be watching an insect on the ceiling, or perhaps considering that in six months time he might buy another pair of jeans. There was a very special Brechtian feel you got from Ray Manzarek. Whenever Ray played I saw two colours: earth brown and purple. So you have the uniqueness of Ray's keyboard platform supporting equally precise, and liquid guitar lines from Robby, given structural integrity by John's very inventive staccato drumming."

What Jim Morrison added, aside from obvious sex appeal, was a dash of unpredictability. There are well-documented episodes throughout The Doors' short but intense career where Morrison's antics went too far for some. This included their appearance on *The Ed Sullivan Show* on September 17 1967, which in reality was a storm in a teacup.

The *Sullivan* show was a big deal on American television, with a prime Sunday-night slot. "If you were going to do national television, you appeared on *Sullivan*," explains Holzman. "It became an even bigger deal when Jim sang the original line: 'Girl we couldn't get much higher.' It was an amusing evening. Sullivan's son-in-law, the producer, came back afterwards and threatened The Doors by saying they would never be on the Sullivan show again, about which the band could care less. Nobody paid the slightest attention to Jim singing 'higher' – only the official network sponsors."

"One of the production people came backstage," Manzarek recalled, "and said, 'Mr Sullivan really liked you, he wanted you on his show for six more performances, and now you'll never play *Ed Sullivan* again.' And Morrison just looks at him and said, 'Well, we just did *The Ed Sullivan Show*.'"

In December of 1967, at a performance in New Haven, Morrison was arrested for a breach of the peace and for badmouthing the police from the stage. Robby Krieger remembers that the band rubbed people the wrong way and that the establishment was wary of them.

"New Haven was the start of people not from LA seeing what could happen at a Doors show," says Krieger. "For us, the first alarm bells didn't sound at New Haven but after the first rehearsal, when Jim almost killed some guy over a dope deal. The Doors' career was always careening out of control, and Jim loved the chaos. New Haven was not his fault – that can be traced to the cop who maced him. Jim started rapping about it on stage, the cops didn't take kindly to it, and they dragged him away."

Krieger says that Elektra were very good about all this and did not criticise the band for what was happening. "They might have been too accommodating. A lot of stuff that Jim did, they let him get away with. He trashed the studio after we did 'The End' at Sunset Sound. Jim was on a lot of acid, and when we finished recording, he didn't want go home. The rest of us left, but he snuck back to the studio and got pissed off that there was no one else around, so he sprayed the place down with a foaming fire extinguisher. The studio owner wanted to slap him in jail, but Elektra paid the damages and cooled things off. And I thought Jim did feel, well, I got away with that – I can get away anything."

Holzman could see the turmoil in Morrison. "They really wanted to make it, and Jim wanted the ride. Jim was both in the middle of it and observing from the outside looking in. Perhaps this was a movie in which he was starring. And he sees all this stuff going down."

The band recorded the *Strange Days* album soon after 'Light My Fire' had lit up the charts, gathering together the remainder of their matchless early repertoire. Released in September 1967, it perfectly uncovered the flip side of the summer of love. It took the feral beauty and potency of *The Doors* even deeper.

"We were feeling the same buzz as the first album, but that was when we began to experiment more," recalled Manzarek. "We went from four-track to eight-track recording, which may seem like nothing today, but it completely freed us."

"Making that record was a hell of a lot of fun," Krieger says. "Jim was no saint, but he was still in check. 'Moonlight Drive' was the song I jammed on before I joined the group, which we hadn't yet recorded. 'People Are Strange' was new. Jim dropped by the house that John and I shared in Laurel Canyon and walked up the hill overlooking the Canyon. He pretty much wrote the whole song there, reflecting how alone and depressed he had been feeling. I wrote the music and we recorded it the next day."

Manzarek remembered that The Doors had become a force. "We created a new American music that was universal: a rock band coming out of America and commenting on America itself. We explored night and day, yin and yang. We loved Orson Welles and the music of Howlin' Wolf, in other words darkness. Or Muddy Waters singing 'Hoochie Coochie Man'. Or listening to Miles Davis's music, with its dark overtones. Music that had deep dark psychological poetry. Allen Ginsberg's opening to *Howl* was very influential: 'I saw the best minds of my generation destroyed by madness.' That's where The Doors come from: city of night, Raymond Chandler's Los Angeles, Nathanael West's *Miss Lonelyhearts* and *The Day Of The Locust*."

This descent into the underbelly of America was wonderfully expressed by *Strange Days* with its Fellini-esque jacket art, featuring a classic full-colour Joel Brodsky shot that Bill Harvey effectively used 12 inches by 24 inches, continuing from the front to the back of the jacket. It conveyed the mood of The Doors in CinemaScope.

The band were constantly touring and made their European debut in the autumn of 1968, memorably playing London's Roundhouse, and a performance there was filmed by Granada TV as *The Doors Are Open*.

They worked themselves through the classic third-album curse, releasing *Waiting For The Sun* just before heading to Europe. It was the first time they found themselves needing to write new songs and, searching for a hit, they delved back to their pre-Elektra demos for 'Hello I Love You'. By their standards this was a trite pop song, but it provided their second Number One.

As Ray Manzarek recalled, The Doors wanted another 'The End' or 'When The Music's Over' as the climax of the new album. "'Celebration Of

The Lizard' was meant to be the album's epic, but the experiment didn't jell, so we were short of songs. 'Hello I Love You' was a ditty on our very first demos. Some people hearing it the first time in England thought we were lightweight. It was like, 'Haven't you heard "The End"? Fuck you, are you kidding me?'"

For drummer John Densmore, *Waiting For The Sun* was a difficult birth. "For the first time, we had to come up with songs to order. We were in transition as a group and having problems with Jim's behaviour. Paul Rothchild bore the brunt of that. He was a perfectionist, to the point of beating the life out of some songs – we did 130 takes of 'The Unknown Soldier'." It was a theatrical Brechtian anti-war song, the antithesis of 'Hello I Love You', and as a single it stalled at 39.

It was a sign of things to come. Morrison often invited his drunken posse to the studio, which interfered with the sessions. This worsened during the recording of the next two albums, and it had the effect of creating constant problems for the exacting Paul Rothchild. "Paul was the only guy who could intimidate all of The Doors," says Bill Siddons, the group's manager. "He could yell and scream in a very direct way. He busted you point by point. He never spoke in generalities."[2]

"The band was being torn apart," says Robby Krieger, "because Jim was going nuts, and he had all these weird friends who he'd invite to the sessions, and they'd be disruptive. One time, Paul said, 'We need something that's rocking hard,' and we went into that opening riff of 'Five To One' and turned it up as loud as we could. By 'Five To One', Jim meant that there were five times as many people under the age of 21 as over. The baby-boomers were taking over."

Waiting For The Sun, for all the wrangles in recording, was the only Doors album to reach Number One. Holzman feels it's often maligned. "Listen to 'Spanish Caravan': wonderfully done. What other band would even attempt that? You have this clear flamenco intro, and then it's seamless the way the band comes in with such enthusiasm. They could take this disparate material and turn it into a Doors song while paying respect to the original source. Jim's voice on 'Spanish Caravan' is almost a croon. He was a big fan of crooners."

The Doors were now playing larger venues, of a size that no American group had played before. Whatever else drove Morrison to excess, he certainly didn't enjoy the mass adulation. Bill Graham, who often promoted the live Doors shows, recalled how after one show in San Francisco, Morrison was scared because he realised that every woman in the crowd wanted to fuck him.

In Graham's opinion, "Adulation came on such a level, but it wasn't just bobby-soxers screaming at Frank Sinatra. People followed him across the country like the crusades – and how do you deal with that responsibility of being an involuntary leader? Think about that. The pressure on you personally. Jim Morrison didn't want to be a leader, a role model who has self doubts and knows that other people think he has all the answers."[3] It's what eventually drove Morrison to destroy his own perceived image, by putting on weight and shrouding himself with hair and a full beard. This was just what Steve McQueen would do, too, a few years later.

Famously, it was during a concert in Miami on March 1 1969 that a drunken Jim Morrison was arrested, and then he was charged four days later. Three of the charges were misdemeanours, the fourth a felony. At the end of the month he was arrested again, on an FBI charge, citing interstate flight to avoid prosecution.

Robby Krieger, like the others, saw trouble in their future. "We had become targets, especially after Miami. There was a body called the Hall Managers Association and they pretty much blackballed us, after that, and we couldn't play anywhere decent for a year or two. There was a reason for it, but we did feel as if we were doing it for everybody else. Like Lenny Bruce taking the lead in doing his kind of comedy and going to jail for obscenity. We felt like marked men."

When they were not touring, the band devoted time to the next record, *The Soft Parade.* The Doors began to veer off course, away from their signature sound. Both Manzarek and Densmore take responsibility for this direction.

"If that album is not satisfactory, that's entirely my fault," said Manzarek. "The Doors were supposed to be a tight quartet – dark, mysterious, and brooding – so what were we doing adding horns and strings? Whatever we did, all The Doors had to agree, everyone had to say OK. We all wanted to make *that* record."

"The idea of using strings and horns had been at the back of my mind, and Ray's, for a while," says Densmore. "Experimenting was fun. Critics were very harsh about the results. It was Catch 22 – if we hadn't tried something different it would have been The Doors Just Stick To The Same Old Formula."

Krieger is less keen. "To me, it didn't sound like The Doors. I'm still not crazy about the orchestrations, but it includes some of our strongest songs. Hell, I wrote a lot of them – 'Touch Me', 'Wishful Sinful' – but I also like 'The Soft Parade', which was pieced together from some of Jim's poems. That album took months. We had to keep things interesting just to get Jim's attention and have him come to the studio."

Holzman admits that Paul Rothchild could be very demanding. "He did have a tendency to do take after take, wearing an artist to the nub. The studio isn't fun any more, and the records suffer. I thought *The Soft Parade* was weaker, but they had the hit single with 'Touch Me' [a Number Three on *Billboard*]. *The Soft Parade* was too much for Rothchild. It did well, but the studio was getting harder for everyone involved. I thought The Doors were drifting too far from their centre, but the problem self-corrected – they made *Morrison Hotel*."

Morrison Hotel was a tough R&B-based collection that excited Morrison, despite his Miami court case and the possibility of jail time. Morrison had meanwhile pleaded innocent to the Miami charge, with the trial set for April 1970. This was the backdrop against which *Morrison Hotel* was recorded, released only a few months before the trial. Holzman knew there was nothing he could do about Miami except to let it run its natural course and support the group. "This would pass, and there'd be lots of finger-pointing and an entire media circus – but I assured them we were totally committed to them. That was what they needed to hear."

Morrison Hotel represented a return to a simpler, bluesier format, but it was still the product of arduous sessions in the studio. Densmore says, "Paul Rothchild suffered desperately as a result of Jim's descent into self-destruction. He had a difficult time pulling vocals out of Jim. *Morrison Hotel* was tough to make because of the confusion going on around the group, particularly Jim. It took a long while for the Miami hysteria to die down, and Jim was deeply concerned about the impending trial. For Jim's sake, we needed to get back to our core, the roots of the music."

Krieger agrees. "We wanted that garage-band sound, and the album definitely has the rugged feel we were after. It was R&B, but if the Doors played the blues there was always some little hook, some twist; it was never just another blues song. Jim came up with most of the songs, unlike *The Soft Parade*, when he was pretty distracted and uninterested."

Surprisingly, *Morrison Hotel* fared less well than *The Soft Parade* and did not yield a hit single. The group had undertaken a short tour around its release and would soon issue their first live recording. *Absolutely Live* was a double album recorded under controlled conditions to be a live album. The initial recordings were pulled from two concerts held at the Aquarius Theater in Los Angeles in July 1969. As a thank-you to the band's fans, Elektra charged only $2 to join the party. In all, shows from six cities were recorded, concluding with four concerts over two nights at the Felt Forum in New York City on January 17 and 18 1970.

The *Absolutely Live* album finally unveiled the previously aborted 'Celebration Of The Lizard' and reached the Top Ten almost simultaneously with the arrival of the verdict from the Miami jury. Morrison was found guilty of indecent exposure and open profanity but innocent of lewd and lascivious behaviour. On October 30 1970, Morrison was sentenced to 60 days hard labour at Dade County Jail but, after appeal, was freed on bail of $50,000.

With that settled, The Doors were feeling more positive about recording again, only to suffer another setback when Rothchild decided he would no longer produce them. He had lost the strength and will to continue. According to Botnick, "It reached a point where Paul couldn't take any more. He needed not to have to go in and deal with the same problems he had been facing in the studio, and the band didn't want to deal with the same thing any more either." Krieger: "It was a shock, because we normally played the new songs to Paul before recording, and he didn't like any of them. He called them cocktail music. He had just completed *Pearl* with Janis Joplin, and perhaps he just thought that The Doors were sliding downhill without a future."

Rothchild's importance to the group can never be denied, but Krieger feels that Rothchild often had a negative influence in the studio as time went on. "If he had a fault, he drowned a lot of the spontaneity sometimes by trying to make it too perfect," says Krieger. "There's two ways to look at it. You can say that Paul really got some great vocals from Jim after hours and hours of takes, but maybe, if he hadn't taken four hours to get a snare drum sound, Jim might not have gone out and got drunk that day. He had a certain way of doing things, but you can't fault the results."

Holzman began to have misgivings about Rothchild producing the *LA Woman* album. When Rothchild told him that he couldn't do it any more, Holzman commended him for performing miracles, telling the producer that the crucial first album in particular owed him a tremendous debt. "Freed of Paul, the band decided they wanted to work with Bruce Botnick. As a producer, Botnick had saved Love's *Forever Changes*, and I enthusiastically supported their decision and kept my fingers crossed." As Botnick recalls, "The boys said to me, 'What are we going to do?' I replied that we can make this album together as partners. They felt, as I felt, free. And that's how Paul felt."

Rather than go into the Elektra studios, they chose to record in the familiarity of rehearsal rooms, bringing in a 16-track console and with Botnick operating out of a small makeshift control booth. Doors manager Bill Siddons asked Holzman not to come to the sessions because they wanted to keep his ears fresh for when it was done. "When they played me the tapes," says Holzman, "the first thing I heard was 'Riders On The Storm', and I nearly jumped out of my skin with delight and relief. The whole album was done in ten days, and it was seamless and stunning, pure and life-affirming."

Krieger describes the set-up for the *LA Woman* sessions. "We recorded live. The 'studio' was downstairs, while Bruce recorded upstairs watching us through a video remote. Jim was in the bathroom, the door removed to create an improvised vocal booth. His level of concentration was at a peak I'd not seen in years. He was present the whole time and stayed focussed. It was the fastest we had recorded since the first album."

John Densmore agrees. "We tried to do each song in a few takes. Jim was definitely empowered by the responsibility of producing the record ourselves. He was able to keep his problems and his alcoholism away from the studio. The first album was done on four-track, then eight-track, but it's the songs that should dictate the required technology, not the other way around. We had lost sight of that until *LA Woman.* We were back to the basics: just the four of us playing in our garage again."

For Holzman, it was a near miracle. "Their pride at having pulled it off on their own was the key. It gave them back their self esteem, which had been eroded by Rothchild's implied power, because he had been so essential at the beginning."

LA Woman wrapped early in 1971 after two pre-Christmas shows in

Dallas and, disastrously, in New Orleans, where a wasted Morrison clung to the mic-stand telling jokes. It was to be The Doors' final live performance. The stereo mixes for *LA Woman* were completed before Morrison left for Paris where, on July 3 1971, he died at the age of 27. *LA Woman* had been out barely a month.

"When the album came out," remembers Densmore, "Jac Holzman put up a billboard, just as he had done for our first album. This one was on the opposite side of the street leading into Laurel Canyon. After Jim died, Jac kept it up for six months. It was a fitting monument to Jim and the group."

"Paul Rothchild used to say, 'Boys, we better record as much as we can because Jim won't be around for too much longer,'" recalls Krieger. "I always thought Jim would last forever. He was indestructible. I think when Paul said that, he actually meant he thought Jim might just go off and live in Africa or somewhere. He wasn't saying he was going to die, but there were times when you didn't know what Jim was going to do the next day. As a group, it meant we did everything for the moment."

Holzman recalls their last meeting. "Elektra had an office-warming party on Wednesday March 3 1971, to celebrate our expansion and new Studio A. Jim dropped by around 7:30, 'To see,' as he said, 'what I helped pay for.' And then we all went to dinner at the Blue Boar down the street. Jim was always fairly quiet in groups, and was unusually so that evening – half there and half somewhere else. I could feel finality in the air.

"As he left, Jim and I hugged each other, and then he turned somewhat awkwardly and walked away. I looked at his shambling gait and wondered if I would ever see him again."

Today, we look back 50 years to The Doors' classic debut. After that, they packed in six studio albums, and so much more, into a staggering and often wildly turbulent five-year period. They notched up their share of firsts: the first American band to earn six Gold records one after another; the first American rock band to play massive arenas, as they brought theatricality and a sense of the unpredictable to those shows, before the arenas became commonplace for rock events.

"We set the scene for punk," Robby Krieger explains. "The Doors was improvisational theatre. You never knew what was going to happen – there was always a sense of danger. Other groups had no idea what we were doing:

we were always ahead of our time. We weren't trying to be this or that or anything."

The Doors were outsiders. Not just Morrison, but as a group. "I think there was a jealousy toward The Doors," says Jac Holzman. "They had come out of nowhere and were on a strange label for that kind of music. People were surprised that Elektra had succeeded in accomplishing this. Their peers didn't show too much interest in them, and they didn't hang together much. They all had their own lives."

In interviews, Morrison talked about The Doors being "the band they love to hate". According to Holzman, "Jim liked that notion. He liked the idea of being the outsider, and I think he felt he wrote better from the outside than the inside. He maintained that for himself: the vagrant poet who has a better view of contemporary happenings than the insider does. Those are clichés that he had some belief in. A lot of Jim's actions were ways he found to keep himself interested."

The Byrds had set Los Angles alight in 1965 and, stylistically, had a far-reaching effect, especially in their home town. But The Byrds never did anything on a scale to match the achievements of The Doors. Roger McGuinn agrees with this notion. "We were established a little before them, so we saw them as a new upcoming act. But they reached greater heights, mainly because of Jim Morrison's antics.

"Morrsion has this iconic image about him," McGuinn continues, "but I think that has tended to be at the expense of the music. His musical talent gets overlooked. I think the same thing is true of Gram Parsons. They're both more celebrated in some circles for their dramatic personal lives and untimely deaths, and sometimes the music just seems to be an afterthought, which is just crazy."

Los Angeles was teeming with bands when The Doors arrived upon the scene, but The Doors always stood apart. They were an intrinsically LA band who reflected upon the city's seductive appeal.

"We liked LA because it was the cutting edge of civilisation for us," Krieger recalls. "Like Jim says, 'the West is the best'. It was the end point. When you come to the West, it's like the newest part of civilisation. It's where everything was heading and where everything was happening. So we felt we were at the forefront, leading a musical revolution."

Happy Sad

> *"I don't think there was much difference between the topical songwriters and the confessional singer-songwriters of the 70s. Every singer-songwriter who signed to Elektra offered their life stories and their point of view. Tim Buckley, David Ackles, and Paul Siebel were their music."* **JAC HOLZMAN**

If any of Elektra's folk acts felt sidelined because of Elektra's new trajectory, it was inevitably Phil Ochs who voiced his complaint, in *Broadside* magazine. He said that Elektra was "reaching out to the commercial market". Holzman defended his label's unwavering commitment to its folk and rock acts in the same magazine, reminding Ochs of Elektra's open attitude in signing him.

Typical of Ochs's chiding, he was simultaneously lobbying Elektra to make an orchestrated pop album with him. "Even at the apogee of Elektra's rock years," says Holzman, "I never stopped recording other genres. Nonesuch continually released what I thought was interesting and right for Nonesuch, and we signed serious voices like David Ackles and Paul Siebel. And I continued to release the purest ethnic material, from *The Bauls Of Bengal* to *Crow Dog's Paradise*, an album of Sioux Indian music."

Judy Collins says that Elektra's inclusion of rock never felt like a betrayal. "There was room for everybody on that label. I loved The Doors, I loved Carly Simon, Bread – it was a great family enterprise, and these wonderfully talented people put Elektra in a stronger position for other artists to achieve hit singles, which had never been an Elektra strength. They were getting smarter. Nonesuch only contributed to the greater good. Collectively, all of Jac's artists became integrated into an ongoing artistic enterprise. It was very renaissance, in a way."

Tom Rush was less convinced at the time. "I have to say that I didn't ever respond on a visceral level to the rock acts. I realised that Jac was very much taken by them, especially The Doors. He was heading in that direction, and I wasn't comfortable. So it was time for us to part company. One of the cool things about Elektra was that if you had a problem, you could go to Jac and work it out. I think the move to the Los Angeles office and his focus on The Doors in particular signalled that there was some distance growing between us. These things happen. I wasn't dropped by Elektra: my contract had expired."

Rush had a better offer on the table from Columbia than Holzman was prepared to match, and Holzman was swayed, in part, because he didn't care for Rush's final Elektra album, *The Circle Game* – regarded by so many as his finest. It's often viewed as the precursor to the 70s singer-songwriter movement, a trend once perfectly described by respected rock writer Greg Shaw as "lifestyle wallpaper music". Rush wrote very little himself, recording new songs by James Taylor ('Sunshine Sunshine', 'Something In The Way She Moves'), Jackson Browne ('Shadow Dream Song'), and Joni Mitchell ('Tin Angel', 'Urge For Going', 'The Circle Game') before other interpreters had even heard them.

"I was two years over deadline and I really needed to get a record out, and I was a bit desperate," says Rush. "In very quick succession, Joni, Jackson, and James came up with these fabulous songs. All three writers were introduced to the world on the same piece of vinyl. People sat up and thought hey, something's going on here. It was three songwriters who I'd not previously heard of, and boom – they were on my album." Rush was hardly prolific himself, and his own songwriting contribution was the poignant 'No Regrets', the definitive version, floating beautifully atop Bruce Langhorne's languid guitar.

In 2009, Rush released his first studio album in 35 years, *What I Know*, sounding just as he did in the 60s. He never joined the pantheon of million-selling confessional singer-songwriters he helped introduce, his three excellent Columbia albums faring only moderately well, on a label where

Rush never felt at home. "Elektra was a small shop where everybody knew everybody," he says. "Columbia operated on layers and layers of bureaucracy. It was hard to figure out who did what."

Wildflowers, released in 1967, continued Judy Collins's association with Joshua Rifkin, begun on the previous year's *In My Life*, although the studio location shifted to Elektra's new creative centre, California. During the sessions for *In My Life*, Collins had begun playing piano again, and it provided a comfort zone within which she began writing her own songs. The purity of 'Since You Asked', 'Sky Fell', and 'Albatross' on *Wildflowers* reveals a remarkable songwriting talent. Yet it was a cover of Joni Mitchell's 'Both Sides Now', which Joni had sung down the phone to her, which became Collins's first hit single, reaching Number Eight in the *Billboard* chart.

"*Wildflowers* was the first completely orchestrated album of the genre," Collins rightly observes. "Not a folk guitar on it. And it had my writing. I was well established and reasonably successful, and I'd been content to sing the great songs of others, to have someone like Leonard Cohen send me a tape of three new songs and say: 'You choose.' After we recorded 'Suzanne', Leonard said I should write. I had never considered that possibility until he encouraged me."

The 1969 album *Who Knows Where The Time Goes* was another departure – and one Judy Collins was unsure of. It was, after all, a country-rock album featuring musicians Van Dyke Parks, James Burton, and her then-beau Stephen Stills, who was inspired by her to write 'Suite: Judy Blue Eyes' for Crosby Stills & Nash.

She moved into the 70s with *Whales & Nightingales* and a tapestry of music more reminiscent of her earlier work. It also yielded an a cappella version of 'Amazing Grace', recorded at St Paul's Chapel in New York City, with her friends in the chorus, which intermittently spent two years in the UK charts and provided her second substantial US hit. Such is her association with that song and its MOR context that the bold, adventurous music she made throughout the 60s is often overlooked.

Collins combined her own material with choice covers and exploratory interpretations, but her albums appeared less frequently. *Judith* in 1975 was her first under the new Elektra regime of David Geffen. She didn't speak to Holzman after he left Elektra in 1973, upset at his departure and wary of his chosen successor.

Ironically, *Judith* became her bestselling album – under David Geffen rather than Jac Holzman and despite her initial reservations. The album provided another impressive hit in 'Send In The Clowns'. A senior Warner Communications officer, upon prompting by some of Frank Sinatra's people, had called Holzman requesting that Sinatra's version of 'Send In The Clowns' be allowed to precede that of Collins. Holzman refused.

Five albums later, *Home Again* (1984) ended Judy Collins's 23-year span with Elektra, equalling that of Holzman himself. Her unassuming artistic perseverance and innate dignity were overshadowed by the turbulent public life and high-profile records of The Doors, Love, and Tim Buckley. Buckley is often seen as the last of Elektra's great 'folk' signings in the connecting line from Collins, Paxton, Neil, and Ochs. He appears to bridge the era of acoustic folk and the influence of rock from Los Angeles, but really he never belonged in either camp.

Born in Washington, DC, on Valentine's Day 1947, Tim Buckley was raised in New York. His family moved to Orange County, California, when he was ten years old. At seventeen, he joined a country & western outfit, Princess Ramona & The Cherokee Riders. He formed simultaneous bands with two friends from Buena Vista High School, Larry Beckett, then playing drums, and bass player Jim Fielder. One was more of a pop combo, The Bohemians; the other, Harlequin 3, more esoteric. They played clubs in LA, where the Mothers Of Invention drummer Jimmy Carl Black befriended them and brought them to the attention of Herb Cohen, who arranged an audition at the Crescendo, on the Strip.

"The band did a set of five or six songs," said Cohen. "Tim was phenomenal. He looked great, and the voice was special even then. But Larry was not really a drummer, and Jim Fielder was nowhere near as good a musician as he would become. I brought Tim to Elektra." Holzman was smitten by Buckley's voice after hearing a six-song demo, and says he thought the voice not of this world. Holzman signed him during the summer of 1966, and the debut album, *Tim Buckley*, was recorded in LA by Paul Rothchild and released later that year, before the first Doors album.

Holzman felt *Tim Buckley*, as interesting as it was, served merely as an introduction to his talent. "It was an exercise in learning the studio and introducing Tim to its possibilities. The first album was training wheels for what followed. There was a mysterious, almost ephemeral quality about

Tim. Some songs are really good – 'Wings', 'Song Of The Magician', perhaps 'Grief In My Soul' – and there were moments of daring. 'Song Slowly Song' has a sparse two-and-a-half-minute intro, so you can see the antecedents of what would come."

Lee Underwood first met Buckley in New York, and he played guitar on that debut and throughout much of Buckley's career. Underwood saw the same adventuresome tilt: "The intimate 'Song Slowly Song' and the dreamlike 'Song Of The Magician' signalled the more improvisational instrumental approach and expansive, atmospheric qualities that Tim would explore in two later Elektra albums, *Happy Sad* and his breakthrough experimental opus, *Lorca*."

Buckley worked hard to promote his album, playing festivals, concerts, clubs, and campuses, a typical campaign designed to build by word of mouth. "Live, he was cotton candy for the girls," says Holzman. "His songs reveal a sensitivity that women pick up on earlier than men. Women always made the connections – gorgeous, waif-like, and sensitive – and they were the first he would lose later with his ambiguous work. *Goodbye And Hello* was a fully realised gem, a miracle."

Buckley's most obvious attraction was that voice, which Robert Shelton described in *The New York Times* as "not quite a counter-tenor, but a tenor to counter with". However, within a year of his tantalising debut, Buckley was preparing something more challenging and sophisticated. He and Larry Beckett, now writing the poetic lyrics, had a solid notion of how they wanted to shape *Goodbye And Hello.*

"The first time I met Tim," recalls Jerry Yester, his newly assigned producer, "was up at Herbie Cohen's house. Tim played for Judy Henske, Fred Neil, and me, and he sang with Jim Fielder on bass. Right out of high school, Tim was wearing a suit, a maroon tie, and his hair was slicked back. He was painfully shy. Fred Neil was his god, and I'm sure he dreamed that his voice could have dropped an octave so that he could sing like Fred. He emulated Fred's tragic side, too."

Yester remembers a wonderful relationship developing between him and Buckley and Beckett. "They just tickled me. They weren't about to let anyone screw them over. Firm in their ideals, they had that album all worked out, even down to the track sequencing. I would make suggestions – some they would take, others they wouldn't, but they were open-minded.

My role was to bring Tim out, his uniqueness and the clarity of his vision."

At its best, such as the dramatic, impassioned 'Pleasant Street' or the mood-shifting 'Hallucinations', *Goodbye And Hello* scores high. Buckley appears most at ease on the two mellower, more laidback songs: 'Morning Glory', with its wonderful understated arrangement, and the simple, dreamy 'Once I Was', inspired by Fred Neil after Buckley visited the sessions for Neil's recording of 'The Dolphins'.

Holzman saw that Buckley was now using his vocal instrument fully. "He was already a considerably improved singer riding above the music. The flow of that album is exquisite. Tim's 12-string guitar-playing is subtle but quietly propelling. It's spiritual and special without being precocious. I was thrilled with *Goodbye And Hello* – I would take that home, get loaded, lie on the floor, and play it as loud as I could. It uplifted me."

The album marked a turning point for its creator. "It was very hard for me to write songs after *Goodbye And Hello* because most of the bases were touched," Buckley said in 1974. "That was the end of my apprenticeship for writing songs. Whatever I wrote after that wasn't adolescent, which means it wasn't easy to write after that, because you can't repeat yourself. The way Jac had it set up, you were supposed to move on artistically, but the way the business is, you're not. You're supposed to repeat what you do, so there's a dichotomy there."[1]

Lee Underwood observed the dichotomy that Buckley had identified. "Tim's approach was very much at odds with the laidback troubadour image. His insights penetrated to the core of issues. He linked disparate concepts in startling ways. His thought processes were as fast as an eye-blink, and his use of language brilliant. That image fit him during the early days, when he was a teenage folkie, but quickly became irrelevant and inappropriate as he matured."

Bruce Botnick, who was the engineer on the first three Buckley albums for Elektra, saw him change before his eyes. "You couldn't contain Tim Buckley's talent – a reflection of all the different sides of his personality. They are what they are, and as a producer you really don't have a lot of control over that. You have to go with it. There were quantum leaps between his albums and an intellectual growth that's the mark of a great artist. It's never really conscious with someone like Tim Buckley, or Bob Dylan – these people don't slice themselves up into pieces. It's all very instinctive: they have a vision."

In the year after *Goodbye And Hello*, Buckley had grown musically through the experience of touring with a pool of musicians who were now exploring jazz roots rather than folk. It was this intimate acoustic-based group of players – featuring Buckley's own 12-string, Lee Underwood on lead guitar, and Carter C.C. Collins on congas, plus acoustic bass and vibes – who entered the studios to record what became *Happy Sad*.

They just let the tape roll while the musicians improvised and weaved minimalist tapestries around six of Buckley's new songs, of which two stretched beyond ten minutes. If you release yourself from judgement, you can be effortlessly drawn into Buckley's hypnotic world. Gone is the elaborate poetic metaphor, gone are the intricate arrangements. *Happy Sad* is the defining album in Tim Buckley's work, replacing romanticism with experimentation. The word groundbreaking is often used glibly, but here it is for once applicable. *Happy Sad* is Tim Buckley's equivalent to Miles Davis's *Kind Of Blue*. It was his highest-charting album, even if it only made Number 81, and it remained in the charts for three months after its release in April 1969.

Happy Sad's producer, Jerry Yester, has less than fond memories. He was in the middle of recording an album with Pat Boone when Buckley asked him to do *Happy Sad*. Yester was working in a production team with Zal Yanovsky, who had left The Lovin' Spoonful (and whom Yester would replace). Buckley's musicians ridiculed them for working with the straight-laced Boone, but there was one bizarre consequence. The Pat Boone album that Yester was producing includes the first-ever recorded version of one of Tim Buckley's most renowned compositions, 'Song To The Siren', which would remain unrecorded by Buckley until *Starsailor* two years later.

"After the rewarding and enjoyable experience with *Goodbye And Hello*, this was oil and water," Yester says of *Happy Sad*. "Not so much with Tim, but with the band. He really didn't need any input from me on arrangements. The band was leading him at times, and I was there to help make it sound as good as possible." Buckley had a different recollection. "I really loved doing that album. It was really a breakout time for me musically, and we had a ball doing that. The trick of writing is to make it sound like it's all happening for the first time. It took a long time for me to write that album, and then to teach the people in the band, but they were all great people so it was really a labour of love – the way it should be."[2]

Critics make much of the influence of Fred Neil on Buckley's new approach. As Lee Underwood has said, the Buckley–Neil relationship has been exaggerated, and this is confirmed by Herb Cohen, who maintains that "the contact that Fred Neil had with Buckley was minimal". Larry Beckett once commented, "Tim and I went to one of Fred's recording sessions, where he was working out 'Dolphins', and from that day on, Tim became obsessed with him. This shows up in his writing on *Goodbye And Hello*, his singing on *Happy Sad*, and it lasted until the end."[3] Holzman says, "I knew that he and Fred had been hanging out, and that worried me, because of Fred's drug habits. If people want to sit around and smoke dope, that's fine with me, but heroin and Tim was a frightening thought. As a writing influence, Fred Neil might be exceptional. I just didn't like what went with Fred."

The music always came first for Buckley, as Holzman knew from the start. "He never felt any desire to be famous. He was purely musical and he wanted people around him who could facilitate his music. He was motivated only by a need for self-expression. When *Happy Sad* made the shift from *Goodbye And Hello*, the audience he had acquired began to drift away. You go to *Lorca* and *Starsailor*, and that process escalates – and he wasn't adding any new audience to compensate for the loss. Tim never cared about the numbers. Just the music."

Holzman wasn't open to the albums that followed *Goodbye And Hello*. He felt that *Happy Sad* had the sense of a humid afternoon in Santa Monica, where *Goodbye And Hello* was dramatic and intense, bypassing the brain. "*Happy Sad* disappointed me at first, because I expect things to take off and go up, not to take off and go nowhere. In retrospect, that was tough for me to understand. Tim was drifting into a looser style, much jazzier, but there are fine, fine songs: 'Buzzin' Fly', and 'Love From Room 109' is compelling. It was something I didn't expect, and I realise more now that it was also very, very good. I did not have the perspective then; I do now."

Herb Cohen, who would continue to manage Buckley into the 70s, is just as rueful. "He committed artistic suicide, in a way – certainly commercial suicide. Because he was trying to become a vocal musician. Of course, he did some stuff that was really good, strange as it was, but he wanted to develop something, and I don't know that he really knew what that was or whether he felt he had ever got there. There was no way that people could relate to albums like *Lorca* and *Starsailor*. People do now try to figure out what that music was and where it was going, but the world at the time wasn't prepared for that. People would come to see him because of what they heard from the first two albums, and they couldn't understand what he was doing any more. And they would stop coming."

Buckley's final Elektra album was the more experimental and near-instrumental *Lorca*. During the autumn of 1969, Buckley recorded both *Lorca* and what became *Blue Afternoon*, plus part of his sixth album, *Starsailor*. Holzman gave Buckley his release, knowing he already had a potential new home with Herb Cohen's Discreet label. Holzman hadn't heard *Lorca* in 40 years, but returned to it and had this response: "I totally blew it with *Lorca*. When I hear it now, I realise I should have paid closer attention at the time. Even for me, so into evolution in music, I was not ready to accept Tim's streams of self-expression and the lack of modality on *Lorca*. 'Nobody Walkin'' astonishes me in the way Tim uses his voice. If that's the last song he recorded for Elektra, he went out in flaming glory. How he got those voices on that album I can't imagine. Hearing it in 2010, I'm proud it is on Elektra. And it is on Elektra through no credit to me."

Herb Cohen released Buckley's *Blue Afternoon* and the extraordinary *Starsailor* on his Straight label. *Starsailor*, appropriately, received a five-star review in the jazz journal *Down Beat* but failed to register with the public. There was a *Rolling Stone* review of one of the handful of shows played by the improv-fuelled Starsailor band, with the headline 'Buckley Yodelling Baffles Audience'. Buckley had the talent and the carefree attitude that he could do anything, and he would never be reined in, certainly not by commercial considerations, as Cohen found. "To be successful you really have to be driven," he says, "and he wasn't. But his attitude was always positive as to what he wanted his music to be. No question. He could actually do anything he wanted to do with that voice."

Buckley's more difficult albums are held in greater esteem today. The accolades and his reputation continued to grow, particularly following his death in June 1975 from a heroin overdose. More albums – some unreleased studio works, and mostly live concerts – have appeared since then than during his lifetime. Holzman regrets that he didn't have a great deal of contact with Buckley toward the end of his Elektra years. "The stylistic shift was a shock to me – I just didn't know who would want those albums. I stepped off the bus at this point and I got off early. I think today I would probably have continued."

* * *

David Ackles is often mentioned in the same breath as Tim Buckley. Like Buckley, he was unusual in not coming from a folk-based tradition. In Ackles's case, prior to recording he had never performed in public as a solo artist. Of all the singer-songwriters signed to Elektra in the later 60s, Ackles was arguably the least typical. He played piano rather than guitar, but it was his voice, a warm but powerful baritone, that caught the ear.

Ackles was born into a showbiz family – his grandfather was a music hall comedian, his grandmother was the leader of an orchestra – and at the age of four he made up one half of a Vaudevillian song-and-dance act with his sister. By his early teens, he had been a Hollywood B-movie child actor, playing a character called Tuck Worden in a series of low-budget films for Columbia directed by future horror-maestro William Castle. While studying drama at UCLA, Ackles met David Anderle. "Then there was a five-year period when I didn't see him," recalls Anderle. "When I settled at Elektra, he was the first person I brought to the label."[4]

Ackles was signed in 1968, although he thought he was being hired as a staff writer. First attempts at recording didn't go well until producers Anderle and Russ Miller handpicked some session musicians who were currently being auditioned for a new Elektra supergroup, which became Rhinoceros. The players included guitarist Danny Weis and bass player Jerry Penrod (both formerly in Iron Butterfly) along with Daily Flash guitarist Doug Hastings, and organist Michael Fonfara. It's Hastings's delicate filigreed guitar and Fonfara's ghostly whistling organ that help define the sound of the album. Their understated playing on Ackles's debut album provides the perfect balance to his own steady, pounding piano. Bruce Botnick was the engineer on those sessions. "They were great musicians but hadn't recorded together at that point," recalls Botnick. "The only element they would lack in Rhinoceros was songs. How well they played on the David Ackles album proves what they could have done with powerful material."

The *David Ackles* debut album was stagey and emotional, the songs intelligent, doomy, and powerful. 'Laissez-Faire' was an orphan from an unrealised Broadway musical; 'Sonny Come Home' was art-house suspense. But the two best remembered songs from the album were world-weary ballads.

"At UCLA," remembers Anderle, "David was a song-and-dance man performing in revues and musicals, Noel Coward type stuff with clever wordplay. Then, years later, he brought me 'The Road To Cairo' and 'Down River'. I was deeply moved by the depth and the darkness. I thought: where did this come from?"[5]

Holzman has his own notions. "David Ackles was fascinating, because he was really a composer of musicals for a very small stage. His albums were like intimate musicals. You could have taken the songs and later written a book around them. He was beset by so many demons, which appear in disguise within his songs – but that's why *he* has to sing them. Ackles was very kind and considerate, an extremely gentle soul who lived within himself and within his music."

Bruce Botnick agrees. "The music may have been intense, but he was a marshmallow: one of the sweetest people. He was obviously conflicted and a complicated person. You don't write about the subjects he engaged with unless it's to deal with demons. He was uniquely Elektra in temperament, with a Jacques Brel quality, dark but also charming. Ackles had the perfect voice for what he was doing, although he was by no means a perfect singer." Holzman says, "I loved the songs for exactly the reasons they did not attract an audience."

Ackles was better appreciated in Britain and by a wide range of fellow artists. Phil Collins selected Ackles's 'Down River' when he appeared on the great BBC Radio institution *Desert Island Discs.* Elton John was astonished to find Ackles supporting him on his first US tour in 1970. "I was topping the bill over David Ackles, but that just seemed inappropriate to me," says Elton. "There was no way anyone could've convinced me that I should have been listed above David Ackles. To see that audience chatting away while he was singing those seductive songs just tore me apart."[6] Elton's writing partner Bernie Taupin agrees. "In the golden age of the singer-songwriter, David was a hybrid disconnected from the troubadour label pinned on others. It's not just that his music was different, *he* was different."[7]

It's tempting to view Ackles's follow-up album, *Subway To The Country*, as transitional, since it displayed a growing sophistication after the sparse, moody palette of his debut, with its evocative jacket photograph of an out-of-focus Ackles gazing through a cracked windowpane. The songs on the second record are no less intense but, musically, they veer from barroom country to deranged gospel. The music draws upon the more atonal style of Kurt Weill, with Ackles's lyrics swinging violently in a manner characteristic of Weill's collaborator Bertolt Brecht. It was influenced as much by country music as avant-garde theatre, while the less brutal songs provide a bridge to the album that followed, which is his most praised work.

Ackles devoted almost two years to plan the cycle of songs that became *American Gothic*, and Bernie Taupin was given the opportunity to produce him. For an album that takes its title from Grant Wood's *American Gothic*, one of the most famous paintings in American art history, it was perhaps surprisingly recorded in England, where Ackles lived for nine months after September 1971. As Ackles himself remarked, "When you are away from it, you have a sharper perspective of your own country."[8]

American Gothic is a dramatic and colourfully orchestrated album that ranges widely over the American music landscape – country, church hymns, ragtime, Aaron Copland, Charles Ives, and Hollywood soundtracks. Taupin is no less in awe today than when it was recorded. "[It is] a body of work so steeped in imagery, [and] everything David is here – from stark noir pieces to sarcastic music-hall parodies. Even his songs of love and loss are branded with originality: the image of the moving van, the itinerant musician, or the simple romantic breathe and move with sadness and timeless wonderment. It's been said many times that his theatrical background was the catalyst for his song styling, the thing that set him apart from everyone else. It's true his work was riddled with homages to Kurt Weill, Bertolt Brecht, and Orson Welles, and in his masterwork, the epic 'Montana Song', never has Stephen Vincent Benét met Aaron Copland with such breathtaking results."[9]

Not for the first time, Jac Holzman had recorded an artist who, even today, has only a dedicated cult following. "We stayed with Ackles," says Holzman, "although nobody really bought the records. He went to Columbia after us for one album. He was just raw talent. In the end, we made three great David Ackles albums, but there is a limit, however much you believe in an artist."

Ackles shared Holzman's viewpoint, as he told *Ptolemaic Terrascope* in 1994. "Well, the thing was, I'd had three strikes at bat with Elektra and got nowhere. The records had all been well reviewed and hadn't done much else, so Jac Holzman and I sat down and decided between us that it might be time to try somewhere new. It was thoroughly mutual. Jac was as frustrated at the lack of sales as I was, and we decided it was an opportune moment to move on. So off I went to Columbia and did *Five And Dime*."

Five And Dime, which Ackles recorded for Columbia in 1973, suffered the same disappointingly poor sales as his Elektra recordings. He would never record again, and he spent the next 25 years of his life working in the arts and education. He returned to writing TV scripts along with work on ballet scores and teaching songwriting. Ackles did complete the score for a musical, *Sister Aimee*, in the early 90s. He settled on a six-acre horse farm near Los Angeles with his wife Janice, and became a professor of theatre for the University of Southern California. He died of lung cancer, at the age of 62, in March 1999.

"There are artists on the label – and David Ackles is one of them – that we were never able to connect to an audience," says Holzman with a deep sigh. "Part of it was the personality of the man. He was so happy to do what he was doing. There were people who didn't want it badly enough, but I saw what was inside the music and believed it had to be recorded and preserved."

Ackles's widow Janice offered a final thought in 2007. "David's overriding dream was to write a musical: direct it; stage it; design the sets, costumes, and lighting; plot the choreography; and play the lead. He could have done it – he had all the talent. I so regretted that this never happened in the way he envisaged. When you listen to David singing his music, you are in that place he intends for you. You can visualise the barroom, smell the grass on the vast Montana plains, and feel the motion of the carousel – all revel in the delirium of newly found love. All you have to do is listen."

By comparison, David Ackles is far better known than Paul Siebel, whose two exceptional albums were released in 1970 and 1971. Born and raised in Buffalo, Siebel headed to New York City in 1959 but was soon drafted into the army. Back in Buffalo in 1962, he hung around the cloistered folk scene for a while, watching the rise of Eric Andersen and Jackson C. Frank. He returned to New York in late 1962, drawn to the folk epicentre of Greenwich Village. He waited until 1969 before a collection of demos he recorded with David Bromberg led to an opportunity to record his Elektra debut *Woodsmoke And Oranges* with a small, intimate ensemble, including Bromberg, Richard Greene, and pedal-steel player Weldon Myrick. Produced by Peter Siegel, the result was unassuming country-folk blessed by Siebel's charming, woodsmoked songs.

It was Peter Siegel who brought Paul Siebel to Jac Holzman, on the recommendation of David Bromberg. "*Woodsmoke And Oranges* was one of the best of my recordings," says Siegel. "Paul Siebel came out of the beat generation, even though it took a while before he came to record. He was a wonderful lyricist, a wonderful singer and musician. Jac knew right away he was good but he wasn't going to spend a lot of money on it. Jac would use the term 'recording fund', which didn't mean just the recording budget; if there was any money left, that was the artist's advance. So we made a $10,000 record. I was really pushed to make a whole album with a folk-rock band for that money, but it sounds well produced and had a lot of spontaneity." Paul Siebel told Jim Allen in the November 2010 issue of *Mojo* that the album actually came in at $8,000, "and they gave me $2,000 – more money than I'd ever seen."

'Any Day Woman' was covered by Bonnie Raitt and 'Louise' by Jerry Jeff Walker and Ian Matthews; Waylon Jennings and Linda Ronstadt also recorded Siebel's songs, but apart from *Live At McCabes*, recorded in 1978, his two Elektra albums are all that remain of his quietly devastating work. Vivid storytelling and stark, melodic songs make him a trailblazer of Americana. Neither *Woodsmoke And Oranges* nor the equally impeccable *Jack-Knife Gypsy* caused more than discreet ripples of appreciation. *Jack-Knife Gypsy*, featuring an entirely different cast, still attracted such highly regarded musicians as Clarence White, Buddy Emmons, and David Grisman, but suffered the same fate. "They were just a cult thing," Siebel told Peter Doggett, who managed to track him down to his local bar for the liner notes of reissues of both albums in 2004. "It kind of depressed me: it just didn't seem to work, or at least that's how I felt about it." "He basically stopped writing songs," says Peter Siegel. "He had writer's block, or lost the ability. One version that I heard was that he stopped drinking and couldn't write anymore. Unfortunately I didn't produce the second album because I had quit my job by then."

"I was never aware of him in the early Village days," Holzman says. "He was just a natural singer-songwriter who wasn't going any place except where his music was going to take him. He wrote in a pure environment which always interests me. He wrote with purity and directness. He was a great craftsman who wanted a record out, and I obliged him and my own taste."

Tim Buckley, David Ackles, and Paul Siebel were all highly individual voices. Siebel's career simply petered out, and by the mid 80s he ceased touring and writing songs altogether. Ackles, too, had turned his back on recording after his fourth album. Buckley went through yet another stylistic about-face when he recorded *Greetings From L.A.* for Warners in 1972 – this time moving toward risqué funked-up soul – and at the time of his death he was planning a live album that revisited his earlier work. "Tim was making music for himself to the very end," said Herb Cohen. "He could achieve pretty much anything within his imagination."

Holzman was simultaneously shifting Elektra away from its proven solid ground at the end of the 60s, and he made a series of signings – some of which promised more than they delivered. They drew from a multiplicity of styles that veered into new territory, from white Southern soul to breathtaking, introspective country and experimental sound collages.

Remembering Elektra
Larry Beckett on Tim Buckley

"I was at the same high school – Loara High School in Anaheim – where I knew Jim Fielder; he knew Tim and thought we should meet. Tim was singing folk songs and I was writing poetry. Jim thought we would get along, and he was right. It was strange because we were opposites: he was careless and passionate and I was disciplined and thoughtful. We admired those opposites in each other.

Tim was obsessed with extending his vocal range. When he heard Fred Neil, he wanted to sing lower; when he heard Yma Sumac* he wanted to sing higher. Tim was singing in hootenannies and he was singing folk songs better than anybody I had ever heard. When I heard him sing with his beautiful Irish tenor voice, it was like standing next to Caruso.

Tim was completely a musician; I was completely a poet. When I

* A popular, exotic Peruvian singer of the 50s with a five-octave range.

suggested we write songs together, he liked the edge of having a poet for a lyricist. He loved poetry – listen to his song 'Lorca'.

We formed The Bohemians to play our electric rock'n'roll songs in between radio hits at dances and bars. The Harlequin Three was a break from too many Top 40 covers, to play acoustic experiments, comedy, and poetry out loud, in folk music clubs. Songs like Fred Neil's 'I've Got A Secret' and Bob Dylan's 'Boots Of Spanish Leather' showed me that you could write songs that were in the vein of folk songs and just as strong. We listened to *Bleecker And MacDougal* by Fred Neil over and over, and it was always fresh. I've called it the *Kind Of Blue* of folk-rock.

Besides the glories of 60s folk, rock, and folk-rock, we listened to blues: *Blues, Rags And Hollers* by Koerner Ray & Glover, *Completely Well* by B.B. King; old-time: *See Reverse Side For Title* by Jim Kweskin & The Jug Band; world: *Music Of Bulgaria*; jazz: *Is That All There Is* by Peggy Lee; spoken word: *912 Greens* by Ramblin' Jack Elliot; classical: *The Well-Tempered Clavier* by J.S. Bach, *Duets With The Spanish Guitar, Piano Music Of Erik Satie*. Tim could sing many more kinds of music than he recorded, like 'Hi Lily, Hi Lo' on *Dream Letter*. Miles Davis turning from *Kind Of Blue* to *Sketches Of Spain* to *ESP* was an inspiration in his boldness to change.

Tim was always moving into a new music; 'Song Slowly Song' was the farthest out on that first album, and it felt like it when we wrote and played it. 'Strange Street Affair Under Blue' – Tim's wife wrote a verse, then Tim gave up trying to finish it and gave me some fragments, and I reworked it completely. Then he set it in Greek syrtaki dance style that starts in one tempo and then accelerates. He listened to all kinds of music; 'Hallucinations' was inspired by Arab street music.

Tim had a dark sense of humour. On *Dream Letter: Live In London 1968*, 'Morning Glory' is introduced by Tim as being "about a hobo beating up on a collegian kid … outside of Dallas, Texas"; he's just kidding around. 'Morning Glory' is in part about time. The morning glory is a flower that opens in the morning and dies later that afternoon; its life is surprisingly brief, like a house that vanishes. The characters in the song could be said to represent Innocence, who is singing, and Experience, who is the hobo. Innocence has had little time, and Experience much: "No more tales of time," says the hobo.

'Pleasant Street' is about addiction in some form or another – perhaps drugs – that is dragging him down, and that is the whole point of the song. He raises his head at some point and sees the straight people with their stone-like exteriors in their black suits. "Christian liquorice" describes people who are wearing suits and think, "Why do I want to be alive in this world?"

'Goodbye And Hello': It was a time when pop art was verging on fine art. Dylan's 'Desolation Row' was one of the finest lyric poems of the decade; 'Eleanor Rigby' by The Beatles was a classical art song. I was obsessed with this, and we were given artistic control over the album. So, with Tim working with me, I dreamed ideas for arrangements, down to the instrumentation. And I loved the music of Bach.

There was 'revolution in the air'. The song 'Goodbye And Hello' gathered up failures we were turning from and ideals we were turning toward. I was influenced in my thinking by ideas voiced on counter-cultural FM radio. The chorus sections were meant to be sung in counterpoint, so that "O the new children dance" and "I am young" would be sung at the same time, and "All around the balloons" with "I will live", and so on. But Tim chose to sing them consecutively. I always wrote the words first, and he'd come back in a few days with amazing music.

I wouldn't say the songs are completely unlike anybody else's. There is a strong connection between 'Once I Was' and 'Dolphins' by Fred Neil. We also loved the songs of Tim Hardin. He was an influence, and he was very concise – one of his great graces is that he gets in and gets out. But there was a lot of originality.

The wonderful people at Elektra – especially Jac Holzman and Paul Rothchild – gave us full creative control. We had a brilliant producer in Jerry Yester, who was very sympathetic. Tim and I worked out the instrumentation for each piece. If there is an oboe or something, then it is there precisely because we decided that there should be an oboe on it.

The *Goodbye And Hello* sleeve is very striking: we went down to the beach to shoot a picture and Tim had no idea what they wanted. He picked up a bottle cap and stuck it in his eye and they thought, That's the shot. ”

Thanks to Spencer Leigh and Andy Morten at Shindig! *magazine for permission to use some of the above comments by Larry Beckett.*

CHAPTER 20

Accept No Substitute

> *"I wanted Elektra to live more on the edge, to encourage experimental music that defied easy definition. If you make these recordings intelligently and at modest cost, a whole new world can open, and sales are not the measure of your success. Such recordings are made not for 'now' but for 'tomorrow'."* **JAC HOLZMAN**

In 1966, Jac Holzman paid $75,000 for a building on La Cienega Boulevard, on the eastern boundary of West Hollywood. After reconstruction, it became Elektra's West Coast headquarters for the next 20 years. It was typical of Holzman's foresight that when he took the wrecking ball to the existing structure he installed extra-strength steel supports to allow for upward expansion (and later acquired adjacent lots). It was something Holzman remembered that publisher William Randolph Hearst had done with a small building on Columbus Circle in New York City, permitting 30 storeys to rise above what had been a two-storey building.

"Acquiring the La Cienega space was our crucial commitment to Elektra as a two-coast enterprise," says Holzman. "The East Coast was the operational centre – legal, financing, everything to do with production and manufacture. The West Coast was A&R, marketing, and a studio. For years I dreamed of building my own studio, and every year that went by before I could begin, my technical wish-list grew larger."

Everything was custom-built, assembled by technicians able to work without budget constraints. "It was the world's finest party living room, and you could change the acoustics and the appearance with sliding panels," Holzman continues. "A kitchen was close by, and the entire complex was locked off from the street. It was very tough to gain access if you didn't belong there. It was an exotic, fun space, ideal for California and catnip for me. God knows what went on when I wasn't there."

By the late 60s, the West Coast more than the East Coast defined Elektra. Elektra had managed to do successfully what few other labels had done: to establish an office where the creative people could thrive.

Paul Rothchild also moved west. His house on Ridpath, which he shared with engineer Fritz Richmond, became a central point for the Laurel Canyon music community. Another Canyon resident was the occasional Elektra producer Barry Friedman, who soon adopted the name Frazier Mohawk. Both offered open-house opportunities for all interested in sex, drugs, and rock'n'roll, Southern California style. "Frazier was a total fruitcake," says Holzman, "but a very engaging fruitcake – there were real nuts and shiny candy pieces in there. Whatever Frazier was doing would always grab my attention." Mohawk soon produced two of Elektra's most searching and unorthodox albums, with Nico and with The Holy Modal Rounders.

Aside from the enticing hedonistic appeal of the Canyon lifestyle, after 1968 Rothchild was spending huge gulps of time in Sunset Sound studios with The Doors. He was still exclusively tied to Elektra, producing further albums in LA with Clear Light, Ars Nova, and Rhinoceros. Holzman later said these were unreasonably complex projects and that Rothchild was "firing blanks".

Ars Nova were thoughtfully conceived, mostly comprising former students of New York City's Mannes Music College, one of America's leading conservatories. Even the band's name was an allusion to an iconoclastic circle of 14th-century church composers. Their one Elektra album, *Ars Nova*, carefully blended a baroque classical approach with a rock sound, but it hits out in so many directions that it invariably missed the target.

Clear Light are invariably remembered for having two drummers, especially as one of them, Dallas Taylor, later joined Crosby Stills Nash & Young; on the evidence of their sole Elektra album, they deserve to be feted for more than just a perceived gimmick. The group combined dramatic rock, flashes of folk-rock, oddball hooks, and sharp shocks of experimentation with a melodic side dish of psychedelia that was never Elektra's strongest suit. They formed in LA, bursting onto the scene around Sunset Strip in 1966 and went through a series of name changes, including The Garnerfield Sanitarium and The Brain Train. After signing to Elektra, they adopted the name Clear Light. The story goes that, high on a hilltop, zonked on acid, the lead singer of another Elektra group turned to Paul Rothchild and said, "Race you into the clear light." Rothchild, who having signed the group also took over their management, thought it would be a great name, and the group deferentially concurred. That other singer was Jim Morrison.

'Black Roses', their first single, was recorded in April 1967 and turned out to be the only one to feature the Clear Light line-up that Rothchild had originally signed: drummers Dallas Taylor and Michael Ney, bassist Douglas Lubahn, and guitarists Bob Seal and Robbie Robison. Within two months, Paul Rothchild brought in actor-turned-singer Cliff de Young, after which, when recording resumed in August, guitarist Robison was ousted in favour of a keyboardist, Ralph Schuckett. The addition of a dramatic singer and Schuckett's keyboard flourishes are a sure indication that Clear Light were being remodelled along the lines of The Doors. When the album was released in November, there was no doubting that several songs brought to mind Elektra's two best known rock acts, Love and The Doors.

"Clear Light was a one off," says Holzman. "They were the first of the double-drumming bands and made an interesting sound. The album actually did very well, sold close to 100,000, coming on the heels of Love and The Doors. And we gave them a terrific logo, which reinforced that connection. They were a band that came together organically but lacked focus. Their lead singer was a very strange guy. Cliff de Young had no real charisma or presence as a singer and got by more because of his acting skills in a very theatrical manner; and he became a good actor.

"Rothchild got the best out of them. None of the material had a great arc. We signed them because we wanted another band to do right away to learn more about the dynamic of bands, and the problems of recording Clear Light were interesting because of the double drumming."

Dallas Taylor remembered Paul Rothchild as a mad genius. "He looked like a leprechaun, with his red hair and green velvet clothes. In the beginning, he tried to mould us into The Doors, and that really didn't work. So tension really grew within the band, and Paul would make us do the same track

50 times over, and we'd be sick to death of it long before that point. Our thing was spontaneity, and in the studio it just got squashed. Clear Light was very much like the Grateful Dead, with a cult following. When we had the right combination of drugs, or the vibe was just right, it was magic and we were amazing. When we were off we just sucked, because we were too high. It was very unpredictable and we really struggled when it came to writing material."[1]

Paul Rothchild's scheming continued while the group were on tour supporting their album; by January 1968, Bob Seal had also been dismissed from the group and replaced by Danny 'Kootch' Kortchmar. In retrospect, the group concluded that Rothchild's manoeuvring was something of a trial run for Rhinoceros. The new line-up toured widely but never recorded anything other than demos for a projected second album. By the end of 1968, they had split up.

"We lost all direction," said Dallas Taylor, "and the family feeling that had made us special in our own way. It felt too much like a business and all the heart was gone. So I contacted Stephen Stills, because I'd heard he needed a drummer, and I was off into something else." Schuckett's later credits include The Peanut Butter Conspiracy, Carole King's early band City, and Jo Mama (with Kortchmar), while Doug Lubahn played on three Doors albums, *Strange Days*, *Waiting For The Sun*, and *The Soft Parade*. Cliff de Young successfully returned to acting, appearing in the musical *Hair* and in countless film and television roles.

"I can see now that Clear Light was subject to a lot of interference from Paul," says Holzman. "The Tom Paxton cover I'm sure was Rothchild's idea; strange but interesting." Tom Paxton had no issues with it. "Paul took me into his room and over his booming stereo he played me the dub of Clear Light performing my song 'Mr. Blue'," he recalls. "He really wasn't sure how I would take it, whether I would object or not, because it was so radically different to my version. But I thought it was fabulous – vocally sinister, the way I wanted it to be. He was so relieved."

Stefan Grossman remembers another of Paul Rothchild's attempts to put a group together during this period, this time inspired by seeing his friends in The Mamas & The Papas storming the charts. Grossman had already recorded his instrumental blues album with Rory Block, which would eventually be released as *How To Play Blues Guitar*. "Paul wanted to get the blend of the acoustic guitars that Rory and I had recorded with some singers up front. Rory and I had broken up and I was in Berkeley, living with Steve Mann, and we played a lot of guitar together – Jorma Kaukonen from Jefferson Airplane was very influenced by Steve, and his tune 'Fate Of Mann' is about Steve.

"So the idea evolved to have Steve and me playing guitars and Paul set up an informal rehearsal at our place. They arranged for Taj Mahal and Janis Joplin to come in as the vocalists. The sound of the four of us was as powerful as you can imagine. The combination of Janis's rough voice and the smooth voice of Taj Mahal was amazing. We left it that Paul and Jac would set us up in LA, where we'd rehearse with a studio bass and drummer. A few weeks later I headed back to New York to check in with Paul to see how things were progressing, and he said it wasn't going to happen as Taj and Janice had taken off in their own solo directions." Janis Joplin joined Big Brother & The Holding Company in June 1966, while a chance meeting with Ed Sanders in the Village resulted in Grossman joining The Fugs for four months at the end of that summer.

No project upset the delicate balance of the Holzman–Rothchild relationship more than Rhinoceros. Rothchild's strategy was to build "a better supergroup, with not-yet-famous people". In the end, it took much longer than his original notion of inviting 50 or so musicians to auditions over a long weekend to see who was left standing. Making the cut were Danny Weis on guitar and bassist Jerry Penrod, both from Iron Butterfly, keyboardist Michael Fonfara, guitarist Doug Hastings, a local hot property after standing in for Neil Young in Buffalo Springfield at Monterey, and, last to join, drummer Billy Mundi, who'd played with Tim Buckley and The Mothers Of Invention.

Holzman was wary of the idea from the outset. "Rhinoceros was a misfire," he says, "contrived from the start. Paul insisted on trying it and I gave him my reluctant blessing. He believed supergroups were a big deal – though none of the music from any of those so-called supergroups is remembered today. I didn't say no to Paul, because he had done so much for Elektra."

Rhinoceros's eponymous debut album was released in October 1968. The instrumental 'Apricot Brandy' was licensed as the theme for a Bob Hope TV special and is the only track anyone ever remembers. Greater than the music was Gene Szafran's stunning, brightly coloured, beaded Rhinoceros image on the jacket. "Ultimately, Rhinoceros could never overcome their paint-by-numbers origins," says Holzman. "You can't manufacture originality. Rhinoceros was an exercise in ego: Paul's for wanting to do it; mine for letting him."

Billy James was another Canyon resident who had been invaluable when the early Elektra West Coast office was set up and in helping convince The Doors that Holzman and Elektra were right for them. James made way for David Anderle, who had been recommended by Judy Collins and was chosen to head up the LA office.

Holzman's immediate impression was that Anderle knew everyone in town. "He had the right look, the sensitivity, and the smarts to attract artists. David was aware of everything happening in LA. He brought in Delaney & Bonnie and David Ackles, and he worked closely with Russ Miller, who ran our music-publishing unit. If David needed to green light something immediately, he had the authority to do it, and I would back him up. He was part chameleon, depending upon who he was with. He was masterful at unruffling feathers: if people were pissed at me or Rothchild, he could smooth it over. He hung out with the artists more, which I was reluctant to do, because you traded your independent view for the price of hanging out."

Anderle's most memorable Elektra production was for Delaney & Bonnie's *Accept No Substitute* album. Holzman regretted making the record – not for the music, but for Delaney Bramlett's boorish attitude.

Delaney and Bonnie Bramlett's vibrant soul sound was evidence of a growing interest in roots music, with The Band's *Music From Big Pink*, Van Morrison's *Moondance*, and Dylan's openly circulating *Basement Tapes* providing the impetus. Delaney & Bonnie were the hottest act in the San Fernando Valley, part of a loose collective that included Gram Parsons, Leon Russell, Mac Rebbenack, and Rita Coolidge. Also in there were the musicians in Delaney & Bonnie's own exciting band, a mix of assorted sessionmen and various ex-Shindogs (from the house band of the TV music show *Shindig*).

The husband-and-wife's country-blues and urban soul was brought boldly to life by this group, under the communal banner Delaney & Bonnie & Friends. They were keyboardist Bobby Whitlock, bassist Carl Radle, drummer Jim Keltner, Jim Price on trumpet, and Bobby Keys on saxophone, and they soon became heavily in demand. Most of them would desert Delaney & Bonnie to join Joe Cocker's Mad Dogs & Englishmen in March 1970, under ringmaster Leon Russell.

"I had seen them play at a little club in Westwood," says David Anderle, "and I was knocked out immediately. I cut a demo with them, and that led to the recording of *Accept No Substitute*, which was not the hit in America that we hoped for. But it reverberated in Britain, with Eric Clapton, The Beatles, and The Rolling Stones as admirers. It was the first album of country blues, American roots music, by white artists. They were originally billed as Bonnie & Delaney, but when they signed to Elektra, Delaney made sure his name came first ... a Southern boy, you know?" The deal itself raised hackles within the Elektra organisation, especially with Bill Harvey for the degree of artistic control they had, including approval of artwork.

Delaney & Bonnie opened for Blind Faith on their 1969 US tour, and the band hit it off immediately with Eric Clapton, who was soon to be seen jamming with them. Once the members of Blind Faith went their separate ways, Clapton joined Delaney & Bonnie full-time, resulting in an album release the following year on Atlantic – *On Tour With Eric Clapton* – that clawed its way into the Top 30 of the American charts, primarily because of Clapton's name in the title.

"*Accept No Substitute* was a successful enough album," says Holzman, "but not as successful as Delaney wanted. I just didn't like him. He was on the label because we made him a good deal, and his manager wanted to be on the label, but Delaney always thought we were small potatoes, unworthy of him. Before the album was even released he surreptitiously offered it to Apple, which he could not do because of his deal with us. He was a captive to his own ego, burning his bridges with everyone."

When Holzman was in England, Bramlett called him to complain about the lack of records in his father's hometown store in Texas and threatened Holzman with shooting if the problem was not corrected immediately. Even David Anderle, Bramlett's earliest supporter, saw the problem. Holzman immediately released Delaney from his Elektra agreement. "Once an artist shows that little respect for you as a person," he says, "to continue a relationship would signal that I had little regard for myself. Do I really think he would have picked up a gun, come over, and shot me? I'd say 60/40 that he would."

Delaney & Bonnie were the first in a stream of Southern acts that mixed country, blues, and Memphis R&B. They included Delaney & Bonnie, Lonnie Mack, and Mickey Newbury, all picked up by Russ Miller. "He had a gift for finding artists and music which look like one thing but are not," says Holzman. "I was introduced to Russ as a potential A&R man. With my A&R team constantly in the studio, I needed someone outside and on the move. Russ was very sensitive to acoustic music and he had taste. He 'got' David Ackles immediately, co-produced his first album with Anderle, and then oversaw the second, *Subway To The Country.* Russ was very talented but always in a minor state of chaos. Elektra was a safe and stable environment for him – and if you can call Elektra a stable environment, well, you can imagine what his life must have been like."

Russ Miller had been a young tent-evangelist and singer before joining Elektra Records, where, over the years, he produced more than 30 albums. He later became a motivational preacher, was ordained as a Religious Science minister in March 2003, and became a founding minister of the Spiritual Centre for Positive Living in Cameron Park, Sacramento. The Reverend Russell G. Miller died in August 2009.

One of Russ Miller's key signings was Lonnie Mack, best known for his Top Five hit in the summer of 1963, a stinging instrumental cover of Chuck Berry's 'Memphis', and its savage follow-up, 'Wham'. Miller produced Mack's three Elektra albums, the two best coming along in rapid succession in 1969: *Whatever's Right* and *Glad I'm In The Band.* They aimed to morph Mack into a soulful country-blues singer while de-emphasising his guitar wizardry.

Bruce Botnick was the engineer on all Mack's Elektra albums. "Working with Lonnie was amongst the most fun I had during my time at Elektra," he says, "especially with Russ, who had a fabulous sense of humour. Here was Lonnie Mack, who could play faster than lightning. He claimed to have learned to play with such verve by listening to 45s at 78rpm speed. We saw him at Winterland on a bill with Johnny Winter, and Fender had populated the stage with Fender Twins and a wall of amplifiers for Johnny Winter. It was beyond loud. Then out comes Lonnie Mack with his one-square-foot Fender Champ amp and a reduced B-3 organ, plus a drummer and bass player all plugged into midget amps. Everyone crowded up to the stage. The Mack sound was pure and better integrated – it was fantastic. Johnny Winter just scratched his head in awe."

Lonnie Mack found himself playing other major rock venues, rather than the usual roadhouse bars, and made a guest appearance on The Doors' *Morrison Hotel.* "It was weird bringing Lonnie in to play bass," says Botnick, "but he certainly knew that style of music, and he participated in probably the world's greatest bar-band song, 'Roadhouse Blues'. He had played them all, let's face it."

Holzman agrees. "He was perfect for The Doors: they loved having Lonnie Mack in the studio and were very respectful. He just did his job and played his bass, but there was something in the pulse that was so authentic, and it helped them to get what they needed for that record. I think it was right he only played bass, because the basic beat was more important than any guitar embellishment on top. He was part of the foundation, and that felt right."

Mack turned Miller on to other Southern acts. "One night, Lonnie Mack came to my house in the Hollywood Hills with two albums under his arm," says Miller. "He said, 'Put your ears between those speakers and smoke one of these and don't say anything.' The first album was by Roberta Flack. I freaked. The second was by Nashville singer-songwriter Mickey Newbury, and I was so moved I cried. Lonnie also led me to Memphis, Tennessee, and to Muscle Shoals, Alabama, and I was gathering up artists: Don Nix, Marlin Greene, and Marlin's wife Jeanie."[2]

Despite Don Nix's celebrated history – he began his musical career playing saxophone for instrumental soul pioneers The Mar-keys and helped define the Memphis sound of the 60s – his sole Elektra album, *Living By The Days*, was unable to elevate him from sideman to frontman. It conjures up a warm brew of fervent country soul aided and abetted by some of Muscle Shoals finest musicians but it failed to sell. Nor did the one-off releases by husband-and-wife team Jeanie & Marlin Greene, who sang so gloriously on Nix's album. Marlin Greene went on to become Russ Miller's A&R assistant in LA.

Holzman understood that they were all Southern artists, although they were not country artists per se. "There was no Southern genre that people readily identified with at that time," he says. "It's a Memphis mix of soul and country, gospel, and R&B, and Russ Miller found and explored those tributaries very well. We went to Nashville and to Muscle Shoals because the studios and the musicians were there and although Marlin and Jeanie

Greene, Don Nix, and Lonnie Mack didn't really connect with people, I think those records still hold up today. They were too difficult to pigeon hole however much there was a growing interest in more natural roots music around the turn of the decade."

Despite containing the blistering guitar-punctuated opener 'Asphalt Outlaw Hero', Lonnie Mack's final album for Elektra album, *The Hills Of Indiana*, was a mellower and distinctly country-headed album recorded mostly in Nashville with the Area Code 615 players. It signs off with a moving, acoustic gospel-flavoured duet between Mack and Don Nix on 'Three Angels', the song they wrote together which first appeared on *Living By The Days*. The two them had been lined up to front a funky music extravaganza that was effectively a knockdown version of Mad Dogs & Englishmen, but without the superstar razzmatazz. It featured Mack's band, a Muscle Shoals band, Don Nix, and Marlin and Jeanie Greene, all under the banner The Alabama State Troupers And The Mount Zion Choir & Band. Mack disappeared six days before the tour. When Miller found him, holed-up on a backwoods farm in Kentucky, Mack refused to join the tour, freaked by a dream in which he and his family were hounded by the devil, and waking to find his Bible open at the passage "Flee ye from Mount Zion." In the end, blues guitarist Furry Lewis was drafted in and the tour went ahead, subsequently released as the Elektra double live album *Road Show – The Alabama State Troupers.*

Holzman looks back on Lonnie Mack – who died on April 21 2016 at the age of 74 – as a fascinating artist. "In recording him, we supported a tradition, and a very different tradition in terms of Elektra's past. Lonnie's history was to release singles for the R&B and pop market, and we tried to turn him into an album artist. He had a terrific voice, but people wanted to hear him play fast guitar."

Russ Miller also brought Mickey Newbury to Elektra. Newbury's 70s Elektra material was fittingly described by the rock writer Ben Fong-Torres as "the troubadour answer to Frank Sinatra's late-50s *Only The Lonely* period". When Newbury signed to Elektra in 1970, he was best known as a writer whose songs had been covered by Willie Nelson, Eddy Arnold, Don Gibson, Roy Orbison, and Kenny Rogers & The First Edition, who scored a major hit with Newbury's atypical 'Just Dropped In (To See What Condition My Condition Was In)'.

Newbury was a major player in the musical revolution that swept through Nashville during the 60s and 70s, but compared to Johnny Cash, Waylon Jennings, Willie Nelson, or Kris Kristofferson, he was a quiet rebel. It was Newbury who introduced Kristofferson to Roger Miller, and Miller was the first to record 'Me And Bobbie McGee'. Kristofferson said of Newbury, "Mickey played the most crucial role of any single songwriter in my life. You could see a change in my writing after I met him."[3]

Newbury insisted that he have control over his albums. "That was so I could produce the album myself, or hire my own producer and choose the musicians I wanted," he said, "which was a remarkable situation for the time. I also didn't want to work the road any more, which makes it hard to promote records, and Elektra was the only label that came through with a deal on that basis. The orchestral sound on *Frisco Mabel Joy* is all pedal steel and some electric guitar. It's all guitars, even though it sounds like there are strings or horns. Players like Charlie McCoy, Weldon Myrick, and Wayne Moss – they're the best. I do a lot of overdubbing: I record by doing the vocal and acoustic guitar first, and build the song from there. Every additional instrument serves a purpose."

Many of the songs on *Frisco Mabel Joy*, his breathtaking 1971 Elektra debut, were written when Newbury was living on a houseboat in Nashville, where he was taken by the sound of rain on the roof mingling with wind chimes. He made shrewd use of atmospheric sound effects to further enhance the despairing mood of his sad songs. "It seemed to rain a lot back then," Newbury explain. "It became sort of a trademark for me, but it does help provide a languid flow to move easily from one track to the next."

Newbury was as individual and distinctive a voice as Tim Buckley and as original as any of the great Nashville country songwriters. Yet he is known popularly for only one song, from *Frisco Mabel Joy*: 'An American Trilogy'. It was an arrangement by Newbury of three songs from separate factions in the Civil War – 'Dixie', 'The Battle Hymn Of The Republic', and 'All My Trials' – and Newbury's inspired bonding of these into 'An American Trilogy' is indelibly associated with Elvis Presley. It was never even a substantial hit for Presley – Newbury's original version charted considerably higher, going to Number 26 in the *Billboard* pop charts – but became a show-stopping, integral part of Presley's stage performances after 1972, almost to the point of caricature.

Elektra released three more albums by Newbury after *Frisco Mabel Joy*: *Heaven Help The Child*, *I Came To Hear The Music*, and *Lovers*. The sequence of albums beginning with *Looks Like Rain*, recorded for Mercury in 1969, through to his final Elektra album, *Lovers*, in 1975, represents the pinnacle of Newbury's recording career. They are spiritual, meditative works that defy categorisation, rooted in folk, country, and soul, but if anything the music was too complex and the themes too ethereal to reach a wide audience. To describe Newbury's recordings as country music is nothing less than a matter of convenience.

Holzman had enormous respect for Newbury as a writer and singer. "The albums were mood pieces, by design. His records sold respectable numbers. I thought I was doing a very big favour for his music publisher, since they were able to use Mickey's own albums to secure covers. Unfortunately, that doesn't always reflect positively on the artist or his label in terms of public awareness." In 1996, Newbury formed his own music-production and distribution company called Mountain Retreat, and released an eight-CD boxed set that included all his Elektra albums. He died at his home in Springfield, Oregon, on September 29 2002, after a lengthy illness.

Unlike Mickey Newbury, Dennis Linde's cache as a successful Nashville songwriter didn't provide the bridge to his own albums catching on. After his death from lung disease at the age of 63, on 22 December 2006, in Nashville, the obituaries remembered him, first and foremost, as the man who wrote Elvis Presley's last Top Ten hit during his lifetime, 'Burning Love'. When producer Felton Jarvis first took the song to Elvis, he didn't want to record it, but it inspired one of Elvis's leanest late-period vocals. Until then, Linde (pronounced Lindy) was barely known as a songwriter outside of Nashville, and even fewer people were aware he had recorded five intriguing, grossly overlooked albums. Three of them were for Elektra: *Dennis Linde*, *Trapped in the Suburbs*, and another with the group Jubal. He also produced Mickey Newbury's *Frisco Mabel Joy* and *Heaven Help The Child*. Newbury had personally requested his former sideman Linde, making full use of his expertise in overdubbing, never bettered than by the grandiose orchestrations on these exquisite Elektra albums, using nothing but layers of guitars and steel guitars.

Linde was born in Abilene and raised in San Angelo, Texas, Miami, and St. Louis. He became hooked on music, learning guitar and joining local outfit Bob Kuban & The In-Men, who enjoyed a 1966 pop hit, 'The Cheater'. He took up writing songs by default: "In 1968 I was playing nights with Bob Kuban and driving a cleaning truck during the day. I received so many speeding tickets that my licence was revoked, so to keep myself busy I wrote some songs. From 1968 until 1970 I wrote about 160 songs and got a few recorded."

Roger Miller and Roy Drusky were early takers, after which Linde's songs were recorded by The Judds, Billy Swann, Alan Jackson, Kenny Rogers, Roy Orbison, Delbert McClinton, Don Williams, Garth Brooks, and The Dixie Chicks. The eccentric Linde would cite such diverse influences as Gershwin, Mark Twain, J.D. Salinger, Fats Domino, Little Richard, John Steinbeck, and Cole Porter. For fun, he'd set himself challenges like writing songs starting with each letter of the alphabet – hence titles like 'X Marks the Spot', 'Zoot Suit Baby', and the baffling 'U-Joints Don't Come Free'. On a wall at home, he hung a map of a fictitious town he'd created where the offbeat characters in his songs lived and worked, drank and died.

"Dennis Linde is an unlikely dude," said Kris Kristofferson in 1972. "He looks like he's just stepped out of a scene from *The Last Picture Show* and may well be a genius; he certainly is weird. He's one of the few gifted producers working today, an exceptional picker, and possibly the most creative and prolific songwriter in the business." In 1969, alongside Kristofferson, Linde became a staff writer at leading Nashville publishing house Combine Music, run by Bob Beckham; he even married the boss's daughter, Pam, inspiring his most famous song. "I was a newlywed, and 'Burning Love' was a great newlywed title," he told *The New York Times* in 2005. "I had it done in 20 minutes."

Linde issued his first album, *Linde Manor*, on the Mercury subsidiary Intrepid in 1970; it's a tastefully unhinged delight. Then, taking a surprising backseat role, mostly playing bass, he joined Jubal, whose self-titled album was released by Elektra in 1972. The following year he released *Dennis Linde*, one of the absolute jewels that Russ Miller brought to Elektra. Carefully constructed in his own time, *Dennis Linde* mixed home recordings done on an eight-track machine in the bedroom of his home in Mt Juliet, Tennessee, with sessions from various Nashville studios. His own Creedence-like take on 'Burning Love' was recorded with the nucleus of hotshot players from Barefoot Jerry. Often more pop than country (see the wonderfully infectious

'Hello I Am Your Heart'), the album is totally and gloriously out of step with the prevailing brand of California country-rock.

As his friend Billy Swann explains, "It took Dennis about a year and a half, working in between his songwriting, playing guitar or bass on different recording sessions, and producing [Kris Kristofferson and Mickey Newbury], to finish this album. He loved recording, building a song from scratch – having begun using a little four-track, just mono to mono."

Linde's second album for Elektra, *Trapped In The Suburbs*, was more conventional, eschewing his debut's layered, constructionist intimacy. Linde made one final album, *Under the Eye*, for Monument in 1977 and thereafter he concentrated on writing, becoming renowned around Nashville for keeping himself to himself.

* * *

In the heady spirit that infused the 1967 Monterey pop festival, Frazier Mohawk approached Holzman with an idea for a secluded, back-to-the-woods studio at Paxton Lodge in the remote wooded mountains of Northern California. "Frazier caught me at a particularly vulnerable moment," says Holzman, "the morning after Monterey, and, in that climate of optimism, I said yes to his idea for Paxton Lodge. I didn't realise that Frazier wanted to get all the boys and girls together in one psychic hot tub and see what might happen. Fuel it well with dope, feed them expansively, in a place where there was not much other entertainment, and invite a lot of women. That I was putting a madman in charge of the madhouse didn't occur to me at the time."

Frazier organised a house band with the intention of forming The Los Angeles Fantasy Orchestra – essentially his musician pals, with other artists coming and going. Among those checking into Paxton Lodge during its six-month existence were house engineer John Haeny, John Koerner, Dave Ray, Lonnie Mack, and troubadours Ned Doheny and Jackson Browne.

Holzman remembers John Haeny. "He was a producer and engineer at Elektra who volunteered out of his affection for Jim Morrison to create the sonic collage famously known as *An American Prayer*. He is an enormously skilled engineer and worked with Mark Abramson and Judy Collins on several of her albums. He was another of those crazy and talented people. He always brought his dog into the studio. Elektra was a benign environment where such people could be creative and crazy at the same time."

Frazier Mohawk recalls that they did try to produce a Jackson Browne record at Paxton. "I don't know quite what happened. Jackson wasn't ready, and I was not at my best. It spun out of control. An incredible psychodrama was unfolding there, and I just escaped to my bedroom and hid under the pillow. Many musicians passed through Paxton. I run across them to this day and they say, 'I was there', but I don't remember them."

Browne was signed to Elektra's publishing arm, Nina Music, and had recorded 20 or so demos (the best of which, 'The Fairest Of The Seasons', Nico recorded for her *Chelsea Girl* album), but the standard of songwriting bears no relation to the high quality, proactive, personal material on his Asylum Records debut of 1972. The album recorded with the communal band at Paxton was called *Baby Browning*, but it never came out – with good reason, says Holzman. "The recordings Jackson did were not releasable, and that had an interesting effect on him. Here he was given the keys to the kingdom, as was everybody: they were eating well, smoking well, everyone was getting laid. But after Paxton, Jackson took charge of his life. None of the exceptional songs he later recorded were in the catalogue we owned."

Browne agrees. "It was poorly played and badly realised. We named it *Baby Browning* after a stillborn child's tombstone that we once saw while we were walking through the local cemetery." After Paxton Lodge, says Browne, "it was humbling to be back on the street and not have a record deal."[4]

Holzman says the best thing to come out of the Paxton Lodge episode was the *Running Jumping Standing Still* album by Spider John Koerner & Willie Murphy. "It's a classic of spaced-out stomping-school-of-roadhouse music," he says. "Dave Ray recorded *Bamboo*, too, with the house band and with Will Donicht sharing vocals." It marked the end of Elektra's association with Koerner Ray & Glover, who were now out of contract individually and collectively, and they had themselves gone their separate ways.

Lonnie Mack arrived up at Paxton, spent a few days there, and ran away, Holzman remembers, calling the residents a bunch of drugged-out crazies. "His manager called and asked if I knew what was going on up there. And that's when I chartered a plane and walked in unannounced." He gave Paxton another month to pull itself together but shut it down after a life of six months. "The tab came to $75,000," says Holzman. "Not a huge amount, considering what could have been."

Holzman has fond memories of Frazier Mohawk, who died in June

2012. "My relationship with him started with a group called Kaleidoscope. I loved their first album, *Side Trips*, which he produced with panache. I found myself charmed and stretched by people like Frazier and Danny Fields. I like to keep such people in orbit. Frazier always had an eye for the unusual." Mohawk's oddball credentials made him ideal to produce two groups for whom the common denominator was drugs. This time, both gained from putting the lunatic in charge of the asylum.

The New York-based Holy Modal Rounders, originally a duo of Peter Stampfel and Steve Weber, were signed to Prestige Records in 1963 by Paul Rothchild, attracted to the label because Rothchild smoked dope, or so they said. Then Rothchild left and almost immediately joined Elektra. It took nearly five years before the Rounders followed him there, where Frazier Mohawk, a fan of the original duo, was assigned to produce them.

According to David Anderle, "This was about as bizarre as they come. Sam Shepard was the drummer." Shepard became the actor, playwright, and director who appeared in movies such as *The Right Stuff* and *Paris, Texas*. "It was a great line-up of eccentrics: one doing speed, another doing smack, the producer doing both, and the only productivity is when the drugs balance each other out."

Mohawk: "They were crazy people. I only knew the original duo and I loved their records, but they turned up with all these people and told me that this was going to be their new band. They said they weren't willing to do a Holy Modal Rounders record, only a Moray Eels record. 'More A' was for 'More Amphetamine', or that was how Peter Stampfel tells it. They tried to complete songs but could never finish one."

One familiar song on *The Moray Eels Eat The Holy Modal Rounders* was a surprise hit. Holzman says that after Elektra released the album, he received a call from the producers of *Easy Rider* asking if he would licence 'Bird Song' for the soundtrack. "The bonus came from the extraordinary sales of the soundtrack album, fuelled by a new audience who identified with the freedom expressed by Jack Nicholson as he flapped his arms, birdlike, riding the pillion behind Dennis Hopper."

Mohawk's East Coast equivalent was the Elektra publicist Danny Fields. In 1969, Fields was responsible for bringing both The Stooges and the MC5 to the label. A year earlier, Fields introduced Holzman to the former Velvet Underground chanteuse Nico. Her first solo album for Verve, *Chelsea Girl*, showed off her chilling voice in a context of carefully arranged pop folk, with songs written by Dylan, Lou Reed, Tim Hardin, and Jackson Browne. She was never happy with way it turned out, once dismissing the producer as an idiot for adding strings. In the interim, through Leonard Cohen, she discovered the harmonium, which would accompany her for the rest of her career.

"I had heard the Verve album and didn't like it," says Holzman. "Danny brought her in, and I had heard her perform the *Marble Index* songs. They were haunting and haunted. I had not considered her as a singer-songwriter. I saw her more as a presence – half voice, half priestess. Frazier later remarked that her songs were not something you listened to but a hole you fell into. Curiously, her music reminded me of Jean Ritchie's dulcimer – three strings and two drones. The harmonium was a support to her voice, which would rise above it. Nico had a fine contralto voice and a vibrato that pulsed softly but rapidly. Most vibrato bothers me – hers didn't."

John Cale was brought in as arranger, his first Elektra assignment before he was asked to produce The Stooges. The production role on *The Marble Index* fell to Frazier Mohawk. Danny Fields considers that Elektra treated her with great respect. "There was the wonderful Guy Webster cover photograph," says Fields, "which was very tasteful. Jac simply recognised good songs – that was the essence of Elektra. He recognised the quality in Nico and saw something beyond the aura that she was an actress, had been in The Velvet Underground, and was associated with Andy Warhol. *The Marble Index* was her wanting to do an album of her own songs on a modest budget. No orchestra was required – not if they had John Cale. Jac was still reticent about turning the whole production over to Cale, and that's how Frazier Mohawk became involved."

The Marble Index was recorded in just a few days during September 1968. "The budget was small and the studio was tiny, and we recorded through the night when the studio was normally dark," Mohawk recalled. "When I met Nico, I immediately fell in love with her. She was a dream to work with. Beautiful, very theatrical, and a marvellous human being. People assume she was icy cold because of that voice, but she was always pleasant and laughed a lot. There was a lot of heroin – Nico and I were stoned the whole time. Being in the same state as her kept me focussed on the music."

According to Mohawk, the reason the album is only 30 minutes long was because that's all he could listen to. "Fifteen minutes a side seemed about right. John Haeny and I spent a day or two mixing it. Huge credit must go to Haeny: he's a brilliant engineer, and we did a lot of special editing and overlapping."

The harmonium dominated the arrangements, underpinning Nico's mesmerising voice, while Cale fleshed out the sound, playing piano, guitar, electric viola, harmonica, bass, glockenspiel, bells, and a bosun's pipe. Speaking in 1977, Cale described *The Marble Index* as "an artefact, not a commodity", adding that "you can't sell suicide".[5] Cale was right: the album didn't sell. But as Holzman says, "Sales are not the only benchmark."

Despite requests, Nico never came back to make another record. "You could never find her," Holzman says. "She'd say, 'I'll be here on Wednesday,' and never show up. She cleaned herself up and became a healthy person, free of drugs."

Asked in 1975 about leaving Elektra, Nico was typically insouciant. "No, that was my mistake. I had gone to Europe and stayed there ever since. I should have stayed in America. It was just my running away."[6] In July 1988, while on holiday in Ibiza, Spain, Nico injured her head following an accident on her bike and died of a severe cerebral haemorrhage.

There were a number of one-offs at this time that illustrate the experimental nature of Elektra, such as David Stoughton's near unclassifiable *Transformer*. Stoughton was a Harvard math major who hung out at Boston's Club 47 where he "learned to play all kinds of folk guitar – bluegrass, blues, fingerpicking, and flatpicking styles". After graduating in 1965 he got a job teaching guitar at the Newton Music School, but he soon came under the spell of the avant-garde musician and composer John Cage and began to compose his own musique concrète, which gives an indication of what to expect on *Transformer.* The album is credited as "produced and created by David Stoughton" and was recorded with the nucleus of Stoughton's group The Cambridge Electric Opera Company, once described by *Newsweek* as at the cutting edge of where modern pop music might be going. Holzman invited Stoughton to his home one Saturday to listen to Stoughton's demos, after learning that Clive Davis, then President of Columbia Records, might be interested. "I wanted to hear what Clive had heard," says Holzman.

"I thought Jac was terrific," says Stoughton, "A truly great personality. Up for anything new. The first song on my demo tape was the most extreme, 'The Anecdote Of Horatio and Julie'. Jac sat through it. Expressionless. 'The

Sun Comes Up Each Day' followed. Jac heard eight bars and stopped the tape. I thought he was going to tell me I was history. 'You've got a deal,' he said. 'What do you want, money or freedom?' 'Freedom,' I said. 'Total control over all aspects of content and production. Did Clive offer you that?' Jac wondered. 'No,' I said. 'One problem,' Jac said. 'I don't like the trumpet and flugelhorn players on your demo. Find out who the best player is in the Boston Symphony and we'll hire him for the recording session.'"

Transformer was David Stoughton's only album for Elektra, or any label. Elektra also released the first of two David Peel & The Lower East Side albums in 1968, the street singer's controversial *Have A Marijuana*, as well as one-offs by Nico, Ars Nova, The Holy Modal Rounders, and Steve Noonan. Noonan is another interesting case. He was a friend of Jackson Browne's from Orange County, and Browne contributes four songs to Noonan's album, including 'Shadow Dream Song', which he taught to Tom Rush – who then recorded it first on *The Circle Game*. Unusually, there are no credits for musicians or production on Noonan's album jacket, apart from one to photographer Linda Eastman (later McCartney). It's likely this was due to a conflict between Noonan and Paul Rothchild, who part-produced the album before Peter Siegel took over – and wanted his name removed. It's certainly one of Elektra's intriguing failures.

The number of one-off albums in 1968 reflects creative bravado on Holzman's part. He knew that Elektra could afford to take risks – none of these artists had the standard three-album contract. At the same time, the extraordinary and rapid success of The Doors was causing Holzman to consider his label's status as an independent and how best to cope with the company's need for more personnel, new responsibilities, and more reliable distribution. He was forced to weigh the pros and cons in what turned out to be a very turbulent year ahead.

Down On The Street

“*Well it’s 1969, OK / All across the USA.*” **THE STOOGES**

The year 1969 was one of high drama for Jac Holzman and Elektra Records. Delaney & Bonnie’s *Accept No Substitute* was released in May and, within months, Holzman had fired Delaney for threatening to shoot him. Holzman also released the MC5 from their contract after an incident when the band took out an offensive ad in a local underground paper excoriating a large Midwest retail chain, Hudson’s, for not stocking their album. In Miami-Dade County on March 1, Jim Morrison was arrested for “lascivious and lewd behaviour”. On April Fools Day, the little-known Stooges were recording their debut album at the Hit Factory, a seedy New York studio off Times Square, marking the first major step for a group to whom controversy was second nature. It was 1969, OK.

The saga of the MC5 and The Stooges began on the weekend of September 21 1968, when Danny Fields flew to Detroit to see MC5 at the Grande Ballroom and caught their “mascot band”, The Stooges. By Monday, both bands had agreed to sign to Elektra. Neither was known outside the Detroit area. Locals, even if they knew about The Stooges, would have tagged them unsignable.

The manager of the MC5 at the time was John Sinclair. He recalls meeting Fields through friends at the East Village newspaper *Cocaine Karma*, “ says Sinclair, “who wrote glowingly about the MC5. “Some of the guys from the paper also hosted a radio show in New York, and that’s how Danny first heard the group. He flew to Detroit and we turned him on to The Stooges, who were playing the following night."

Fields wanted both bands, so he called Holzman and said he'd found two that Elektra should sign. "I described them to him," says Fields, "with both managers sitting there in the kitchen at the MC5's house. It was easy to explain the MC5, who had just sold out a 3,000-capacity ballroom, but the magic of The Stooges was a harder sell. They had no following, even in Detroit. They had a singer who defied description. Jac said to see if the MC5 will take $15,000 and the baby band $5,000. He was prepared to make this signing offer over the phone and take my word for it. Both managers said they'd take it."

Holzman's decision met with resistance in New York, especially from Bill Harvey. Holzman recalls that Elektra staffers who eventually heard the two bands thought he was out of his mind. "I am normally left-of-centre musically, and my outreach depends upon the people I'm working with, who nurse me along until I understand the new music, which is a physical as well as intellectual perception. I respected Danny Fields. He was bringing us something that he believed in deeply. I suspended my own judgement and trusted his instinct."

Sinclair had no reservations about signing to Elektra. "What they had done with the Butterfield Blues Band was impressive, although I think the MC5 were equally attracted by the Number One success Elektra had enjoyed with The Doors. Elektra didn't play safe in the way that most record companies did."

Originally part of Detroit's Trans-Love Energies commune, MC5 became the house band for Sinclair's White Panther party, founded in Detroit on November 1 1968 – the day after the MC5 recorded their Elektra debut album live at the Grande Ballroom. Reaction against the Panthers and leader Sinclair's revolutionary ideology cast the MC5 in a political light and obscured their music – which was a fusion of raw punk and high energy rock'n'roll, all fired up with blasts of free jazz and heavy blues. The MC5 was a classic dual-guitar band with a line-up now well known and respected by discerning rock'n'roll fans: Rob Tyner on vocals, Wayne Kramer and Fred 'Sonic' Smith on guitars, Michael Davis on bass, and drummer Dennis Thompson.

Bruce Botnick was assigned to engineer and produce them. "The MC5 were a bunch of kids who really wanted to make a Detroit blues album," he says, "and they didn't fully grasp what was going on with John Sinclair. I liked what they were doing. Listen to the songs – they're about teenage sex, a trip on a spaceship – and they were playing jazz in the way they knew best. Very, very loud. This was a combination of hard blues, rock, and Sun Ra. Flat out, pedal to the metal, let's get drunk, get high – that's what they were about."

Danny Fields was struck dumb by their high-octane performances, built upon loose music fired up by plenty of hollering and ranting. According to Botnick, "They attracted attention, but they were a great and mischievous rock'n'roll band. They were not so much troublemakers themselves, but they attracted a retinue of rabble-rousers. Their first appearance in New York at the Fillmore East turned into a riot and, although this wasn't a Bill Graham show, but sponsored by Elektra, he blackballed them – and that was a warning to every venue in America."

While the group was allegedly inciting mayhem, the Panthers talked their talk: "We will do anything we can to drive people out of their heads and into their bodies. Rock'n'roll is the spearhead of our revolution because it's so effective and so much fun." Much of their politics was extreme, centred on "the collapse of the obsolete social and economic forms which presently infest the earth".[1] Holzman had no problem with the group's politics, which at the beginning were interchangeable with Sinclair's stance. "I thought what they were doing as an adjunct to the White Panthers was interesting and worth documenting. John Sinclair was very amiable. You could sit down and talk politics with John. He wouldn't scream at you or shake his fist in your face. I never bought into their revolution. I was only interested in the integration of the music with their politics."

Holzman, Botnick, and the band decided to record their first album live on home turf at Detroit's Grande Ballroom, as Sinclair recalls. "The MC5 were a dazzling performing unit. Their live shows were the basis of their reality, and it's not always easy to put that across isolated from your audience. Also, a live album cost less and was truer to their ideals."

Neither Holzman nor producer Botnick had any idea what to expect when they first saw them. Botnick recalls having the presence of mind to bring along a mono cassette recorder with a built-in microphone. "We went to the concert that night and I put the recorder on a stool in the Grande Ballroom. They were the loudest thing I'd ever heard, so loud that neither Jac nor I could tell if there was any music. It was white noise. When we were safely back at the hotel I said, 'Let's listen,' and we couldn't believe there were songs."

They recorded two shows in a single evening, and then the next day recorded them again at the same venue. "They were more cohesive and there was more clarity," says Botnick of day two. "We brought it back to LA and pieced it together." Holzman says, "Live albums are really hard to carry off, but our recording did that. It was how they wanted to sound, an accurate reflection of that band."

On that second day, they recorded an alternative intro to the band's infamous opening shout, "Kick out the jams, motherfuckers," replacing "motherfuckers" with "brothers and sisters". Sinclair explains, "Jac Holzman easily convinced us. It was our big number in Detroit, but we were willing to do the 'brothers and sisters' version because it was essential for FM radio."

Released in early spring 1969, the *Kick Out The Jams* album reeked of controversy from day one. The MC5's rallying call, complete with motherfuckers, and John Sinclair's manifesto-cum-liner-notes were both removed after the initial pressings caused offence. Sinclair believes they still sold 90,000 copies before that, and the album landed in the *Billboard* Top 40.

So-called riots at the Fillmore East were one thing, but a run-in with the major retail chain Hudson's led to Elektra dropping the band. Danny Fields explains. "Hudson's wouldn't carry the album in Detroit, so the MC5 took an ad in an underground paper [the *Ann Arbor Argus*] featuring a picture of Rob Tyner with an angry fist in the air. The copy read, 'Fuck Hudson's.' And at the bottom of the ad was an Elektra logo – which was very naughty of them. In response, Hudson's threw out all their Judy Collins, Doors, Paul Butterfield, and Nonesuch albums, along with the MC5."

It was a tough call for Holzman – the first time he ever released a band because of 'inappropriate activity'. Looking back now, he describes the MC5 as a political movement expressed through music. "I liked John Sinclair. I think, today, if they took out a 'Fuck Hudson's' ad, I would find it troubling but not a threat. But at the time, it was not amusing. I told John Sinclair I would give them a release so they could record elsewhere, and Sinclair responded, 'That's righteous, Jac.' We shook hands, and that was the end of it. He never badmouthed me. Of course, it would be Danny who had the final word. One day he came into my office and said, 'I guess it's OK for Jim to take out his dick, but the MC5 can't take out their ad.' It was a whopper of a non sequitur, but I thought it was hysterical. Bill Harvey, who had been in the army in World War II, thought Danny was insubordinate."

The MC5 immediately signed with Atlantic, working with producer and rock journalist Jon Landau, who produced a stripped-down frenetic rock'n'roll album, *Back In The USA*, as disciplined as *Kick Out The Jams* was chaotic. More outwardly commercial, it failed to convey what the band stood for, and flopped. Holzman feels a tinge of regret. "However far away the edge is, there resides a complexity, and that's what everything moves towards. Though I may not 'get' some music, my work is to try and connect that music to an audience. Sometimes the audience finds it before I do. Sometimes never. You cannot use conventional means to connect unconventional music to an audience. You create a space and a climate and hope that others will discover it."

Record companies were not queuing up to sign The Stooges in 1968, but Elektra had a lot to recommend it, not least The Butterfield Blues Band, who were an immediate plus. The pre-Iggy Pop, James Osterberg, had already played hard-edged blues in The Prime Movers and, in 1966, befriended former Butterfield drummer Sam Lay in Chicago. Lay helped set him up to play drums with Big Walter Horton. It was seeing The Doors that convinced Iggy to come out from behind his drum set. According to Paul Trynka, "[Jim Morrison] had entranced [Iggy] as he staggered around drunk at the University of Michigan on October 20 1967, howling like a gorilla and 'enraging the frat boys'. Morrison's antics and his provocation of the audience convinced [Iggy] that he too could become a singer."[2] Stooges guitarist Ron Asheton explained in 2007, two years before his death, that Fields went to Elektra. "He said you've got to just sign these guys. And Jac Holzman trusted him: he was a younger pair of ears on the street. He talked Jac into something good."

Asheton said they were big fans of the Butterfield Band and The Doors, so Elektra was a cool, hip label. The Stooges recorded their second album, *Fun House*, at Elektra's studios in Hollywood, and the group saw Los Angeles for the first time. "We were staying at the Tropicana Motel," recalled Asheton, "and it was like, this is too fucking cool. The Doors still had an office near there. I saw Jim Morrison at the corner liquor store, and he wanted to see what our guitarist Bill Cheatham and I were buying – and he stood, looked through the window, walks in, checks out our liquor, and leaves. I don't think any stage would have been big enough for the two Jims together." Holzman agrees. "Iggy was beyond Jim Morrison. You had to be ready for something beyond stock outrageous."

Like The Velvet Underground, The Stooges' music and attitude has cast a longer shadow over every generation since. Led by the charismatically degenerate Iggy Pop, with guitarist Ron Asheton, his brother Scott on drums, and bassist Dave Alexander, they had first performed as The Psychedelic Stooges in Ann Arbor on Halloween night in 1967. By the end of that year they'd abandoned the Psychedelic as too much of a cliché. Iggy was a wilder, snottier, and more threatening take on Mick Jagger, and the band's three-chord pulse gave him free rein.

Danny Fields loved them. "It was a revelation. I thought The Stooges were the best rock'n'roll band in the history of the world. But they had zero following. They were just too bizarre. The first time Elektra came to see them, they were awful and played to only about seven people, so it's just as well they were already signed. The Stooges weren't just about Iggy – everyone fastened on to Iggy, but it takes five seconds to know if a band is good, and that whole package was riveting. Iggy was menacing and the music sounded dangerous – and seven years or so later, that's what came to be called punk."

Iggy was definitely a man with a mission. "We were a forward-looking rock band who were different where other bands were not," says Iggy, "and we would be around when they were gone. I think the rest of the band had some trouble with this notion. But, little by little, it began to happen."[3]

"When Jac and Danny came out to Ann Arbour after our signing," recalled Ron Asheton, "we were doing jams and a lot of free-form stuff, and Jac asked Iggy if we had any songs. He says, 'Well, yeah!' So, after that, I just sat down with my guitar and started coming up with tunes, and Jim was getting ideas and writing the lyrics, but we were still short when we arrived in New York. We needed three more songs, and we wrote them at the Chelsea Hotel in a few hours – 'Little Doll', 'Not Right', and 'Real Cool Time'. We recorded each song in one take: very loose, very much on the fly. We blasted that whole album out in under a week."

Recording in New York with John Cale producing was on-the-job experience for The Stooges, and Cale knew his mandate was to capture in the studio what they did on stage. "That was my first recording session, and as far as we were concerned all we could do was play loud," explained Asheton. "We stacked up our Marshalls and John Cale is screaming at us. So he says no one plays at 10 any more, and it was like sit-down strike, sit-down strike. And Jim goes, 'That's what we do, that's how we play.' I think our compromise was to turn it to 9."

Cale has said since that he doesn't remember any strike. Elektra had wanted him to produce The Stooges because they believed the band sounded similar to The Velvet Underground. Cale's aim was "not to turn them into us". And he didn't. The resulting album, *The Stooges*, was as uncompromising as the Velvets, but the band's gloriously banal sound set them apart, and songs like 'No Fun', '1969', and 'I Wanna Be Your Dog' conveyed an enigmatic but hypnotic reverie.

The Stooges was released the same weekend as the Woodstock Festival, in a jacket that mirrored the first Doors album. It sold a modest 32,000 copies, but enough for Elektra to send them back to the studio within six months, this time with a whole bunch of songs. Don Gallucci was installed as producer for *Fun House.* He had just produced the very antithesis of The Stooges in Crabby Appleton, a power-pop group. He told Holzman he thought The Stooges unrecordable. Gallucci did have his own punk credentials: he had played keyboard with The Kingsmen on the immortal 'Louie Louie', once Iggy's set-piece number in his high school band, The Iguanas.

By now, The Stooges were showing greater rock'n'roll intent, adding the local tenor-saxophone ace Steve Mackay to the band and bringing in a second guitarist, Bill Cheatham. Significantly, the new songs had been road-tested. Gallucci's aim was to just capture their adrenaline-soaked classics – 'Loose', '1970', 'T.V. Eye', and 'Down On The Street'. "By the time we came to record *Fun House*," says Stooges drummer Scott Asheton, "Don Gallucci knew he had to capture that vibe, that live set, and that feeling. Iggy even set up a PA in the studio. It was recorded flat out. It's not letter perfect, it's not super tight, and it's not supposed to be ... the power and the looseness."

One unsavoury consequence of their stay at the Tropicana was that most of the band moved heavily into heroin. *Fun House* was released within a year of their debut, but the band were now ravaged by drugs and hell-bent on excess. Bassist Dave Alexander left, along with Cheatham. Eventually, guitarist James Williamson came in. He would play a key role in the newly reconstituted Iggy & The Stooges, but his arrival did not reverse their drug-saturated downward spiral.

Elektra rejected the option for a third album. Scott Asheton has no doubt why. "People were afraid of Iggy & The Stooges: what we represented, or what people thought we represented. Elektra associated us closely with the MC5, and they had reasons to be wary of them, because they were so

Elektra
Jean Ritchie
singing the traditional songs of her kentucky mountain family
MEXICAN FOLK SONGS
Sung by Cynthia Gooding
FOLK BLUES
SONNY TERRY
LOS GITANILLOS DE CADIZ
FOLK SONG KIT
PANORAMIC STEREO
BLOOD BOOZE 'n BONES
ED McCURDY
Tenderly
NORENE TATE
Susan Reed
JOSh WHITE
Sabicas
NEW YORK JAZZ QUARTET
NEW YORK JAZZ QUARTET
a midnight session
JAZZ MESSENGERS
ART BLAKEY
JOSH WHITE
ED McCURDY
SIN SONGS
pro con
COURTIN'S A PLEASURE
JEAN RITCHIE OSCAR BRAND TOM PALEY
Jean Ritchie
Cynthia Gooding
SPANISH MEXICAN and TURKISH FOLK SONGS
mister CALYPSO
featuring LORD FOODOOS and his CALYPSO BAND
QUEEN OF HEARTS
CYNTHIA GOODING
"HERE WE GO BABY!"
GLENN YARBROUGH
THE DELTA RHYTHM BOYS
The Original Trinidad
STEEL BAND
THE SHANTY BOYS
BASS
GLENN YARBROUGH
MARILYN CHILD
THEODORE BIKEL
SINGS JEWISH FOLK SONGS
SHALOM!
PANORAMIC STEREO
SABICAS
FESTIVAL GITANA
THEODORE BIKEL
SONGS OF A RUSSIAN GYPSY
FULL STOP
erik darling

THE FOLK SINGERS
COME HEAR
ELEKTRA
PANORAMIC STEREO
JOSH WHITE
CHAIN GANG SONGS
GOLD COAST SATURDAY NIGHT
SAKA ACQUAYE
JEAN SHEPHERD
and other foibles
PANORAMIC STEREO
hairy JAZZ
SHEL SILVERSTEIN AND THE RED ONIONS
PANORAMIC STEREO
SKI SONGS
SUNG BY BOB GIBSON
PANORAMIC STEREO
OUT OF THE BLUE
MORE AIR FORCE SONGS BY OSCAR BRAND
the Limeliters
the exciting artistry of WILL HOLT
BONUS PAK
A TREASURE CHEST OF AMERICAN FOLK SONG
featuring ED McCURDY
FASTEST BALALAIKA IN THE WEST
SASHA POLINOFF
PANORAMIC STEREO
S. HUROK PRESENTS
THE VIRTUOSO GUITARS OF PRESTI & LAGOYA
STEREO
FOLK BANJO STYLES
STEREO
The TRAVELERS 3
STEREO
JUDY COLLINS
THE DILLARDS
BACK PORCH BLUEGRASS
JUDY HENSKE
DEAN & THE GREENBRIAR BOYS
KOTO
THE MUSIC OF JAPAN
PLAYED BY
WHERE I'M BOUND
BOB GIBSON
AND HIS 12-STRING GUITAR
STEREO
JUDY HENSKE
high flying bird
PANORAMIC STEREO
THEODORE BIKEL
SONGS OF RUSSIA OLD & NEW
the songs of FRED ENGLEBERG
STEREO
the EVEN DOZEN JUG BAND
TEAR DOWN THE WALLS
MARTIN & NEIL
STEREO
The Irish Ramblers
The Patriot Game
STEREO
THE DILLARDS
LIVE
!!!almost!!!
LOTS MORE
BLUES, RAGS AND HOLLERS
STEREO
The IAN CAMPBELL FOLK GROUP
PHIL OCHS
All the News that's Fit to Sing
WOODY GUTHRIE
LIBRARY OF CONGRESS RECORDINGS
happy ALL THE TIME
Joseph Spence

Laddie Lie Near Me
JEAN REDPATH
TOM PAXTON
SNAKER'S HERE!
DAVE RAY
PHIL OCHS
I ain't marching any more
TOM RUSH
FRED NEIL
THE CORRIE FOLK TRIO with Paddie Bell
string band project
Tom Paley & Peggy Seeger
TOM PAXTON
ain't that news!
NEGRO FOLKLORE from TEXAS STATE PRISONS
Leadbelly
Jimmy Davis
SINGER SONGWRITER PROJECT
TOM RUSH
The IAN CAMPBELL FOLK GROUP
EAST-WEST
the BUTTERFIELD BLUES BAND
TOM PAXTON
FROST AND FIRE
The WATERSONS
The Incredible String Band
LOVE
What's Shakin'
THE LOVIN' SPOONFUL
DAVID BLUE
goodbye and
TIM BUCKLEY
da capo
LOVE

TOM RUSH
TOM PAXTON
morning again
JUDY COLLINS
WHO KNOWS WHERE THE TIME GOES
The Moray Eels Eat The Holy Modal Rounders
HAVE
A
MARIJUANA
Recorded Live On The
Streets Of New York
David Peel & the lower east side
lonnie mack
RUNNING JUMPING STANDING STILL
THE THINGS I NOTICE NOW
TOM PAXTON
tim buckley / happy sad
bread
nico
the marble index
Judy Collins
RECOLLECTIONS
RHINOCEROS

the stooges
fun house
RENAISSANCE
David Peel & the lower east side
THE AMERICAN REVOLUTION
TIM BUCKLEY
LORCA
FOR COLLECTORS ONLY
LONNIE MACK
WHAM
MEMPHIS
On The Waters
bread
The Doors
13
PAUL SIEBEL
jack-knife gypsy
CARLY SIMON
SHOW OF HANDS
RADIO FREE NIXON
DAVID FRYE
bread
Manna
SIREN
TIMBER
BRING AMERICA HOME
Lindisfarne
AUDIENCE
CRABBY
APPLETON
rotten to the core!
DON NIX
LIVING BY THE DAYS
Bridget St John
Songs for the gentle man
MICKEY NEWBURY

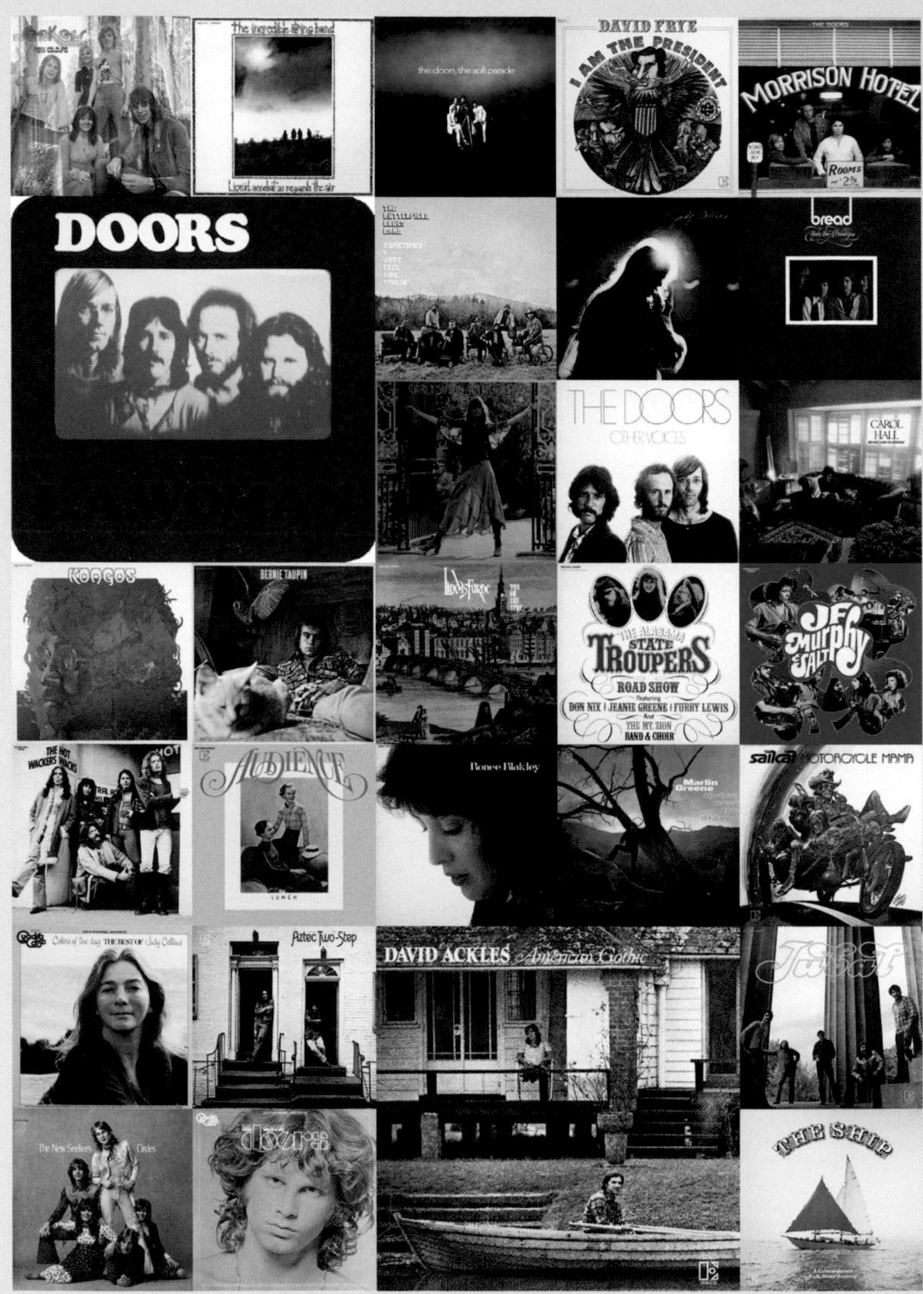
The Incredible String Band
Liquid Acrobat as Regards the Air
the doors the soft parade
DAVID FRYE
I AM THE PRESIDENT
MORRISON HOTEL
ROOMS
DOORS
THE BUTTERFIELD BLUES BAND
SOMETIMES I JUST FEEL LIKE SMILIN
bread
THE DOORS
OTHER VOICES
CAROL HALL
KONGOS
BERNIE TAUPIN
Lindisfarne
THE ALABAMA STATE TROUPERS
ROAD SHOW
Featuring
DON NIX JEANIE GREENE FURRY LEWIS
And
THE MT. ZION
BAND & CHOIR
JF Murphy & Salt
AUDIENCE
LUNCH
Ronee Blakley
Marlin Greene
sailcat MOTORCYCLE MAMA
Colors of the day THE BEST OF Judy Collins
Aztec Two-Step
DAVID ACKLES American Gothic
The New Seekers Circles
doors
THE SHIP

Casey Kelly
Lindisfarne Dingly Dell
Plainsong
The Wackers
Shredder
Carly Simon
No Secrets
bread
guitar man
Veronique Sanson
The Best of The New Seekers
Dana Cooper
Judy Collins
Billy Mernit Special Delivery
the best of bread
the best of bread
Don Agrati
Stardrive
Ian Matthews
Linda Hargrove
Queen
Harry Chapin
short stories
Dennis Linde
Dennis Coulson
jobriath
Pipedream Alan Hull
Buzz Rabin
Lindisfarne
Roll On, Ruby
Ian Matthews
Melba Montgomery
No Charge

blatantly political. We scared people in a different way. Iggy was different, really wild, and he did things that more normal people would never think of. It wasn't Elektra's fault that they didn't push the band hard enough. We were tough to handle."

David Bowie intervened to get 1973's *Raw Power* made, this time for Columbia. In absentia, The Stooges became increasingly relevant through the 70s and beyond, an irrefutable inspirational force. They were the engine for punk, grunge, and whatever the next wave of edgy, threatening rock'n'roll will be.

Danny Fields is unrepentant about taking them to Elektra. "The Stooges were unmanageable. It was like a John Waters movie. But it's remarkable that they could dance to the same rhythm – and I mean that on every metaphorical level. They were so disorganised, but they came up with such brilliant stuff. The songs on those two albums speak for themselves. When they signed, they had no songs, and after Jac sent them away to write, they came up with *those* songs. Each one is an acknowledged classic. It's peculiar to be in a position of now boasting about bands you got rid of rather than nurturing them, although there's no denying that both The Stooges and the MC5 contributed to their own downfall."

Holzman had few pangs about releasing them. "It was another contention with Bill Harvey. He claimed The Stooges were destroying the label, and I said well, no one's going to hear it anyway. It was typical of the arguments we'd have about The Stooges, and I was wrong. It just took a few more years before the right people heard it, and then everyone got it. They were difficult to work with because they were so strung out, but we got two classic albums."

The mainstream will eventually catch up – as Holzman himself observes today after listening again to The Stooges' albums. "I was just charmed – an odd word, perhaps, but it was so in-the-groove. And I have always thanked Danny for being so supportive of them and me. Danny was let go by Bill Harvey, who said: 'I can't stand Danny Fields, he's wrecking the label, either he goes or I go.' And I said, 'OK, you have to fire him.' I now deeply regret having allowed it. Danny Fields was smart, with excellent taste: highly outspoken, frequently outrageous. And if you were the record company, you also had to respond to your staff, your distributors, and the audience. You *were* somewhat of an establishment operation."

Elektra signed Bread in 1969 – but about the only thing Bread have in common with The Stooges and the MC5 was how quickly the deal was done. Bread came to Holzman's attention in a roundabout way. After releasing the first Love album, Arthur Lee had threatened to walk away from his contract because he was a minor when he signed it. Lee's lawyer Al Schlesinger appreciated the way Holzman handled the situation and promised that if ever anything came through his office that could be good for Elektra, he'd be in touch. That 'anything' was Bread, and although Holzman recognised only one name in the group's line-up, David Gates, he immediately asked David Anderle to cut a demo.

David Gates was born in Tulsa, Oklahoma, and began recording in 1962 for maverick producer Gary S. Paxton when he was teamed with Leon Russell as David & Lee, an Everly Brothers soundalike. Like Russell, he worked behind the scenes, offering his skills as a songwriter, producer, and arranger to others. Which is how, in 1968, Gates found himself producing a group called The Pleasure Fair. The Carpenters' third hit, 'For All We Know', was written by James Griffin and Robb Royer, both members of The Pleasure Fair. The sessions for the group's album (released on Uni in 1967) ultimately led to Bread's formation, as a trio of Gates, Royer, and Griffin. According to Gates, "We played some songs together. James and I harmonised well: our phrasing was just a little country. Within the group there were two writers, two lead singers, and we could all sing killer harmonies." An occasion when the group was stuck in traffic behind a slow-moving Wonder Bread truck gave them their name.

Bruce Botnick was called in. He'd first met Gates after finishing high school and starting work at Liberty Records. "David was a contract songwriter with Leon Russell," says Botnick. "I hadn't seen him since he produced the first Captain Beefheart single, 'Diddy Wah Diddy'. David Anderle asked me to record the demos, and when David came walking in the studio, it was a surprise. They were a group in name only, but that demo did have a special well-crafted edge to it."

The demos were couriered to Holzman. "I thought they were great," he says. "Utterly fresh and likeable, with harmonising vocals that wove in, out, and around each other. It was a softer, more considerate sound than the hard rock that was then everywhere. I heard the tape 24 hours after it was recorded, listened to it twice, and immediately called Al Schlesinger and made an offer." The deal worked well both ways, says Gates. "Elektra did not have an act on its roster like us. Crosby Stills & Nash were on Atlantic, so we felt if we were on Elektra we might be unique in our style of music, and at the same time they would be unique to us."

Signing Bread caused almost as much bewilderment as when Holzman green-lit the MC5 and The Stooges. "Many in my office – not Bill Harvey this time – felt Bread was a total anachronism," says Holzman. "I took a lot of kidding by Danny Fields and Frazier Mohawk, and not just those two. The first Bread album just sold about 30,000 copies, but I knew I had learned enough about the craft of songwriting to know it was not easy to write melodic, uncluttered, direct, and memorable songs. I loved the first album, but Crosby Stills & Nash had come out two weeks earlier and they were all the rage. Deep down, I knew that if we kept them writing and recording, the hit singles would emerge."

Holzman wasn't entirely alone in his assessment. Reviewing the album in *Rolling Stone*, leading rock critic Lester Bangs commented that Bread should be compared to The Beatles, Byrds, Bee Gees, and Buffalo Springfield. He described the group's sound as "a highly refined amalgam of the sweetest, most successful elements in both rock and country. Bread's songs are mostly about love and just good old rock'n'roll, but they have not shut their eyes to all the misery and injustice in the world".

That debut, *Bread*, was blessed with melodic soft-rock and smooth harmonies that belied sharp and clever lyrics. The first single, 'Dismal Day', flopped, but with their signature sound firmly established, Bread began recording *On The Waters*, which included the worldwide million-seller 'Make It With You', selected by Holzman as a single before the album was completed. 'If', 'Baby I'm-A Want You', and 'Everything I Own' followed, all Top Ten global hits. By 1972, Bread had released four Gold albums.

After top session drummer Jim Gordon played on the debut album, Mike Botts joined Bread for *On The Waters* and they set out on their first major tour. Yet Bread never managed to establish a performing presence as recognisable as their sound, unlike the already individually famous Crosby Stills & Nash, the name on everyone's lips. The members of Bread were anonymous mister nice guys. Holzman had already decided that if it didn't work after the second album, that would be that. Gates felt the same. "I was going to dissolve the group," he says, "because I had to feed my family, so I'd go back to doing arrangements and producing for others."

Holzman recalls the Bread recording method as completely civilised. "Most groups would shuffle into the studio by late afternoon, if you were lucky, and nothing would be laid down until mid evening. And then you'd work until two in the morning, leaving the studio drained. Bread would arrive at nine sharp, David with his attaché case, as if he were heading to a Beverly Hills bank. They would record until lunch, break for an hour, work all afternoon, and they would go home to their families at five. I stayed out of their way, wanting to hear the finished tapes. I rarely requested any changes, although I might ask to eliminate a fade – nothing more."

Robb Royer left Bread after their third album, *Manna*, to be replaced by top session player Larry Knechtel, known for his strong contributions to sessions by The Byrds, The Beach Boys, and The Monkees and playing bass on 'Light My Fire' by The Doors. Bread recorded two further albums, *Baby I'm A-Want You* and *Guitar Man*, before a rift between Gates and James Griffin over the division of royalties saw the band break up in 1973. They reunited briefly in 1977, but after one album, *Lost Without Your Love*, the tensions resurfaced and the band dissolved a second time.

Bread were the best exemplars of a musical genre that floated freely onto the AM airwaves in the early 70s: blissful singing, hooks to die for, and immaculate arrangements. This was all fine with Holzman. "Everyone says, 'Jac, they are *pop*.' But I love those songs, the simplicity of their lyrics. We always had enough bedrock curiosity to go after the odd thing and record it, and nobody would raise an eyebrow, but people were surprised to hear Bread on Elektra. In the end, Bread won respect, because they had beautifully crafted gems and displayed intriguing writing qualities."

Bruce Botnick appreciates why people on the outside were baffled. "It did cast a different light on Elektra, with Bread becoming a pop sensation, because Elektra was not known for anything as mainstream as that. I'm not sure Elektra would have been as successful with Carly Simon but for Bread pointing the way. Bread helped Elektra understand and work Top 40 radio."

"I had no problems having Bread on my label," says Holzman. "They were a superb group who produced a stream of high-end hits. Nothing was ever measured only in dollars. There had to be an emotional bang, and Bread had that for me."

Bread proved to be a dream band for Holzman to work with, especially in a year when, even in the light of experience, he had been required to deal with a whole slew of so-called difficult artists and situations. He says he didn't usually see them as being difficult with him or the company. "They sometimes did foolish things or were self-defeating but all of those so-called difficult artists had very different 'problems'. Phil Ochs was trying to be better than Dylan; Arthur Lee didn't want to leave LA, thus severely truncating his career; Jim hated authority or constriction and loved to see how far he could test the limits. Iggy was trying something so new in a world that didn't get him at the beginning but he was a sweet guy. I didn't discount sticking with Iggy after we had let the group go, but he had already moved on and we never had the conversation."

Although Holzman was much more at arm's length with them, trouble was soon brewing with another new Elektra signing, Soft White Underbelly, who had begun recording in Elektra's New York studios in November 1968, with Peter Siegel assigned to produce them. Elektra arranged several New York shows for the band and Holzman committed to signing them after seeing the group in the Ballroom of the Hotel Diplomat in New York. Richard Meltzer and fellow *Crawdaddy* magazine critic Sandy Pearlman managed the group, all of them residing in a run-down communal house where they came together as students or part-time students at Stony Brook University in Long Island.

The housemates played their first gig in the University's Gymnasium in October 1967, as a backing band for Elektra singer songwriter Steve Noonan. It was Pearlman who christened them Soft White Underbelly, after "Winston Churchill's description of Italy as the soft white underbelly of the axis". Six months later, they were joined by aspiring songwriter Les Braunstein, who took over vocal duties, which the group had never entirely settled upon. Braunstein's writing pedigree included a frivolous song called 'I'm In Love With A Big Blue Frog' that Peter Paul & Mary had covered on 1967's *Album 1700*.

"I heard Soft White Underbelly," says Peter Siegel, "and they had a young, good-looking singer called Les Braunstein who had a dark, brooding personality, and I thought they were going to be the next Doors." Indeed, Elektra's early publicity buzz centred round the notion that Soft White Underbelly were the 'East Coast Doors'.

"Les had that kind of star power," says Siegel. "We proceeded to make a rock album; we laid down all the tracks, and he was going to over dub all the vocals – we had only done scratch vocals. At this time an argument took place between Les and the rest of the band. Les was difficult; his mood swings were unbelievable. He was living in the band's communal house but he wanted his own house, and he wanted the band to rent him or buy him a house to live in alone. So it became, 'If you don't get me my own house, I'm going to quit.' And they didn't get him his own house, and he quit, and that was pretty much the end of my involvement with them. I thought somebody was going to back down. Maybe the rest of the band wanted him out; most of them had known each other from high school so he was always an outsider."

The stories surrounding Braunstein are legion, including one about how he didn't like his vocals and crept into the studio one night and wiped them. "That didn't happen any time I was around," says Siegel. "I would have known, trust me. We made an album, we spent $30,000, and I thought they were great tracks but with just guide vocals for the band to hold on to. It was very frustrating because the recordings and the songs were great but it was just never finished. If Les been able to hold it together he was a fine singer, but that star quality came from the same place his mood swings came from. It's one of those great rock'n'roll tragedies. They eventually brought in another singer but by that time I was on to something else."

Drummer Albert Bouchard told his side of the story to Max Bell in 2015. "What it boiled down to was that Les wasn't as serious about the music as the rest of us. He was gifted and talented but when he did the vocals it all got fucked up. He started by lying down on the floor twelve feet from the mic or he'd insist on singing when we weren't there."[4]

Whatever version of the story, the singer – on whose strength Holzman had essentially signed them – was no longer in the group. After bringing in their road manager, Eric Bloom, the group – Bloom on lead vocals and guitar, Donald Rosen (aka Buck Dharma) on lead guitar, Andy Winters on bass, Allen Lanier on keyboards and guitar, and Albert Bouchard on drums – recorded a substantially different-sounding album under the Mexican appellation Oaxaca, before switching again to Stalk-Forrest Group. Their second shot at recording, this time with Pearlman co-producing, took place in Elektra's Los Angeles Studios in February 1970, under the supervision of company man Danny Murphy. The completed album was scheduled for summer 1970, with 'What Is Quicksand' and 'Arthur Commix' pressed up as a promotional single. According to Meltzer, the group thought it was a mistake to release the album in the middle of the summer, so they did their best to delay the release. In the end, Holzman decided not to release it at all. The following summer, re-christened again, this time as Blue Öyster Cult, they were brought to the attention of Columbia's Clive Davis, who auditioned and signed them.

The Stalk-Forrest Group's *St Cecelia* was released by Rhino in 2003 but included nothing from the recordings with Les Braunstein. "I thought that the eventual recordings I heard were less than I expected from having seen them," says Holzman. "I just felt they didn't measure up to the other great groups we had on the label. It wasn't there but it happened for them later. Those unreleased recordings eventually came out purely because, in retrospect, they had become more interesting to people, but that doesn't make them any better."

Remembering Elektra
Peter Rowan / Earth Opera

After dropping out of college in upstate New York, Peter Rowan went to Boston, where he became part of the scene around Club 47, playing with the likes of Bob Siggins, Jim Rooney, Bill Keith, and The Charles River Valley Boys.

"I was the youngest of that crowd around Club 47 in Cambridge and played in both the Keith & Rooney Band and The Charles River Valley Boys. My mentor there was Joe Val, the great mandolin player and tenor vocalist. He taught me to hear and sing the harmony parts of The Monroe Brothers, Delmore Brothers, the Louvins, and The Blue Sky Boys.

The Mother Bay State Entertainers was an old timey-style string band that centred around Bob Siggins's activities in Harvard Square. Bob was co-leader of The Charles River Valley Boys with John Cook. I toured with them one summer and we formed the Mother Bay State Entertainers with Ethan Signer on fiddle and Johnny Shawn on bass. We played Uncle Dave Macon and Charley Poole's kind of rollicking pre-bluegrass music. I played mandolin and my first 'away-from-home' music experience to go to New York and record three songs for Elektra's *String Band Project* LP with the band.

I was on my way to Nashville to play with Bill Monroe on the *Grand Ole*

Opry. It was mostly in my travels with Bill Monroe [during 1964–67] that I assimilated the roots of bluegrass, which covers Cajun, blues, and Western swing. We are all following in some very big footprints; Bill Monroe teaches you to removes the limits or boundaries to any type of music.

When I left Bill Monroe & The Bluegrass Boys in March of 1967 I left Nashville and went back to New England to meet up with an old friend, David Grisman, who had been a member of the Even Dozen Jug Band. We got together as an acoustic duo.* I had written many songs while I was with Bill Monroe and David; I arranged them as a duo and rehearsed every day. Songs like 'Time and Again', 'The Child Bride', 'As It Is Before' [from *Earth Opera*], 'The Great American Eagle Tragedy', and 'Mad Lydia's Waltz' were already taking shape while I was a Bluegrass Boy, but I was told they weren't "dumb enough" for country.

David's childhood friend, Peter Siegel, had become a producer for Elektra and Nonesuch Records, and he came up to Boston and recorded us as a duo with my vocals, mandocello, and guitar. He took the demo tapes from Boston to Jac Holzman who decided to sign us as a new act.

Jac arranged a meeting for us with Simon & Garfunkel's management, but they wanted to take our demo and orchestrate the material as it stood with rock drumming, violins – the whole treatment. They wanted something commercial, but of course, coming from bluegrass, we thought the whole idea preposterous, even slightly immoral, in a musical sense. We spent an agonising afternoon in the management offices before finally turning Jac's idea down. He signed us anyway.

Peter Siegel really championed us, although we had no recording experience outside of bluegrass, and our band knew even less. I watched the simplicity of what David and I called Earth Opera devolve into a democracy-of-dunces as a result of "band input".†

The bluegrass intuitive approach was alien to them and required more musical training to lead than I had had thus far. David acted as musical director and helped translate my songs into band arrangements. It was just too weird for the band, God bless 'em. The vocals were also a nightmare, just impossible, but now it all sounds strange and wonderful.

---

* Sometimes under the name The Bluegrass Drop-outs.

† The musicians were John Nagy (bass), Bill Stevenson (piano, organ and vibraphone), and the last man to join, toward the end of the first album sessions, Paul Dillon (drums).

My original songs began to take shape as an underground sound that would later be dubbed 'art rock', 'folk jazz', and 'Gothic rock' by some writers of the time, and we received a lot of coverage in the press, especially from Jon Landau in *Crawdaddy*. We had nothing to do the 'Bosstown Sound', which was pure poppycock.

David and I believed that the validity of jazz, and the playing of musicians like Eric Dolphy and John Coltrane was similar to the 'truth' in bluegrass music; it was spontaneous and direct. After the first album we scandalised the band by adding two saxophone players who shared our vision – Richard Grando on tenor sax and flute and Jack Bonus on alto sax. We began to include free jazz jams on stage; the horn players were way into it but the rest of the band was freaked out. They saw it as an incomprehensible left turn, but to David and me it was all the great free-flowing music that existed in space.

Elektra allowed us to record as a sextet for *The Great American Eagle Tragedy*.* We had a vision of the music as evolving, spontaneous, and free, and we followed that; the recordings sound interesting to me now. We were much closer to the vision than I realised.

We opened for The Doors on many shows, which was great exposure. We played all over the Northeast with them and we did OK; they were noisy crowds, just waiting for Jim Morrison, but we held our own.

We kept going through 'Home To You'† and the release of *The American Eagle Tragedy*, but it was difficult to keep the band together. There was not a lot of money happening. We were not commercial enough to make it as a rock band and we were too rock'n'roll to be folk.”

After Earth Opera disbanded, Rowan joined Sea Train, where he teamed up with Richard Greene (another String Band Project alumnus); he and Grisman worked together in both Muleskinner (with Clarence White) and Jerry Garcia's bluegrass spin-off project Old And In The Way. After that, Rowan relocated to Nashville, recording three albums with The Rowan Brothers, before embarking on an ongoing career that has proven compellingly diverse in scope without ever abandoning his bluegrass roots.

* A long, free-form, four-saxophone intro was edited out of the ten-minute title track.
† A very near hit which crept into the *Billboard* Top 100.

CHAPTER 22

Anticipation

> “*There are a lot of exciting ideas running around: some of them might be right, some of them might be cockeyed, but they are affecting all our lives. I want to know how I stand, how I fit into the picture, what's it all going to mean to me? I can't find that out sitting behind a desk in an office. So, as soon as I get enough money together, I'm going to knock off for a while. Quit. I want to save part of my life for myself. There's a catch to it, though. It's got to be part of the young part. Retire young; work old. Come back when I know what I'm working for. Does that make sense to you?*” **JOHNNY CASE (PLAYED BY CARY GRANT) IN *HOLIDAY*, 1938, ONE OF JAC HOLZMAN'S FAVOURITE MOVIES.**

In 1968, Jac Holzman boarded the *SS President Roosevelt*, a slow boat to Hong Kong. During the journey, the ship's purser recommended that he visit the Hawaiian island of Maui, so he disembarked at Honolulu and flew to the island, planning to catch up with the *Roosevelt* in Yokohama. Maui was a revelation to Holzman. “As I travelled across the isthmus of the island,” he says, “the world turned green and tranquil. It was more peace than I had ever experienced.”

Early that evening, he sat in a charming thatched restaurant in Maui, watching the sun drift slowly behind the western fringe of Lanai. “I stared at the point where the sun had disappeared below the horizon, saying to myself,

'I can't keep up this pace forever. There are other good things out there for me.' I could hear the Cary Grant character who wants to take a long break in midlife, to understand why he's working and where he fits in. I made a promise to myself. In five years I'll be done – I will move here and begin again."

Elektra was thriving as an independent and spirited label, but Holzman, who was still very hands-on, realised that record-making was changing. As late as 1969, he considered keeping the company small and flexible by staying at the same level of 15 to 20 people as when The Doors broke through. If, however, he chose to develop the label further, he knew that he had to control his own distribution.

Starting in the 50s and continuing through to the mid 60s, independent distributors were the primary suppliers of independent recordings to dealers. Once powerful, these distributors were becoming less so as the major labels grew. The majors were propelled by rock'n'roll signings and their tightly integrated systems for branch distribution. "In 1969, after Atlantic was sold to Warner Seven Arts," says Holzman, "they joined Warner's house-owned distributors in LA. I asked Atlantic's Jerry Wexler about how the company branch compared to his indie experience. He replied, 'Jac, the worst branch distribution is better than the best independent distribution.' That was something I didn't forget."

Artists, their managers, and the lawyers who cosseted them began asserting their influence, and the advances, guarantees, and marketing costs all moved in one direction: upward. "If we had stayed independent," reflects Holzman, "it would have required distribution through one of the major labels, and they would have had tremendous leverage over me. Independent distribution was showing stress fractures. If you were a dealer or rack-jobber, you paid the majors first. Elektra could not survive without predictable cash flow."

Holzman knew that by joining Elektra with Warners and Atlantic, the future of the label was secure. "My brother labels were run by people who I knew, respected, and liked – at Atlantic you had Ahmet Ertegun, Jerry Wexler, and I admired Ahmet's brother, Nesuhi. I had enormous affection for Mo Ostin and Joe Smith at Warners, who said, 'You're one of us.' After the merger, both Warner Brothers and Atlantic still projected an indie image. In comparison, Elektra was a bijou label, so I knew we could chart our own destiny.

"When the opportunity came to join people for whom I had such high regard," Holzman continues, "there was no twinge of doubt. After blessedly short negotiations – just two days – I agreed to the merger. I felt a sigh of relief being on the inside of a strong organisation. What I didn't anticipate were the unexpected opportunities that this would open for me."

The deal covered both the Elektra and Nonesuch labels, soon consolidated under the umbrella of Warner Communications Inc with Warners and Atlantic. "There was never a hint of interference from WCI chairman Steve Ross. He promised me autonomy and he kept his word, never once questioning a decision or a release. It was still 'my company' and I was running it as I always did – without the threat of a large distributor suddenly filing bankruptcy. Even though we were the boutique label of the group, and wanted to remain so, we still competed in A&R, marketing, sales, and radio play. Warners and Atlantic had loud voices. Elektra had to make itself heard."

The ink was barely dry on the deal when Holzman had to resolve the fragmentation in his relationship with Paul Rothchild. Holzman missed the crazies like Danny Fields and Frazier Mohawk who were no longer around. David Anderle had gone, and Nina Holzman's involvement in Elektra ended after the WCI sale. "No team stays together forever. They move toward their own interests," says Holzman. "Rothchild's a star producer, and he was receiving offers elsewhere. He continued to produce for us as an independent, but when he left The Doors, he left the company. It's a mistake to try and hold on to people when they get that itch. You let them move on."

Holzman knows that Rothchild made an enormous contribution to Elektra. "It's almost beyond measurement. He was clearly the perfect producer for The Doors. I can't think of anyone else I could have trusted with that band. He was as smart as they were, and Bruce Botnick played a pivotal role, too. He hears so well."

After Rothchild and Holzman parted, they stayed close. "When, much later, he became seriously ill," says Holzman, "I was one of only three people he told. When we were younger, we were both more foolish, more ego-driven. The thread of the friendship and our high mutual regard never wavered. But in 1970, both our heads had swelled, and it was time to move on."

Rothchild made a fleeting return, bringing the *Goodthunder* album to Elektra in 1972. "That was Paul wanting to get back in under the awning," says Holzman about the group's only album, a throwback to the heavy folk and psych days of Clear Light, with crunching guitars, a driving bass, and swirling keyboards. "Before his death in 1995, Paul produced a terrific album for my Discovery label – the first of our very successful *Jazz At The Movies*

Band series, released in 1993. In remission from lung cancer, he was still the Paul of old, agonising over the minutiae of detail."

Holzman had always believed in a strong core of resident staff producers. Elektra could call upon Rothchild, Mark Abramson, David Anderle, Peter Siegel, and Russ Miller, as well as engineers who could double as producers, such as Bruce Botnick and John Haeny. The team he'd built by the mid to late 60s was hard to beat. "It was never as good again, but as the record industry grew, with more artists and multiple genres, we could no longer maintain enough staff producers to handle that volume and variety. When Elektra dipped into the pool of non-affiliated producers, that decision became the most important creative decision I would make. When it comes to matching the artist to the ideal producer, you have to get it absolutely right."

This was nowhere better illustrated than Holzman's matchmaking efforts with Carly Simon. The process of finding producers is arduous, he says. He thought Eddie Kramer was right for Simon's debut, because he knew Kramer could teach her the studio and get a fully rounded sound from her voice when it was mixed with instruments. Simon had grown up in a family where everyone was expected to achieve, so it took a strong presence in the studio to deal with that level of attention.

For Simon's second album, 1971's *Anticipation*, Holzman wanted somebody with a more thorough sense of song. "So we went with Paul Samwell-Smith, from The Yardbirds, who had a more holistic approach. For album number three, I brought in Richard Perry, who was one of the most talented producers of the time. I thought he could confront Carly and develop the major hit single we needed to take her to the next level. Between them, they built 'You're So Vain', about which I had no expectations when I heard an early audition track."

Carly Simon's songs had done the rounds of various labels before Holzman saw something intriguing. He initially toyed with the idea that, like Judy Collins, Simon might be a gifted interpreter of songs by other writers. "Based on her demo tape, I was more struck by her ability to wrap her voice around a song than her ability to write one. I normally pre-recorded an artist, running through all the material and then listening to it over and over, studying their work, learning all about their artistic choices, and talking with the musicians who had been with them in the studio. I didn't do that with Carly. I wanted to see what would happen."

Simon was another child of folk music. "From the time I was in high school," she says, "all the records I felt close to were on Elektra. I had a big library of Nonesuch. I knew and liked Theodore Bikel, I loved Judy Henske: so solidly earthy. I adored her 'Wade In The Water'. And the Butterfield Band. Judy Collins was one of the women I emulated, and the fact that she was on Elektra meant something. Elektra had standards."[1]

Carly Simon was born into a wealthy publishing family in New York City in 1945, and she first performed and recorded with her sister Lucy as The Simon Sisters. Their angelic voices blended beautifully, and they even achieved a minor hit in 1964 with 'Winkin' Blinkin' And Nod'. They played around Greenwich Village and in New York, while Simon was still at college. Her mentors at the time were Odetta and Judy Collins. When Lucy married, they stopped performing together, and Carly began tentatively writing songs at the end of the 60s. When her debut album, *Carly Simon,* was released in 1971, the era of new singer-songwriters was unfolding, although she hardly fitted in. Her songs had a strong intellectual spine, as the *Rolling Stone* review of that first album noted, "Some of these songs sound like Updike or Salinger – short stories set to music."[2]

Having taken one risk by signing Simon when no one else was interested, Holzman knew that her album was a gem. "The songs were sophisticated and openhearted," he says, "which is a rare combination. Some of the lyrics reminded me of Stephen Sondheim, with their keen sense of the crosscurrents of life and the human condition. Though Carly sang with a rock backing, her well-bred voice was of a kind rarely heard in that context."

Holzman picked 'That's The Way I've Always Heard It Should Be' as the first single. "That song meant so much to me," says Simon about her breakthrough hit, a collaboration with screenwriter Jacob Brackman, the words written by him but from her point of view. "Jac was always able to pick songs that were most true to the artist. It was a very smart choice, because it introduced me to the public with a song that wasn't typical Top 40 radio. Jac took a chance."[3]

"Carly had an easy story to tell," says Holzman. "She was a long-stemmed rose, she wrote these terrific songs, and she was extremely sexy. The albums had been well produced, but she was real. The emergence of the women's movement and the consciousness that brought about made me think that the choice of Carly's single was so right. She was questioning the role that the evolution of society had placed upon her – not finger-pointing like Helen Reddy's 'I Am Woman'. I thought women would identify with that. She had it both ways, because every red-blooded male knew who Carly was."

Simon saw 'That's The Way I've Always Heard It Should Be' become a respectable hit in the summer of 1971. "I left for London to record with Paul Samwell-Smith a few months later," she says. "We made *Anticipation*. It was one of the best memories I shall ever have of recording. I had a band. The entire album was just that band – Andy Newmark [drums], Jimmy Ryan [guitars], Paul Glanz [keyboards] – and myself. Cat Stevens did some vocals, and there were strings on a few songs, but on the whole it was sparse, and I loved it. *Anticipation* was a hit, and then [it was] back to England to make *No Secrets* with Richard Perry in 1972."[4]

She had perfected her own brand of melodiously laidback adult pop, and *Carly Simon* and *Anticipation* both had irresistibly come-hither jackets. The records were perfect for those who had bought Carole King's *Tapestry* in such large numbers. Simon's great attribute has always been her intelligence, allied with her looks, but on *No Secrets* that voice was given a shimmering rock production. Holzman says that during the recordings in London there were rumblings about problems between her and Perry. "But from an ocean away, I kept my fingers crossed. I'm sure they pushed each other, but out of that pairing came 'You're So Vain'."

By now, Simon was married to James Taylor, the pre-eminent male singer-songwriter of the era. As a high-profile couple, their life together and eventual separation in 1983 played out with none of the media frenzy that would accompany it today. Simon's Elektra career carried through until *Spy* in 1979. *No Secrets*, propelled by 'You're So Vain', had been a Number One album, and she had continued with Richard Perry for two more Top Ten albums, *Hotcakes* (1974) and *Playing Possum* (1975).

Like Carly Simon, Harry Chapin was an Elektra singer-songwriter who came up through the folk circuit, performing with brothers Tom and Stephen as The Chapin Brothers, and even briefly teaming with Carly and Lucy Simon and known as Brothers & Sisters. Chapin found success writing unconventional songs with an affinity to folk. He differed from other current singer-songwriters in that his songs were rarely about himself. Harry sang about real or imaginary characters in elaborate narratives.

Holzman gives the example that Carly Simon wrote mostly from her own experience, where Chapin was an observer. "I always kidded him that he had his craft down so he ought to reach more for art. But Carly was closer to the art than Harry was. Harry was almost a troubadour, in the traditional sense, and that he did so well on Top 40 radio fascinated me. He was masterful at working the stations, better than anyone at Elektra, including the radio promotion department. He'd call programme directors and, after his successful single 'Taxi', they'd take his calls. He knew the sports teams they supported, the names of their family members, so when something like 'Cat's In The Cradle' was released they were quickly on board. Harry wasn't fawning, he was just a good guy, and he adored human contact." On second thoughts, says Holzman, he didn't think Chapin was such a good guy when he said he was signing with Clive Davis at Columbia and not with Elektra.

Harry Chapin was born in December 1942, the son of a big-band drummer. He packed a wide variety of experiences into his early life: he flew planes, was sharp at pool, and had earned a 1968 Academy Award nomination for a short boxing film he wrote and directed, *Legendary Champions*. He returned to music, forming a group based on his storytelling songs, animated by an unusual line-up – two guitars, bass, and cello – that revelled in complex arrangements without sounding contrived.

Holzman found that he and Clive Davis were chasing the same act. "I thought we had a deal," Holzman bristles, "but the way Harry went about telling me face-to-face was to his credit. He and his manager, Fred Kewley, met me at the airport prior to a trip to LA. They told me Harry had decided to sign to Columbia. I was crushed, but I knew that, because of the massive Columbia paperwork, it would take some time to be sorted. It was a tough one to lose. That made me even angrier. I did what I always did in that situation. I ramped up my determination."

Clive Davis, who had been the company lawyer at Columbia Records, was made president when Goddard Lieberson retired. Holzman recalls that Davis worked hard to learn about the artistic and A&R side of the business, the parts with which he was least familiar. "Clive had shown Harry the figures of some of his singer-songwriters: Paul Simon and Bob Dylan – heady company. Then he told Harry his numbers should fall in the same range."

Obsessed by his failure to get a commitment from Chapin, Holzman caught the red-eye to New York City the following weekend and hammered on Chapin's door early that Sunday. He told the musician that he was not leaving until they worked out an arrangement for Chapin to sign to Elektra. Unlike Columbia, Elektra had flexibility, and that was an asset. As he had done with The Doors, Holzman committed to releasing no other album during the month Chapin's debut would appear. He also volunteered to produce the record himself, which helped clinch the deal. "I loved producing," says Holzman, "especially great artists, and I knew that personally taking charge would get the attention of my staff. I was determined to capture the authentic Harry Chapin who had so impressed me."

At over six minutes long, 'Taxi', from Chapin's 1972 debut *Heads & Tales*, was a sizable enough hit to launch him, with help from alternative FM radio, which played a wide range of songs from the album. 'Taxi' became his signature song, first introduced to the American public on Johnny Carson's *Tonight* show. Carson invited Chapin back for an unprecedented repeat of the song the following night. In itself, that was certification of his everyman appeal and his ability to create an atmosphere and have the listener feel it too.

Chapin would become a popular and much-loved Elektra artist, recording ten albums for the label until he left at the end of the 70s. 'Cat's In The Cradle', from the 1974 *Verities & Balderdash* album, gave Elektra its fifth Number One single. Critically undervalued, Chapin was like a character from a Frank Capra movie who spoke both to and for the people. If Carly Simon was a continuation of Judy Collins for a newer decade, Harry Chapin was its Tom Paxton. He, too, wrote children's songs, for 70s kids TV series *Make A Wish*. Tragically, on July 16 1981, Chapin was killed when his Volkswagen was demolished by a truck in Jericho, New York.

Chapin had become increasingly interested in politics and deeply involved with raising awareness about the fight against world hunger, standing as a delegate to the 1976 Democratic Convention. He played benefits tirelessly, raising millions for his causes. In 1987, Chapin was posthumously awarded the Congressional Gold Medal for his humanitarian efforts. "My continuing challenge to Harry," says Holzman, "was over the difference between craft and art. He was a brilliant craftsman, but I knew he was capable of so much more. Writing seemed to come so easily, and I wanted him to dig deeper. After his death, I came to understand that how he lived his life and what he stood for was Harry's art."

Bread, Harry Chapin, and Carly Simon were the new face of Elektra Records. By 1971, almost every artist associated with the label from the previous decade had moved on, including Love, Tom Paxton, Phil Ochs, Tim Buckley, Koerner Ray & Glover, The Incredible String Band, Paul Butterfield, Tom Rush, and, however brief their stay, The Stooges and the MC5.

Jim Morrison's death was the most tragic loss, in July of that year. Yet a few months later, the remaining trio released *Other Voices*. "That was my way of saying to Ray, Robby, and John that it hadn't all been about Jim," explains Holzman. "Despite some superb tracks, *Full Circle* was as far as it could go. They had performed a fabulous show in New York in a packed Carnegie Hall, but it missed the theatricality and the danger level without Morrison." Reflecting on the two post-Morrison albums, John Densmore told *Uncut* magazine in 2015, "I hadn't listened to them in quite a while. Boy, excuse my patting ourselves on the back but this is a really tight band instrumentally but I do miss hearing that great voice tone … nobody had Jim's voice. This is a guy who never had any proper singing instruction, and to be able to scream from the bowels of his soul and not rip up his vocal cords…"[5]

"Jim would have loved the atmosphere of his poetry released as *An American Prayer* in 1978," Holzman continues. "I thought it was done with great taste – as sensitive as Jim – and was very smartly put together by John Haeny. It was a completion of the kind Jim would have appreciated. And Haeny brought forth Jim the poet within an ideal musical context: music by The Doors."

Joshua Rifkin had been a strong member of the Nonesuch team, rising to become associate director of the label, second in command to Tracey Sterne, when he left in 1975. Rifkin witnessed the transformation of Elektra. "When I first visited them, the office and its staff were still fairly small, and you could drop in and chat with Jac at leisure," he says. "Both the underlying music and the company style shifted. Everyone – I don't necessarily exclude myself – was dazzled by the glitz and the potential riches. The edges of the operation had become harder, the bottom line more important."

Holzman understood this. He knew he was playing in a game with smart people – namely Mo Ostin and Ahmet Ertegun. "I wanted to do well for the company and for chairman Steve Ross, although he earned his entire investment back many times over from the signing of Queen alone [in 1972]. The period from 1970 to 1973 marked the most commercially successful era of all the Elektra years. I could play at their level while still reaching out for unusual artists and records. As I look back at the Elektra catalogue of that period, I should have made fewer albums and trimmed the staff. In the last six months, knowing I would be leaving, I probably paid less attention."

FM radio helped 70s audiences broaden their tastes, and Holzman looked to Britain as a source, where the new independent labels respected Elektra and knew that he understood them, their artists, and the spirit that drove them. Accordingly, Elektra licensed albums from Island (by Renaissance), B&C and Charisma (Lindisfarne, Audience, Atomic Rooster, John Kongos), and Dandelion (Siren and Bridget St John).

Plainsong was a rare direct signing, and the band featured Ian Matthews. He was already established, following his departure from Fairport Convention and a surprise UK Number One with his band Matthews Southern Comfort and their cover of Joni Mitchell's 'Woodstock'. Matthews's main collaborator in Plainsong was the ex-Liverpool Scene musician Andy Roberts, an accomplished singer-songwriter and criminally underrated guitarist. The later solo albums Roberts made for Elektra, *Urban Cowboy* and *The Great Stampede*, fell foul of the changes within its corporate structure and received little attention, while a second Plainsong album went unreleased, of no interest to a label under David Geffen, who was installed after Holzman moved on in 1973.

"I loved Ian's records," says Holzman, "but he had become more of an Englishman trying to make American-sounding records rather than exploring a native uniqueness in the manner of The Incredible String Band. I later suggested former Monkee Mike Nesmith to produce Ian's *Valley Hi*. It's a wonderful, graceful record, and you hear Nesmith's deft touches throughout."

The Charisma albums that Elektra released all had connections with the producer and engineer Gus Dudgeon. "Sometimes you pick an artist because of the producer," says Holzman, "like Audience." Elektra released two of their albums, *The House On the Hill* and *Lunch*. "Audience were meticulous," he says, "a rolling tapestry, very singular material, well behaved in a rock'n'roll context. I am still flummoxed that it didn't happen for them, but what was most unfortunate for all the British acts was that they rarely toured America. I was attracted to Lindisfarne's strong folk roots, and Alan Hull was an excellent writer, but for British groups to make an impact, they had to be seen. America is so damn big and very expensive to tour. In Europe, you threw everything in the back of a Transit van and went on the road."

By now, Clive Selwood was running Elektra UK, and through his close relationship with DJ John Peel he was simultaneously looking after Peel's

Dandelion label, which Elektra occasionally tapped into. Holzman singles out Siren's *Strange Locomotion*, which he describes as typical of Dandelion's invention and flair, although he found the recordings less polished than Elektra was used to. "Clive Selwood was a grand Elektra personality. He understood me and was close to the highly respected John Peel, who had an abiding affection for Elektra. Clive not only had taste, but he would run stuff by Peel, and Peel had unerring taste."

In October 1970, Elektra released *Right On Be Free* by The Voices Of East Harlem. "Talk about energy!" says Holzman of this 20-strong Afro-American youth choir. "They were genuine, likable, and overpowering. Urban radio played the album in New York, but I didn't know if they would get radio play in Detroit. American urban communities are very diverse in terms of their local cultures. It needed to break out from New York, and that didn't happen. Elektra was as white a label as you could sign to, and although we had done a lot of funky stuff, we could not deliver on The Voices Of East Harlem."

In the early 70s, Elektra embraced a sweeping spectrum of contrasting artists and styles, ranging from *Right On Be Free* to three albums by The New Seekers, licensed from Philips in the UK, or the power-pop of The Wackers and Crabby Appleton. Elektra made four albums with The Wackers, including their debut as Roxy. Holzman kept faith in them, trying different producers – including Gary Usher on their debut, *Wackering Heights*, and *Hot Wacks* – but to no avail. At least Crabby Appleton almost broke with a hit, the wonderful hook-laden 'Go Back' from the first of their two Elektra albums. Both bands suffered the curse of power-pop, recapturing the giddy flavour of 60s pop without the commercial validation.

Crabby Appleton's self-titled debut was well received, with Lester Bangs writing that it was "as satisfying a definition of the mainstream rock band as we've had this year" in *Rolling Stone*. "Folks at Elektra were supportive," says Michael Fennelly, who wrote all of the group's material, "but there was too much turnover at the label to know who our champion was at any given time." Nor did they have the management to keep on top of things. "So we'd arrive some places where we'd have the Number Two record at the local radio station and be unknown at others. When we played it was the same – we'd draw huge crowds one night and next night be playing to five bored guys seated at the bar just sixty miles drive away. Our commercial success was just too erratic to sustain the group in the end."

Clive Selwood thought that Holzman had a tough time dealing with the now more corporate set-up. "Elektra started to lose its singularity," says Selwood, "but that's almost inevitable when a label grows from a handful of people to become a small empire. I don't think Jac signed any dummies. He liked smart people, both on the label and around him. But by 1970, Elektra had grown, and for anyone in Jac's position it requires your full attention to take care of the business side, however much it was a music-driven label. Ironically, when you're running something hand-to-mouth, it's much simpler than being part of a huge enterprise."

Holzman doesn't consider this as like the end of the 50s, when he was looking for a direction. "In the 70s, we had become very successful, so I could indulge myself in music that David Geffen would have considered a distraction. I didn't think of David Ackles or The Wackers as distractions. Those LPs had staying power, even if they didn't connect at the time."

He spotlights *A Child's Garden Of Grass*, an album that targeted aging dope-smokers, as a fun record to make. It was an audio companion to a book of the same name by Jack S. Margolis and Richard Clorfene, and was recorded under the guidance of California's Top 40 radio hotshot, Ron 'Whodaguy' Jacobs, with help from Cyrus Faryar, in whose home studio it was recorded. Faryar is the voice of the Indian guru on the album, spoofing instruction cassettes with straightfaced narration and sound 'dope' advice spoken over a mostly electronic score. Various members of The Firesign Theatre also participated.

"Elektra was a label that tolerated dope," says Holzman, "but not in the offices. In the studio, we had installed a secret compartment in our mixing console into which you could immediately make everything disappear, but you first had to touch the panel at exactly the right spot for it to open."

Country music was an obvious direction for Elektra. Their most successful acts, certainly as writers, were Dennis Linde and Mickey Newbury. Mike Nesmith's Countryside label was an intriguing venture based, in part, on the premise that Nesmith thought it possible to develop a label in California based upon a Western take on country music, and he cited Buck Owens as a model. Holzman thought it worth exploring the idea of a small ancillary label working a potent vein of American music, separate from Elektra's offices.

"Nesmith could bring unusual, talented people together and create a supportive environment," says Holzman. "He was whip-smart and a pro in the studio. Countryside was an effort to develop a different kind of country music, where country and cowboy and folk merges. We built Michael his own studio around the same analogue mixing console that recorded *LA Woman*. Unfortunately, Countryside was the first thing David Geffen dismantled when he took over." Only two albums appeared: Garland Frady's splendid *Pure Country* and one by Nesmith's renowned steel guitarist Red Rhodes, *Velvet Hammer In A Cowboy Band.*

There are recognisable patterns in Elektra's catalogue during Holzman's final three years: the British licenses; the self-confessed indulgences; a toehold in country; and a continued commitment to songwriters. Despite the successes of Carly Simon and Harry Chapin, there were other deserving releases that didn't catch on.

Cyrus Faryar made two delightful and gently swaying albums, *Cyrus* and *Islands*, both recorded in his home studio in North Hollywood (part constructed by a young carpenter and struggling actor named Harrison Ford).

Carol Hall had the misfortune to clash in the release schedules with Carly Simon's debut, but Hall's album, *If I Be Your Lady*, warranted greater attention. She later achieved recognition by writing the music and lyrics for the musical *The Best Little Whorehouse In Texas*, first produced on Broadway in 1978.

Another overlooked release from the period is the album by Ronee Blakley, whose sole self-titled Elektra album in 1972 made far less of a splash than her appearance three years later in Robert Altman's *Nashville* as the fragile country star Barbara Jean. She was discovered by Senior Staff Producer Robert Zachary while he was screening prospective songs for Judy Collins. The assumption is always that this is a country-rock album, but its sparse, piano-driven instrumentation and dramatic balladry edges it closer to David Ackles at times, such as on the mawkish 'I Lied'; Linda Ronstadt lightens the mood, adding harmony to 'Bluebird'.

"My attention was now divided," explains Holzman, "and the label suffered at times. From being the only thing I thought about 24 hours a day, for 23 years, even in my sleep, it had changed. I was no longer 'just running a record company'. Being part of Warner Communications Inc meant other opportunities, other commitments."

Holzman was aware that WCI was moving into new areas of entertainment. "They invited me to help build their future from the ground up. I wasn't going to make records forever, and I knew that I could now have a career going beyond music – and in ways I never anticipated."

CHAPTER 23

Goodbye & Hello

> *"Looking back 60 years, I must have seemed a very odd duck in the music business. I was an oddity in taste and attitude, but it became an advantage. My view was less conventional and I drew upon all my instincts and interests: a talent and passion for electronics, folk music, graphics, the blessing of the LP record, and a lot of raw nerve. I was a self-appointed midwife to the music, a surrogate for the audience, with a commitment to draw the best from every artist who trusted me and recorded for Elektra."* **JAC HOLZMAN**

In July 1970, within a few months of merging his company with Atlantic and Warner Bros to form the Warner Music Group (WMG) within the parent Warner Communications Inc (WCI), Jac Holzman had become deeply involved in high-level planning at the parent company. Steve Ross, chairman of WCI, understood that with a vertically integrated record group, film company, magazine distribution, and both music and book publishing, he had the platform to support a communications empire. Holzman was invited to join a forward-planning group that included only four other senior executives. They were: Steve Ross, Ted Ashley (who was chairman of the Warner Bros film studios), Spencer Harrison (Ashley's right-hand man and a lawyer), and Peter Goldmark (one of Holzman's heroes, the co-inventor of the LP, who was now building a research lab for Warner Communications).

"I was ecstatic to up the ante on myself," says Holzman. "We were a think-tank with a mandate to define the future and to prepare for that future. Very early, we decided to look carefully at cable television. Steve Ross preferred not to make the errors and missteps of early start-ups but to buy existing cable companies and build upwards."

It proved a smart choice. "Infrastructure, experience, and institutional memory already existed," says Holzman, "and we worked within the system to build the systems. When the more established MSOs [Multi System Operators] noticed our rapid growth, they encouraged the large equipment manufacturers to place our equipment orders at the end of the line behind them. This was topic number one for the next meeting of the forward-planning group. We were already partners in a joint venture with Pioneer Electronics in Japan, who owned half of our Japanese record company. As a Pioneer director, I knew the inner workings of the company and its capabilities."

Holzman wanted to sidestep the equipment manufacturers entirely. He didn't want to be held up by domestic American manufacturers when they could get the equipment they needed built in Japan to their own needs and specifications. Together with the head of Warner's cable operations, he jumped on a plane to Japan and began talks with Pioneer. Within 90 days they had impressive prototypes, and within six months they had full delivery. "We were free of the American obstructionists," says Holzman, "and had designed a better product."

In 1970, Holzman saw the original glass master prototype for what became the optical LaserDisc. Developed by the Philips electronics company in The Netherlands, it was a game-changer. The optical disc could store digital or analogue encoding for music, films, or both. It was the innovation at the core of what would become the CD and the DVD. Historically, format changes in media advance in 25 to 35 year cycles. The LP record was introduced in 1948, 25 years after the introduction of electrically recorded sound for 78rpm records. Optical memory, however, was more than a change, and its many possibilities were a radical shift that Holzman yearned to be a part of.

He supervised the technical evaluation for Warner Communications' acquisition of Atari in 1976 and became a working member of the Atari board, focussing on product planning. Holzman co-wrote Warner's business plan for early entry into home video and the development of the first interactive cable system, QUBE, in Columbus, Ohio.

It's hard to recall a time when MTV wasn't an essential part of the music scene. Holzman jump-started the idea and was responsible, in 1979, for connecting the senior executives who would lead that effort. The genesis of the idea came in 1967, when he filmed a video clip for The Doors' debut single 'Break On Through'. Shot by staff producer Mark Abramson, it eased them into mainstream pop TV without demystifying the group's potent image.

"You could call that one of the first music videos," says Holzman. "We could not afford to tour The Doors at the beginning, and I didn't want them performing in front of distracted teenagers on shows like *Bandstand* and *Hullabaloo*. I thought it would shift the focus away from the music. I wanted the exposure, but in a controlled situation. What Jim might have done in front of an audience of nubile teenage girls was a risk I was unwilling to take."

Years later, Holzman saw the beautifully produced and imaginative clip that Mike Nesmith filmed for his single 'Rio' in 1977. The potential for linking up a music track to a powerful visual component was immediately clear. Holzman showed it to Steve Ross, who agreed this was an area WCI should explore, and connected Nesmith with John Lack at Warner Amex (a joint venture between Warners and American Express's cable aspirations).

Holzman and Nesmith met John Lack, and Nesmith agreed to produce ten half-hour shows called *PopClips* at his studio in Carmel, California. *PopClips* was given a trial run on Nickelodeon in 1980, a Warner-Amex owned children's TV channel. The concept was further developed and MTV: Music Televison was fully launched on August 1 1981. Holzman could see, just as with the Doors clip all those years before, that the advantage of what became MTV was to present the artist the way the label and the artist wanted, under tightly controlled circumstances. There is no better example of this than Queen's global 1975 hit 'Bohemian Rhapsody', which helped to establish the music video as a powerful tool to promote singles and led to Queen's unassailable US breakthrough with *A Night At The Opera*.

In 1972, when Holzman had one foot in the advancement of technological ideas within WCI and another in Elektra, he wrote an internal memo to his staff. "I have seen the future of pop music, and it is a band called Queen," he said. He was desperate to sign them. "I knew in my bones they were it and that Queen would thrive at Elektra and we were the perfect label for them," he says. "There was the added thrill of the chase, going up against Columbia yet again. I had been told that deal was completed, but discovered through my own sources that Queen had yet to see the first draft of the Columbia contract. And there was no deal memo."

Holzman kept up the pressure on the band's management, visiting them in London, and he slowly began to convince Queen and their manager, Jack Nelson, of his commitment. "We offered the same lure that worked so well with The Doors and Harry Chapin: we wouldn't release any other album the same month as Queen's debut appeared. Elektra could do that, but Columbia, because of their enormous size and obligations, could not. Although we were now part of the Warner Music Group, we were still flexible. We eventually signed Queen for over 60 percent of the world. EMI had Europe. We sold far more Queen records than EMI."

Holzman never doubted that Queen would make a worldwide impression. After all, they were so dramatic and so self-assured. "The third album, which was the one that broke them, hadn't come out when I left, but I knew it was there. It took a while before their stage act dazzled – they grew into that and became the most outlandish act out there – but the records were powerful and inventive from the first. Although I could see some parallels with The Doors, I did not conjure Freddie Mercury as a Jim Morrison figure, because there was more inherent tragedy in Jim, although it ended the same way for them both. The group dynamic was excellent: they liked and respected each other. Each member of Queen was brilliant, and you have no idea how much that excites me. The relationship ripens and deepens when you can talk with the guitarist about celestial mechanics."

Signing Jobriath was less auspicious. Like The Stooges or the MC5, Jobriath only later found a following, including major-league fans such as Morrissey and Pet Shop Boys. He was the first openly gay rock star, dramatic and theatrical, and his decadent lyricism and trashy glamour pre-dated groups like The New York Dolls. At the time Elektra signed Jobriath, Holzman knew he was leaving the company. He had faith in Jobriath's manager, Jerry Brandt, who had turned Elektra on to Carly Simon. "I knew I wouldn't be the one to suffer the consequences if Jobriath didn't connect with an audience," says Holzman, "and, from that standpoint, it was a mistake. The total advance was $50,000, including recording costs. Nowhere near the numbers bandied about in later years."

Jobriath's debut was recorded at Electric Lady studios with Eddie Kramer and presents a hybrid of *Hunky Dory* Bowie, early Elton John, and Mick Jagger at his most faux-camp. To its credit, however, the electronic bedrock of the *Jobriath* album anticipated Bowie's future direction on *Low* and *Heroes.* Jobriath's debut is best remembered for the media blitz that surrounded its release in October 1973, with a hefty $30,000 advertising spend capped by a huge billboard in Times Square.

Holzman had indeed left the company when the album was released. Looking back now, he thinks the record not totally devoid of value. "I just had no emotional investment in the music. Unfortunately, signing Jobriath gave some people a chance to say that I didn't pay attention at the end." A second Jobriath album, endorsed by David Geffen, *Creatures Of The Street,* was released just six months after *Jobriath*, this time with a zero advertising spend. A revival of interest in the 90s came too late for Jobriath, who died from AIDS-related illness in 1983.

Lenny Kaye, a highly regarded journalist and, later, leader of The Patti Smith Group, once described Holzman as an anthropologist who visited uncharted regions and brought back rare specimens – which is why Kaye took on Holzman's idea for an album of singles by American garage bands. It became *Nuggets: Original Artyfacts From The First Psychedelic Era 1965–1968.* Holzman knew he could trust Kaye to select material and, since no one else was interested in these quite recent but forgotten gems, Elektra easily obtained the licences. Holzman says they were so forgotten, it did seem like musical archaeology, even though they went back only seven or eight years. "It's amazing how fast the layers of neglect obscure music that has passed its useful life," he says.

Holzman believes the secret of *Nuggets* was that it elevated something that appeared 'less' into something that was clearly 'more'. It focussed on a strand of music where no one noticed the connecting threads. "Garage bands were the natural outgrowth of high-quality, inexpensive recording gear that they could set up in the garage, where they rehearsed and recorded. Only Lenny Kaye had noticed the musical trend-lines that connected these bands to The Stooges and the MC5, who were fuelled by the same energy as classic garage bands."

Holzman had asked Kaye to act as a freelance talent scout for Elektra in 1979, although Kaye says, "There wasn't much I brought to the label that they liked; I remember recommending not signing Hall & Oates while trying to get Jac to keep The Stooges on the label and release the Stalk-Forrest Group album. I don't think *Nuggets* turned out the way Jac originally envisaged it when he first outlined the concept, but he gave me the opportunity to back my instincts. So I went against the grain, and because Elektra had a reputation for being art for art's sake in signing groups like Ars Nova and Earth Opera, when it came to drawing up a list I thought, well, these are bands that Elektra might have signed, but they didn't. Most of the tracks I included would have been heard on Top 40 radio, so they weren't obscure when they came out, but were none too obvious either.

"Mostly the idea was to make a record that was listenable and not turn it into either a collectors' album or a golden-oldies album, which was the norm as far as catalogue releases went. The project did drag on a while, and I figured it was never going to happen, so I put more of my own spin on the selections; then they got all the rights to almost everything, bar a couple of things – that's why '96 Tears' didn't make the final cut. It was a pretty broad selection because it covered that transitional time between the three-minute single and albums becoming the artistic statement, and there was a sense of 'anything goes' in that era."

Nuggets was also the beneficiary of a stunning album jacket: an eye-catching painting by Abe Gurvin, who had illustrated Elektra's striking *Zodiac Cosmic Sounds* in 1967. The *Nuggets* art was as classic a piece of illustration as ever had graced an Elektra record and marked it out as one of Elektra's most memorable packages, annotated and authenticated by Lenny Kaye's engagingly erudite notes. Holzman says, "Elektra had assembled and released the Library Of Congress recordings for Woody Guthrie and Leadbelly. This was a similar endeavour – not an Oldies But Goodies collection but so much more. *Nuggets* was an immediate success. Everyone wanted it; everyone wished they had come up with the idea. *Nuggets* pointed directly toward the birth of Rhino Records and their revitalisation of worthy back catalogue."

By 1973, Holzman was feeling that Elektra was less about the music and more about the profit margins. It was not the amiable enterprise he had created. "If I was leaving," he says, "it was important to have some input as to my successor. I was criminally delinquent in not training anyone to take over from me. Was it ego, or did I think I was indispensable? Any chief executive should intuitively understand that one of their major responsibilities is to prepare someone to take over in their absence – and I didn't. But I knew that once you anointed that person, your influence in the company you created would bleed out in days."

Holzman suggested to Steve Ross that David Geffen should bring in his Atlantic-distributed label Asylum, combine it with Elektra, and head up a joint Elektra–Asylum operation.

Until it was announced in August 1973, no one knew Holzman was leaving. "Under my agreement with Steve Ross," he explains, "1973 was the completion of my three-year obligation to him and to Elektra. There was a two-year option period, and if it was picked up, I was required to serve another two years, which felt like a prison sentence."

The lawyer responsible for exercising contract options on behalf of the company was ill, and the pick-up letter never arrived. "So I called Mo Ostin," says Holzman. "I told him they hadn't picked up my option and asked if he knew if they intended to extend it. And Mo said yes, of course, and that he'd call Steve Ross. I said to him, as my friend, 'I know this puts you in a terrible position, but please do nothing.' And I asked Irwin Russell, my close friend and lawyer, if there was a provision in the contract which could allow WCI to cure that breach. When Irwin said there wasn't, I knew I was free, if I had the guts to leave."

Steve Ross, always composed and unflappable, understood Holzman's passion for moving to Maui and changing his life. Nevertheless, he still asked if Holzman would remain as WCI's Chief Technologist since, as he put it, "nobody around here knows how to change a light bulb".[1] Holzman agreed, as long as he could do it from the islands. "It was perfect for me. I was halfway between Silicon Valley and Japan, the hot spots where technology was happening."

Holzman's departure was announced in August 1973 at an event at the 21 Club in New York City. "The press was invited," he says. "I was there with David Geffen, Ahmet Ertegun, and Steve Ross, and it was all hugs and kisses and happy photographs. I felt relieved, but something was missing deep inside that would take distance and time to replace."

Geffen, says Holzman, was laser-like in his objectives. "He wanted stars and an organisation that produced cash flow. There were Elektra artists he was delighted to nurture, who were attracted to him. If you had Geffen's support, you had no better person on your side."

With the backing of Ahmet Ertegun and Atlantic Records, Geffen had begun Asylum Records in 1971. In its first two years, it greatly resembled Elektra's developmental approach, signing singer-songwriters like Judee Sill and David Blue, who both failed commercially, before acquiring four acts that didn't: Jackson Browne, Linda Ronstadt, Joni Mitchell, and The Eagles. Geffen's rise from the mailroom at the William Morris Agency as a guiding light in Laura Nyro's early career, and then as part of a management team with Elliot Roberts, gave him a reputation for being ambitious, an astute businessman, and very supportive of the artists he personally cared about.

Geffen moved Asylum into Elektra's offices on La Cienega Boulevard and immediately set about 'refreshing' the staff and the roster. Bewilderingly, from Holzman's perspective, Geffen demolished the Elektra studios, turning that space into an accounts department. Geffen fired Bill Harvey and all the radio promotion and publicity staff. Mel Posner became president of the two labels. Geffen trimmed the roster from 45 to 13 acts. The press release about the merger mentioned that Elektra had retained Carly Simon, Harry Chapin, Bread, Judy Collins, Mickey Newbury, and Ian Matthews. Queen, just flying in for their first American tour, also survived. The Asylum list included The Eagles, Jackson Browne, Joni Mitchell, Linda Ronstadt, and the lacklustre reformed Byrds. Geffen's biggest coup, within a year, was to briefly lure Dylan away from Columbia.

In a clear swipe at Holzman, Geffen commented to *Time* magazine that Elektra had been "overly technology devoted" and "overly intellectual".[2] "Geffen was right on both counts," says Holzman. "But he missed the point that both these directions had served me and the company well. Elektra Records never 'suffered' from that kind of focus. I'm proud that we were smart: it's what attracted so many artists to the label, like The Doors, Judy Collins, or Queen, who remained backbones of the company after I left."

Paul Rothchild, angry when Geffen pushed him out of the Crosby Stills & Nash deal he helped broker, expressed it incisively. "When David Geffen enters the California waters as a manager, the sharks have entered the lagoon and the entire vibe changes. It became 'let's make money, music is a by-product'."[3]

"The dynamic was shifting," says Holzman, "and that shift would bring with it excesses and insensitivities that would take what I considered a calling and demote it to a career path. What I had fought for, to keep the music ahead of the money, would change. The galoots were coming to the party. The mystery and the wonder had gone. The excitement can't continue: you've had your first Top 40 single, your first Number One single and album – all the firsts you can have in music. I loved the risk, to see how long I could keep it going, but, as with everything in life, there also comes a time to let go."

"My only real career disappointment was being out here [in LA] when Bob Dylan was in New York. I missed Dylan. I was living out here and I never heard Dylan; it was a heartbreak, but it's not who you didn't sign that counts, it's who you did sign. I would love to have worked with Neil Young – he did some demos for us but then he fell under the spell of Ahmet and Atlantic. I think Jackson Browne was tainted by the Paxton Lodge experience, but the demos he did for us were not the Jackson we know and love today. Joni Mitchell, it was a conscious decision not to sign her because of Judy. I admired Joni but I also knew she was a handful.

"When the Doors took off I had already been on this 17-year marathon, and finally here was the finish line. I had finally reached the top, but the question was how long I could stay at the top, because that would be historically important to me. By the 70s Elektra was turning into a label with a high percentage of success with each record; by then we had Carly Simon, Bread, Harry Chapin, and Queen. That was the right time to pick my laurel and rest on it."

What is remarkable, and far less publicly known, is how much Holzman has accomplished since he left Elektra in 1973 – and mostly it is outside of music. He felt that it was time to find out whether his experience in building a business could be applied to a non-music enterprise. "When I started Elektra, I didn't know what I was doing. All the 'making it up' was gone from music by the early 70s, because I knew *exactly* what I was doing. So I welcomed every opportunity, whether it was as a director of Pioneer Electronics, becoming Chairman and CEO at Panavision, or buying and running Cinema Products, developers and manufacturers of Garrett Brown's camera stabiliser, the Steadicam."

Holzman found he could not keep away from music-making forever, and in June 1991 the Warner Music Group retained him, yet again as Chief

Technologist, to help define and co-ordinate Warner's expanding music interests. Later that year, he was back running a small record company. Through his FirstMedia investment vehicle, Holzman had acquired the Discovery, Trend, and Musicraft jazz labels from the estate of Albert Marx, and he overhauled Discovery into a fully contemporary label.

When the Warner Music Group needed someone to design a new digital-only label for the emerging world of the internet, they turned to Holzman, who created Cordless Recordings in 2005. Who else but the 70-something Holzman would see in the digital opportunity what he calls "a more level playing field, with similarities to those when Elektra was founded in 1950".

It's a measure of his vision and commanding authority that, for millions of music fans, Holzman is most renowned for the founding and shaping of Elektra Records. His other outstanding achievements beyond the music industry notwithstanding, Jac Holzman is one of *the* great record men.

Afterword
Jac Holzman

It was 60 years ago that I impetuously started a tiny indie label that grew way beyond my most vivid imagining.

Looking back, I can see the shape of my Elektra years far more clearly than when I was living them. As a sculptor begins with a simple block of stone, knowing that a work of art lies within, I laboured to bring forth something exceptional. I shaped Elektra, and Elektra shaped me.

In the first decade, the effort was enormous and the successes were few. But those years excited and energized me. I came to understand that the only sure reward was in the journey itself. As Harry Chapin sang in 'Greyhound': "It's got to be the going / Not the getting there that's good. "All that followed, in my 23 hyperactive Elektra years and in every executive position I later held, was built on what I learned about process during those early times.

My former Elektra associates and I talk frequently. Every one of them regards Elektra as formative in their lives and as their most cherished work experience. This is true for me, too.

In 1970, I helped found Warner Music Group, with Mo Ostin and Ahmet Ertegun, two of the great names in recorded music. In 1973, I moved on. In 2004, I returned to Warner.

Working as part of the new WMG team reawakened forgotten memories and skills. I realized how much I missed record-making and that a significant part of me had gone undernourished. Lessons from my past became alive again and available for me to draw upon.

Those lessons were a perfect preparation for the many gratifying hours I spent working with Mick Houghton and the fine people at Jawbone Press for this book. *Becoming Elektra* tells the story with accuracy and flair, and I am grateful to all those who lavished their time and talent, their art and their craft, on the volume you now hold in your hands.

Appendix 1
A 70s Miscellany

This intention here is to highlight the wide and sometimes unfathomable range of Elektra releases between 1970 and 1973. This 70s Miscellany – arranged in catalogue order – doesn't include any obvious commercially successful albums, nor anything that was licenced from the UK. For the most part, it also excludes albums already discussed in the final chapters of the book.

CRABBY APPLETON *CRABBY APPLETON* (1970)

Signed by David Anderle and produced by Don Galluci, who also produced The Stooges *Fun House* that year, this group switched names from Stonehenge to Crabby Appleton after Michael Fennelly joined; he had been a member of Millennium with Curt Boettcher, and was also on Sagittarius' *Present Tense*. According to Fennelly, Galluci hadn't wanted to record 'Go Back', the group's irresistible Top 40 hit, which he thought was bubble-gum. It has since come to define them, as perfect a power-pop song as anything by The Raspberries. Crabby Appleton had a pre-Cheap Trick hard-rock edge but moved away from inventive, melodious post-Beatles pop to a style more heavily rooted in blues-rock and country on their second Elektra album, *Rotten To The Core* in 1971. They disbanded soon after.

GULLIVER *GULLIVER* (1970)

A good example of a horses-for-courses policy in choosing outside producers, Gulliver were a blued-eyed soul four-piece from Philadelphia whose sole album was recorded at Sigma Sound Studios, home of Philly soul and the sound of Gamble & Huff's Philadelphia International Records and Thom Bell. *Gulliver* was engineered by Joe Tarsia, the founder and owner of the studio. Daryl Hall, later of Hall & Oates, was one of Gulliver's featured members; the duo were later under consideration at Elektra but signed to Atlantic. Gulliver's dominant frontman, though, was Tim Moore, who had a long apprenticeship in Philadelphia pop and rock bands, including a liaison with Todd Rundgren, before Frank Zappa tried to sign him to his Bizarre label. Moore turned him down and went back to Philadelphia, where he and Daryl Hall became staff writers and session men for Thom Bell and Gamble & Huff. After the break-up of Gulliver, Moore found success as a songwriter before signing with David Geffen and releasing five albums for Asylum and Elektra during the 70s.

SUITE STEEL *THE PEDAL STEEL GUITAR ALBUM* (1970)

This album was brought to Elektra as a concept by John Boylan, a producer Jac Holzman admired; Boylan had produced The Dillards' *Copperfields*, the group's most commercial sounding album, which had effectively mapped a broader sound beyond their bluegrass roots. He was also the architect of Rick Nelson's revival with The Stone Canyon Band before teaming Linda Ronstadt with a handpicked bunch of relative unknowns, later the founding members of The Eagles. *Suite Steel* was a throwback to the sort of multi-artist instrumental albums (such as *Folk Banjo Styles* or *New Dimensions in Banjo & Bluegrass*) that Elektra released in the 60s, here featuring Nashville veterans Jay Dee Mayness and Buddy Emmons, Rusty Young from Poco, Sneaky Pete from The Flying Burrito Brothers, and Red Rhodes, who was then adding exquisite authenticity to Mike Nesmith's First and Second National Bands. The top-notch steel ensemble tackle recent hits as well as Boylan's own 'Suite Steel' with a band featuring prolific session guitarist and Byrd-man Clarence White.

DAVID FRYE *RADIO FREE NIXON* (1971)

Elektra had a long history of releasing comedy albums, whether it was nightclub counter-cultural performers like Jean Shepherd and David Steinberg or re-packaging Lord Buckley's outrageous jive-talking narratives from the early 50s. David Frye had made a name impersonating and satirising Richard Nixon on *The Tonight Show*, having started out taking off assorted personalities on *The Smothers Brothers Comedy Hour*. His second album for Elektra was brilliantly framed as a radio show, complete with authentic jingles from the heart of Dallas 'radioland'. Frye voices contemporary politicians including Agnew, Johnson, and Humphrey, saving the best till last, Nixon's wonderfully disingenuous 'My Way'. He released two further albums but eventually the veracity of Nixon's career went beyond satire. Frye made a comeback during the Clinton administration, mining a rich comic vein on *Bill Clinton: An Oral History*.

SWAMP DOGG *RAT ON* (1971)

The infamous soul producer/songwriter Jerry Williams was recommended to Russ Miller by Lonnie Mack; Williams had adopted the name Swamp Dogg for his debut album *Total Destruction Of Your Mind* in 1970. *Rat On*, his second, began a pattern where he'd release an album almost every year for a different label through the decade. His tenure at Elektra was, indeed, over within six months, accelerated by a distasteful album cover photograph that depicted the smiling Swamp Dogg sitting astride a giant rat. Elektra had no track record in the world of Stax-influenced black R&B with deep bass and punchy horns, let alone songs that mixed outspoken views on race, sex, religion, and war. There was some conflict over the anti-Nixon administration song 'God Bless America For What?', a powerfully drawn-out cry for freedom whose title appeared merely as 'God Bless America' on the reverse of the original jacket. Swamp Dogg was invariably misunderstood for his daring songs – sometimes direct, sometimes satirical – and for juxtaposing classic soul and R&B against white rock stylings. Ads for his debut had proclaimed, 'Swamp Dogg is Underground & Progressive Rock & R&B & Pop & Jazz'. He covered all bases without ever finding a settled home for them and has only recently begun achieving recognition. *Rat On* is a regular contender among 'Worst Album Covers' lists; Swamp Dogg is both proud and pleased that such a "left-handed accolade" has helped it avoid obscurity.

HENRY & LEONARD CROW DOG WITH AL RUNNING *CROW DOG'S PARADISE* (1971)

This album was originally commissioned by Tracey Sterne at Nonesuch, who brought Peter Siegel back to produce it, before Holzman commandeered it for Elektra. "It was pure indulgence," he said, "and although we had Nonesuch for certain types of releases that would once have come out on Elektra, I thought *Crow Dog's Paradise* was fascinating and pure Elektra. I'm sure that music made a lot more sense when you were loaded." As with *The Bauls Of Bengal*, released just as Elektra was about to launch a new direction with Love and Tim Buckley, this album made a statement during Elektra's most commercially successful era. The music is plaintive and compelling, capturing authentic Sioux chants and sparse percussive accompaniment and it was housed in an elaborate, informative gatefold sleeve. "Crow Dog came into the office one day," recalls Holzman, "he blessed the record and we smoked a peace pipe. I don't know what he put in it – certainly not peyote – but it tasted awful."

THE RAINBOW BAND *THE RAINBOW BAND* (1971)

Immediately following Crow Dog in the Elektra catalogue, cynics might see The Rainbow Band as a more opportunistic way of exploiting the hippie counter-culture; the satirical *A Child's Garden Of Grass* was a further take on it. The Rainbow Band were husband-and-wife duo Mahesh and Parvathi looking suitably blissed out on the cover. They lived in Topanga Canyon and crafted a warm, whimsical, quasi-religious brew of Eastern-tinged, spiritual, gentle folk-rock, aided and abetted by musicians, some of whom appeared in the credits as themselves, such as Colin Walcott of jazz-folk group Oregon (who later recorded for Elektra) and Dave Brubeck's son Darius. The Incredible String Band offer a reference point, and they might well have sounded more like this if they lived in a rural Californian commune. The project was supervised by staff producer Robert Zachary.

DON NIX *LIVING BY THE DAYS* (1971)

Introduced to Russ Miller by Lonnie Mack, Don Nix was the perfect foil for him in helping assemble a series of albums that culminated in the Alabama State Troupers roadshow. Nix was a prolific soul/blues songwriter, producer, and arranger who cut his teeth as a Stax/Memphis/Ardent executive and musician on numerous key records of the 60s and 70s. After recording his debut album, *In God We Trust*, for Leon Russell's Shelter label, he left claiming he was tired of people comparing his voice to Russell's. Nix retained many of his Shelter associates, including vocalists Jeanie and Marlin Greene, as well as country-bluesman Furry Lewis, who was later brought in to replace Lonnie Mack for the roadshow. Although Nix's sanctified mix of country soul, barrelhouse blues, and gospel-dipped Americana failed to connect, it was the catalyst for Elektra's journey South, and specifically for the sole albums recorded by Jeanie and Marlin Greene.

JEANIE GREENE *MARY CALLED JEANIE GREENE* (1971)

Don Nix was the driving force behind the only album Jeanie Greene would ever record. Greene had a long if obscure history recording for Chet Atkins at RCA in 1965, and for Atlantic's Atco subsidiary, and along with Donna Thatcher (later the Grateful Dead's Donna Jean Godchaux) had recorded under the name Southern Comfort. She also sang the high parts on Elvis's 'Suspicious Minds', as well as overdubbing the four harmonies on *Live In Las Vegas*. "She was white, but she sang black," says Russ Miller. "She heard voices and truly believed she was the reincarnation of Mary Magdalene."[1] That's the backdrop to her Elektra album, which is, in essence, an album of Christian songs delivered with intense feeling. *Mary Called Jeanie Greene* teamed her with producer Don Nix (who also wrote several of the tracks, one with Dan Penn) and Muscle Shoals Studio founders Barry Beckett, Roger Hawkins, David Hood. Aside from the expected mix of Southern soul, gospel, and rock, often sounding like a secular Janis Joplin, 'Swaziland Remembered African Folk Chant' is a fine atypical African-influenced piece.

THE WACKERS *HOT WACKS* (1972)

Jac Holzman is said to have described The Wackers as a cross between Crosby Stills & Nash and the Grateful Dead, and he has a point. It's certainly a more apt description than power-pop. *Hot Wacks* is rock everyman Bob Segarini and Randy Bishop's finest hour; The Wackers can be heard channelling the Dead, and most definitely CSN's harmonies ('Time Will Carry On', for example) while neatly marrying *Rubber Soul*-era Beatles with *Abbey Road*'s lofty ambition right from sprightly opener 'I Hardly Know Your Name'. The group stylishly cover Lennon's 'Oh My Love', but it's the McCartney bass lines and *Abbey Road*-style medley that make this such an enjoyable record. The elusive hit never came, but third album *Shredder*, produced by Mark Abramson (replacing Gary Usher), came closest, yielding a Canadian hit, 'Day and Night'. As with all three Wackers albums, they invariably found favour with America's most noted rock critics. It's a critic's curse whereby they often end up championing lost causes; Segarini was left to rue that The Wackers' timing was always either "five years too early or five years too late".

MARLIN GREENE *TIPTOE PAST THE DRAGON* (1972)

Some time in late 1965, Marlin Greene started a recording studio with Quin

Ivy, where he played guitar and co-produced Percy Sledge's 'When A Man Loves A Woman'. Called up for basic training with the National Guard, Greene had no idea the song was a hit until he heard it on a jukebox. It opened up a career for him as part of the Muscle Shoals studio scene, his name popping up in collaboration with the likes of Dan Penn, Spooner Oldham, and Eddie Hinton, until Russ Miller recruited him through Don Nix. Greene later became Miller's A&R assistant, "ferreting out promising candidates from the slush of bric-a-brac that arrived every day." *Tiptoe Past The Dragon* appeared in April 1972 and takes on a very different character to the earlier albums by his now ex-wife Jeanie Greene, Don Nix, and the Alabama State Troupers. He mines a more laid-back, late-night country-rock groove that rejects the Muscle Shoals template. *Tiptoe Past The Dragon* is one of the overlooked gems of Holzman's swansong years. It's wonderfully arranged and played (by Chuck Leavell, Eddie Hinton, Wayne Perkins, and Ardent's Larry 'Glimmer' Nicholson), delivering atmospheric songs, sweetly sung and steeped in post-hippie idealism, often reminiscent of Mac Gayden's mystical soul and Michael Nesmith's uplifting country reboot.

SAILCAT *MOTORCYCLE MAMA* (1972)

Another Muscle Shoals album that broke the mould. After a stint in a shortlived studio band called Sundown with future Allman Brothers keyboard player Chuck Leavell, Courtland Pickett formed Southern-rock group Sailcat with songwriter and local rock-scene hustler John Wyker (who co-wrote James & Bobby Purify's hit 'Let Love Come Between Us'). Sailcat signed to Elektra in 1972 after Wyker played Russ Miller an unfinished version of 'Motorcycle Mama' on a Dictaphone machine. The album was hastily recorded, taking on a loose biker-themed concept, and produced by Muscle Shoals guitarist and songwriter Pete Carr. The title track became a one-hit wonder, shooting to Number 12 in *Billboard*, the album breaking into the Top Forty in its wake. The distinctive jacket featured paintings by graphic artist David Mann, whose work celebrated biker culture. Sailcat were then dropped by Elektra after Wyker dissed his own hit single before unleashing a torrent of insults against his LA record company on stage at Carnegie Hall. Courtland Pickett's services were retained, and he recorded the intermittently pleasing *Fancy Dancer* the following year, again produced by Carr.

THE SHIP *A CONTEMPORARY FOLK MUSIC JOURNEY* (1972)

Gary Usher was another producer briefly brought under the Elektra umbrella; his earlier production credits included The Hondells and The Surfaris, and he also collaborated with Brian Wilson on a dozen early songs, including 'In My Room'. He later produced three albums by The Byrds, including *Younger Than Yesterday* and *The Notorious Byrds Brothers*, while working in house at Columbia. Holzman asked him to produce the first two Wackers albums before he took on The Ship's somewhat arcane concept, a contemporary 'folk suite' the group had debuted at Chicago's Channing-Murray School. Initially a folk trio of former high-school friends who were now at the University of Illinois, they adopted the name The Ship in April 1972. The influential William Morris Agency signed them up and encouraged an Elektra deal. The album is an odyssey of country-tinged folk-pop, heavy on Crosby Stills & Nash-style harmonies, following the ship's voyage – a rather cumbersome metaphor for life itself. Gary Usher provides a steady hand on the tiller but can't prevent the music becoming becalmed. The album is well executed all round but buckles under the weight of its ambition. The group rarely played beyond Chicago; they self-released a second album, *Tornado*, in 1976 before disbanding.

CURT BOETCHER *THERE'S AN INNOCENT FACE* (1972)

Another of Usher's Columbia jobs had been to produce *Present Tense* by Curt Boettcher's group Sagittarius and *The Blue Marble* for Together Records, a label he formed with Boettcher in 1969. Holzman admired Boettcher's earlier Millennium album *Begin* and wanted him on the label. Usher is credited as executive producer on *There's An Innocent Face*, but compared to the gloriously ornate harmonies and measured psychedelic flights that marked the Sagittarius and Millennium recordings, *There's An Innocent Face* presents a prevailing California country-rock style. The best track by far is the opener, 'I Love You More Each Day,' which is typical of Boettcher's graceful melodic pop confections but one of only two co-written songs by him here. Boettcher worked throughout with little known multi-instrumentalist Web Burrell, credited as co-producer on an album lacking the adventurousness of his earlier work. The record was two years in the making – Boettcher had warned Holzman he didn't work fast. Boettcher visited a noted numerologist during the recording, who told him things would go better if dropped one of the letter 't's from his name. He also suggested that Burrell lose an 'l'. It's the only album in Boettcher's canon of work thus credited.

PLAINSONG *IN SEARCH OF AMELIA EARHART* (1972)

Plainsong developed out of an occasional working relationship between former Liverpool Scene guitarist Andy Roberts and Ian Matthews, late of Fairport Convention, and by then with five albums under his belt (three with Matthews Southern Comfort). After a certain amount of managerial horse-trading, Plainsong secured a rare deal with Elektra in the UK. Produced by Sandy Roberton, whose September Productions specialised in British folk-rock, it's often assumed that *Amelia* is a concept album, but it's merely housed in a related graphic sleeve. Half the songs were provided by Matthews, while two of the covers connected with Elektra's history: Paul Siebel's 'Louse' and 'Raider', co-written by Judy Henske (from *Farewell Aldebaran*). While working on a follow-up, Matthews was lured to California, where he recorded *Valley Hi*, and the group broke up. Roberts remained on Elektra's books but still smarts about Matthews having been 'encouraged' to leave Plainsong. He still feels his Elektra career went sour very quickly. Of the two UK-only Elektra releases, the piecemeal *Urban Cowboy* included unused Plainsong recordings and *The Great Stampede* more or less sank without trace after David Geffen took over. Matthews survived the axe, releasing *Some Days You Eat The Bear* in 1974.

SWEET SALVATION *SWEET SALVATION* (1972)

Russ Miller discovered and co-produced Sweet Salvation's sole album in Los Angeles, their forward-looking sound built around long-established New Orleans drummer 'Big John' Thomassie, keyboard player Wayne DeVillier, and guitarist Don Normand creating a heavy mix of gospel, soul, R&B, and funk. They played the LA circuit before Lowell George and Little Feat brought funk to the forefront on *Dixie Chicken*. Sweet Salvation featured two fine female singers; DeEtta Little delivers a full-tilt vocal on the album's closing cover 'Rock Steady'. Her brother was the actor Cleavon Little, and she found fame singing on 'Gonna Fly Now', the theme from *Rocky*. Her co-singer in Sweet Salvation was Fritz Baskett, later a successful songwriter (notably for Deniece Williams) who had sung in 60s groups The HiFi's and The Intervals with Marylin McCoo and Lamonte McLemore, founder members of The Fifth Dimension. Thomassie toured with Tom Waits and plays on his 1980 album *Heartattack And Vine*. There's one curious link to Elektra's past: engineer Fritz Richmond plays jug on one track.

DANA COOPER *DANA COOPER* (1973)

CASEY KELLY *CASEY KELLY* (1973)

Between 1971 and 1973, Holzman was keen to move back into publishing, and he says he was "constantly drawn to discover new writers but it was very tough to find any who had magnetism and who could capture an audience". Elektra signed two singer-songwriters in 1973, both through Marlin Greene: Dana Cooper, who was from Kansas, and Casey Kelly, who moved to LA after touring with Tom Rush. Both recorded self-titled albums in the Elektra studios, utilising such leading session players as Leland Sklar, Russ Kunkel, Joe Osborn, and Al Perkins. The single to herald Cooper's album was 'Lover Baby, Friend', an obvious choice in that it sounded just like Bread. Yet Cooper displayed a far more original talent, with 'Sweet City Man and 'Jesse James' distinguished by a vocal dexterity recalling Terry Reid and post-Elektra Tim Buckley. Kelly's album was judiciously assigned to producer Richard Sanford Orshoff, the engineer Peter Asher often used for singer-songwriter projects, including James Taylor's *Mudslide Slim*; Orshoff had only recently engineered and produced Jackson Browne's *Saturate Before Using*. Kelly's album opens with a blistering cosmic-country song, 'Silver Meteor', featuring Burritos steel player Sneaky Pete, but neither artist was able to rise above the level of also-ran singer-songwriters seemingly arriving daily in LA.

STARDRIVE FEATURING ROBERT MASON *INTERGALACTIC TROT* (1973)

'Love it or hate it' is a common way to describe some of Elektra's 1971–73 output. Holzman himself included Stardrive in a list of albums he says he doesn't know "why I approved them", alongside *Portland, Homegrown* (by former *My Three Sons* actor Don Agrati), *Capital City Rockets*, and *Jobriath*. *Stardrive* offers an amalgam of synthesizer-driven rock and jazz fusion that isn't spontaneous enough for fans of the genre unless they are Michael Brecker completists. Franks Zappa's *Hot Rats* and keyboard-driven British prog-rock are contrasting touchstones, but *Intergalactic Trot* lacks a strength of original material to underpin the music. The standout is 'Strawberry Fields Forever'. Stardrive was Robert Mason's brainchild; the liner notes claim he had "built the world's first multi-voice synthesizer that can be played like a real keyboard instrument with full chords and tonal clusters. All the music on this album was performed live on the Stardrive synthesizer … never before have man and machine come so close together with such intimate rapport". The end result is part Wendy Carlos and part Keith Emerson overkill. Unusually for an album hinged around the Moog, Mason eschews both experimental noodling and novelty approaches, preferring a punchier jazz-rock sound that continues to divide critics.

CAPITAL CITY ROCKETS *CAPITAL CITY ROCKETS* (1973)

PAINTER *PAINTER* (1973)

After neither The Wackers nor Crabby Appleton could build careers on the back of singles that failed to make it nationally, Elektra continued to search in vain for decent rock groups to break on through. Capital City Rockets were fronted by Jamie Lyons from The Music Explosion, whose 'Little Bit O' Soul' made the cut on *Nuggets*, but Capital City Rockets could only muster a minor hit single in the Midwest and parts of the South with 'Breakfast In Bed'. A curious hybrid of Anglophile glam-rock and flamboyant proto-punk, the group has its latter-day admirers. Painter were formed in Calgary from the ashes of another 60s garage band, The 49th Parallel, and had an equally limited impact at radio with 'West Coast Woman' and a sound that only sprung to life around Danny Lowe's muscular guitar. If both groups' riff-laden rock fires only sporadically, the unimaginative artwork and appalling band photos uphold Holzman's comment that he didn't feel he was paying enough attention in 1973, in the knowledge that he was going to leave. Capital City Rockets' image almost beggars belief as they try to look menacing in rugby shirts and roller skates.

LINDA HARGROVE *MUSIC IS YOUR MISTRESS* (1973)

Linda Hargrove was far more a product of classic Nashville than most of Russ Miller's signings, even if she arrived in Music City from Florida, where one of her songs for local group After All was picked up by Sandy Posey. Producer and pedal-steel player Pete Drake took her under his wing and she is credited as the first female studio guitarist in Music City. In 1973, Leon Russell recorded a couple of her songs for his country album *Hank Wilson's Back*, and Drake introduced her to Michael Nesmith; the pair co-wrote the song 'Winonah', which Nesmith recorded on *Pretty Much Your Standard Ranch Stash.* He also signed Hargrove to his shortlived, Elektra-funded Countryside label, but the album was shelved. Russ Miller brought her over to Elektra and released *Music Is Your Mistress*, produced by Pete Drake, swiftly followed by *Blue Jean Country Queen*. The album is knee deep in Nashville session giants – Drake himself, Grady Martin, Chip Young, Hargus 'Pig' Robbins, among then – but falls short of that classic Nashville sound while being unable to snare the new country-rock audience already embracing Linda Ronstadt and Emmylou Harris.

JOHN BARHAM & ASHISH KHAN *JUGALBANDI* (1973)

John Barham first met sarod player Ashish Khan during the sessions for George Harrison's *Wonderwall.* Ravi Shankar had introduced Barham to Harrison, and Barham contributed to the London sessions, playing piano, harmonium, and flugelhorn. Eighteen months later, Barham and Khan began collaborating on *Jugalbandi*, which was facilitated by Jonathan Clyde, label manager for Elektra in the UK. The recordings that combined the sarod with Western arrangements were inspired by Barham's involvement with Ravi Shankar on his *Concerto For Sitar & Orchestra*, released in 1971. The sessions for *Jugalbandi* – Zakir Hussain and Pranesh Khan added tabla accompaniment – eventually resulted in four pieces. The pair wouldn't record together again, although both have enjoyed successful and wide-ranging careers since. Barham continued his relationship with Harrison on *All Things Must Pass*, *Living In The Material World*, and Harrison and Shankar's *Chants Of India* recordings. *Jugalbandi* – with a recommendation from Harrison – was released only in the UK, but would not have been out of place on Elektra or Nonesuch during the 60s. Elektra in the UK was clearly no less schizophrenic than its parent company; in 1973, Clyde also supervised the release of *Patrick Kavanagh: At The King's Head* – a series of readings from a collection of the late Irish poet's work, recorded at an Islington theatre pub.

Appendix 2
Elektra 1973–2010

DAVID GEFFEN (1973–75)

Jac Holzman knew that when he left Elektra in 1973, the label would change. Every label takes on the character and ideas and obsessions and working methods of its head, but a label also has to adjust to the changing climate – just as Elektra had in the 23 years that Holzman was at the tiller. Holzman announced he was leaving in August 1973, and three months later he was gone, replaced, at his own urging, by David Geffen. Geffen became head of a combined Elektra/Asylum label. He made his presence felt immediately (see chapter 23) by trimming the Elektra artist roster and sacking many long-term staffers. In the end, his own stay was brief. Geffen left the label in 1975 to branch out into the movie business, becoming Vice Chairman of WCI's Warner Bros Pictures unit. Combining Elektra/Asylum had created a strong powerbase, and Geffen's achievements were crowned when he lured Bob Dylan away from his longtime home, Columbia Records. *Planet Waves*, Dylan's sole studio album for Asylum, earned him his first *Billboard* Number One, although his interlude with Elektra/Asylum proved even shorter than Geffen's.

SELECTED ALBUMS

Bob Dylan *Planet Waves* 1974
Bob Dylan/The Band *Before The Flood* 1974.
Joni Mitchell *Court And Spark* 1974.
Jackson Browne *Late For The Sky* 1974.
Judy Collins *Judith* 1974.

JOE SMITH (1975–82)

WCI was determined to retain the highly successful Warner/Elektra/Atlantic triumvirate, and tapped Joe Smith, then president of Warner Bros Records, to move over to the Elektra/Asylum division as its new chairman. He officially assumed his new post in December. Smith had guided Warners through the tough times of the early 60s and, as with Elektra, folk music had helped set the tone, especially when the label signed Peter Paul & Mary. Smith had created an artist-friendly environment at Warners and helped the label's transition into the rock era by building a strong team of musicians, producers, and A&R people at its core, including Lenny Waronker, Ted Templeman, Van Dyke Parks, Ry Cooder, and Randy Newman. Smith's challenge at Elektra/Asylum was to preserve artist-centred eclecticism and diversity while operating on a much larger scale. In 1972, Elektra (not including Nonesuch) released 35 albums; in 1979, Elektra/Asylum released nearly 90. It was a reflection not only of the expansion from Elektra's independent roots into a major label but also of the increasingly corporate nature of the music industry.

SELECTED ALBUMS

Queen *A Night At The Opera* 1975; *News Of The World* 1977.
The Eagles *One Of These Nights* 1975; *Hotel California* 1976.
Joni Mitchell *The Hissing Of Summer Lawns* 1975; *Hejira* 1976.
Jackson Browne *The Pretender* 1976; *Running On Empty* 1977.
Tom Waits *Small Change* 1976.
Linda Ronstadt *Hasten Down The Wind* 1976; *Simple Dreams* 1977.
Television *Marquee Moon* 1977.
The Cars *The Cars* 1978.
Warren Zevon *Excitable Boy* 1978.
Eddie Rabbit *Horizon* 1980.
Urban Cowboy: Original Motion Picture Soundtrack 1980.
Grover Washington, Jr. *Winelight* 1981.
Patrice Rushen *Straight From The Heart* 1982.

BOB KRASNOW (1983–94)

When Joe Smith moved over to WCI's new Sports Division, the company turned to Warner Bros Records' "executive without portfolio" Bob Krasnow, who had been with the company in Burbank since 1975. Appointed Elektra's chairman, Krasnow relocated the label's headquarters back to New York City and began to re-establish Elektra's pop credentials, with an emphasis on black music, one of his specialties. Krasnow quickly signed soul singers Teddy Pendergrass, Peabo Bryson, and Howard Hewett to strengthen his new roster – after cutting it by more than half to correct what he saw as an overbalanced emphasis on singer-songwriters. The few remaining Holzman-era singer-songwriters – Harry Chapin, Carly Simon, and, finally, Judy Collins – had already moved on. Under Krasnow, Asylum was soon folded into Elektra. Krasnow's appointment of Robert Hurwitz at Nonesuch (see chapter 14) came after Keith Holzman elected to leave, preferring to remain in LA. Hurwitz's arrival signalled a shift toward building a roster of contemporary artists while adhering to the label's core of modern classical and world music. When Krasnow departed in 1994, Nonesuch left the Elektra fold, 30 years after its foundation by Holzman. It stayed within the Warner Music Group, shifting initially to Atlantic and then to Warner Bros, its home at the time of writing.

SELECTED ALBUMS

Simply Red *Picture Book* 1985.
The Cure *The Head On The Door* 1985.
Teddy Pendergrass *Love Language* 1984.
Anita Baker *Rapture* 1986; *Giving You The Best That I Got* 1988.
Metallica *Master Of Puppets* 1986; *... And Justice For All* 1988; *Enter Sandman* 1991.
10,000 Maniacs *In My Tribe* 1987; *Blind Man's Zoo* 1989.
Tracy Chapman *Fast Car* 1988.
Mötley Crew *Girls Girls Girls* 1987; *Dr. Feelgood* 1989.
The Sugarcubes *Life's Too Good* 1988.
Dokken *Back For The Attack* 1987.
Keith Sweat *Make It Last Forever* 1987.
Natalie Cole *Unforgettable: With Love* 1991.
Björk *Debut* 1993.
Phish *Hoist* 1994.

SYLVIA RHONE (1994–2004)

The merger of the two media giants Warner Communications and Time Inc in 1989 was seen by Wall Street as a great match. Yet the new Time Warner combination disrupted the music division, unleashing a stricter scrutiny of artistic choices and some business deals that rankled WMG veterans. The rank and file on both sides found the corporate cultures of Time and Warner less compatible than the way the people who originated the deal imagined. Bob Krasnow, quietly recovering from a serious illness and accustomed to being his own boss, grew impatient with the layers of politics and, in the midst of major corporate restructuring, left the company.

Sylvia Rhone – who had been running Atlantic's Atco/EastWest division after a long career working her way up through the ranks at both Elektra and Atlantic – became the first black woman chairman of a major label. She formed the Elektra Entertainment Group, which combined the Elektra and Atco/EastWest rosters to create one of the broadest-based companies in the industry. Rhone brought with her many of the artists she had been nurturing and working with at Atco/EastWest, ranging from R&B stars En Vogue and Gerald Levert to hard rockers AC/DC. She blended them into the Elektra roster, together with Atco's rich back catalogue (Otis Redding, Bobby Darin, Buffalo Springfield, and so on).

In 2000, Time Warner merged with AOL, in an attempt to merge traditional content with new media. It proved to be a failure of epic proportions. It was only a matter of time before senior AOL Time Warner executives were desperate to shed assets to generate income. They decided that music, historically their most consistent earner and producer of cashflow, was no longer a core business. In 2004, AOL-Time Warner finalised the sale of the entire Warner Music Group (including the Warner, Elektra, and Atlantic divisions) to a group of private investors led by Edgar Bronfman Jr, who was a music aficionado, songwriter, and architect of Vivendi Universal's entertainment division, including the Universal Music Group.

The Warner Music Group became the largest standalone music company in the world, but the music business was buckling under the strain of declining CD sales, the threat posed by illegal digital file-sharing, and competition from other media for consumer attention. The decision was made to streamline and consolidate the two East Coast-based WMG labels – Atlantic and Elektra – into a single company. Elektra was folded into the larger Atlantic, and Sylvia Rhone left to join Universal as head of its Motown label. For the first time since its formation 54 years earlier, Elektra was no longer an active enterprise.

SELECTED ALBUMS

Natalie Merchant *Tigerlily* 1996.
Keith Sweat *Keith Sweat* 1996.
Third Eye Blind *Third Eye Blind* 1997.
Busta Rhymes *The Coming* 1996; *When Disaster Strikes* 1997.
Missy Elliott *Supa Dupa Fly* 1997; *Da Real World* 1999.
Yolanda Adams *Mountain High … Valley Low* 1999.
Staind *Break The Cycle* 2001.
Jason Mraz *Waiting For My Rocket To Come* 2002.

REBIRTH (2009–)

In June 2009, it was announced that Elektra was to be relaunched under Mike Caren, an A&R executive at Atlantic, and John Janick, founder of the prominent indie label Fueled By Ramen. Elektra would operate as a freestanding label within the Atlantic Records Group. Its first signings included Cee-Lo, of the Grammy-winning duo Gnarls Barkley, Little Boots, and the French electronic music duo Justice. Jac Holzman, now the senior advisor to Edgar Bronfman Jr, could look back happily at his newly restored label. "Each new label head reverentially built on the accomplishments of their predecessor," he said, "zealously guarding Elektra's magical reputation. In 2004, Elektra was allowed to go dormant until bright new talents could be found to re-energise and rebirth it as the 'artists label' for a new century. I'm fortunate to have yet another chance to watch Elektra bloom."

SELECTED ALBUMS

Little Boots *Hands* 2009.
True Blood: Music From The HBO Original Series 2009.
Charlotte Gainsbourg *IRM* 2010.
Bruno Mars *Doo-Waps & Hooligans* 2011.

Thanks to Mark Leviton and Bob Kaus for help in compiling this section.

Appendix 3
Discography by Andy Finney

MAIN ELEKTRA CATALOGUE

EKLP 1 *New Songs By John Gruen* Georgiana Bannister (Soprano) & John Gruen (Piano), 1951

EKLP 2 *Jean Ritchie Singing The Traditional Songs Of Her Kentucky Mountain Family* Jean Ritchie, 1952

EKLP 3 *American Folk Songs And Ballads* Frank Warner, 1952

EKLP 4 *British Traditional Ballads In America Vol 1* Shep Ginandes, 1953

EKLP 5 *Voices Of Haiti* Various Artists (not credited), 1953

EKLP 6 *Turkish And Spanish Folksongs* Cynthia Gooding, 1953

EKL 7 *There Was A Little Tree... American Folksongs For Children* Shep Ginandes, 1953

EKL 8 *Mexican Folk Songs* Cynthia Gooding, 1953

EKL 9 *French Traditional Songs* Shep Ginandes, 1953

EKL 10 *O' Lovely Appearance Of Death* Hally Wood, 1953

EKL 11 *The Queen Of Hearts: Early English Folk Songs* Cynthia Gooding, 1953

EKL 12 *Folk Songs From The Southern Appalachian Mountains* Tom Paley, 1953

EKL 13 *Songs And Ballads Of America's Wars* Frank Warner, 1954

EKL 14 *Folk Blues* Sonny Terry & Alec Stewart, 1954

EKL 15 *City Blues* Sonny Terry & Alec Stewart, 1954

EKL 16 *Bad Men And Heroes* Ed McCurdy, Jack Elliot & Oscar Brand, 1955

EKL 17 *Italian Folk Songs* Cynthia Gooding, 1954

EKL 18 *Pirate Songs And Ballads* Dick Wilder, 1954

EKL 19 *Songs Of The Abbaye* Gordon Heath & Lee Payant, 1954

EKL 20 *Russian Folk Songs* Hillel Raveh, 1954

EKL 21 *Once Over Lightly: Folk Songs* Alan Arkin, 1955

EKL 22 *Courting Songs* Jean Ritchie & Oscar Brand, 1954

EKL 23 *Nova Scotia Folk Music* Various Artists, 1955

EKL 24 *Sin Songs – Pro And Con* Ed McCurdy, 1955

EKL 25 *Kentucky Mountain Songs* Jean Ritchie, 1954

EKL 26 *Old Airs From Ireland, Scotland, And England* Susan Reed, 1954

EKL 27 *Goin' Down The Road* Clarence Cooper, 1955

EKL 28 *Flamenco Guitar Solos* Jim Fawcett, 1955

EKL 29 *Encores From The Abbaye* Gordon Heath & Lee Payant, 1955

EKL 30 *Festival in Haiti* Jean Léon Destiné & Ensemble, 1955

EKL 31 *French Troubadour Songs Of The 12th And 13th Centuries* Yves Tessier, 1955

EKL 32 *Folksongs Of Israel* Theodore Bikel, 1955

EKL 35 *Elektra Playback System Calibration Record*, 1956

EKL 701 *The Story Of John Henry ... A Musical Narrative / Ballads, Blues And Other Songs* Josh White, 1955

CC 1 *Code Course* Ray Antinolfini (W2WFC), 1956 (Morse code training disc)

EKS 7099 *In The Gloryland* Ken Davern & His Salty Dogs, 1958

EKS 7100 *Gypsy Magic* Edi Csoka & His Gypsy Orchestra, 1958

EKS 7101 *The Neue Deutschmeister Band In Stereo* Neue Deutschmeister Band, 1958

EKL 102 *Josh At Midnight* Josh White, 1956

EKL 103 *Los Gitanillos De Cadiz: Songs And Dances Of Andalucia* Los Gitanillos de Cadiz, 1956

EKL 104 *Songs Of Montmartre* Suzanne Robert, 1956

EKL 105 *An Actor's Holiday* Theodore Bikel, 1956

EKL 106 *The Unabashed Virtuoso* Stephen Kovács, 1956

EKL 107 *Of Faithful Lovers And Other Phenomena* Cynthia Gooding, 1957
EKL 108 *Blood Booze 'n Bones* Ed McCurdy, 1956
EKL 109 EKS 7109 *A Young Man And A Maid* Theodore Bikel & Cynthia Gooding 1956
EKL 110 *When Dalliance Was In Flower* Ed McCurdy, 1956
EKL 111 *Tiger On The Keys* Stephen Kovács, 1956
EKL 112 *Songs Of The Old West* Ed McCurdy, 1957
EKL 113 EKS 7113 *Tenderly* Norene Tate, 1957
EKL 114 *Josh (Sings Ballads And Blues)* Josh White, 1957
EKL 115 EKS 7115 *Adam's Theme* The New York Jazz Ensemble (Quartet), 1957 (Stereo version 1960)
EKL 116 *Susan Reed* Susan Reed, 1957
EKL 117 EKS 7117 *Sabicas (The Greatest Flamenco Guitarist)* Sabicas, 1957
EKL 118 EKS 7118 *The New York Jazz Quartet Goes Native* The New York Jazz Quartet, 1957
EKL 119 *An Evening At L'Abbaye* Gordon Heath & Lee Payant, 1957
EKL 120 EKS 7120 *A Midnight Session With* ... The Jazz Messengers, 1957
EKL 121 *Sabicas Vol II* Sabicas, 1957
EKL 122 *Courtin's A Pleasure* Jean Ritchie, Oscar Brand & Tom Paley, 1957
EKL 123 *25th Anniversary Album* (also known as *The Story Of John Henry...*) Josh White, 1957
EKL 124 *Sin Songs – Pro And Con* Ed McCurdy, 1957
EKL 125 *Songs Of Her Kentucky Mountain Family* Jean Ritchie, 1957
EKL 126 *Old Airs* Susan Reed, 1957
EKL 127 *Calypso!* Lord Foodoos & His Calypso Band, 1957
EKL 128 *Turkish, Spanish, And Mexican Folk Songs* Cynthia Gooding, 1957
EKL 129 *Badmen, Heroes, And Pirate Songs* Ed McCurdy, Oscar Brand, Jack Elliot & Dick Wilder, 1957
EKL 130 *Festival In Haiti* Jean Léon Destiné & Ensemble, 1957
EKL 131 *Queen Of Hearts* Cynthia Gooding, 1957
EKL 132 EKS 7132 *Folk Songs Of Israel* Theodore Bikel, 1957
EKL 133 *Shep Ginandes Sings Folk Songs* Shep Ginandes, 1958
EKL 134 EKS 7134 *4 French Horns Plus Rhythm* 4 French Horns Plus Rhythm, 1958
EKL 135 *Here We Go Baby* Glenn Yarbrough, 1958
EKL 136 *Vibe-Rant* Teddy Charles, 1957
EKL 137 *Of Maids And Mistresses* Tom Kines, 1957
EKL 138 *Delta Rhythm Boys* Delta Rhythm Boys, 1957
EKL 139 EKS 7139 *Original Trinidad Steel Band* Original Trinidad Steel Band
EKL 140 *When Dalliance Was In Flower Volume II* Ed McCurdy, 1957
EKL 141 EKS 7141 *Jewish Folk Songs* Theodore Bikel, 1958
EKL 142 *Off-Beat Folk Songs* The Shanty Boys, 1958
EKL 143 *Marilyn Child & Glenn Yarbrough Sing Folk Songs* Marilyn Child & Glenn Yarbrough, 1958
EKL 144 *Gene & Francesca* Gene & Francesca, 1958
EKL 145 *Sabicas Vol III* Sabicas, 1958
EKL 146 EKS 7146 *Shalom!* Oranim Zabar Israeli Troupe Featuring Guela Gill,1958
EKL 147 *Unholy Matrimony* Paul Clayton, 1958
EKL 148 *The Many Sides Of Sandy Paton* Sandy Paton, 1958
EKL 149 EKS 7149 *Festival Gitana* Sabicas & Los Trianeros, 1958
EKL 150 EKS 7150 *Songs Of A Russian Gypsy* Theodore Bikel, 1958
EKL 151 *Our Singing Heritage Vol I* Various Artists, 1958
EKL 152 *Our Singing Heritage Vol II* Various Artists (Not issued)
EKL 153 *Our Singing Heritage Vol III* Frank Warner, 1958
EKL 154 *Erik Darling* Erik Darling, 1958
EKL 155 *Bobby Burns' Merry Muses Of Caledonia* Paul Clayton, 1958
EKL 156 EKS 7156 *On The Road To Elath* Oranim Zabar Israeli Troupe, 1958
EKL 157 *The Folk Singers* The Folk Singers, 1958
EKL 158 EKS 7158 *Chain Gang Songs Spirituals And Blues* Josh White, 1958
EKL 159 EKS 7159 *Cuadro Flamenco* Cuadro Flamenco, 1959
EKL 160 EKS 7160 *When Dalliance Was In Flower Volume III* Ed McCurdy, 1959

EKL 161 EKS 7161 *Folk Songs From Just About Everywhere* Theodore Bikel & Geula Gill, 1959
EKL 162 EKS 7162 *The Catch Club* Randolph Singers, 1958
EKL 163 *Songs For The Wee Folk* Susan Reed, 1959
EKL 164 *Love And War Between The Sexes* Gene & Francesca, 1959
EKL 165 EKS 7165 *More Jewish Folk Songs* Theodore Bikel, 1959
EKL 166 EKS 7166 *Around The Campfire* Oranim Zabar, 1959
EKL 167 EKS 7167 *Gold Coast Saturday Night* Saka Acquaye & His African Ensemble, 1959
EKL 168 EKS 7168 *The Wild Blue Yonder* Oscar Brand featuring the Roger Wilco Four, 1959
EKL 169 EKS 7169 *Every Inch A Sailor* Oscar Brand, 1960
EKL 170 *Son Of Dalliance* Ed McCurdy, 1959
EKL 171 *A Concert With Hillel & Aviva* Hillel & Aviva, 1959
EKL 172 *Jean Shepherd And Other Foibles* Jean Shepherd, 1959
EKL 173 EKS 7173 *Donkey Debka! –Young Israel Sings* Ron & Nama, 1959
EKL 174 EKS 7174 *Tell It To The Marines* Oscar Brand, 1960
EKL 175 EKS 7175 *Bravo Bikel! Theodore Bikel Town Hall Concert* Theodore Bikel, 1959
EKL 176 EKS 7176 *Hairy Jazz* Shel Silverstein & The Red Onions, 1959
EKL 177 EKS 7177 *Ski Songs* Bob Gibson, 1959
EKL 178 EKS 7178 *Out Of The Blue* Oscar Brand, 1961
EKL 179 EKS 7179 *The World In My Arms* Anita Ellis, 1960
EKL 180 EKS 7180 *The Limeliters* The Limeliters, 1960
EKL 181 EKS 7181 *The Exciting Artistry Of Will Holt* Will Holt, 1960
EKL 182 EKS 7182 *We Sing Of The Sea* The Seafarers Chorus Featuring Eugene Brice, 1960
EKL 183 EKS 7183 *Boating Songs And All That Bilge* Oscar Brand & The Sea Wolves, 1960
EKL 184 *Presenting Joyce Grenfell* Joyce Grenfell, 1960
EKL 185 EKS 7185 *Songs Of Russia Old And New* Theodore Bikel, 1960
EKL 186 EKS 7186 *Hora – Songs And Dances Of Israel* Oranim Zabar Troupe featuring Guela Gill, 1960
EKL 187 EKS 7187 *Sabra – The Young Heart Of Israel* Ron & Nama, 1960
EKL 188 EKS 7188 *Sports Car (Songs For Big Wheels)* Oscar Brand, 1960
EKL 189 EKS 7189 *Newport Folk Festival, 1960* Theodore Bikel, Oscar Brand, Will Holt, Oranim-Zabar Troupe, 1960
EKL 190 EKS 7190 *Spook Along With Zacherley* Zacherley, 1960
EKL 191 EKS 7191 *Caledonia* The MacPherson Singers And Dancers Of Scotland, 1960
EKL 192 EKS 7192 *Goin' Places* Casey Anderson, 1960
EKL 193 EKS 7193 *Spirituals & Blues* Josh White, 1961
EKL 194 EKS 7194 *Balalaika* Sasha Polinoff & His Russian Gypsy Orchestra, 1961
EKL 195 *Will Failure Spoil Jean Shepherd?* Jean Shepherd, 1961
EKL 196 EKS 7196 *The Dudaim* Ben & Adam, 1961
EKL 197 EKS 7197 *Yes I See* Bob Gibson, 1961
EKL 198 EKS 7198 *Up In The Air – Songs For The Madcap Airman* Oscar Brand, 1961
EKL 199 EKS 7199 *Go To Blazes – The Outrageous Wit Of Peter Myers & Ronnie Cass* Peter Myers & Ronnie Cass, 1960
EKL 200 EKS 7200 *From Bondage To Freedom* Theodore Bikel, 1961
EKL 201 EKS 7201 *A Town Hall Concert* Oranim Zabar & Geula Gil, 1961
EKL 202 EKS 7202 *The Pulsating Sounds Of Paraguay* Los Chiriguanos, 1961
EKL 203 EKS 7203 *The House I Live In* Josh White, 1961
EKL 204 EKS 7204 *For Doctors Only* Oscar Brand, 1961
EKL 205 *A Treasure Chest Of American Folk Song* Ed McCurdy, 1961
EKL 206 EKS 7206 *The Whole World Dances* Geula Gill with Oranim Zabar, 1961
EKL 207 EKS 7207 *At The Gate Of Horn* Bob Gibson & Bob Camp, 1961
EKL 208 EKS 7208 *The Virtuoso Guitars Of Presti & Lagoya* Ida Presti & Alexandre Lagoya, 1961
EKL 209 EKS 7209 *A Maid Of Constant Sorrow* Judy Collins, 1961

EKL 210 EKS 7210 *A Harvest Of Israeli Folksongs* Theodore Bikel, 1961
EKL 211 EKS 7211 *Empty Bed Blues* Josh White, 1962
EKL 212 EKS 7212 *Fastest Balalaika In The West* Sasha Polinoff & His Russian Gypsy Orchestra, 1962
EKL 213 *The Best Of Dalliance* Ed McCurdy, 1961
EKL 214 *Scottish Ballad Book* Jean Redpath, 1962
EKL 215 *Bob Grossman* Bob Grossman, 1961
EKL 216 EKS 7216 *The Travelers 3* Travelers 3, 1962
EKL 217 EKS 7217 *Folk Banjo Styles* Eric Weissberg, Marshall Brickman, Tom Paley & Art Rosenbaum, 1962
EKL 218 *A Treasury Of Spanish And Mexican Folk Songs* Cynthia Gooding, 1962
EKL 219 EKS 7219 *Sing Along In Hebrew* Dov Seltzer Conducting The Maccabee Singers, 1962
EKL 220 EKS 7220 *The Poetry And Prophecy Of The Old Testament* Theodore Bikel, 1962
EKL 221 *French And Italian Folksongs* Cynthia Gooding & Yves Tessier, 1962
EKL 222 EKS 7222 *Golden Apples Of The Sun* Judy Collins, 1962
EKL 223 *A Treasury Of Folk Songs For Children* Various Artists, 1962
EKL 224 *Songs Of Love, Lilt, And Laughter* Jean Redpath, 1962
EKL 225 EKS 7225 *The Best Of Bikel* Theodore Bikel, 1962
EKL 226 EKS 7226 *Open House* Travelers 3, 1962
EKL 227 EKS 7227 *Olé La Mano* Juan Serrano, 1962
EKL 228 EKS 7228 *A Snow Job For Skiers* Oscar Brand, 1962
EKL 229 *A Treasury Of Music Of The Renaissance* La Societe De Musique D'Autrefois, 1963
EKL 230 EKS 7230 *Theodore Bikel On Tour* Theodore Bikel, 1963
EKL 231 EKS 7231 *Judy Henske* Judy Henske, 1963
EKL 232 EKS 7232 *Back Porch Bluegrass* The Dillards, 1963
EKL 233 EKS 7233 *Dián & The Greenbriar Boys* Dián & The Greenbriar Boys, 1963
EKL 234 EKS 7234 *Art Of The Koto – The Music Of Japan* Kimio Eto, 1963
EKL 235 EKS 7235 *Flamenco Fenomeno* Juan Serrano, 1963
EKL 236 EKS 7236 *Live! Live! Live!* Travellers 3, 1963
EKL 237 EKS 7237 *Songs Fore Golfers* Oscar Brand & His Sand Trappers, 1963
EKL 238 EKS 7238 *New Dimensions In Banjo And Bluegrass* Eric Weissberg & Marshall Brickman, 1963
EKL 239 EKS 7239 *Where I'm Bound* Bob Gibson, 1964
EKL 240 *Blues, Rags And Hollers* Koerner, Ray & Glover, 1963
EKL 241 EKS 7241 *High Flying Bird* Judy Henske, 1964
EKL 242 EKS 7242 *Cough! Army Songs out Of the Barracks Bag* Oscar Brand & The Short Arms, 1963
EKL 243 EKS 7243 *Judy Collins 3* Judy Collins, 1963
EKL 244 *20th Century Music For the Guitar* Rey De La Torre, 1964
EKL 245 EKS 7245 *Adventures For 12-String, 6-String And Banjo* Dick Rosmini, 1964
EKL 246 EKS 7246 *The Even Dozen Jug Band* The Even Dozen Jug Band, 1964
EKL 247 *The Songs Of Fred Engleberg* Fred Engleberg, 1964
EKL 248 EKS 7248 *Tear Down The Walls* Vince Martin & Fred Neil, 1964
EKL 249 EKS 7249 *The Patriot Game* The Irish Ramblers, 1964
EKL 250 EKS 7250 *A Folksinger's Choice* Theodore Bikel, 1964
EKL 251 EKS 7251 *Authentic Sound Effects Vol 1*, 1962
EKL 252 EKS 7252 *Authentic Sound Effects Vol 2*, 1962
EKL 253 EKS 7253 *Authentic Sound Effects Vol 3*, 1962
EKL 254 EKS 7254 *Authentic Sound Effects Vol 4*, 1964
EKL 255 EKS 7255 *Authentic Sound Effects Vol 5*, 1964
EKL 256 EKS 7256 *Authentic Sound Effects Vol 6*, 1964
EKL 257 EKS 7257 *Authentic Sound Effects Vol 7*, 1964
EKL 258 EKS 7258 *Authentic Sound Effects Vol 8*, 1964
EKL 259 EKS 7259 *Authentic Sound Effects Vol 9*, 1964

EKL 260 EKS 7260 *Authentic Sound Effects Vol 10*, 1964

EKL 261 EKS 7261 *Authentic Sound Effects Vol 11 (Paris And Venice)*, 1964

EKL 262 EKS 7262 *Authentic Sound Effects Vol 12 (Rome and Madrid)*, 1964

EKL 263 EKS 7263 *Authentic Sound Effects Vol 13 (London)*, 1964

EKL 264 EKS 7264 *The Blues Project* Various Artists, 1964

EKL 265 EKS 7265 *Live!!! Almost!!!* The Dillards, 1964

EKL 266 EKS 7266 *The Folk Fiddler Who Electrified The Newport Folk Festival* Jean Carignan, 1964

EKL 267 EKS 7267 *Lots More Blues, Rags And Hollers* Koerner, Ray & Glover, 1964

EKL 268 EKS 7268 *The Ian Campbell Folk Group* The Ian Campbell Folk Group, 1964

EKL 269 EKS 7269 *All The News That's Fit To Sing* Phil Ochs, 1964

EKL 270 EKS 7270 *Swing Hallelujah* The Christian Tabernacle Church Of New York City With Reverend W.M. O'Neil, 1964

EKL 271/2 *Library Of Congress Recordings* Woody Guthrie, 1964

EKL 273 *Happy All The Time* Joseph Spence, 1964

EKL 274 EKS 7274 *Laddie Lie Near Me* Jean Redpath, 1964

EKL 275 EKS 7275 *Bravo Serrano!* Juan Serrano, 1964

EKL 276 EKS 7276 *Old Time Banjo Project* Various Artists, 1964

EKL 277 EKS 7277 *Ramblin' Boy* Tom Paxton, 1964

EKL 278 EKS 7278 *Paths Of Victory* Hamilton Camp, 1964

EKL 279 *The Iron Muse* Various Artists, 1964

EKL 280 EKS 7280 *The Judy Collins Concert* Judy Collins, 1965

EKL 281 EKS 7281 *Yiddish Theatre And Folk Songs* Theodore Bikel, 1964

EKL 282 *Music Of Bulgaria* Ensemble Of Bulgarian Republic, 1965

EKL 283 EKS 7283 *Five And Twenty Questions* Mark Spoelstra, 1965

EKL 284 EKS 7284 *Snaker's Here* Dave 'Snaker' Ray, 1965

EKL 285 EKS 7285 *Pickin' And Fiddlin'* The Dillards With Byron Berline, 1965

EKL 286 EKS 7286 *Classical Music Of Japan* Various Artists, 1965

EKL 287 EKS 7287 *I Ain't Marching Anymore* Phil Ochs, 1965

EKL 288 EKS 7288 *Tom Rush* Tom Rush, 1965

EKL 289 EKS 7289 *Kathy & Carol* Kathy & Carol, 1965

EKL 290 EKS 7290 *Spider Blues* John Koerner, 1965

EKL 291 EKS 7291 *Corrie Folk Trio With Paddie Bell* Corrie Folk Trio With Paddie Bell, 1965

EKL 292 EKS 7292 *The String Band Project* Various Artists, 1965

EKL 293 EKS 7293 *Bleecker And MacDougal* Fred Neil, 1965

EKL 294 EKS 7294 *The Paul Butterfield Blues Band* The Paul Butterfield Blues Band, 1965

EKL 295 EKS 7295 *Tom Paley & Peggy Seeger* Tom Paley & Peggy Seeger, 1965

EKL 296 EKS 7296 *Negro Folklore From Texas State Prison* Various Artists, 1965

EKL 297 EKS 7297 *Sounds Of Japan* Actuality Sounds, 1965

EKL 298 EKS 7298 *Ain't That News!* Tom Paxton, 1965

EKL 299 EKS 7299 *Singer Songwriter Project* Various Artists, 1965

EKL 300 EKS 7300 *Judy Collins' Fifth Album* Judy Collins, August 1965

EKL 301/2 *The Library Of Congress Recordings* Leadbelly, 1965

EKL 303 *Maxwell Street Jimmy Davis* Maxwell Street Jimmy Davis, 1965

EKL 304 EKS 7304 *The Promise Of The Day* Corrie Folk Trio With Paddle Bell, 1966

EKL 305 EKS 7305 *The Return Of Koerner, Ray & Glover* Koerner, Ray & Glover, 1965

EKL 306 EKS 7306 *The Baroque Beatles Book* Baroque Ensemble Of the Merseyside Kammermusikgesellschaft, 1965

EKL 307 EKS 7307 *State Of Mind* Mark Spoelstra, 1966

EKL 308 EKS 7308 *Take A Little Walk With Me* Tom Rush, 1966

EKL 309 EKS 7309 *The Rights Of Man* The Ian Campbell Folk Group, 1966

EKL 310 EKS 7310 *Phil Ochs In Concert* Phil Ochs, 1966

EKL 311 EKS 7311 *Light Of Day* Pat Kilroy, 1966

EKL 312 EKS 7312 *How To Play Electric Bass* Harvey Brooks, 1967

EKL 313/4 EKS 7313/4 *Elektra Library Of Authentic Sound Effects*, 1966
EKL 315 EKS 7315 *East-West* The Butterfield Blues Band, 1966
EKL 316 EKS 7316 *Oliver Smith* Oliver Smith, 1966
EKL 317 EKS 7317 *Outward Bound* Tom Paxton, 1966
EKL 318 EKS 7318 *Goodbye And Hello* Tim Buckley, 1967
EKL 319 EKS 7319 *Fine Soft Land* Dave 'Snaker' Ray, 1967
EKL 320 EKS 7320 *In My Life* Judy Collins, 1966
EKL 321 EKS 7321 *Frost & Fire* The Watersons, 1967
EKL 322 EKS 7322 *The Incredible String Band* Incredible String Band, 1966
EKL 324 *How To Play Blues Guitar* Stefan Grossman, 1967
EKL 325 EKS 7325 *The Bauls Of Bengal* The Bauls Of Bengal, 1967
EKL 326 EKS 7326 *Songs Of The Earth* Theodore Bikel & The Pennywhistlers, 1967
EKL 4001 EKS 74001 *Love* Love, 1966
EKL 4002 EKS 74002 *What's Shakin'* Various Artists, 1966
EKL 4003 EKS 74003 *David Blue* David Blue, 1966
EKL 4004 EKS 74004 *Tim Buckley* Tim Buckley, 1966
EKL 4005 EKS 74005 *Da Capo* Love, 1966
EKL 4006 EKS 74006 *Beatle Country* The Charles River Valley Boys, 1966
EKL 4007 EKS 74007 *The Doors* The Doors, 1967
EKL 4008 EKS 74008 *Sea Drift* Dusk 'Til Dawn Orchestra Conducted By Mort Garson, 196
EKL 4009 EKS 74009 *The Zodiac Cosmic Sounds* Composed, Arranged And Conducted By Mort Garson: Words By Jacques Wilson, 1967
EKL 4010 EKS 74010 *The 5000 Spirits Or The Layers Of The Onion* Incredible String Band, 1967
EKL 4011 EKS 74011 *Clear Light* Clear Light, 1967
EKL 4012 EKS 74012 *Wildflowers* Judy Collins, 1967
EKL 4013 EKS 74013 *Forever Changes* Love, 1967
EKL 4014 EKS 74014 *Strange Days* The Doors, 1967
EKL 4015 EKS 74015 *The Resurrection Of Pigboy Crabshaw* The Butterfield Blues Band, 1967
EKS 74016 *Earth Opera* Earth Opera, 1968
EKS 74017 *Steve Noonan* Steve Noonan, 1968
EKL 4018 EKS 74018 *The Circle Game* Tom Rush, 1968
EKS 74019 *Morning Again* Tom Paxton, 1968
EKS 74020 *Ars Nova* Ars Nova, 1968
EKS 74021 *The Hangman's Beautiful Daughter* The Incredible String Band, 1968
EKS 74022 *David Ackles* David Ackles, 1968
EKS 74023 *Eclection* Eclection, 1968
EKL 4024 EKS 74024 *Waiting For The Sun* The Doors, 1968
EKS 74025 *In My Own Dream* The Butterfield Blues Band, 1968
EKS 74026 *The Moray Eels Eat The Holy Modal Rounders* The Holy Modal Rounders, 1968
EKS 74027 *In My Life* Judy Collins, 1967 (Reissue of 300-series disc)
EKS 74028 *Goodbye And Hello* Tim Buckley, 1967 (Reissue of 300-series disc)
EKS 74029 *The Marble Index* Nico, 1968
EKS 74030 *Rhinoceros* Rhinoceros, 1969
EKS 74031 *Early Morning Blues And Greens* Diane Hildebrand, 1969
EKS 74032 *Have A Marijuana* David Peel & The Lower East Side, 1968
EKS 74033 *Who Knows Where The Time Goes* Judy Collins, 1969
EKS 74034 *Transformer* David Stoughton, 1968
EKS 74035 *Wheatstraw Suite* The Dillards, 1968
EKS 74036 *Wee Tam* The Incredible String Band, 1968
EKS 74037 *The Big Huge* The Incredible String Band, 1968
EKS 74038 *The Great American Eagle Tragedy* Earth Opera, 1969
EKS 74039 *The Original Delaney & Bonnie (Accept No Substitute)* Delaney & Bonnie, 1969
EKS 74040 *Glad I'm In The Band* Lonnie Mack, 1969
EKS 74041 *Running Jumping Standing Still* 'Spider' John Koerner & Willie Murphy, 1967
EKS 74042 *Kick Out The Jams* MC5, 1969
EKS 74043 *The Things I Notice Now* Tom Paxton, 1969

EKS 74044 *Bread* Bread, 1969
EKS 74045 *Happy Sad* Tim Buckley, 1968
EKS 74046 (CD) *St Cecilia* Stalk-Forrest Group, 2001 (Not released until 2001)
EKS 74047 *The Best Of Lord Buckley* Lord Buckley, 1969
EKS 74048 *Bamboo* Bamboo, 1968
EKS 74049 *Four Sail* Love, 1969
EKS 74050 *Whatever's Right* Lonnie Mack, 1969
EKS 74051 *The Stooges* The Stooges, 1969
EKS 74052 *Matthew, Mark, Luke And John* Methuselah, 1969
EKS 74053 *Keep On Moving* The Butterfield Blues Band, 1969
EKS 74054 *Copperfields* The Dillards, 1970
EKS 74055 *Recollections* Judy Collins, 1969
EKS 74056 *Satin Chickens* Rhinoceros, 1969
EKS 74057 *Changing Horses* The Incredible String Band, 1969
EKS 74058 *Love Revisited* Love, 1970
EKS 74059 *Partyin'* Wild Thing, 1969
EKS 74060 *Subway To The Country* David Ackles, 1970
EKS 74061 *I Looked Up* The Incredible String Band, 1970
EKS 74062 *Classic Rush* Tom Rush, 1971
EKS 74063 *Roxy* Roxy, 1969
EKS 74064 *Woodsmoke And Oranges* Paul Siebel, 1970
EKS 74065 *Disguised As A Normal Person* David Steinberg, 1970
EKS 74065 *Relics Of The Incredible String Band* The Incredible String Band, 1971 (UK release re-using number)
EKS 74066 *Tom Paxton 6* Tom Paxton, 1970
EKS 74067 *Crabby Appleton* Crabby Appleton, 1970
EKS 74068 *Renaissance* Renaissance, 1969
EKS 74069 *The American Revolution* David Peel & The Lower East Side, 1970
EKS 74070 *Gulliver* Gulliver, 1970
EKS 74071 *Fun House* The Stooges, 1970
EKS 74072 *Suite Steel: The Pedal Steel Guitar Album* Various Artists, 1970
EKS 74073 *Little Bit Of Rain* Fred Neil, 1970
EKS 74074 *Lorca* Tim Buckley, 1970
EKS 74075 *Better Times Are Coming* Rhinoceros, 1970
EKS 74076 *On The Waters* Bread, 1970
EKS 74077 *For Collectors Only* Lonnie Mack, 1970
EKS 74078 *If I Be Your Lady* Carol Hall, 1971
EKS 74079 *13* The Doors, 1971
EKS 74080 *Right On Be Free* Voices Of East Harlem, 1970
EKS 74081 *Jack-Knife Gypsy* Paul Siebel, 1971
EKS 74082 EQ 4082 *Carly Simon* Carly Simon, 1971
EKS 74083 *Farquahr* Farquahr, 1970
EKS 74084 *Formerly Anthrax* Show Of Hands, 1970
EKS 74085 *Radio Free Nixon* David Frye, 1971
EKS 74086 *Manna* Bread, 1971
EKS 74087 *Strange Locomotion* Siren, 1971
EKS 74088 *Beautiful People* New Seekers, 1971
EKS 74089 *Rat On!* Swamp Dogg, 1971
EKS 74091 *Crow Dog's Paradise* Henry & Leonard Crow Dog With Al Running, 1971
EKS 74092 *The Rainbow Band* The Rainbow Band, 1971
EKS 74093 *Smiling Men With Bad Reputations* Mike Heron, 1971
EKS 74094 *Death Walks Behind You* Atomic Rooster, 1971
EKS 74095 *Bring America Home* Timber, 1971
EKS 74096 *The Quinaimes Band* The Quinaimes Band, 1971
EKS 74097 *The Uncle Dirty Primer* Uncle Dirty, 1971
EKS 74098 *Wackering Heights* The Wackers, 1971
EKS 74099 *Nicely Out Of Tune* Lindisfarne, 1971
EKS 74100 *The House On The Hill* Audience, 1971
EKS 74101 *Living By The Days* Don Nix, 1971
EKS 74102 *The Hills Of Indiana* Lonnie Mack, 1972
EKS 74103 *Mary Called Jeanie Greene* Jeanie Greene, 1971
EKS 74104 *Songs For The Gentle Man* Bridget St John, 1971
EKS 74105 *Cyrus* Cyrus Faryar, 1971
EKS 74106 *Rotten To The Core* Crabby Appleton, 1972
EKS 74107 EQ 4107 *Frisco Mabel Joy* Mickey Newbury, 1971
EKS 74108 *New Colours* New Seekers, 1972
EKS 74109 *In Hearing Of* Atomic Rooster, 1971
EKS 74112 *Liquid Acrobat As Regards The Air* The Incredible String Band, 1971
EKS 74115 *I'd Like To Teach The World To Sing* New Seekers, 1971

EKL 5000 *The Golden Apple* Original New York Cast, 1960
EKL 5001 *The Folk Song Kit/How to Play Folk Guitar* Billy Faier & Milt Okun, 1958
EKL 5002 EKS 75002 *Dramatic Cue Music & Mood Music: Volume 1* Orchestra Conducted By Robert Kreis, 1964
EKL 5003 EKS 75003 *Dramatic Cue Music & Mood Music: Volume 2* Orchestra Conducted By Robert Kreis, 1964
EKL 5004 EKS 75004 *Dramatic Cue Music & Mood Music: Volume 3* Orchestra Conducted By Robert Kreis, 1964
EKS 75005 *The Soft Parade* The Doors, 1969
EKS 75006 *I Am The President* David Frye, 1969
EKS 75007 *Morrison Hotel* The Doors, 1970
EKS 75008 *The Best Of Josh White* Josh White, 1970
EKS 75009 *13* The Doors (Venezuela only!)
EKS 75010 *Whales and Nightingales* Judy Collins, 1971
EKS 75011 *LA Woman* The Doors, 1971
EKS 75012 *A Child's Garden Of Grass* Various Artists, 1971
EKS 75013 *Sometimes I Just Feel Like Smilin'* The Butterfield Blues Band, 1971
EKS 75014 *Living* Judy Collins, 1972
EKS 75015 EQ 5015 *Baby I'm – A Want You* Bread, 1972
EKS 75016 *Anticipation* Carly Simon, 1971
EKS 75017 *Other Voices* The Doors, 1971
EKS 75018 *Beads And Feathers* Carol Hall, 1972
EKS 75019 *Kongos* John Kongos, 1972
EKS 75020 *Bernie Taupin* Bernie Taupin, 1971
EKS 75021 *Fog On The Tyne* Lindisfarne, 1972
EKS 75022 *Road Show* Alabama State Troupers Featuring Don Nix, Jeanie Green, Furry Lewis, And The Mt Zion Band And Choir, 1972
EKS 75023 *Heads & Tales* Harry Chapin, 1972
EKS 75024 *J.F. Murphy & Salt* J.F. Murphy & Salt, 1972
EKS 75025 *Hot Wacks* The Wackers, 1972
EKS 75026 *Lunch* Audience, 1972
EKS 75027 *Ronee Blakley* Ronee Blakley, 1972
EKS 75028 *Tiptoe Past The Dragon* Marlin Greene, 1972
EKS 75029 *Motorcycle Mama* Sailcat, 1972
EKS 75030 EQ 5030 *Colors Of The Day – The Best Of Judy Collins* Judy Collins, 1972
EKS 75031 *Aztec Two-Step* Aztec Two-Step, 1972
EKS 75032 *American Gothic* David Ackles, 1972
EKS 75033 *Jubal* Jubal, 1972
EKS 75034 *Circles* New Seekers, 1972
6E 5035 EQ 5035 *Greatest Hits* The Doors, 1973
EKS 75036 *The Ship* The Ship, 1972
EKS 75037 *There's An Innocent Face* Curt Boetcher, 1973
EKS 75038 *Full Circle* The Doors, July 1972
EKS 75039 *Made In England* Atomic Rooster, 1972
EKS 75040 *Casey Kelly* Casey Kelly, 1972
EKS 75041 *Goodthunder* Goodthunder, 1972
EKS 75042 *Sniper And Other Love Songs* Harry Chapin, 1972
EKS 75043 *Dingly Dell* Lindisfarne, 1972
EKS 75044 *In Search Of Amelia Earhart* Plainsong, 1972
EKS 75045 *Sweet Salvation* Sweet Salvation, 1972
EKS 75046 *Shredder* The Wackers, 1972
EKS 75047 *Guitar Man* Bread, 1972
EKS 75048 *Portland* Gary Ogan & Bill Lamb, 1972
EKS 75049 EQ 5049 *No Secrets* Carly Simon, 1972
EKS 75050 *Veronique Sanson* Veronique Sanson, 1973
EKS 75051 EQ 5051 *Best Of The New Seekers* New Seekers, 1973
EKS 75052 *Dana Cooper* Dana Cooper, 1973
EKS 75053 *True Stories And Other Dreams* Judy Collins, 1973
EKS 75054 *Special Delivery* Billy Mernit, 1973
EKS 75055 *Heaven Help The Child* Mickey Newbury, 1973
EKS 75056 EQ 5056 *Best Of Bread* Bread, 1973
EKS 75057 *Homegrown* Don Agrati, 1973
EKS 75058 EQ 5058 *Intergalactic Trot* Stardrive, 1973
EKS 75059 *Capital City Rockets* Capital City Rockets, 1973
EKS 75060 *Fancy Dancer* Courtland Pickett, 1973
EKS 75061 *Valley Hi* Ian Matthews, 1973
EKS 75062 *Dennis Linde* Dennis Linde, 1973
EKS 75063 *Music Is Your Mistress* Linda Hargrove, 1973
EKS 75064 *Queen* Queen, 1973

EKS 75065 *Short Stories* Harry Chapin, 1973
EKS 75066 EQ 5066 *First* David Gates, 1973
EKS 75067 *Dennis Coulson* Dennis Coulson, 1973
EKS 75068 *Islands* Cyrus Faryar, 1973
EKS 75069 *Melba Montgomery* Melba Montgomery, 1973
EKS 75070 *Jobriath* Jobriath, 1973
EKS 75071 *Painter* Painter, 1973
EKS 75072 *For Sale* Casey Kelly, 1974
EKS 75073 *Skymonters With Hamid Hamilton Camp* Skymonters, 1973
EKS 75074 *IV* Atomic Rooster, 1973
EKS 75075 *Pipedream* Alan Hull, 1974
EKS 75076 *Cross Country Cowboy* Buzz Rabin, 1974
EKS 75077 *Roll On Ruby* Lindisfarne, 1974
EKS 75078 *Some Days You Eat The Bear* Ian Matthews, 1974
EKS 75079 *No Charge* Melba Montgomery, 1974
EKS 75081 *Soakin' With Tears* Randy Lee, 1974
EKS 75082 *Queen II* Queen, 1974
EKL 9001 *The Folk Box* Various Artists, 1964 (four disc boxed set)
EKS 9002 *Absolutely Live* The Doors, 1970 (double album)
8E 6001 *Weird Scenes Inside The Gold Mine* The Doors, 1972 (double album)
7E 2001 *Live* The Butterfield Blues Band, 1971 (double album)
7E 2002 *U* Incredible String Band, 1970 (double album)
7E 2003 *The Compleat Tom Paxton* Tom Paxton, 1971 (double album)
7E 2004 *Relics Of The Incredible String Band* The Incredible String Band, 1971 (double album)
7E 2005 *Golden Butter: The Best Of The Paul Butterfield Blues Band* The Paul Butterfield Blues Band, 1972 (double album)
7E 2006 *Nuggets* Various Artists, 1973 (double album)
7E 2007 *Live at Montezuma Hall/Looks Like Rain* Mickey Newbury, 1973 (double album)
7E 1002 *Hotcakes* Carly Simon, 1974
7E 1007 *I Came To Hear The Music* Mickey Newbury, 1974

EARLY STEREO DISCS

EKL 201 X *In The Gloryland* Ken Davern & His Salty Dogs, 1958
EKL 202 X *Gypsy Magic* Edi Csoka & His Gypsy Orchestra, 1958
EKL 203 X *The Neue Deutschmeister Band In Stereo* The Neue Deutschmeister Band, 1958
EKL 204 X *The Catch Club* The Randolph Singers, 1958

SAMPLER DISCS

FMS 1 *A Folk Music Sampler* Various Artists, 1954
SMP 2 *Folk Sampler* Various Artists, 1956
SMP 3 *Folk Pops 'n Jazz Sampler* Various Artists, 1957
SMP 4-X *Around The World In Stereo* Various Artists, 1958
SMP 5 *Folk Sampler 5* Various Artists, 1959
SMP 6 *The Folk Scene* Various Artists, 1961
SMP 7 SMP 7-ST *Sound Effects Sampler*, 1963
SMP 8 S 78 *Folksong '65* Various Artists, 1965

PROMOTIONAL DISCS

EPK 1001/2 *Theodore Bikel* Theodore Bikel (double EP)
JC 1 *Judy* Judy Collins, 1967
DS 1 *Untitled* David Steinberg, 1970
EB 1 *Elektra's Best: Volume 1, 1966 Through 1968* Various Artists, 1971
S3 10 *Garden Of Delights* Various Artists, 1971
CGG 1 *Excerpts From 'A Child's Garden Of Grass – A Pre-Legalization Comedy'*, 1971
UDP 1 *The Uncle Dirty Primer* Uncle Dirty, 1971
BRD 1 *Bread* Bread, 1971
EK-PROMO 1 *1/71* Various Artists, January 1971
EK-PROMO 2 *2/71* Various Artists, February 1971
EK-PROMO 3 *4/71* Various Artists, April 1971
EK-PROMO 4 *5/71* Various Artists, May 1971
EK-PROMO 5 *Elektra July Releases* Various Artists, June 1971
EK-PROMO 6 *Elektra September Releases* Various Artists, August 1971
EK-PROMO 7 *Elektra October Releases* Various Artists, September 1971
EK-PROMO 8 *Elektra January Releases* Various Artists, January 1972
EK-PROMO 9
EK-PROMO 10

EK-PROMO 11 *Elektra March Releases* Various Artists, March 1972

EK-PROMO 12 *Elektra April Releases* Various Artists, April 1972

EK-PROMO 13 *Elektra May Releases* Various Artists, May 1972

EK-PROMO 14 *Elektra June Releases* Various Artists, June 1972

EK-PROMO 15 *Elektra August Releases* Various Artists, August 1972

EK-PROMO 16 *Elektra September Releases* Various Artists, September 1972

EK-PROMO 17 *Elektra October Releases* Various Artists, October 1972

EK-PROMO 18 *Something Out Of The Ordinary: January, 1973* Various Artists, December 1972

EK-PROMO 19 *Elektra July Releases* Various Artists, July 1973

EK-PROMO 20 *Recorded Live At Montezuma Hall* Mickey Newbury, 1973

DS 500 *Judy* Judy Collins, 1969 (Special compilation for the Columbia Record Club)

Nina Music Publishing 3/4 *Songs By ...* Jackson Browne and Steve Noonan, 1967 (Music publisher demos)

FM 102 (CD) *Follow The Music* Various Artists, 2000 (slipped into the trade paperback of Jac's autobiography *Follow The Music*)

(No Number) *The History Of Elektra (The Elektra Project)* BBC Radio London 'Fresh Garbage' Series, 1973 (Limited edition promotional pressing of radio documentary)

BOXED SETS

60381 *Bleecker And MacDougal (The Folk Scene Of The 1960s)* Various Artists, 1984 ('The Jac Holzman Years' retrospectives)

60383 *Crossroads (White Blues in The 1960s)* Various Artists, 1984 ('The Jac Holzman Years' retrospectives)

60402 *O Love Is Teasin' (Anglo-American Mountain Balladry)* Various Artists, 1985 ('The Jac Holzman Years' retrospectives)

60403 *Elektrock (The Sixties)* Various Artists, 1985 ('The Jac Holzman Years' retrospectives)

Rhino *Forever Changing: The Golden Age Of Elektra, 1963-1973* Various Artists, 2006 (Retrospective 5CD box)

ELEKTRA UK RELEASES

EUK 251/2 *The Folk Box* Various Artists, 1966

EUK 253 *A Cold Wind Blows* Various Artists, 1966

EUK 254 EKS 254 *The Incredible String Band* The Incredible String Band, 1966

EUK 255 *Alasdair Clayre* Alasdair Clayre, 1967

EUK 256 EUKS 7256 *AMMMusic* AMM, 1967

EUK 257 EUKS 257 *The 5000 Spirits Or The Layers Of The Onion* The Incredible String Band, 1967

EUK 258 EUKS 258 *The Hangman's Beautiful Daughter* The Incredible String Band, 1968

EUK 259 *Fantastic Folk* Various Artists, 1968

EUK 260 EUKS 260 *Good Time Music* Various Artists, 1967

EUK 261 EUKS 261 *Select Elektra* Various Artists, 1968

EUKS 262 *Begin Here* Various Artists, 1969

EUKS 263 (CD) *Selections From 'Forever Changing'* Various Artists, October 2006 (Promotional release)

K 32003 *Patrick Kavanagh At The King's Head* John Welsh & Patrick Magee, 1973

K 42094 *Brand New Day* Dorothy Morrison, 1971

K 42129 *Jugalbandi* John Barham & Ashish Khan, 1973

K 42136 *Plainsong 3* Plainsong (not released)

K 42139 *Urban Cowboy* Andy Roberts, 1973

K 42151 *Andy Roberts And The Great Stampede* Andy Roberts, 1973

K 22002 *New Magic In A Dusty World* Various Artists, 1971

K 22005 *The One That Got Away* Various Artists, 1973

ESP 9001 *Garden Of Delights* Various Artists, 1972 (double album)

EPK 801 *Lord Of The Dance* Sydney Carter, 1966 (EP)

EPK 802 *Tom Paxton* Tom Paxton, 1967 (EP)

DANDELION

D9 101 *Ask Me No Questions* Bridget St John, 1970

D9 102 *I'm Back And I'm Proud* Gene Vincent, 1970

D9 103 *Soundtrack* Principal Edwards Magic Theatre, 1970

D9 104 *Siren* Siren, 1970

COUNTRYSIDE

CM 101 *Pure Country* Garland Frady, 1973

CM 102 *Velvet Hammer In A Cowboy Band* Red Rhodes, 1973

Bibliography and Sources

Kevin Avery *Everything Is An Afterthought: The Life And Writings Of Paul Nelson* (Fantagraphics 2011)

Joan Baez *And A Voice To Sing With* (Arrow 1989)

Theodore Bikel *Theo* (Harper Collins 1994)

Joe Boyd *White Bicycles* (Serpents Tail 2005)

Oscar Brand *The Ballad Mongers: Rise Of The Modern Folk Song (*Greenwood Press 1979)

Mark Brend *American Troubadours* (Backbeat 2001)

Simon Broughton, Mark Ellingham, David Muddyman, Richard Trillo *World Music: The Rough Guide* (Rough Guide 1994)

John Broven *Record Makers And Breakers* (University Of Illinois Press 2009)

David Browne *Dream Brother* (Fourth Estate 1988)

Robert Cantwell *When We Were Good* (Harvard University Press 1996)

Peter M. Coan *Taxi The Harry Chapin Story* (Carol Publishing Group 1990)

Ronald D. Cohen *Rainbow Quest* (The University Of Massachusetts Press 2002)

Stan Cornyn *Exploding* (Harper Entertainment 2002)

David Crosby, Carl Gottlieb *Long Time Gone* (Doubleday 1988)

Clive Davis (with James Willwerth) *Clive Inside The Record Business* (William Morrow And Company 1975)

John Densmore *Riders On The Storm* (Bloomsbury 1990)

David Deturk, A. Poulin Jr (ed) *The American Folk Scene* (Laurel 1967)

Peter Doggett *There's A Riot Going On* (Canongate 2007)

Bob Dylan *Chronicles Volume 1* (Simon & Schuster 2004)

Jonathan Eisen (ed) *Twenty-Minute Fandangos And Forever Changes* (Vintage 1971)

Ben Fong-Torres (ed) *The Doors By The Doors* (Hyperion 2006)

Bob Gibson, Carole Bender *I Come For To Sing* (Firebird 2008)

Charlie Gillet *The Sound Of The City* (Sphere 1971)

Fred Goodman *The Mansion On The Hill* (Vintage 1998)

Max Gordon *Live At The Village Vanguard* (Da Capo 1980)

Michael Gray *The Bob Dylan Encyclopaedia* (Continuum 2006)

David Hajdu *Positively Fourth Street* (Bloomsbury 2001)

Phil Hardy, Dave Laing *Encyclopaedia Of Rock 1955–1975* (Aquarius 1977)

Richie Havens *They Can't Hide Us Anymore* (Avon 1999)

Clinton Heylin *Bob Dylan – A Life In Stolen Moments* (Music Sales 1996)

Christopher Hjort *So You Want To Be A Rock And Roll Star: The Byrds Day-By Day 1965–1973* (Jawbone 2008)

Jac Holzman, Gavin Daws *Follow The Music* (FirstMedia 1998)

Jerry Hopkins, Danny Sugerman *No One Gets Out Of Here Alive* (Plexus 1980)

Jerry Hopkins *The Lizard King: The Essential Jim Morrison* (Plexus 2006)

Barney Hoskyns *Waiting For The Sun* (Viking 1996)

Barney Hoskyns *Hotel California* (Fourth Estate 2005)

Mick Houghton *I've Always Kept A Unicorn* (Faber & Faber 2015)

Bernie Krause *Into A Wild Sanctuary* (Heyday 1998)

Dave Laing *The Electric Muse: The Story Of Folk Into Rock* (Methuen 1975)

Ronald Lankford *Folk Music USA* (Schirmer 2005)

Ray M. Lawless *Folk Singers And Folk Songs In America* (Greenwood 1965)

Ray Manzarek *Light My Fire* (Arrow 1998)

J Marks, Linda Eastman, *Rock And Other Four Letter Words* (Bantam 1968)

Domenic Priore *Riot On Sunset Strip* (Jawbone 2007)

Rolling Stone *The Rolling Stone Record*

Review Volumes One And Two (Pocket Books 1971/1974)
Suze Rotolo *A Freewheelin' Time* (Aurum 2008)
Lillian Roxon *Roxon's Rock Encyclopaedia* (Universal Library 1971)
Ellen Sander *Trips* (Scribners 1973)
Jon Savage *1966: The Year The Decade Exploded* (Faber & Faber 2015)
Michael Schumacher *There But For Fortune: The Life Of Phil Ochs* (Hyperion 1996)
Joel Selvin *Summer Of Love* (Penguin 1994)
Clive Selwood *All The Moves (But None Of The Licks)* (Peter Owen 2003)
Irwin Stambler, Grelun Landon *Encyclopaedia Of Folk, Country, And Western Music* (St Martins 1969)
Martin C. Strong *The Great Folk Discography: Pioneers & Early Legends* (Polygon 2010)
Michael Stuart-Ware *Love Behind The Scenes On The Pegasus Carousel* (Helter Skelter 2003)
Phil Sutcliffe *Queen* (Voyager Press 2009)
Paul Trynka *Iggy Pop: Open Up And Bleed* (Sphere 2007)
Lee Underwood *Blue Melody: Tim Buckley Remembered* (Backbeat 2002)
Richie Unterberger *Turn! Turn! Turn!* (Backbeat 2002)
Richie Unterberger *Eight Miles High* (Backbeat 2003)
Dave Van Ronk *The Mayor Of MacDougal Street* (Da Capo 2006)
Eric Von Schmidt, Jim Rooney *Baby Let Me Follow You Down* (University of Massachusetts Press, 1994)
Elijah Wald *Josh White: Society Blues* (Routledge 2002)
Elijah Wald *How The Beatles Destroyed Rock'n'roll* (Oxford University Press 2009)
Neil Warwick, John, Kutner, Tony Brown *The Complete Book Of The British Charts Singles And Albums* (Omnibus 2004)
Dick Weissman *Which Side Are You On* (Continuum 2005)
Sheila Weller *Girls Like Us* (Ebury 2008)
Joel Whitburn *The Billboard Book Of Top 40 Hits* (Billboard 2005)
Adrian Whittaker (ed) *Be Glad: An Incredible String Band Compendium* (Helter Skelter 2003)
Jan Mark Wolkin, Bill Keenom *Michael Bloomfield* (Miller Freeman 2000)
Joe Ziemer *Mickey Newbury Crystal And Stone* (Authorhouse 2004)

A lifetime of newspapers and specialist music publication past and present, including *Broadside*, *Classic Rock*, *Comstock Lode*, *Crawdaddy*, *Creem*, *Dark Star*, *Fusion*, *Hit Parader*, *Hot Wacks*, *Let It Rock*, *Melody Maker*, *Mojo*, *NME*, *Omaha Rainbow*, *Ptolemaic Terrascope*, *Q*, *Record Collector*, *Record Mirror*, *Rolling Stone*, *Shindig*, *Sing Out*, *Sounds*, *Swing 51*, *Uncut*, *Who Put the Bomp*, *The Word*, *Zigzag*, and the invaluable rocksbackpages.com.

Endnotes

These endnotes provide credits for the relevant quotes in the text. All quotes in the text without credits are from the author's own interviews.

CHAPTER 2

1 *Follow The Music* transcripts, Gavan Daws

CHAPTER 3

1 John Broven *Record Makers And Breakers* (University Of Illinois Press 2009)
2 Elijah Wald *How The Beatles Destroyed Rock'n'Roll* (Oxford University Press 2009)
3 *Follow The Music* transcripts, Gavan Daws
4 Ronald D Cohen *Rainbow Quest* (University of Massachusetts Press 2002)
5 Theodore Bikel *Theo* (Harper Collins 1994)
6 David Hajdu *Positively Fourth Street* (Bloomsbury 2001)
7 *Jac Holzman's Elektra Story* (BBC Radio 2, April 2008)
8 Theodore Bikel *Theo* (Harper Collins 1994)
9 *Jac Holzman's Elektra Story* (BBC Radio 2, April 2008)
10 *Follow The Music* transcripts, Gavan Daws
11 *Follow The Music* transcripts, Gavan Daws
12 *The New York Times* November 7 2008
13 *Follow The Music* transcripts, Gavan Daws

CHAPTER 4

1 Dick Weissman *Which Side Are You On* (Continuum 2005)
2 *Follow The Music* transcripts, Gavan Daws
3 *Follow The Music* transcripts, Gavan Daws
4 *Follow The Music* transcripts, Gavan Daws

5 *Follow The Music* transcripts, Gavan Daws
6 *Follow The Music* transcripts, Gavan Daws
7 Theodore Bikel *Theo* (Harper Collins 1994)
8 *Follow The Music* transcripts, Gavan Daws
9 *Follow The Music* transcripts, Gavan Daws

CHAPTER 5

1 David Hajdu *Positively 4th Street* (Bloomsbury 2001)
2 Max Gordon *Live At The Village Vanguard* (Da Capo 1980)
3 Dave Van Ronk *The Mayor Of MacDougal Street* (Da Capo 2006)
4 Robert Cantwell *When We Were Good* (Harvard University Press 1996)
5 Theodore Bikel *Theo* (Harper Collins 1994)
6 *Follow The Music* transcripts, Gavan Daws
7 Theodore Bikel *Theo* (Harper Collins 1994)
8 Bob Dylan *Chronicles Volume One* (Simon & Schuster 2004)
9 www.erikdarling.com
10 *Guitarist* December 2003 by Neville Marten
11 Booklet notes Various Artists *Forever Changing*
12 *Follow The Music* transcripts, Gavan Daws

CHAPTER 6

1 Ronald D. Lankford Jr. *Folk Music USA: The Changing Voice Of Protest* (Schirmer 2005)
2 *Follow The Music* transcripts, Gavan Daws
3 *Follow The Music* transcripts, Gavan Daws
4 *Follow The Music* transcripts, Gavan Daws
5 Dave Van Ronk *The Mayor Of MacDougal Street* (Da Capo Press 2006)
6 Dave Van Ronk *The Mayor Of MacDougal Street* (Da Capo Press 2006)
7 *Follow The Music* transcripts, Gavan Daws

CHAPTER 7

1 *Follow The Music* transcripts, Gavan Daws
2 *Hearings Regarding Communist Infiltration of Minority Groups*, Part 1, 81st Congress
3 Elijah Wald *Josh White – Society Blues* (Routledge 2002)
4 Max Gordon *Live At The Village Vanguard* (Da Capo 1980)
5 Robert Cantwell *When We Were Good* (Harvard University Press 1996)
6 Elijah Wald *Josh White – Society Blues* (Routledge 2002)
7 The Estate of Josh White and the Josh White Archives; Douglas A. Yeader Productions Ltd
8 *Follow The Music* transcripts, Gavan Daws
9 *The Independent* January 15 1999 by Jennifer Rodger
10 Elijah Wald *Josh White – Society Blues* (Routledge 2002)
11 David Crosby & Carl Gottlieb *Long Time Gone* (Doubleday 1988)

CHAPTER 8

1 Robert Cantwell *When We Were Good* (Harvard University Press 1996)
2 Theodore Bikel *Theo* (Harper Collins 1994)
3 Liner notes Theodore Bikel *Songs Of Russia Old & New/Songs Of A Russian Gypsy* (Collectors Choice 2005) by Richie Unterberger
4 Liner notes Theodore Bikel *Songs Of Russia Old & New/Songs Of A Russian Gypsy* (Collectors Choice 2005) by Richie Unterberger
5 *Jac Holzman's Elektra Story* (BBC Radio 2, April 2008)
6 *Follow The Music* transcripts, Gavan Daws
7 *Follow The Music* transcripts, Gavan Daws

CHAPTER 10

1 *Phil Ochs: Still Marching* (BBC Radio 2, 2008)
2 Michael Schumacher *There But For Fortune: The Life Of Phil Ochs* (Hyperion 1996)
3 Bob Gibson & Carole Bender *I Come For To Sing* (Firebird 2008)
4 Bob Gibson & Carole Bender *I Come For To Sing* (Firebird 2008)
5 Bob Gibson & Carole Bender *I Come For To Sing* (Firebird 2008)
6 Bob Gibson & Carole Bender *I Come For To Sing* (Firebird 2008)
7 Liner notes Bob Camp *Paths Of Victory* (Collector's Choice 2001) by Richie Unterberger
8 Bob Gibson & Carole Bender *I Come For To Sing* (Firebird 2008)
9 *Follow The Music* transcripts, Gavan Daws

CHAPTER 11

1 *Follow The Music* transcripts, Gavan Daws
2 *Follow The Music* transcripts, Gavan Daws
3 *Follow The Music* transcripts, Gavan Daws
4 Robert Cantwell *When We Were Good* (Harvard University Press 1996)
5 Dave Van Ronk *The Mayor Of MacDougal Street* (Da Capo 2006)

CHAPTER 12

1 *Follow The Music* transcripts, Gavan Daws
2 Dave Van Ronk *The Mayor Of MacDougal Street* (Da Capo 2006)
3 *Rock'n'Reel* June 2008 by Johnny Black
4 Bob Gibson & Carole Bender *I Come For To Sing* (Firebird 2008)
5 Booklet notes Various Artists *Forever Changing* (Rhino 2006) by Peter Doggett
6 Booklet notes Various Artists *Forever Changing* (Rhino 2006) by Peter Doggett
7 Booklet notes Various Artists *Forever Changing* (Rhino 2006) by Peter Doggett
8 *Follow The Music* transcripts, Gavan Daws
9 Booklet notes Various Artists *Forever Changing* (Rhino 2006) by Peter Doggett
10 *Follow The Music*

CHAPTER 13

1 *Follow The Music* transcripts, Gavan Daws
2 *Follow The Music* transcripts, Gavan Daws
3 Booklet notes Various Artists *Forever Changing* (Rhino 2006) by Peter Doggett
4 Booklet notes Koerner Ray & Glover *Lots More Blues Rags And Hollers* (Red House 1998) by Tony Glover
5 *Follow The Music* transcripts, Gavan Daws
6 Richie Havens *They Can't Hide Us Anymore* (Avon 1999)
7 *Follow The Music* transcripts, Gavan Daws
8 Booklet notes Various Artists *Forever Changing* (Rhino 2006) by Peter Doggett
9 *Mojo* February 2000 by Ben Edmonds
10 *Mojo* February 2000 by Ben Edmonds
11 Booklet notes Various Artists *Forever Changing* (Rhino 2006) by Peter Doggett
12 Interview by Max Bell, November 2009
13 *Mojo Collections*

CHAPTER 14

1 *Follow The Music* transcripts, Gavan Daws
2 *Follow The Music* transcripts, Gavan Daws
3 *Follow The Music* transcripts, Gavan Daws

CHAPTER 15

1 J. Marks & Linda Eastman *Rock And Other Four Letter Words* (Bantam 1968)
2 *Follow The Music* transcripts, Gavan Daws
3 *Follow The Music* transcripts, Gavan Daws
4 *Follow The Music* transcripts, Gavan Daws
5 *Rolling Stone* October 1971 by Aaron Fuchs
6 *Follow The Music* transcripts, Gavan Daws
7 *Follow The Music* transcripts, Gavan Daws

CHAPTER 16

1 Ellen Sander *Trips* (Scribners 1973)
2 Michael Stuart-Ware *Love Behind The Scenes On The Pegasus Carousel* (Helter Skelter 2003)
3 *Follow The Music* transcripts, Gavan Daws
4 *Follow The Music* transcripts, Gavan Daws
5 *The Big Takeover* Summer 2012 by Daniel Coston
6 *The Big Takeover* Summer 2012 by Daniel Coston
7 *The Big Takeover* Summer 2012 by Daniel Coston
8 Sandy Pearlman in Jonathan Eisen (editor) *Twenty-Minute Fandangos And Forever Changes* (Vintage Books 1971)
9 *The Big Takeover* Summer 2012 by Daniel Coston
10 *The Big Takeover* Summer 2012 by Daniel Coston
11 *The Big Takeover* Summer 2012 by Daniel Coston
12 *Rolling Stone* February 1968 by Jim Bickhart
13 Barney Hoskyns *Waiting For The Sun* (Viking 1996)
14 *The Big Takeover* Summer 2012 by Daniel Coston

CHAPTER 17

1 Ken Hunt *Joe Boyd, The Unpublished Interview*, March 2006
2 Booklet notes *Elektrock/The Sixties* (Elektra, 1985), by Lenny Kaye
3 Joe Boyd *White Bicycles* (Serpents Tail Press 2005)
4 Joe Boyd Newsletter January 2016
5 *Sound On Sound* November 2011
6 Booklet notes *Elektrock/The Sixties* (Elektra, 1985) by Lenny Kaye
7 Jon Savage *1966: The Year The Decade Exploded* (Faber 2015)
8 *Rock History* (rockhistory.co.uk) August 2012 by Mark Rye

CHAPTER 18

1 *Follow The Music* transcripts, Gavan Daws
2 *Follow The Music* transcripts, Gavan Daws
3 *Follow The Music* transcripts, Gavan Daws

CHAPTER 19

1 *Zigzag* No. 44, No. 48 1974 by Andy Childs
2 *Zigzag* No. 44, No. 48 1974 by Andy Childs

3 www.timbuckleyandfriends.com
4 *Uncut* July 2007 by Dave Cavanagh
5 *Uncut* July 2007 by Dave Cavanagh
6 *Zigzag* No. 25 1972 by John Tobler
7 Essay for unreleased set David Ackles *There Is A River* (Rhino 2007) by Bernie Taupin
8 Elektra press release for *American Gothic*
9 Essay for unreleased set David Ackles *There Is A River* (Rhino 2007) by Bernie Taupin

CHAPTER 20

1 Booklet notes Various Artists *Forever Changing* (Rhino 2006) by Peter Doggett
2 *Follow The Music* transcripts, Gavan Daws
3 Joe Ziemer *Mickey Newbury Crystal And Stone* (Authorhouse 2004)
4 *Follow The Music* transcripts, Gavan Daws
5 Booklet notes Nico *The Frozen Borderline 1968–1970* (Rhino 2007) by Simon Goddard
6 *Zigzag* No. 50 1975 by Kenneth Ansell

CHAPTER 21

1 Liner notes to MC5 *Kick Out The Jams* by John Sinclair
2 Paul Trynka *Iggy Pop Open Up And Bleed* (Sphere 2007)
3 Roy Wilkinson July 2009
4 *Classic Rock* July 2015 by Max Bell

CHAPTER 22

1 *Follow The Music* transcripts, Gavan Daws
2 *Rolling Stone* April 1971 by Timothy Crouse
3 *Follow The Music* transcripts, Gavan Daws
4 *Follow The Music* transcripts, Gavan Daws
5 *Uncut* November 2015 by Tom Pinnock

CHAPTER 23

1 Stan Cornyn *Exploding: The Highs, Hits, Hype, Heroes, And Hustlers Of The Warner Music Group* (Harper Entertainment 2002)
2 Stan Cornyn *Exploding: The Highs, Hits, Hype, Heroes, And Hustlers Of The Warner Music Group* (Harper Entertainment 2002)
3 Fred Goodman *The Mansion On The Hill* (Vintage 1998)

APPENDIX 1

1 *Follow The Music* transcripts, Gavan Daws

Index

Words *in italics* indicate album titles unless otherwise stated. Words 'in quotes' indicate song titles. Page numbers in **bold** indicate photographs.

Abramson, Mark, 9, 50, **102**, 105, 120, 122–4, 126, 159–60, 180, 189, 209, 219, 292, 325, 337, 350
Abramson, Robert, 68
Absolutely Live, 258
AC/DC, 360
Accept No Substitute, 284–5, 298
Ackles, David, 8, 17, 228, 245, 262, 271–4, 276, 284, 286, 333–4
Ackles, Janice, 107, 180
Acquaye, Saka & His African Ensemble, 107, 180
Adagio For Strings & Organ, 177
Adventures For 12-String, String And Banjo, 60
Adventures Of A Ballad Hunter (book), 45
Ain't That News!, 143
'Alabama Song', 15
Alabama State Troupers & The Mount Zion Choir & Band, The, 288
'Albatross', 264
Alexander, Dave, 303–4
'All My Trials', 289
All The News That's Fit To Sing, 114, 138, 147, 156
Allen, Woody, 54, 131, 217
Almanac Singers, The, 33, 37, 48, 52–3, 76, 192
'Almost Grown', 200
'Alone Again Or', 8, 224–5
'Always See Your Face', 227
Amazing Blondel, 245
'Amazing Grace', 118, 264
Amdurski, Benny, 106
American Folk Songs, 34, 45, 50, 144
American Gothic, 273
American Prayer, An, 292, 330
American Revolution, The, 191
'American Trilogy, An', 289
AMM Music, 240
Ancient Voices Of Children, 184

Anderle, David, 10, **204**, 225, 271, 284–5, 294, 314, 324–5, 346
Andersen, Eric, 120, 123, 141, 144, 274
Anderson, Laurie, 187
'Andmoreagain', 222
'Anecdote Of Horatio And Julie, The', 296
Angel, David, 222, 224
Anglo, Steve, *see* Winwood, Steve
Animals, The, 197, 236
Anka, Paul, 170
Anthology Of American Folk Music, The, 55, 65, 132, 161
Anticipation, 325, 327
'Any Day Woman', 275
'Apricot Brandy', 283
Arkin, Alan, 58, 68, 95, 114
Arnold, Eddy, 288
Arnold, Jerome, 200
Ars Nova, 280, 297, 340
Ars Nova, 280
Art Of The Five-String Banjo, 58
Art Of The Koto, 72, 107, 180
Arthur Lee And Love, 4, 9, 228
Asch, Moe, 32, 63, 73, 76, 85, 132–3, 151, 181, 189
Ash Grove (club), 89
Asheton, Ron, 10, 302–3
Asheton, Scott, 10, 304–5
Ashley, Ted, 335
Asylum (label), 127, 293–4, 341–2, 347, 357–9
Atlantic (label), 8, 11, 17, 28, 187, 235, 285, 302, 315, 323–4, 335, 341–3, 347, 350, 357, 359–61
Atomic Rooster, 331
Audience, 331
Au-Go-Go Singers, The, 109
'August', 227
Authentic Sound Effects, 14, 96, 175–6
Axton, Hoyt, 60, 170

Baby Browning, 293
Baby I'm-A Want You, 315
'Baby I'm-A Want You',
Back In The USA, 302
Bad Men And Heroes, 66–7
Baez, Joan, 10, 13, 51, 68, 88, 111–12, 117, 120–1, 125, 129, 135–6, 139–40, 146, 150–1, 234
Baker, Etta, 134
Baker, Ginger, 200, 238
Balalaika, 90, 106, 235
'Ballad Of Sammy's Bar', 237
Ballad Record, The, 67
Bamboo, 293
'Banana Boat Song, The', 96, 114
Bannister, Georgiana, 24
'Barbara Allen', 34
Barber, Chris, 83
Barham, John, 12, 356
Baroque Beatles Book, The, 162, 187–8
Baroque Trumpet, The, 177
Barrett, Syd, 241
Bartók, Bela, 25
Bartók, Peter, 25, 79
'Battle Hymn Of The Republic', 289
Bawdy Songs And Backroom Ballads, 69
Beach Boys, The, 182, 215, 316
Beatle Country, 164
Beatles, The, 162, 187–8, 196–9, 213, 278, 285, 315
Beaver, Paul, 184–6, 193–5
Beckett, Larry, 11, 265–6, 269, 276, 278
Beefeaters, The, 199
Beefheart, Captain, 314
Belafonte, Harry, 53, 69, 74, 81, 96
Bell Ringing In The Empty Sky, A, 182
Bell, Thom, 346–7
Berry, Chuck, 168, 200, 228, 286
Best Little Whorehouse In Texas, The (musical), 334
Best Of Lord Buckley, The, 128
Bethlehem (record label), 31, 107
Better Days, 213
Bido Lito's (club), 14, 217
'Big Rock Candy Mountain', 34
Bikel, Theodore, 9, 14, 35, 38, 45, 50, 54, 57, 58, 60, 72, 84–7, 92–3, **99**, **100**, 105–6, 112, 119, 128, 234, 326
'Bird Song', 294
Bishop, Elvin, 10, 200, 209–14
Bishop, Randy, 350
Bither, David, 187
Bitter End (club), 140, 149, 171
Bizarre (label), 131, 347
Black Beauty, 228
'Black Is The Color', 34
Blackwell, Bumps, 115
Blakey, Art, 107
Blakley, Ronee, 334
Bleecker & MacDougal, 168, 170, 172
Block, Allan, 35, 164
Block, Rory, 190, 282
Blood 'N Bones, 67
Bloomfield, Mike, 196, 209, 235, 252
'Blowin' In The Wind', 122, 139, 151
Blue Afternoon, 270
Blue Angel (club), 54, 75
Blue Note (label), 107, 234
Blue Oyster Cult, 180, 319
'Blue Tail Fly', 22, 34
Blue Thumb (label), 227
Blue, David, 164, 198, 342
'Blues On The Ceiling', 171
Blues Project, The (band), 137, 198
Blues Project, The, 163–4, 238
Blues, Rags And Hollers, 158, 160–2, 277
Blues Till Dawn, 75
Bobby Burns' Merry Muses Of Caledonia, 66
Boetcher, Curt, 352
'Bohemian Rhapsody', 337
Bohemians, The, 265, 277

Bolcom, William, 184
Bonny Bunch Of Roses, The, 134
Boone, Pat, 268
Boone, Steve, 199
Bootleg Series, 123
'Born In Chicago', 209
'Both Sides Now', 125, 264
Botnick, Bruce, 5, 8, 10, **201**, **202**, 219, 220, 222, 248, 251, 259, 267, 271–2, 286, 299, 314, 316, 324–5
Botts, Mike, 315
Bouchard, Albert, 318
Bowie, David, 231, 313, 339
'Boy Named Sue, A', 108
Boyd, Joe, 10–12, 18, 200, 229–30, 233–4, 236, 240–2
Brackman, Jacob, 326
Bramlett, Delaney, 168, 284–5
Brand, Oscar, 39, 42, 54–5, 58, 62, 66, 68, 71, 74, 79, 81, 111, 114, 135, 140–1, 161, 234
Brandt, Jerry, 338
Braunstein, Les, 317, 319
Bread, 17, 262, 313–16, 329, 342–2, 354
Bread, 315
'Break On Through', 17, 248–50, 337, 335
'Breakfast In Bed', 355
Brickman, Marshall, 56, 59
Broadside (magazine), 74, 122, 132, 147, 262
Brodsky, Joel, 92, 254
Bromberg, David, 274–5
Bronfman Jr, Edgar, 360–1
Broozny, Big Bill, 53, 74, 83
Brothers & Sisters, 327
Brothers Four, The, 109
Browne, Jackson, 190, 263, 292–3, 295, 297, 342–3, 354, 357–8
Bruce, Jack, 200, 238
Bruce, Lenny, 54, 89, 130, 170, 256
Bryson, Peabo, 359
Buchanan, Ian, 164
Buckley, Lord, 128, 347
Buckley, Tim, 4–5, 7, 9, 11, 17–18, 124, 150, 168, 172, 181, **203**, 228, 239–41, 245, 262, 265, 267–8, 271, 276, 283, 289, 330, 349, 354
Buffalo Springfield, 109, 216–17, 283, 315, 360
Bunyan, Vashti, 238
Burdon, Eric, 236
'Burning Love', 290–1
Burrell, Web, 352
Burton, James, 264
Bushler, Herb, 191
Butler, Joe, 199
Butler, Michael, 228
Butterfield, Paul, 4–5, 7, 14–16, **104**, 151, 160, 196, 200, 210, 213, 234, 301, 330
'Buzzin' Fly', 269
Byrds, The, 4, 109, 116, 121, 131, 185, 196, 198, 215, 217, 219, 235, 251, 261, 316, 352

Caedmon (record label), 30–1 134
Café Society (club), 53, 74, 77, 80–1
Café Society Uptown (club), 48, 53
Cale, John, 231, 295, 303
Cambridge Electric Opera Company, The, 296
Camp, Hamilton (aka Bob Camp), 113–14, 116–118
Campbell, Ian, Folk Group, The, 152, 236
Canby, Edward Tatnall, 36
'Candy Man', 171
Cannon, Gus, 59, 165
'Cantata For The Third Saturday After Shea Stadium', 188
Cantrelli, Tjay, 220
Capital City Rockets, 355
Capital City Rockets, 354
Caren, Mike, 361
Carignan, Jean, 152
Carl & The Passions, 182
Carly Simon, 326, 327, 334
Carolinians, The, 33, 76, 80
Carpenters, The, 314
Carter, Elliott, 184
Carter, Sydney, 237
Carthy, Martin, 236–7
Casey Kelly, 354
Cash, Johnny, 108, 289
'Castle, The', 221
'Cat's In The Cradle', 328–9
Cee-Lo, 361
'Celebration Of The Lizard', 258
Chain Gang, 33
Chain Gang Songs, 33–4, 80, 83
Challenge, 241
Chandler, Len, 91, 170
Changes, 199
'Changes', 147, 156
Chapin Brothers, The, 327
Chapin, Harry, 4, 17, **206,** 327–9, 334, 338, 342–3, 345, 359
Chapin, Stephen, 327
Chapin, Tom, 327
Charles River Valley Boys, The, 135, 164, 319
Charles, Ray, 82, 170
Charles, Teddy, 107
Cheatham, Bill, 302, 304
Chelsea Girl, 293–4
Chess, Leonard, 28, 83
Chess, Phil, 28, 83
Child, Marilyn, 110
'Children Of Tomorrow' 244
Child's Garden Of Grass, A, 333, 349
'Chords Of Fame', 150
'Cindy Oh Cindy', 96, 170
Circle Game, The, 168, 263, 297
'Circle Game, The', 263
Clancy Brothers, The, 32, 54–5, 119–20, 134
Clancy Brothers & Tommy Makem, The, 55, 134
Clapton, Eric, 32, 81, 200, 236, 238–9, 285
Clapton, Eric & The Powerhouse, 200, 238
Clark, Gene, 109, 199
Clayre, Alasdair, 237–9
Clayton, Paul, 57, 66, 134–5
Clear Light, 8, 280–2, 324

Clear Light, 281
Clorfene, Richard, 333
Club 47 (club), 112, 135, 155, 165, 296, 319
Clyde, Jonathan, 356
Coasters, The, 200
Cohen, David, *see* Blue, David
Cohen, Herb, 10, 17, 88–9, 130–1, 169–71, 173, 218, 226, 265, 269–70, 276
Cohen, John, 56–7, 63, 150, 164
Cohen, Leonard, 4, 124, 264, 295
Cohen, Mike, 56
Cold Wind Blows, A, **203**, 236, 237
Collection Of Ballads, Folk And, Country Songs, A, 34
Collins, Carter C.C., 268
Collins, Judy, 4, 10, 13–14, 16, 18–19, 34, 51, **101**, **102**, 105, 112–13, 116, 118–20, 124–5, 127, 142, 165, 198, **204**, **207**, 234–5, 238, 241, 262, 264–5, 268, 284, 292, 301, 325–6, 329, 334, 342, 357, 359
Collins, Phil, 272
Coltrane, John, 11, 210, 321
Columbia (record label), 4–5, 7, 16–17, 28, 33, 39, 49, 76, 80, 119, 132, 134, 151, 179, 199, 218, 228, 263, 271, 273, 274, 296, 313, 319, 328–9, 338, 342, 352, 357
'Come Away Melinda', 91, 120,
Conka, Don, 219
Contemporary (record label), 31, 220
Contemporary Folk Music Journey, A, 352
Conway, Gerry, 11–12, 242–4
Cooder, Ry, 82, 154, 187, 358
Coolidge, Rita, 284
Cooper, Dana, 354
Copperfields, 129, 347
Cosmo Alley (club), 89, 110, 130
Cough! Army Songs Out Of The Barracks Bag, 71
Country Blues, The, 161
Country Joe & The Fish, 137, 211
Countryside (label), 333–4, 356
Court, John, 212
Cowboy Songs And Negro Spirituals, 34
Crabby Appleton, 304, 332, 346, 355
Creatures Of The Street, 339
Crestview (label), 108, 128
Crosby Stills & Nash, 172, 264, 315, 342, 350, 352
Crosby, David, 82, 109, 115, 172–3, 199
Crow Dog's Paradise, 262, 348
Crumb, George, 184
'Cryin'', 171
Cullinan, Ralph, 48
Cumberland Three, The, 109
Cuney, Waring, 33
Cynthia Gooding Sings Turkish And Spanish Folk Songs, 50

D'Amato, Maria, 59, 165
D'Urfey, Thomas, 67–8
Da Capo, 7, 13, 124, 220–2, 239
'Daily Planet, The', 222–3
Dana Cooper, 354
Dandelion (label), 331–2
Dane, Barbara, 60, 134
Darin, Bobby, 120, 170, 360
Darling Family, The, 129
Darling, Erik, 56, 58–9, 68, 95, 114, 120, 134
David & Lee, 314
David Blue, 164, 198, 342
Davis, Clive, 296, 319, 328
Davis, Maxwell Street Jimmie, 154
Davis, Michael, 299
Davis, Miles, 199, 254, 268, 277
Davis, Reverend Gary, 54
Dear You, 228
Decca (label), 7, 28–9, 34–5, 53, 74–5, 235
Delaney & Bonnie, 284–6, 298
Denny, Sandy, 11, 229, 239, 244
Densmore, John, 4, 6, 10, 12, 255, 259, 330
Deren, Maya, 72
DeShannon, Jackie, 60
Dián & The Greenbriar Boys, 129
Dickson, Jim, 118, 128
Diddley, Bo, 168
'Diddy Wah Diddy', 314
Dillard, Doug, 60
Dillard, Rodney, 129
Dillards, The, 129, 347
Dinwiddie, Gene, 212
'Dismal Day', 315
Divine Horsemen (book), 72
'Dixie', 289, 291, 353
'Dixie Chicken', 353
'Do Re Mi', 154
Doheny, Ned, 292
Dolenz, Micky, 185
'Dolphins, The', 171, 267, 269, 278
Donegan, Lonnie, 82
Donicht, Will, 293
Donnellan, Jay, 227
'Don't Be Long', 199
Doors Are Open, The (TV show), 246, 254
Doors, The, 4–5, 7–9, 13–18, 61, 88, 92, 124, 144, 148, 151, 160, 163, 176, 180, 197, **201**, 209, 215, 217–19, 225–6, 239–41, 245–265, 280–2, 284, 287, 297, 299, 301–2, 304, 316–17, 321, 323–4, 328, 330, 337–8, 342–3
Doors, The, 4, 124, 248–9, 253
'Dorogoy Dalnoyu', 88
'Down On The Street', 298, 304
'Down River', 272
Drake, Nick, 229, 239
'Dream', 227
'Dress Rehearsal Rag', 124

Dry City Scat Band, The, 164
Dudaim, 106
Dudaim, The, 106
Dudgeon, Gus, 331
Dueling Banjos, 52, 59
'Dueling Banjos', 59
Dyer-Bennet, Richard, 21–2, 34, 53–4, 69, 74
Dylan, Bob, 19, 22, 33, 51, 57, 69, 81, 88, 91, 115–18, 120, 122, 138–140, 146–7, 150, 160, 164, 196, 214, 235, 267–7, 328, 343, 357

Eagles, The, 342, 347, 358
'Early Morning Rain', 123
Earth Opera, 164, 181, 191, **206**, 319–21, 340
Earth Opera, 181, 320
East-West, 7, 160, 210, 212
'East-West', 210–11
Echols, John, 217, 219–21, 224, 228
Eclection, 242–4
Ed McCurdy Sings Songs Of The Canadian Maritimes And Newfoundland, 67
Ed Sullivan Show, The (TV show), 252–3
Efron, Marshall, 192
Electra Glide In Blue (movie), 151
Electric Flag, The, 212
Electric Music For The Mind And Body, 137
Elektra Playback System Calibration Record, 96
Elektra UK, **203**, 229, 233–6, 238–9, 241–2, 245–6, 331, 355, 356
Elliott, Cass, 129
Elliott, Ramblin' Jack, 19, 54, 57, 66, 135, 277
Emmons, Buddy, 275, 347
Empty Bed Blues, 81, 83
En Vogue, 360
Encores From The Abbaye, 94
'End, The', 155, 248, 252, 253, 254–5
English And American Folksongs, 110
Ennis, Seamus, 134
'Epstein Variations, MBE 69a', 188
Erik Darling, 56, 58–9, 68, 95, 114, 120, 134
Ertegun, Ahmet, 17, 28, 323, 330, 341–2, 345
Ertegun, Nesuhi, 323
Eto, Kimio, 107
Even Dozen Jug Band, The, 59, 160, 164–6, 179, 189, 192, 235, 320
Evening With Salvador Allende, An, 157
Everly Brothers, The, 168, 314
Every Inch A Sailor, 58, 71
'Everybody's Talkin'', 170–1, 173
'Everything I Own', 315

Faier, Billy, 56, 58, 135
'Fairest Of The Seasons, The', 293
Fairport Convention, 8, 229, 231, 244, 331, 353
Faithfull, Marianne, 163, 230, 235
False Start, 227
Fantasy (record label), 31
Farewell Aldebaran, 131, 353
Fariña, Richard, 120, 122–3, 151, 164
Faryar, Cyrus, 10, 60, 168, 185–6, 333–4
Fastest Balalaika In The West, 106
Fawcett, Jim, 72
Feiten, Buzz, 212
Felix, Julie, 142
Festival In Haiti, 72
Field Trip, 40, 43
Fielder, Jim, 265–6, 276
Fields, Danny, 10, 17, 61, 191, 294–5, 298–301, 303, 313, 315, 324
Fifth Album, 71, 120, 122–3
Fireside Book Of Folk Songs, 45
Five And Dime, 274
Five & Twenty Questions, 151
Five String Serenade, 228
5000 Spirits Or The Layers Of The Onion, The, 7, 230
'Five To One', 255
Flamenco Guitar Solos, 72
'Flower Lady', 156
Foc'sle Songs And Shanties, 66
Foggy Foggy Dew, The, 22, 34
Folk Banjo Styles, 59, 64, 235, 347
Folk Music Sampler, The, 95
Folk Song Kit, 58
Folk Songs (And 2 1/2 That Aren't) – Once Over Lightly, 96
Folk Songs From Just About Everywhere, 58, 88, 93
Folk Songs From The Southern Appalachian Mountains, 57
Folk Songs Of Israel, 84, 86
Folklore Center (music store), 59, 140, 154
Folksinger's Choice, A, 91
Folksingers Choice (radio programme), 51
Folksingers, The, 51, 59
Folksong Festival (radio programme), 42, 69
Folksong '65, 209
Folkways (record label), 32–3, 40, 55, 64, 66, 73, 132–3, 137, 150, 161, 183, 189, 238
'Follow The Drinking Gourd', 110
Fonfara, Michael, 271, 283
Fool, The, 230
'Fooled Around And Fell In Love', 213
'For All We Know', 314
Forever Changes, 4, 18, 164, 221–2, 224–5, 227–8, 259
Forrsi, Ken, 219
Fotheringay, 240, 244,
Four Freshmen, The, 109
Frady, Garland, 334
Frank Warner Sings American,
Folk Songs And Ballads, 45
Fred Neil, 170, 172

Freewheelin' Bob Dylan, The, 139, 172
Friedman, Barry, *see* Mohawk, Frazier
Frisco Mabel Joy, 289–90
Frost And Fire, 152
Frye, David, 347
Full Circle, 330
Fun House, 302, 304, 346
Furay, Richie, 109

Gallucci, Don, 304
'Galveston Flood', 168
Gamble & Huff, 346–7
Gandharva, 185
Garcia, Jerry, 211, 321
Garson, Mort, 185, 194, 239
Gaslight, The (club), 140–1, 143, 145
Gate Of Horn, The (club), 80, 108, 113, 115–16, 119, 134, 139, 170
Gates, David, 10, 314
Gateway Singers, The, 109–10
Geffen, David, 264, 331, 333–4, 339, 341–2, 347, 353, 357
Gellert, Lawrence, 34
Genuine Rosmini, A, 60
George, Lowell, 210, 353
Gerde's Folk City (club), 138, 140
'Get Together', 43, 118
Gibson, Bob, 9, 54, 56, 60, **101**, 108, 111–14, 117, 135, 144, 170, 197, 235
Gibson, Don, 288
Gibson & Camp At The Gate Of Horn, 108
Gilbert, Ronnie, 35
Gill, Geula, 58, 88
Glad I'm In The Band, 286
Glanz, Paul, 327
Glenn Yarbrough, 55, **100**, 110, 115
'Gloomy Sunday', 80
Glover, Jim, 146, 199
Glover, Tony 'Little Sun', 161
Gnarls Barkley, 361
'Go Back', 332, 346
'Gob Is A Slob, A', 69
'God Bless America For What?', 348
'Going To The Zoo', 145
Gold Coast Saturday Night, 72, 107
Golden Apple, The (musical), 108, 120–1
Golden Apples Of The Sun, 120
Golden Rain, 182
Goldmark, Peter, 29, 335
Goldstein, Ken, 32, 41, 46, 49–50, 62, 134
'Gonna Fly Now', 353
'Good Old Wagon', 130
'Good Time Music', 200
Goodbye And Hello, 8, 18, 266–9, 278
Gooding, Cynthia, 9, 36, 42, 48–9, 51, 55, 65, 74, 88, 99, **105**, 111
'Goodnight Irene', 106
Goodthunder, 324
Gordon, Jim, 315
Gordon, Max, 52, 54, 76
Gorson, Arthur, 146–7
Gospel Pearls, The, 115
Gottlieb, Lou, **100**, 110
Graham, Bill, 256, 300
Grateful Dead, The, 154, 211, 231, 251, 282, 350
Graubard, Susan, 180, 191
Grauer, Bill, 32, 134
Gravenites, Nick, 200
Great American Eagle Tragedy, The, 181, 320, 321
Great Stampede, The, 331, 353
Greatest Hits (Phil Ochs), 148–9
Greenbriar Boys, The, 129
Greene, Jeanie, 287–8, 349, 350
Greene, Marlin, 287–8, 349, 350–1, 354
Greene, Richard, 164, 275, 321
Grenfell, Joyce, 108
'Grief In My Soul', 266
Griffin, James, 314, 316
Grisman, Dave, 164–5
Grossman, Albert, 88, 112, 115, 122, 139, 212, 247
Grossman, Bob, 129
Grossman, Stefan, 11–12, 59, 158, 165–6, 180, 190, 282
Gruen, John, 24–7
Guard, Dave, 130
Guercio, James, 151
'Guess I'm Doin' Fine', 118
Guitar Man, 316
Gulliver, 346–7
Gulliver, 346
Gurvin, Abe, 186, 340
Guryon, Adam, 106
Guthrie, Arlo, 19
Guthrie, Woody, 19, 21, 32–4, 37, 43, 45, 48, 53, 57, 66, 69, 73, 75–6, 82, 91, 122, 133, 144, 146, 154–5, 167, 192, 340
'Guy Is A Guy, A', 69
'Gypsy Rover, The', 34

Haeny, John, 292, 296, 325, 330
Hall, Annie, 131
Hall, Carol, 334
Hall, Daryl, 346–7
'Hallucinations', 267, 277
Hamilton, Diane, 32, 65, 134
Hamilton, Frank, 56
Hammer In A Cowboy Band, 334
'Hammer Song, The', 35, 110
Hammond, John, 33, 80, 119, 132, 198
Handle, Johnny, 236
Hangman's Beautiful Daughter, The, 18, 230
Happy All The Time, 151, 153–4, 181
Happy Sad, 262, 266, 268–9
Hard Day's Night, A (movie), 197
Hardin, Tim, 137, 278, 295
Hargrove, Linda, 355
Harris, Emmylou, 187, 356
Harris, Steve, **102**, 220, 250

Harrison, George, 162, 185, 356
Harrison, Spencer, 335
Harvest Of Israeli Folksongs, A, 86
Harvey, Bill, 9–10, 55, 67, 95, 99, 101–2, 104, 121, 126–8, 176, 178, 219, 240, 249, 254, 285, 299, 301, 313, 315, 342
Hassilev Alex, **101**, 110, 185
Hastings, Doug, 271, 283
Have A Marijuana, 61, 191, 297
Havens, Richie, 10, 82, 113, 115, 131, 137, 164
Hays, Lee, 33, 35, 74, 193,
'He Come Down', 182
Heads & Tales, 329
Heath, Gordon, 93–4
Heaven Help The Child, 290
Hellerman, Fred, 13, 33, 35, 58, 90–1, **100**, 120
'Hello I Love You', 245, 255
Henske, Judy, 129–30, 171, 197, 266, 326, 353
Herald, John, 129
Here We Go, Baby!, 110
Heron, Mike, 10, 203, 229–31
Hester, Carolyn, 68
Hewett, Howard, 359
'Hey Joe', 217, 249
High Flying Bird, 131
'High Flying Bird', 131
High Llamas, The, 228
Highway 61 Revisited, 162, 196, 198
Highwaymen, The, 109
Hillel & Aviva, 105, 107
Hills Of Indiana, The, 288
Hobday, Stuart, 245
Holdridge, Barbara, 30
Holly, Buddy, 168, 170–1
Holman, Libby, 75
Holy Modal Rounders, 280, 294, 297
Holzman, Jac: birth, 20; education, 20–1; founds Elektra, 24–5; opens record store, 26; invents the sampler album, 95; launches Nonesuch, 177–8; starts Elektra UK, 229; opens West Coast office and studio, 279–80; merges Elektra with Warner Bros and Atlantic, 322–4; leaves Elektra, 340–2; post-Elektra career, 343–4; photographs of, **98**, **100**, **102**, **104**, **202**, **205**, **206**, **207**, **208**
Holzman, Keith, **102**, 177, 182, 187, 359
Holzman, Nina (née Merrick), 95, **102**, 127, 324
Home Again, 265
'Home To You', 321
Hootenanny (TV show), 137, 139
Hopkins, John, 229, 237, 240
Hopkins, Lightnin', 134, 158
Hot Wacks, 332, 350
Hotcakes, 327
'House I Live In, The', 76
House On The Hill, The, 331
How To Play Blues Guitar, 190, 282
How To Play The Five-String Banjo (book), 45
Hull, Alan, 331
hungry i (club), 80, 139
Hurok, Sol, 106–8, 179
Hurwitz, Bob, 182, 187

'I Ain't Got No Home', 154
I Ain't Marching Anymore, 147
'I Ain't Marching Anymore', 146, 198
'I Am Woman', 327
'I Bid You Goodnight', 231
I Came To Hear The Music, 290
'I Can't Help But Wonder Where I'm Bound', 143
I Come For To Sing (book), 114
'I Got A Mind To Give Up Living', 210
'I Wanna Be Your Dog', 304
'I Wanna Hold Your Hand', 196
'I Wonder As I Wander', 34
Ian Campbell Folk Group, The, 152, 236
Ian, Janis, 137
'If', 315
If I Be Your Lady, 334
'I'll Keep It With Mine', 123, 235
In A Wild Sanctuary, 185, 195
In Concert, 146–8, 189
In My Life, 122–4, 200, 238, 264, 289
'In My Life', 197
In My Own Dream, 212
In Search Of Amelia Earhart, 353
'In This White World', 115
'In This Wide World', 115
Incredible String Band, The, 7, 9, 18, 154, 203, 229–32, 237, 239–42, 330–1, 349
Incredible String Band, The, 7, 9
Intergalactic Trot, 354
Iron Muse, The, 152, 236
Italian Folk Songs, 50
Ives, Burl, 21–2, 32, 34, 53, 69, 71, 74–5, 77, 85

'Jack-A-Roe', 58
Jack-Knife Gypsy, 275
Jackson, Aunt Molly, 75
Jacobs, Ron 'Whodaguy', 333
Jagger, Mick, 222, 230, 303, 339
James, Billy, 284
James, Dián, 128
Janick, John, 361
Jazz At The Movies Band, 234–5
Jazz Messengers, The, 107
Jazzology (record label), 31
Jean Ritchie Singing The Traditional Songs Of Her Kentucky Mountain Family, 36
Jean Shepherd And Other Foibles, 108
Jefferson Airplane, 131, 171, 211, 246, 251, 283

'Jelly Jelly', 76
Jenner, Peter, 240–1
'Jennifer's Rabbit', 145
Jennings, Waylon, 275, 289
Jim & Jean, 146, 199
Jobriath, 9, 338–9
Jobriath, 339, 354
John, Elton, 272, 339
John Henry (musical show), 78
Johnson, Lonnie, 170
Jones, David A., 105, 126
Jones, Paul, 200, 238
Joplin, Janis, 258, 283, 350
Joplin, Scott, 183
Josh At Midnight, 79, 235
Josh Sings Ballads And Blues, 80
Josh White Guitar Method, The (book), 82
'Joshua Gone Barbados', 168
Journeymen, The, 45, 109
Jubal, 290–1
Judith, 264–5, 357
Judy Collins 3, **101**, 120, 127
Judy Collins Concert, 120
Judy Henske, 129–30
Jugalbandi, 356
'Just Dropped In (To See What Condition My Condition Was In)', 288

Kagan, Michael, 88
Kalb, Danny, 137, 164
Kajanus, Georg, 11–12
Kaleidoscope, 244, 294
Kathy & Carol, 160
Kathy & Carol, 151
Katz, Steve, 165
Kaye, Lenny, 10, 12, 339–40
Keep On Moving, 212
Keepnews, Orin, 134
Keith, Bill, 135, 165, 319
Keith, Bill & Rooney, Jim, 135, 319
Kelly, Casey, 354
Keltner, Jim, 284
Kentucky Mountain Songs, 40
Kettle Of Fish, The (club), 140, 145, 148
Kewley, Fred, 328
Keynote (record label), 33, 76
Keys, Bobby, 284
Khan, Ashish, 356
Kick Out The Jams, 17, 301–2
Kilberg, Lionel, 56
Kilroy, Pat, 17, 180–1, 190–1
Kingsmen, The, 304
Kingston Trio, The, 31, 47, 109–11, 116, 130, 137, 139
'Kisses Sweeter Than Wine', 144
Knechtel, Larry, 316
Koerner Ray & Glover, 14, 16, 137, 158, 160–3, 277, 293, 330
Koerner, 'Spider' John, 162, 164, 234, 241, 293
Kongos, John, 331
Kooper, Al, 137, 168, 200, 213
Kossoy Sisters With Erik Darling, The, 134
Kottke, Leo, 60
Kramer, Eddie, 325, 339
Kramer, Wayne, 299
Krasnow, Bob, 187, 227, 358, 360
Krause, Bernie, 11–12, 184–5, 192, 195
Krieger, Robby, 5, 10, 16, 160, 163, 248, 251, 253, 255–6, 260
Kristofferson, Kris, 289, 291–2
Krupa, Gene, 49
Kweskin, Jim, 135, 153, 165

'La Bamba', 50
LA Woman, 259–60, 334
Laddie Lie Near Me, 153
'Laissez-Faire', 271
Landau, Jon, 302, 321
Langhorne, Bruce, 263
Larisch, Kathy, 151
LaserDisc, 336
'Last Night I Had The Strangest Dream', 68
'Last Thing On My Mind, The', 143
'Later During A Flaming Riviera Sunset', 240–1
'Laughing Stock', 226
Lay, Sam, 200, 209, 302
Leadbelly, 21–2, 32–3, 39, 45, 48, 52, 69, 73–5, 82, 91, 113, 133, 154–5, 160–2, 170, 192, 340
Leaves, The, 249
Led Zeppelin, 231
Lee, Arthur, 4, 9,13, 217–20, 222, 224–5, 227–8, 314, 317
Lee, Arthur & Band Aid, 227
Lee, Bill, 122
Lennon, John, 60, 122, 162, 192, 197
Les Baxter's Balladeers, 109
Leventhal, Harold, **100**, 122, 142
Levert, Gerald, 360
Leviathan, 244–5
Lew, Harry, 177
Lewis, Furry, 288, 349
Lewiston, David, 182
Library Of Congress Recordings (Leadbelly), 22, 154, 340
Library Of Congress Recordings (Woody Guthrie), 22, 340
Lieberson, Goddard, 328
'Light My Fire', 5, 8, 15, 17–18, 92, 249–51, 253, 316
Light Of Day, 180–1
Lightfoot, Gordon, 116, 120, 123
'Like A Rollin' Stone', 196, 198, 234
Limeliters, The, 100, 109–10, 116, 185, 234
Linde, Dennis, 290–1, 333
Lindisfarne, 331
Lindley, David, 164
'Linin' Track', 161
'Little Bit Of Rain', 171
Little Boots, 361
'Little Doll', 303
Little Sandy Review, The (magazine), 160, 167

Live At McCabes, 275
Live At The Village Vanguard (book), 52
Living By The Days, 287–8, 349
LL Cool J, 40
Lloyd, A.L., 143, 152
Lomax, Alan, 34, 39, 46–8, 52, 74–5, 85, 91, 154–5, 189, 213
Lomax, John, 45, 47
'Loose', 304
Lorca, 184, 266, 269–70, 277
'Lord Of The Dance', 237
Los Angeles Fantasy Orchestra, The, 292
Lost Without Your Love, 316
Lots More Blues, Rags And, Hollers, 161–2
'Louise', 130, 275
Love, 4, 7–9, 14–16, 18, 92, **104**, 124, 148, 176, 180, 216–21, 223, 225–8, 235, 239–41, 250, 259, 265, 281, 314, 330, 349
Love, 219
Love Four Sail, 227
'Love From Room 109', 269
'Love Henry', 58
'Love Me, I'm A Liberal', 147
'Love Me Two Times', 163, 249
'Lover Baby Friend', 354
Lovers, 290
Lovin' Spoonful, The, 163, 165, 171, 199, 268
'Low Down Alligator', 130
Lucas, Trevor, 242, 244
Lunch, 331
Lyman, Mel, 165
'Lyndon Johnson Told The Nation', 143

MacColl, Ewan, 64, 134
Mack, Lonnie, 286–8, 292–3, 348–9
Mackay, Steve, 304
MacLean, Bryan, 217, 219, 223–4, 228
Madaio, Steve, 212,
Maid Of Constant Sorrow, A, 120
'Make It With You', 315
Makem, Tommy, 55, 134
Mamas & The Papas, The, 215–16, 251, 282
Mandel, Steve, 59
Mann, David, 351
Mann, Herbie, 107
Manna, 316
Manzarek, Ray, 10, 15, 226, 248, 250, 252, 254
Mapes, Jo, 55
Marais, Josef & Miranda, 34
Marat/Sade (play), 122–3
Marble Index, The, 17, 295–6
Margolin, George, 56
Margolis, Jack S., 333
Marshall, Jack, 131
Martin, Vince, 96, 168–71
Martyn, John, 229, 239
Mary Called Jeanie Green, 350
Mason, Robert, 354
Masterpieces Of The Early French & Italian Renaissance, 177
'Masters Of War', 121
Matthew, Mark, Luke & John, 245
Matthews Southern Comfort, 331, 353
Matthews, Ian, 275, 331, 342, 353
Matthews, Onzy, 130
Matusow, Harvey, 63
MC5, 4–5, 17, **204**, 294, 298–302, 304, 313–15, 330, 338–9
McCarthy, Senator Joe, 73
McCartney, Paul, 88, 187, 188, 230, 297, 350
McComb, Carol, 151–2
McCoy, Charlie, 289
McCurdy, Ed, 36, 39, 54–5, 58, 66–70, 93, 111, 119, 133–4, 141
McGhee, Brownie, 48, 54, 83, 111
McGuinn, Jim (aka Roger), 60, 91, 109, 118, 197, 199, 216
McGuire, Barry, 109, 215
McKenzie, Scott, 109
'Me And Bobby McGee', 289
Melcher, Terry, 17
'Memphis', 286
Mercury, Freddie, **208**, 338
Merrick, Nina, *see* Holzman, Nina
Methuselah, 245
Mexican Folk Songs, 50
'Mighty Day', 114
Mike Stuart Span, The, 244–5
Miller, Mitch, 39, 43
Miller, Roger, 289, 291
Miller, Russ, 271, 284, 286–8, 291, 325, 348–51, 353, 355–6
Minkoff, Fran, 91, 120
'Mr Blue', 282
'Mr Tambourine Man', 122, 196, 199
Mitchell, Chad Trio, The, 109, 115, 120, 142
Mitchell, Joni, 4, 243, 263–4, 331, 342–3, 357–8
Modern Folk Quartet, The, 60, 168
Mohawk, Frazier, 10, 280, 292–5, 315, 324
'Monday Morning', 237
Monkees, The, 185, 215, 316
Monkey Music, 182
Monroe, Bill, 319–20
'Montana Song', 273
'Moonlight Drive', 17, 251, 254
Moore, Tim, 347
Moray Eels, 294
Moray Eels Eat The Holy Modal Rounders, The, 294
Morning Again, 144, 180, 191
'Morning Glory', 267, 277
Morrison Hotel, 151, 257–8, 287
Morrison, Jim, 4–5, 15, 18, 201, 249, 251–2, 256–7, 261, 281, 292, 298, 302, 330, 338
Morse Code Course, 96
Moss, Wayne, 289

Mother Bay State Entertainers, The, 164, 319
Motorcycle Mama, 351
Mount Auburn (label), 135
MTV, 337
Muldaur, Geoff, 32, 135, 164–5
Muldaur, Maria (née D'Amato), 59, 165
Mundi, Billy, 283
Murdoch, Bruce, 164
Murdoch, Iris, 238
Murphy, Willie, 293
Music From Bulgaria, 140
Music From The Morning Of The World, 182
Music Is Your Mistress, 355–6
'My Favorite Things', 249
'My Little Red Book', 15, 217–19, 235, 241, 250
Myrick, Weldon, 275, 289

Naftalin, Mark, 200, 212
Nashville (movie), 334
N'Dour, Youssou, 187
Neil, Fred, 9, 82, 101, 113, 115–16, 120, 143, 160, 168–73, 197, 266–7, 269, 276–8
Nelson, Jack, 338
Nelson, Paul, 160, 167, 190
Nelson, Willie, 288–9
Nesmith, Mike, 331, 333, 337, 347
New American Songbook, 45
New Christy Minstrels, The, 109
New Concepts (agency), 115
New Dimensions In Banjo & Bluegrass, 59, 347
New Lost City Ramblers, The, 56–9, 62–4, 111, 129, 137, 150
New Seekers, The, 332
New Songs, 24–7, 36, 110
New York Jazz Quartet, 107
Newbury, Mickey, **205**, 287–90, 292, 333, 342
Newman, Randy, 187, 358
Newmark, Andy, 327
Newport Folk Festival, 50, 82, 91, 100, 111–12, 136, 139, 213, 230
Nico, 17, 280, 293–6
Night At The Opera, A, 337, 358
Niles, John Jacob, 21–2, 33–4, 111
'1969', 304
'1970', 304
Nix, Don, 287–8, 349–51
'No Fun', 304
'No More Songs', 148
'No Regrets', 263
No Secrets, **208**, 327
'Nobody Walkin'', 270
None But One, 40
Nonesuch (label), 4, 14, 18, 61, **102**, **104**, 107, 124, 153, 165, 174, 177–84, 186–8, 194, 231, 234–5, 262–3, 301, 320, 324, 326, 330, 348, 356, 358–9
Nonesuch Explorer (label), 11, 72, 92, 181–3, 189
Nonesuch Guide To Electronic Music, The, 184, 186, 194
Noonan, Steve, 190, 297, 317
'Norwegian Wood', 197
'Not Right', 303
'Nothing', 227
Nova Scotia Folk Music, 65
'Nowhere Man', 197
Nuggets: Original Artifacts From The First Psychedelic Era, 339–40, 355
Nyro, Laura, 342

O' Lovely Appearance Of Death, 55, 99
Ochs, Michael, 130, 141
Ochs, Phil, 9, 14, 19, 60, 103, 113–14, 120, 137–8, 141–3, 145–50, 155, 160, 168, 198–9, 216, 234–5, 262, 317, 330
Ochs, Sonny, 11–12, 155
'October Song', 229
Odetta, 19, 111, 122, 134, 171, 326
Odetta At The Gate Of Horn, 134
Odetta Sings Ballads And Blues, 134
Off-Beat Folk Songs, 56
'Oggie Man, The' 237
Okum, Milt, 140
Old And In The Way, 321
Old Time Banjo Project, The, 163–4, 192
On The Road To Elath, 105
On The Waters, 315
On Tour With Eric Clapton, 285
'Once I Was', 267, 278
One Foot In The Groove, 162
'One For My Baby', 80
'One Meat Ball', 76, 79
'One More Parade', 114
One Sheridan Square (club), 80, 108
'One Time And One Time Only', 198
Ono, Yoko, 60
Oranim Zabar Israeli Troupe, 88, 105
Orbison, Roy, 170–1, 288, 291
Original Lost Elektra Sessions, The, 209
Osterberg, James, *see* Pop, Iggy
Ostin, Mo, 206, 323, 330, 341, 345
Other Side Of This Life, 170
'Other Side To This Life', 171
Other Voices, 330
Out Here, 227, 343
'Outside Of A Small Circle Of Friends', 148
Outward Bound, 143, 160
Özbekhan, Hasan, 50

Pacific Jazz (record label), 31, 220
'Pack Up Your Sorrows', 122
Page, Jimmy, 60, 231–2
Painter, 335
Painter, 335
Paley, Tom, 11–12, 54, 56–9, 61, 63–4, 99, 236

Palmer, Clive, 229, 232
Palmer, Earl, 131
'Panama Limited, The', 167
Pappalardi, Felix, 169
Parks, Van Dyke, 10, 15, 60, 147–8, 154, 215, 264, 358
Parsons, Gram, 129, 172, 261, 284
'Party, The', 156
Paths Of Victory, 113, 118
'Paths Of Victory', 118
Patti Smith Group, 339
Paul Butterfield Blues Band, The, 4, 14–16, **104**, 160, 196, 200, 234
Paul Butterfield Blues Band, The, 210
Paupers, The, 247
Paxton, Gary S., 314
Paxton Lodge, 245, 292–3, 343
Paxton, Tom, 10, 14, 19, **103**, 114, 116–17, 120, 122–3, 137–8, 141–2, 145, 147–50, 160, 180, 191, 198, 234, 241–2, 282, 329–30
Payant, Lee, 93–4
Pearl, 258
Pedal Steel Guitar Album, The, 347
Peel, David, 60–1, 180, 191–2, **205**
Peel, David & The Lower East Side, 61, 191, 297
Peel, John, 7, 230, 242, 331–2
Pendergrass, Teddy, 359
Pennywhistlers, The, 92
Penrod, Jerry, 271, 283
'People Are Strange', 254
Pepper, Bob, 164
Perry, Richard, 325, 327
Peter Paul & Mary, 88, 115–16, 139, 142, 317, 358
Pfisterer, Snoopy, 219
Phillips, Glenn, 12, 210
Phillips, John, 45, 109, 216
Piano Rags By Scott Joplin, 183
Pickow, George, 36, 40, 43–4, 47, 54
'Piece Of My Heart', 212
Pink Floyd, 8, 230, 239–41
'Pirate Jenny', 122
Plainsong, 331, 353
'Play With Fire', 249
Playing Possum, 327
'Pleasant Street', 267, 277
'Please Let Me Love You', 199
Pleasure Fair, The, 314
Pleasures Of The Harbor, 148
Polinoff, Sasha, 90
Polinoff, Sasha & His Russian Gypsy Orchestra, 106
'Poor Wayfaring Stranger', 34
Pop, Iggy, 5, 302–4, 313, 317
PopClips (TV show), 337
Posner, Mel, **102**, 126, 128, 342
'Power And The Glory', 146
Present Tense, 346, 352
Presenting Joyce Grenfell, 108
Presley, Elvis, 289–90
Presti & Lagoya, 107
Prestige (record label), 31–2, 34, 135, 158–9, 167, 188, 294
'Pretty Boy Floyd', 66, 154
Price, Jim, 284
'Pride Of Man', 118
Prime Movers, The, 302
Public Enemy, 40
'Puff The Magic Dragon', 139
Pulsating Sounds Of Paraguay, The, 72
Puma, Joe, 115
Pure Country, 334

'¡Que Vida!', 176, 221
Queen, 4, 9, 208, 229, 330, 337–8, 342–3, 358
Queen Of Hearts: Early English Folk Songs, 50
Quicksilver Messenger Service, 118, 251
Radio Free Nixon, 347
Radle, Carl, 284
Ragovoy, Jerry, 212
Raim, Walter, 91, 120
Rainbow Band, The, 349
Rainbow Band, The, 349
Raitt, Bonnie, 275
Ramblin' Boy, 142–3
Raskin, Gene, 88
Rat On, 348
Raw Power, 313
Ray, Dave 'Snaker', 161
RCA Victor (record label), 28, 33
Real Bahamas, The, 181, 189, 231
'Real Cool Time', 303
Rebbenack, Mac, 284
Recorded At Club 47, 151
Red Onion Jazz Band, 108
'Red Sox Are Winning, The', 181
Redding, Otis, 360
Reddy, Helen, 327
Redpath, Jean, 152
Reed, Susan, 21–2, 33, 48–9, 53, 72, 74
Reel To Real, 227
Renaissance, 68, 107, 151, 177, 263, 331
Renbourn, John, 10–12, 81–3
Resurrection Of Pigboy Crabshaw, The, 212
Return Of Koerner Ray & Glover, 162
'Revelation', 221
Rhinoceros, 271, 280, 282–4
Rhodes, Red, 334, 347
Rhone, Sylvia, 359–60
Richards, Keith, 81
Richmond, Fritz, 153, 165, 167, 280, 354
Rickolt, Paul, 24, 26, 45, 72
'Riders On The Storm', 176, 259
Rifkin, Joshua, 10, **104**, 124, 165–6, 179, 180, 183, 188, 264, 330
Right On Be Free, 332
Rinzler, Ralph, 129, 189
'Rio', 337

Ripley, Leonard, 45, 67, 80, 92, 94, 96, 105, 126
Rising Of The Moon, The, 120, 134
Ritchie, Jean, 9–12, 14, 27, 36–45, 47–8, 50, 54–5, 62, 69–70, 97, 110–11, 119, 135, 152, 295
Riverside (record label), 31–2, 40, 58, 61, 66–7, 107–8, 114, 132, 134–5, 141
Road Show – The Alabama State Troupers, 288
'Road To Cairo, The', 272
'Robert Montgomery', 227
Roberton, Sandy, 353
Roberts, Andy, 331, 353
Roberts, Elliot, 342
Rogers, Kenny & The First Edition, 288
Rolling Stones, The, 7, 83, 212, 231, 285
Ron & Nama, 105
Roney, Marianne, 30
Ronstadt, Linda, 275, 334, 342, 347, 356, 358
Rooftop Singers, The, 59, 134, 136
Rosen, Michael, 242–3
Rosenbaum, Art, 59, n.64,
Rosmini, Dick, 60, 91, 101, 117
Ross, Steve, 324, 330, 335–7, 341
Rothchild, Paul, 5, 8–9, 14, 16, 32, **102**, **104**, 112, 116, 120, 127, 135–7, 143–4, 151–2, 158–61, 163, 165, 167–8, 180, 188–90, 200, 201, 209, 213–14, 220–21, 228–9, 233, 235, 239–40, 247, 252, 255, 257, 260, 265, 278, 280–2, 294, 297, 324, 342
Round And Roundelays, 39
Rowan, Peter, 11–12, 164, 319
Rowles, Gary, 227
Roxy, 332; *see also* The Wackers
Royer, Robb, 314, 316
Rubber Soul, 196–7, 350
Rundgren, Todd, 213, 347
Running Jumping Standing Still, 293
Rupe, Art, 28
Rush, Tom, 8, 10, 32, 103, 135, 150–1, 158–60, 166–9, 200, 229, 234, 263, 297, 330, 354
Russell, Irwin, 341
Russell, Leon, 284–5, 314, 349, 355
Rustin, Bayard, 34
Ryan, Jimmy, 327

Sabicas, 16, 45, 93, 105
Sacks, Bob, 21–2, 24
'Sacred Life', 151
Sagittarius, 346, 352
Sailcat, 351
'St James' Infirmary', 79
St John, Bridget, 331
Sainte-Marie, Buffy, 10, 141
Salazar, Marcelo, 50
Samwell-Smith, Paul, 325, 327
Sanborn, David, 212–13
Sandburg, Carl, 34, 45–8, 66
Sander, Ellen, 216
'Scarlet Begonias', 81
Schlesinger, Al, 314
Scott, Mike, 175
Scottish Ballad Book, 153
Scruggs, Earl, 111
Sea, The, 185, 239
'Searchin'', 200
Sebastian, John, 59, 113, 120, 122, 137, 143, 163–5, 169–70, 172, 199–200
Segarini, Bob, 350
Seeger, Mike, 56–8, 63
Seeger, Peggy, 58, 64, 99, 134, 236–7
Seeger, Pete, 13, 19, 33–5, 37, 39, 45, 50, 53, 56–7, 59, 66, 68–70, 73–5, 81, 91, 111, 113, 120–1, 122, 133, 141, 144, 184, 193
Seeger, Toshi, **100**
Seltzer, Dov, 88
Selwood, Clive, 241, 245, 331–3
'Send In The Clowns', 265
Sendak, Maurice, 36
Serendipity Singers, 109
Serrano, Juan, 105, 234
'7 And 7 Is', 8, 220–1, 235
Shack, 228
'Shadow Dream Song', 263, 297
Shankar, Ravi, 210, 230, 356
Shanty Boys, The, 56, 62, 110
Shapiro, Benny, 199
Sharp, Cecil, 37, 39–40
'She Comes In Colors', 221
Shelton, Robert, 138, 141, 266
Shepard, Sam, 294
Shepherd, Jean, 108, 347
Ship, The, 352
Shredder, 350
Siddons, Bill, 255, 259
Side Trips, 294
Siebel, Paul, 17, 180, 192, 262, 274–6, 353
Siegel, Peter, 61, 144, 153, 164–5, 180, 182, 275, 297, 317, 320, 325, 348
Siggins, Bob, 164, 319
Sill, Judee, 342
Silver Apples Of The Moon, 186
Silver, Roy, 115
Silverstein, Shel, 108, 114–15
Simon & Garfunkel, 68, 116, 320,
Simon, Carly, 4, 17, **208**, 262, 316, 325–9, 34, 338, 342–3, 359
Simon, Lucy, 327
Simon, Paul, 328
Simon Sisters, The, 326
Sin Songs Pro/Con, 67
Sinatra, Frank, 29, 66, 76, 185, 224, 251–2, 256, 265, 288
'Since You Asked', 264
Sinclair, John, 10, 298–301
Singer Songwriter Project, 163–4, 354
Singing Family Of The Cumberlands (book), 37
Siren, 268, 331–2

Sister Aimee (musical), 274
Ski Songs, 114–15, 197
'Sky Fell', 264
Sky, Patrick, 141, 164
Skymonters, 118
Smith, Fred 'Sonic', 299
Smith, Harry, 52, 55, 65, 132
Smith, Joe, 206, 323, 357–8
Smith, Oliver, 153, 180, 190
Snaker's Here, 162
Soft Parade, The, 201, 256–8, 282
'Soft Parade, The', 257
Soft White Underbelly, 191, 317
Solomon, Bernard, 134
Solomon, Maynard, 31, **100**, 112, 125, 129, 136, 178
Solomon, Seymour, 31
'Something In The Way She Moves', 263
Sometimes I Just Feel Like Smilin', 213
Son Of Dalliance, 68
'Song Of The Magician', 266
'Song Slowly Song', 266, 277
'Song To The Siren', 268
Songs And Ballads Of America's Wars, 45
Songs Of A Russian Gypsy, 89–90, 92
Songs Of Love, Lilt, Laughter, 153
Songs Of Mark Spoelstra, The, 151–2
Songs Of Russia Old And New, 90
Songs Of The Abbaye, 45, 93–4
Songs Of The Earth, 92
'Sonny Come Home', 271
Sons Of Adam, The, 217
'Soul Kitchen', 17
'Soulless Blues', 151
Southbound Train', 163
Southern Exposure: An Album Of Jim Crow Blues, 33
'Spanish Caravan', 255
Specialty (record label), 28, 115
Spence, Joseph, 151, 154, 160, 181, 189, 192, 231
Spider Blues, 162
Spoelstra, Mark, 150–1, 160, 164, 190
Spontaneous Music Ensemble, 241
Spook Along With Zacherley, 108
Springsteen, Bruce, 33
Sprung, George, 56
Sprung, Roger, 58, 61
Spy, 327
Stafford, Jo, 34
Stalk-Forrest Group, 180, 318–19, 340
Stampfel, Peter, 294
Stardrive, 354–5
Starsailor, 268–70
State Of Mind, 190
Sterne, Tracey, **104**, 179–80, 182–4, 187, 330, 348
Stevens, Cat, 327
Stevens, John, 241
Stills, Stephen, 109, 131, 172, 264, 282
Stone Monkey, 231
Stooges, The, 4, **204**, 228, 294–5, 298–9, 302–3, 313–15, 330, 338–40, 346
Stooges, The, 17, 304
Story Of John Henry, The, 78–80
Stoughton, David, 10, 296–7
Strange Days, 7, 18, 225, 253–4, 282
Strange Locomotion, 332
'Strange Street Affair Under Blue', 277
String Band Project, The, 163–4, 192, 319, 321
Stuart, Michael, 217, 220, 222, 227–8
Subotnick, Morton, 186
Subway To The Country, 272, 286
'Suite: Judy Blue Eyes', 264
Suite Steel, 347
'Sun Comes Up Each Day, The', 297
'Sunshine Sunshine', 263
'Super Skier', 115
Susan Reed, 49
Susan Reed Sings Old Airs, 49
Susan Reed Sings Old Airs From Ireland, Scotland And England, 49
'Suzanne', 124, 264
Swamp Dogg, **206**, 348
Swann, Billy, 291–2
Swann, Donald, 237
Sweet Salvation, 353
Sweet Salvation, 353
Szafran, Gene, 284

Tahiti: The Gauguin Years, 231
Taj Mahal, 154, 283
Take A Little Walk With Me, 167
Tape From California, 148
Tarriers, The, 59, 95–6, 109, 114,
Taupin, Bernie, 272–3
Tawney, Cyril, 236–7
'Taxi', 90, 327–9
Taylor, Dallas, 280–2
Taylor, James, 263, 327, 354
Tear Down The Walls, 169–70
Tedesco, Tommy, 115
Tell It To The Marines, 71, 101
Templeman, Ted, 358
Terry, Sonny, 32, 48, 54, 74, 82–3, 111
'That's The Way It's Gonna Be', 114
'That's The Way I've Always Heard It Should Be', 326–7
Theodore Bikel Sings Jewish Folk Songs, 86
Theodore Bikel Sings Songs Of Israel, 86
'There But For Fortune', 146–7, 150, 235
There's An Innocent Face, 352
'Thirsty Boots', 123
'This Land Is Your Land', 146
Thomassie, Big John, 353–4
Thompson, Dennis, 299

Thompson, Richard & Linda, 229 240
'Those Were The Days', 84, 88
Tijuana Brass, The, 224
Tim Buckley, 4–5, 7, 9, 11, 17–18, 124, 150, 168, 172, 181, 203, 228, 239–41, 245, 262, 265, 267–8, 271, 276, 283, 289, 330, 349, 354
'Time Is On My Side', 212
'Tin Angel', 263
Tiptoe Past The Dragon, 350–1
'Tom Dooley', 46, 48, 109
Tom Paley & Peggy Seeger, 58, 64, 236
Tom Rush, 8, 10, 32, **103**, 135, 150–1, 158–60, 166–9, 200, 229, 234, 263, 297, 330, 354
'Tomorrow Is A Long Time', 122, **103**
'Too Late', 151
'Touch Me', 257
'Town Crier's Song, The', 116
Tradition (record label), 32, 40, 58, 61, 66–7, 132, 134–5, 141
Train, John, 149, 157
Transformer, 296–7
Traum, Happy, 57
Travelers, The, 109, 129
Treasure Chest Of American Folk Song, A, 68
Treasury Of Music Of The Renaissance, A, 107
Treasury Of Spanish And Mexican Folk Song, A, 51
'Try', 212
'Turn Turn Turn', 120–1
Tyner, Rob, 299, 301
'Tzena, Tzena, Tzena', 106

Underwood, Lee, 10, 266–9
Unholy Matrimony, 66
Unicorn, The (club), 89, 130
Unknown Soldier, The, 255
Urban Cowboy, 331, 353, 358
'Urge For Going', 263
Usher, Gary, 332, 350, 352

Valente, Dino, 118, 170
Valley Hi, 331, 353
Van Ronk, Dave, 35, 54, 57, 71, 114, 133, 142, 158, 164–5
Vanaver, Bill, 164
Vanguard (record label), 31–2, 58–9, 61, 112, 119, 125, 127, 129, 132, 134–7, 140–1, 145, 164–5, 174, 177, 179, 193
Vaya (label), 128
Velvet Underground, The, 228, 294–5, 302, 304
Venet, Nik, 172
Verities & Balderdash, 329
'Very Cellular Song, A', 230–1
Village Gate, The (club), 14, 119, 131, 139–40
Village Vanguard (club), 52–3, 75, 141
Vindicator, 227
Voices Of East Harlem, The, 332
Voices Of Haiti, 25, 71–2
Von Schmidt, Eric, 32, 135, 164, 168

Wackering Heights, 332
Wackers, The, 332–3, 350, 352, 355
Waiting For The Sun, 254–5, 288
'Walk Right In', 59, 136
Walker, Jerry Jeff, 275
'Walkin' Blues', 210
'War Is Over, The', 148–9, 156–7
Warhol, Andy, 295
Warner, Frank, 42, 45–8, 54, 66, 109, 111
Waronker, Larry, 358
'Wars Of Germany', 120
'Water Is Wide, The', 169
Waters, Muddy, 83, 158, 210, 229, 235, 254
Watersons, The, 152, 236
'Waves Roll Out, The', 116
Weavers At Carnegie Hall, The, 31, 135, 144
Weavers, The, 13, 34–5, 53, 59, 74, 106, 109, 184, 192–3
Weber, Steve, 294
Webster, Guy, 295
Wednesday Morning 3AM, 68
Wee Tam And The Big Huge, 230
Wein, George, 139, 229
Weinstock, Bob, 135
Weis, Danny, 271, 283
Weissberg, Eric, 56, 59, 64, 122, 129
Weissman, Dick, 45
Welding, Pete, 235
'Well Well Well', 114
Wexler, Jerry, 28, 323
Whales & Nightingales, 264
Whaling And Sailing Songs From The Days Of Moby Dick, 66
'Wham', 286
'What Did You Learn In School Today', 143
What I Know, 263
Whatever's Right, 286
What's Shakin', 200, 238
Wheatstraw Suite, 129
Wheeler, Billy Edd, 120, 133
When Dalliance Was In Flower And Maidens Lost Their Heads, 67
When Dalliance Was In Flower Volume II, 58
'When The Music Starts To Play', 229
'When The Music's Over', 17, 254
'Where Did My Baby Go', 212
Where I'm Bound, 112, 115, 117, 143
Whiskeyhill Singers, The, 130
Whisky A Go Go (club), 4, 13, 217
White, Clarence, 275, 321, 347
White, Josh, 9, 14, 16, 21–2, 32–4, 39, 52–4, 72–4, 76–8, 80–3, 92, **99**, 112, 119, 133, 160–1, 170, 234–5

'White Rabbit', 251
Whitlock, Bobby, 284
Who Knows Where The Time Goes, **204**, 264
Wilco, 187
Wild Blue Yonder, The, 70–1
'Wild Child In A World Of Trouble', 170
Wildflowers, 18, 264
Will Failure Spoil Jean Shepherd?, 108
Williams, Jerry, 348
Williamson, James, 304
Williamson, Robin, **203**, 229
Wilson, Brian, 181, 199, 352
Wilson, Jacques, 185
'Wings', 266
'Winkin' Blinkin' And Nod', 326
Winston, Julian 'Winnie', 164
Winter, Johnny, 286
Winwood, Steve, 200, 231, 238
'Wishful Sinful', 257
Wit And Mirth; Or, Pills To Purge Melancholy (songbook), 67
Wood, Hally, 44, 55, **99**
Woodsmoke And Oranges, 192, 274–5
'Woodstock', 212–13, 304, 331
'Work Song', 210
World Gone Wrong, 58
Wrecking Crew, 222
Wyker, John, 351

Yamaguchi, Goro, 183
Yanovsky, Zal, 199, 268
Yarbrough, Glenn, 55, **100**, 110, 115
Yardbirds, The, 197, 325
Year In The Life, A (documentary), 245
Yellin, Bob, 129
Yes I See, 115
Yester, Jerry, 131, 266, 268, 278, 352
Yiddish Theatre And Folk Songs, 86, 91
York, Pete, 200, 238
'You Can Tell The World', 116
Young Man And A Maid, A, 50, 88, 131
Young, Izzy, 59, 63, 140, 154, 166
Young, Neil, 190, 222, 283, 343
'Your Mind And We Belong Together', 226
'You're Lost Little Girl', 249
'You're So Vain', 325, 327
Youth International Party, 149

Zacherley, John, 108
Zappa, Frank, 17, 180, 210, 347
Zodiac Cosmic Sounds, The, 8, 103, 185–6, 193–4, 340

Photo Credits

The photographs used in this book come from the following sources, and we are grateful for their help. If you feel there has been a mistaken attribution, please contact the publisher.

Jacket front *Iggy Pop* Lenny Kaye Collection; *billboard* William S. Harvey archive; **spine** Joel Brodsky; **97** *Ritchie*, George Pickow; *Record Loft*, Holzman family archive; **98** Holzman family archive; **99** *Paley/Seegar*, Brian Shuel; *Gooding*, Elektra; **100** *Limelighters*, Michael Ochs Archive/Getty Images; *Newport*, David Gahr; **101** *Rosmini/Neil/Gibson* bobgibsonlegacy.com; *Holzman*, Holzman family archive; **102** Elektra; **103** *Rush/Paxton/Ochs*, Michael Ochs Archives/Getty Images; **104** *Love*, William S. Harvey archive; *Nonesuch team*, New York Times; *Butterfield*, David Gahr; **201** Rhino; **202** *Botnik*, Bruce Botnik; **203** *Buckley*, *Incredible String Band*, Michael Ochs Archives/Getty Images; **204** *Collins/Anderle*, Elektra; **205** *Peel*, Tina Tinan; *Newbury/Holzman*, Elektra; **206** *Chapin*, Michael Ochs Archives/Getty Images; *Holzman/Ostin/Smith*, Elektra; **207** *Holzman/Collins*, Elektra; **208** *Panavision*, Holzman family archive; *Queen*, Chris Walter/WireImage/Getty Images.

The 10 Rules Of Rock And Roll: Collected Music Writings 2005–11 Robert Forster

Just Can't Get Enough: The Making Of Depeche Mode Simon Spence

Glenn Hughes: The Autobiography Glenn Hughes with Joel McIver

Entertain Us: The Rise Of Nirvana Gillian G. Gaar

Adventures Of A Waterboy Mike Scott

She Bop: The Definitive History Of Women In Popular Music Lucy O'Brien

Solid Foundation: An Oral History Of Reggae David Katz

Read & Burn: A Book About Wire Wilson Neate

Big Star: The Story Of Rock's Forgotten Band Rob Jovanovic

Recombo DNA: The Story Of Devo, or How The 60s Became The 80s Kevin C. Smith

Neil Sedaka, Rock'n'roll Survivor Rich Podolsky

Touched By Grace: My Time With Jeff Buckley Gary Lucas

A Sense Of Wonder: Van Morrison's Ireland David Burke

Bathed In Lightning: John McLaughlin, The 60s And The Emerald Beyond Colin Harper

My Bloody Roots: From Sepultura To Soulfly And Beyond Max Cavalera with Joel McIver

What's Exactly The Matter With Me? Memoirs Of A Life In Music P.F. Sloan and S.E. Feinberg

Who Killed Mister Moonlight? Bauhaus, Black Magick, and Benediction David J. Haskins

Confessions Of A Heretic: The Sacred & The Profane, Behemoth & Beyond Adam Nergal Darski with Mark Eglinton

Throwing Frisbees At The Sun: A Book About Beck Rob Jovanovic

Lee, Myself & I: Inside The Very Special World Of Lee Hazlewood Wyndham Wallace

Long Promised Road: Carl Wilson, Soul of The Beach Boys Kent Crowley

Eyes Wide Open: True Tales Of A Wishbone Ash Warrior Andy Powell with Colin Harper

Eternal Troubadour: The Improbable Life Of Tiny Tim Justin Martell with Alanna Wray McDonald

Complicated Game: Inside The Songs Of XTC Andy Partridge and Todd Bernhardt

Seeing The Real You At Last: Life And Love On The Road With Bob Dylan Britta Lee Shain

Tragedy: The Ballad Of The Bee Gees Jeff Apter

The Monkees, Head, And The 60s Peter Mills

Perfect Day: An Intimate Portrait Of Life With Lou Reed Bettye Kronstad

ALSO AVAILABLE IN PRINT AND EBOOK EDITIONS FROM JAWBONE PRESS

Strange Brew: Eric Clapton & The British Blues Boom Christopher Hjort

Metal: The Definitive Guide Garry Sharpe-Young

Lennon & McCartney: Together Alone John Blaney

Riot On Sunset Strip: Rock'n'roll's Last Stand In Hollywood Domenic Priore

Million Dollar Bash: Bob Dylan, The Band, and The Basement Tapes Sid Griffin

Bowie In Berlin: A New Career In A New Town Thomas Jerome Seabrook

Beatles For Sale: How Everything They Touched Turned To Gold John Blaney

So You Want To Be A Rock'n'roll Star: The Byrds Day-By-Day Christopher Hjort

Hot Burritos: The True Story Of The Flying Burrito Brothers John Einarson with Chris Hillman

Million Dollar Les Paul: In Search Of The Most Valuable Guitar In The World Tony Bacon

The Impossible Dream: The Story Of Scott Walker And The Walker Brothers Anthony Reynolds

To Live Is To Die: The Life And Death Of Metallica's Cliff Burton Joel McIver

Jack Bruce Composing Himself: The Authorised Biography Harry Shapiro

White Light/White Heat: The Velvet Underground Day-By-Day Richie Unterberger

Return Of The King: Elvis Presley's Great Comeback Gillian G. Gaar

Forever Changes: Arthur Lee & The Book Of Love John Einarson

The 100 Greatest Metal Guitarists Joel McIver

Seasons They Change: The Story Of Acid And Psychedelic Folk Jeanette Leech

Won't Get Fooled Again: The Who From Lifehouse To Quadrophenia Richie Unterberger

Crazy Train: The High Life And Tragic Death Of Randy Rhoads Joel McIver

A Wizard, A True Star: Todd Rundgren In The Studio Paul Myers

The Resurrection Of Johnny Cash: Hurt, Redemption, And American Recordings Graeme Thomson